MW01268447

MUSIC FROM THE MIDDLE AGES
THROUGH THE
TWENTIETH CENTURY

MUSICOLOGY: A BOOK SERIES
Edited by F. Joseph Smith

Additional volumes in preparation

ISSN 0275-5866
This book is part of a series. The publisher will accept continuation orders which may be
cancelled at any time and which provide for automatic billing and shipping of each title in
the series upon publication. Please write for details.

MUSIC FROM THE MIDDLE AGES THROUGH THE TWENTIETH CENTURY
Essays in Honor of Gwynn McPeek

Edited by

Carmelo P. Comberiati
Manhattanville College

and

Matthew C. Steel
Western Michigan University

Gordon and Breach Science Publishers
New York   London   Paris   Montreux   Tokyo   Melbourne

Gordon and Breach Science Publishers

Post Office Box 786
Cooper Station
New York, New York 10276
United States of America

Post Office Box 197
London WC2E 9PX
England

58, rue Lhomond
75005 Paris
France

Post Office Box 161
1820 Montreux 2
Switzerland

3-14-9, Okubo
Shinjuku-ku, Tokyo
Japan

Private Bag 8
Camberwell, Victoria 3124
Australia

Library of Congress Cataloging-in-Publication Data
Music from the Middle Ages through the twentieth
   century.
   (Musicology, ISSN 0275-5866; v. 7)
   Includes index.
   1. Music—History and criticism. 2. McPeek, Gwynn S.
I. Comberiati, Carmelo P., 1952–   . II. Steel,
Matthew C., 1948–   . III. McPeek, Gwynn S.
IV. Series: Musicology (New York, N.Y.); v. 7.
ML55.M38   1988   780'.9   88-2567
ISBN 2-88124-216-2 (France)

It is perhaps not a coincidence nor a mere play on words that "Polyphony" offered to an eager public each year at the Abbey Fair and at the Christmas Festival of Carols is the musical medium through which the sensitive and masterful musicianship of Dr. Gwynn McPeek calls forth the "many voices" of a Monastic Choir expressing the true spiritual experience of a great Religious Art. The words from T.S. Eliot's East Coker *come to mind when one recalls the unique quality of Dr. McPeek's teaching and conducting, for in complement with him the "many voices" evoke*

> *Not the intense moment, isolated,*
> *with no before and after,*
> *But a lifetime burning in every moment*
> *And not the lifetime of one man only*
> *But of old stones that cannot be*
>   *deciphered.*

Lady Abbess and Community
Abbey of Regina Laudis
Bethlehem, Connecticut

CONTENTS

MEDIEVAL MUSIC

PROVINCIAL PERSPECTIVES

INTRODUCTION TO THE SERIES

The Gordon and Breach *Musicology* series, a companion to the *Journal of Musicological Research,* covers a creative range of musical topics, from historical and theoretical subjects to social and philosophical studies. Volumes thus far published show the extent of this broad spectrum, from *Music and Its Social Meanings* to *Late Renaissance Music at the Habsburg Court* to the present volume, *Music from the Middle Ages through the Twentieth Century: Essays in Honor of Gwynn S. McPeek.* Forthcoming titles will include works on musical biography, the history of the trombone, and the music of Mendelssohn and Stravinsky. The editors also welcome interdisciplinary studies, ethnomusicological works, and performance analyses. With this series, it is our aim to expand the field and definition of musical exploration and research.

Gwynn S. McPeek

PREFACE

The preparation of a *Festschrift* for Gwynn S. McPeek has been a gratifying experience. The editors, with the help of Mrs. Mary McPeek, compiled an initial list of possible contributors in 1983, drawn from Professor McPeek's friends, colleagues, and former students. The response to our inquiries was very positive, with a wealth of promised articles, and warm wishes from several of the McPeeks' friends.

Unfortunately, due to grave illnesses, neither Professor Albert Seay nor Robert C. Warner was able to finish articles started for this volume. These close, respected friends had very kind words for Professor McPeek, and the volume would have been honored with their contributions. Similarly, Professor Willi Apel sent kind regards just before his ninetieth birthday, and was not able to contribute.

As a scholar and teacher, Gwynn S. McPeek has contributed much to musicology. His monographs on *The Laborde Chansonnier* and the *British Museum Ms Egerton 3307* were particularly exemplary, and he contributed much to both national and international musicological and learned societies. It is most appropriate that colleagues and former students join together to honor Professor McPeek with a volume of essays.

We especially honor Professor McPeek's work as a teacher. His career brought him to Tulane University, the University of Wisconsin, and finally to the University of Michigan, where he chaired the Department of Music History and Musicology. Every former student contacted by the editors enumerated "Mac's" fine qualities, including selflessness, dedication, and the high standards to which he adhered.

xiii

The variety of topics in this volume demonstrate Professor McPeek's inquiring mind and his wide range of interests. Whether concerning western, nonwestern, secular, or sacred topics, these works touch upon areas in which Professor McPeek is conversant. The editors note that much of the correspondence accompanying these submissions mentions ways that the research had been aided by McPeek's insights.

Gwynn S. McPeek has touched his colleagues and we are the better for it. He will continue to influence and to help people in his current work as a Catholic Deacon. Mac, we praise and honor you, and wish you birthday greetings.

As this project draws to a close, the editors wish to thank the participants and supporting institutions. Dean Paul Boylan at The University of Michigan provided initial funds for contacting contributors. Western Michigan University and Manhattanville College provided the further support neccessary to bring this volume to fruition. Finally, we wish to thank Dr. F. Joseph Smith, general editor of the Gordon and Breach Monographs in Musicology Series. Dr. Smith knows Professor McPeek as a colleague, and has been very supportive of the project from its inception.

C.P.C. and M.C.S.

MEDIEVAL MUSIC

CHAPTER ONE

A FRANKISH BISHOP'S BOOK IN THE VERONA CAPITULAR LIBRARY: COD. LXXXVIII AND ITS CONTEXT

James M. Borders

University of Michigan

The Biblioteca capitolare di Verona possesses one of the most distinguished collections of medieval liturgical manuscripts in Europe. Veronese codices are listed among the principal sources for a number of modern critical editions including the Sacramentarium Gregorianum, the Corpus Antiphonalium Officii, and the Ordines Romani.[1] The value of the library's holdings is enhanced by the fact that a large percentage of its manuscripts were copied locally. They are reference points from which we may depart in our examination of the liturgy at a medieval center in northern Italy.[2]

Considering the importance of the Biblioteca capitolare, it is unfor-

---

[1] Jean Deshusses, *Le Sacramentaire grégorien: Ses principales formes d'après les plus anciens manuscrits*, Spicilegium Friburgense, XVI and XXIV (Friburg, Switz.: Editions universitaires, 1971, 1979); Michel Andrieu, ed., *Les Ordines romani du haut moyen âge (VIII–X siècle)*, Spicilegium Sacrum Lovaniense, Études et documents, 5 vols. (Louvain: Spicilegium Sacrum Louvaniense Bureau, 1931–61); René-Jean Hesbert, *Corpus Antiphonalium Officii*, 6 vols. (Rome: Herder, 1963–79).

[2] See James M. Borders, "The Cathedral of Verona as a Musical Center in the Middle Ages: Its History, Manuscripts, and Liturgical Tradition" (Ph. D. diss., University of Chicago, 1983).

Plate 1 Verona Capitular Library, Cod. Ms. LXXXII: fol. 75v–76r

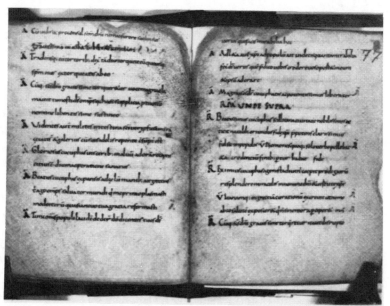

Plate 2 Verona Capitular Library, Cod. Ms. LXXXII: fol. 76v–77r

tunate that a catalogue of the collection has never been published.[3] The most complete guide to the manuscripts is a two-volume, handwritten shelf-list compiled by Rev. Don Antonio Spagnolo, the director of the library at the turn of the century. Obviously, this format limits the catalogue's accessability to scholars, but an even greater problem lies in Spagnolo's cursory treatment of many sources, perhaps understandable considering the scope of the collection. Occasionally his comments concerning the dating of manuscripts, details of their collation, or their inventories are inaccurate and thus continue to mislead modern scholars. Viewed by current standards, Spagnolo's work is due for revision.[4]

The following description of a tenth-century Veronese liturgical manuscript, Bibl. cap. LXXXVIII, supplements and in most respects supersedes Spagnolo's brief catalogue entry. By reviewing the contents and accounting for the irregularities preserved in this and other sources, we come to a fuller understanding of the development and context of the Franco-Roman liturgy in northern Italy.

Cod. LXXXVIII is one of five extant Office books copied in the Verona cathedral scriptorium during the early Middle Ages.[5] The relatively small (145 x 115 mm.) manuscript, which consists of eighty leaves, is a miscellany of liturgical plainchants, hymns, prayers, readings, and poetic verses. An inventory of these items appears in Table 1.

The combination of secular verses and liturgical items in the same manuscript is exceptional for a book copied in the Veronese cathedral scriptorium and therefore deserving of comment. Closely related is the matter of dating. Finally, the liturgical questions raised by the codex must be addressed. These concern the order of chants for Matins on the feast of St. John the Evangelist, and the appearance of antiphons and responsories for the feast of St. Cucufatis, the celebration of which was never incorporated into the northern Italian *Sanctorale*.

Like many medieval manuscripts, Verona Cod. LXXXVIII records layers of accretions. In this case the writing of three hands may be distinguished (see Physical Description, Appendix A). The principal and

---

[3] G.B. Carlo Giuliari, "La Capitolare Biblioteca di Verona e Storia monumentale letteraria, paleografica della stessa," *Archivio veneto*, X–XIV (1875–1877), was to have served as the introduction to such a catalogue but the project was never completed.

[4] A catalogue of seventeen medieval liturgical manuscripts appears in Borders, *op. cit.*, 96–154; 429–484.

[5] *Ibid.*, 158.

TABLE I. Inventory, Verona Bibl. cap. cod. Ms. LXXXVIII

Folio	Contents
fol. 1r	void
fol. 1v	Oration. Inc. "ORATIONE. Domine sancte pater omnipotens aeterna deus, qui es auctor sanctorum . . ." Exp. ". . . ut nullus vie nostrae subripiet inimicis procula nobis sit malignorum accessus et comes nobis dignetur esse spiritus sanctus. Per dominum." Oration (Deshusses, *Le Sacramentaire grégorien* 1:312, sec. 842) Inc. "ORATIONE [PRO PECCATIS]. Exaudi quaesumus domine supplicium preces . . ." Exp. ". . . tribuas benignus et pacem. Per dominum." Oration (ibid., 325, sec. 919). Inc. "ORATIONE [COTIDIANAE]. Concede quaesumus omnipotens deus, ut vitam tuam . . ." Exp. ". . . subripientium delictorum laqueos evadamus. Per dominum." Oration (ibid., 445, sec. 1346). Inc. "ORATIONE [PRIMA, MISSA PRO QUACUMQUE TRIBULATIONE]. Ineffabilem misericordiam tuam domine nobis . . ." Exp. ". . . et a menis quas prohis meremur eripias."
ff. 2r–6r	Litany. Inc. "Kirie. .iii. Christe. .iii. Christe audi nos .iii. Sancte conditor mundi. Miserere nobis . . ." Exp. ". . . Agnus dei, qui tollis peccata mundi, dona nobis pacem."
ff. 6v–8v	Invitatory antiphon plus ten antiphons for Matins on the feast of St. John the Evangelist (see below, Table 2).

ff. 9r–56v	Lessons for the choral office beginning with the four Sundays of Advent (Inc. "INCIPIUNT LECTIONES ANNI CIRCULI. IN PRIMIS DE ADVENTU DOMINI. Ecce enim dominus egredietur de loco sancto suo . . .") and for the following feasts:
	
	    DE NATALE DOMINI (13r)
	    IN SANCTI IOHANNIS EVANGELISTAE (13v)
	    DE INNOCENTIS (14r)
	    DE EPIPHANIA (14v)
	    DE QUADRAGESIMO (15v)
	    DE ASCENSA DOMINI (25v)
	    DE PENTECOSTEN (28r)
	    IN SANCTI IOHANNES (31r)
	    IN SANCTI PETRI (32v)
	    IN OMNIUM APOSTOLORUM (34r)
	    IN UNIUS SACERDOTIS (37v)
	    IN PLURIMORUM CONFESSORUM (40v)
	    IN UNO MARTYRE (42r)
	    IN PLURIMORUM MARTYRUM (44r)
	    DE VIRGINIBUS (47v)
	    IN SANCTAE MARIAE PROPRIE (50r)

TABLE I. *Continued*

Folio	Contents
	IN DEDICATIONE TEMPLI (51r) DE COTIDIANO (52r).
fol. 57r	Closing verses of a hymn without musical notation; the top of the folio is illegible. The hymn has the refrain: "Sanctus Paulus admonuit." Inc. "—salvus fieri—Sanctus Paulus admonuit—." Exp. "Sanctus [Paulus admonuit]. Kanamus domino cum fide corde amore, ut eius nobis indulgentiam. Sanctus [Paulus admonuit]."
fol. 57v	*Versus Waldrammi ad Dadonem Episcopum a Salomone Episcopo Missis* (Paul de Winterfeld, ed., *Poetae Latini Aevi Carolini: Monumenta Germania Historica inde ab anno Christi quingentesimo usque ad annum millesimum et quingentesimum*, 4 [Berlin, 1899]: 311, lines 19–38 [hereinafter cited as *PLAC* 4]). Inc. "Aspera conditio et sors irrevocabilis ore . . ." Exp. ". . . Legifer ipse iacet Moyses Aaronque sacerdos allosquusque [sic] dei dignus amicus obit."
fol. 58r	Verses, Boethius (Consolation of Philosophy?). Inc. "METRUM BOETII. Heu quam praecipiri mens profundo mens . . ." Exp. ". . . Cogitur heu stolidam cernere terram."
fol. 58v	Hymn (Clemens Blume, Guido Maria Dreves, and Henry Marriott Bannister, eds., *Analecta Hymnica Medii Aevi* 50: 38 [hereinafter cited as *AH*]). Inc. "O crucifer bone lucis sator . . ." Exp. ". . . Funditopes ager ingenuans . . . ubi hac aviret."
fol. 59r	Versus, fragment. Inc. "Vestibunt filii tenera ramorum virgulta suis onerata ponis canunt . . ." Exp. ". . . Illa de celo concepit salvatorem, ista de campis fingit natos plures repletque vasa melet favum Christi sapore."
fol. 59rv	Versus, Paulinus of Aquileia (Ernest Dümmler, ed., *Poetae Latini Aevi Carolini*, 2 vols., *Monumenta Germaniae Historica* [Berlin, 1881, 1884], 1: 462, lines 1–11 [hereinafter cited as PLAC 1; 2]). Inc. "Fuit domini dilectus . . ." Exp. ". . . Ecce domine quem amas . . . heu relinquit germanas et obiit."
ff. 59v–60r	*Versus de Iacob et Ioseph* (*PLAC* 4: 462, lines 1–11). Inc. "Tertio in flore mundus . . ." Exp. ". . . Cumque eum fratres . . . occidamus et colemus sanguinem."
ff. 60v–61v	Lessons for the choral office (DE COTIDIANO?).
fol. 61v	Verses of a religious poem. Inc. "Quamvis setyrio superbus ostro commeret . . ." Exp. ". . . Quis illos igitur patet beatos quos miseri tribuunt honores."
fol. 62r	Versus, Boethius (*PLAC* 4: 421). Inc. "Qui se volet esse potentem . . ." Exp. ". . . non posse potentia non est."

TABLE I. *Continued*

Folio	Contents
	Versus, Boethius (Consolation of Philosophy?) Inc. "ITEM VERSUS BOETII. Eheu que miseros tramite devios . . ." Exp. ". . . et cum falsa gravimole paraverint, tum vera cognoscant bona."
ff. 62r–63r	Versus, Paulinus of Aquileia (*PLAC* 1: 144); ff. 62v–63r are palimpsests. Inc. "DE NATIVITATE DOMINI. Gloriam deo in excelsis hodie caelestis primum cecinit exercitus; pax angelorum . . ." Exp. ". . . Gloria sancte trinitati unicae patri natoque . . . per immensa saecula sit semper. Amen."
fol. 63r	Hymn (*AH* 50: 52); palimpsest. Inc. "Cantemus, socii, domino cantemas honore, dulcis amor christi personet ore pio. Primus . . ." Exp. ". . . Agnus ab hoste sacer revocavit sanguine patres, sanguine nosque, refert agnus ab hoste sacer."
ff. 63r–64r	*Versus de Iudit et Olofernum* (*PLAC* 4: 459); palimpsest. Inc. "Anno tertio in regno cum esset et decimo, Nabucondonsur coepit excitare . . ." Exp. ". . . Ille deus, qui percussit tunc castra Assyrii . . . perdat gentes nunct paganas auro [?] introitu."
fol. 64r	Versus (*PLAC* 4: 600); palimpsest. Inc. "Alexander puer magnus circumivit patriam usque ad mare oceanum . . ." Exp. ". . . Ibi fecit civitatem qui dicunt Alexandriam . . . per quem binus nominatur magnus Alexanderius."
fol. 64v	*Versus de laude dei* (*PLAC* 4: 524); palimpsest. Inc. "Adpropinquat finis secli, declinantur tempora . . ." Exp. ". . . Helias inheremo longo vite tempora covis defentibus sacro pane quis dedit? Benedictus [Dominus Christi Dei Filius] —/
fol. 65r	Hymn (*AH* 50: 31). Inc. "HYMNI PRUDENTII. Inventor rutili, dux bone . . ." Exp. ". . . Regnum contineat nomine [sic] triplici. Texens perpetuis saecula saeculis. Amen."
ff. 65v–68r	Lessons for the choral office.
ff. 68r–75v	Lessons from the Book of the Apocalypse.
ff. 76r–79r	Antiphons and responsories (without musical notation) for Matins, feast of St. Cucufatis.

earliest scribe (I) copied the lessons to be read at the choral office by the officiator. These cover the major feasts of the *Sanctorale* and *Temporale,* the Common of Saints, and the dedication of a church. They begin on fol. 9r, continue uninterrupted through the last leaf of gathering VII (fol. 56v), and pick up again on ff. 60v–61v, 65r–75v. Scribe I was also responsible for the antiphons and responsories (without musical notation) in honor of St. Cucufatis (ff. 76r–79r). The expert tenth-century miniscule executed by Scribe I, the small size and excellent grade of parchment employed for the original corpus, and, of course, the contents of the leaves, suggest that the book was intended for a high ecclesiastical dignitary, probably a bishop.

Scribe II copied hymns (without musical notation) and verses selected from the works of Fortunatus, Prudentius, Boethius, and others on ff. 57r–60r and 62r–65r. These items were added by someone other than the book's original owner since ff. 62v–64r are palimpsests; unwanted texts from the original corpus — probably sacred hymns or religious verses — were scraped away to make room for new ones. Yet, judging by the style of script and abbreviation techniques, these accretions were made during the tenth century, a relatively short time after Scribe I completed the original corpus. A comparison of this distinctive script with the writing in coeval Veronese sources further reveals that Scribe II was very likely Bishop Ratherius, the controversial tenth-century prelate of Verona.[6] If this be the case, then the additions of Scribe II probably date from the last period of Ratherius's episcopate, 961–968, since most of the bishop's earlier years were spent in exile or in prison.[7] The addition of poetic verses to a book for personal use, albeit one with liturgical texts, is consistent with the bishop's erudition.

Scribe III added the material comprising the first gathering of Cod. LXXXVIII (ff. 1–8): four orations, a litany sung during a para-liturgical procession through the city,[8] and the antiphons for the feast of St. John the Evangelist. Four of these were provided with musical notation — the Invitatory Antiphon *Valde honorandus est*, plus *Iohannes apostolus*, *Super pectus Domini*, and *Quasi unus* — although ample space for neumes was provided above the remaining texts. The style of Carolingian minuscule employed by Scribe III is generally ascribed to the early eleventh century (see

---

[6] G. Ongaro, "Cultura e Scuola calligrafica veronese del secolo X," *Memorie de R. Instituto veneto di Scienze, Lettere ed Arti*, XXXIX (1925), 50–57, describes the characteristics of Ratherius's script and discusses the role the bishop played in the development of the Veronese cathedral scriptorium.

[7] Guglielmo Ederle, *Dizionario cronologico bio-bibliografico dei Vescovi di Verona* (Verona: Edizioni di "Vita veronese," 1965), 30.

[8] G.G. Meersseman, E. Adda, and J. Deshusses, *L'Orazionale dell-'Arcidiacono Pacifico e il Carpsum del Cantore Stefano*, Spicileqium Friburgense, XXI (Friburg: Editions universitaire, 1974), 72.

TABLE 2. The Order of Matins Antiphons for the Feast of St. John the Evangelist

Cod. LXXXVIII		Cod. XCIV	
Inv. Ant. Valde honorandus est		Inv. Ant Adoremus regem, or Regem apostolorum	
1	Ant. Iohannes apostolus	1	Ant. Iohannes apostolus
2	Ant. Super pectus Domini	2	Ant. Super pectus Domini
3	Ant. Quasi unus	3	Ant. Quasi unus
4	Ant. In ferventis	4	Ant. In ferventis
5	Ant. Propter insuperabilem	5	Ant. Propter insuperabilem
6	Ant. Apparuit	6	Ant. Occurrit
7	Ant. Occurrit	7	Ant. Apparuit
8	Ant. Expandens	8	Ant. Expandens
9	Ant. Dominine suscipe	9	Ant. Domine suscipe

Appendix A). The musical notation (in the same brown ink), which combines northern Italian and French traits and is therefore unique among medieval Veronese sources, is also characteristic of the period.[9] The most unusual feature of the notation, and one which tends to confirm the early date, is the appearance of the *salicus*, the liquescent *scandicus*, a neume form that falls out of use in later Veronese plainchant manuscripts.[10]

Corroborating evidence for the proposed dating of gathering 1 derives from a comparison of the Matins formulary for the feast on St. John in Cod. LXXXVIII with the list of chants for the same service contained in the cathedral's eleventh-century *Liber ordinarius*, called the Carpsum, Bibl. cap. XCIV[11] (see Table 2). First, the sources assign to the Matins service different Invitatory antiphons: *Valde honorandus est* in Cod. LXXXVIII, *Adoremus regem* or *Regam apostolorum* in the Carpsum. Moreover, although the order of the next five antiphons is identical, *Apparuit* occurs sixth in Cod. LXXXVIII, seventh in XCIV. Since Scribe III did not observe the order of chants prescribed in the Carpsum, it is probable that he completed his additions prior to its compilation around 1050 (*terminus post quem*).[12]

---

[9] Bruno Stäblein, *Schriftbild der Einstimmigen Musik*, Musikgescnichte in Bildern IV, no. 3 (VEB Deutscher Verlag für Musik, 1975), 36.

[10] See Borders, *op. cit.*, 227–287.

[11] See Meersseman *et al.*, *op. cit.*, 229.

[12] *Ibid.*, 97.

It remains to account for the liturgical anomaly presented by cod. LXXXVIII, namely the incorporation of antiphons and responsories for the feast of St. Cucufatis into the original corpus of the manuscript. (The texts are edited below in Appendix B.) This is puzzling because, although the cult of this patron of Barcelona flourished in medieval Spain and France, July 27, the date which marks the saint's feast in the Barcelona[13] and Mozarabic[14] traditions, is vacant in all medieval Veronese calendars.[15] Therefore, to explain why these texts appear in a Veronese book, we must look beyond the local sanctoral cycle, turning our attention to the medieval cult of saints.

In the late eighth century, Abbot Fulrad of Saint-Denis (d. 784) procured the remains of St. Cucufatis for his abbey. For reasons now unclear, they were shortly transferred to the Benedictine priory at Lièvre in Alsace. Finally, in 835, the relics were returned to Saint-Denis where they were interred in the crypt of the abbey church.[16] Perhaps as a result of these exchanges, legends concerning the relics began to circulate, and during the tenth century, a cult of St. Cucufatis evolved among West Frankish monks.[17]

It is likely that the Veronese lectionary was prepared according to the specifications of a bishop from the western regions of the Frankish Empire who was also a Benedictine monk. Such a request may have come from Bishop Ilduinus, Ratherius's predecessor, a Benedictine from Corvej and bishop of Verona from 928 to 931.[18] This hypothesis is in keeping with the paleographical evidence, which indicates that the original corpus dates from the first half of the tenth century.

Thus the history of Verona Cod. LXXXVIII may be summarized as follows. The manuscript originally belonged to a Frankish bishop of Verona who was also a Benedictine monk, the most likely candidate being Ilduinus. Apparently Ilduinus's devotion to the cult of St. Cucufatis endured despite his assignment to a northern Italian episcopal see; perhaps the bishop was able to gather a small group of his fellow monks

---

[13] Jacques Paul Migne, *Patrologia cursus completus . . . Series latina*, LXXXV, col. 1053.

[14] *Ibid.*, col. 1170.

[15] See Borders, *op. cit.*, 288–321. Readings for the Office of St. Cucufatis were included in the Mozarabic Orationale, Verona Bibl. Cap. Cod. LXXXIX, ff. 118v–119r, a manuscript which reached Verona from Spain during the eighth century. A direct relation between the books may be ruled out however, since the Orationale does not contain chant texts.

[16] *Biblioteca Sanctorum*, s.v. "Cucufatis."

[17] *Ibid.*, col. 387.

[18] Ederle, *op. cit.*, 29–30.

to perform Matins on the feast day. Upon the bishop's death, the small liturgical book passed to his successor Ratherius, another Frankish Benedictine, who copied devotional as well as secular verses of his own choosing into the manuscript.

The contents of added gathering 1 suggest that Cod. LXXXVIII remained in the possession of a local ecclesiastical dignity into the early eleventh century. Since the bishop and the cathedral clergy were, by statute, required to celebrate the Office and Mass at the church of S. Giovanni in Valle on three feasts — among them the feast of St. John the Evangelist[19] — a small, portable book containing the chants for Matins seems quite practical. Perhaps the clergy performed these items at various churches in the course of a procession from the cathedral to the dependent church, which stood just outside the city walls. Although no incontrovertible evidence survives, local custom may have dictated the singing of the litany of saints[20] during such processions, perhaps accounting for its appearance before the formulary for Matins.[21] In any case, the litany, along with the four prayers for votive Masses on fol. 1v, were not assigned to a specific feast, but were performed on various occasions for special intentions.

Thus by taking scribal practices, local customs, and ecclesiastical history into consideration, we stand in a favorable position to explain many of the apparent irregularities preserved in medieval and Renaissance liturgical books. With care, the unraveled threads may be rewoven into a rich and colorful fabric representative of the history of western European liturgy.

APPENDIX A

Physical Description

Verona, Biblioteca capitolare, Cod. LXXXVIII

1. Number of leaves:
   80, plus 4 modern parchment flyleaves added at restoration, plus a

---

[19] For documentary evidence of this custom, see Giambatista Biancolini, *Notizie storiche della Chiese di Verona*, 8 vols. (Verona, 1749–1771), 4: 633.

[20] This litany lacks any mention of the patrons of Verona; it invokes categories of saints, apostles, martyrs, confessors, and virgins rather than individuals. Meersseman *et al.*, *op. cit.*, 72.

[21] The Carpsum prescribes processions from the cathedral to St. Giovanni in Valle on other feasts. Meersseman *et al.*, *op. cit.*, 229, sec. 105, 230, sec. 117.

single paper flyleaf (nineteenth century?).
2. Parchment:
   a. Size: 145 × 115 mm.
   b. Quality: good; light brown on both sides; color varies to white on skin side; few imperfections; many later folios have been damaged.
3. Binding and restoration:
   Wood and maroon leather with shelf number LXXXVIII stamped on the lowest portion of the spine. Modern pagination in Arabic numbers in upper right corners of recto leaves.
   Restored in Verona in 1962.
4. Writing area: 95 × 65 mm.
   a. Number of lines per folio: 15, corpus; 15–16, added leaves; drypoint.
   b. Space between lines: 6 mm., corpus.
   c. Marginal ruling: double bounding lines, 9 mm. apart, at both margins, corpus.
5. Foliation (quire numbers which appear at the bottom of leaves are indicated in parentheses): see Table 3.
6. Decoration: none.

TABLE III. Foliation of Bibl. cap. cod. LXXXVIII

Gathering	Structure/Description
Y²	two modern parchment flyleaves plus one paper folio
I⁸	ff. 1–8
II⁸	ff. 9–16
III⁸	ff. 17–24
IV⁸	ff. 24–32
V⁸	ff. 33–40 (vi, 40v)
VI⁸	ff. 41–48
VII⁸	ff. 49–56
VIII⁸	ff. 57–64
IX⁸	ff. 65–72
X⁸	73 74 75 76 77 ——————— 78 79 80
	[restored]
Z²	two modern parchment flyleaves

Scribe I

[Contribution to the MS:
   ff. 9r–56v, 60v–61v, 65v–71v, readings for the choral Office;
   ff. 76r–79r, antiphons and responsories (without musical notation)
   for the feast of St. Cucufatis; fol. 80v, aphorism.]
7. Script:
   a. Color of ink, text: light brown; rubrics: red (Rustic capitals).
   b. General characteristics: Carolingian minuscule; tall ascending
      traits, tend to be clubbed.
   c. Ligatures: ET, OR (in -*orum*), RA (ᴙᴀ), ST.
   d. Abbreviations: *nomina sacra*, abbreviation stroke for m or n, ƀ
      (-*bis*), b; (-*bus*), ē (*est*), n̄ (*non*), p (*per*), p" (*per*, fol. 44r), p̄
      (*prae*), q̄ (*quae*), qⁱ (*qui*), sup" (*super*), superscript ꝰ (-*us*).
      Extensive Tironian abbreviations in a later hand appear through-
      out the readings.
   e. Specific letter forms:
      a Uncial form only.
      d occasionally curved.
      f vertical trait dips below the line.
      g both bows are open.
      m spiked vertical traits; final stroke sometimes has foot.
      n majuscule form appears occasionally, especially at the ends of
         lines (iN, fol. 45v).
      r spiked vertical trait, finishes on the line.
      s vertical trait stops on the line.

Scribe II

[Contribution to the MS:
   ff. 57r–60r, 62r–65r, hymns and verses. (Fol. 62v is a
   palimpsest.)]
7. Script:
   a. General characteristics: Carolingian minuscule of inferior qua-
      lity; ruled lines on the folios are typically ignored. The writing of
      Scribe II has a cursive quality — note the loops on the ascenders:
      "in excel*sis* ho*di*e cae*l*estis," fol. 62v, line 2, and elsewhere. Other
      ascending traits have clubs. Initials in the text are done in Rustic
      capitals.
   b. Ligatures: EC, ET, EX, OR (in -*orum*), NT (occideNTis, fol. 63v,
      line 4), ST.
   c. Abbreviations: *nomina sacra*, abbreviation stroke for m or n, ƀ
      (-*bis*), b; (-*bus*), ē (*est*), g° (*ergo*), n̄ (*non*), p̣ (*per*), p̄ (*prae*), ꝓ
      (*pro*),

q̄ (*quae*), q; (*que*), qⁱ (*qui*), q° (*quo*), qđ (*quod*), supᵃ (*supra*).
d. Specific letterforms:
   e eye rises well above the minim line; this feature is exaggerated in ligatures (&).
   f horizontal trait dips below line.
   g upper bow is round and closed.
   n majuscule form sometimes was employed, especially in the abbreviation for *Domini* (dNi).
   s vertical trait rests on the line.

Scribe III

[Contribution to the MS:
   fol. 1v, four prayers;
   ff. 2r–6r, litany of the saints;
   ff. 6v–8v, antiphons for St. John the Evangelist, four with musical notation.]

7. Script:
   a. Color of ink, text: brown.
   b. General characteristics: Carolingian minuscule, probably of the early eleventh century. Note the ticks on the final traits of m and n, and on the letter i.
   c. Ligatures: AE, ET, OR (in -*orum*), ST.
   d. Abbreviations: *nomina sacra*, abbreviation stroke for m or n and for the suspension of words, ꝓ (*pro*), q̄s̄ (*quaesumus*), nob (*nobis*).
   e. Specific letterforms:
      a Uncial form only.
      d tall form exclusively.
      e long finishing stroke which touches the adjacent minim.
      g both bows are closed; upper bow sometimes made in two traits (ℊ).
      m,m feet on final traits.
      r horizontal trait dips below the line regularly.
      s frequently stops on the line.

8. Musical notation:
   a. Style and general characteristics: combines traits of French, northern Italian, and Milanese styles.
   b. Specific neumeforms:
      punctum: somewhat elongated dash.
      virga: simple stick; ductus slopes about 35 degrees to the right; sometimes with thickening at the top.

podatus (*pes*): forma recta (⌐).
clivis: cursive neume with slight tick on the final stroke (⌐).
scandicus: only the liquescent form *salicus* (⌐) appears.
climacus: *virga* plus two *puncta* (⌐).
torculus: resembles a *podatus* plus *clivis* (⌐).
Liquescent neumes: in addition to the *salicus*, the notation of these leaves includes the *epiphonus* (⌐), and two forms of the *cephalicus* (⌐ ,). The latter appears to be related to the Milanese form.
quilisma: (⌐ ⌐).

APPENDIX B

Antiphons and Responseries for the Feast of Saint Cucufatis, (texts only), Bibl. cap. cod. Ms LXXXII

fol. 76r*   Ant. Egregius Christi martyr Cucuphas oravit Deum et dixit: Domine meus Ihesu Christe qui creasti omnia, exaudi me certantem cum diabolo, et ostende incredulis mirabilia tua. Ps. Beatus vir.
(Mobritius 1: 354, lines 5–6: "Domine Iesu Christe ostende virtutem tuam super incredulis.")
Ant. Beatissimus Cucuphas Scillitana civitate nobilissimis exstitit natalibus oriundus, fide Christi praepotens, clarissimus fulsit in populis.
(Mombritius 1: 353, lines 28–29: "Sanctus Cucufatus ex Scillitana civitate nobilissimis ac ditissimis natalibus oriundus.")
Ant. Eximius Cucuphas agonista divinus coepit prodigiorum resplendere miraculis in nomine Domini et virtute Christi.
(Mombritius 1: 353, lines 42–44: "Sanctus autem Cucufatus in Barcinona urbe populosa remanens una cum constantissima et apertissima fide et praedicatione etiam miraculis resplendere coepit.")
Ant. Ita namque in gratiam curationum excrevit, ut nemo ab eo salutem exposceret, qui non sine mora perciperet.
(Mombritius 1: 353, lines 44–46; ". . . et in omni gratia

---

* See Plate 1.

curationum excrevit: daemones solo verbo expellebat: et
virtutem Domini confitentes etiam a credentium finibus
perturbabat.")

Ant. Quae audiens iudex, directis militibus suis
tribunalibus, iussit eum offerri.

(Mombritius 1: 353, lines 46–47: "Hoc audiens proconsul
Gallerius directis militibus eum sibi offerri iussit.")

fol. 76v ** Ant. Cum vidisset proconsul Sanctum Domini nimio
furore succensus, gravissimam eum iubet subire
sententiam.

(Mombritius 1: 354, lines 1–2: "Hac responsione Gallerius
nimio furore succensus: et seipsum ab ira con capiens
. . .")

Ant. Tradensque eum tortoribus dixit: Tamdiu torquete
eum, quousque spiritum eius extorqueatis ab eo.

(Mombritius 1: 354, lines 2–3 ". . . tortoribus eum tradidit
dicens: Tamdiu torquete eum: quamdiu extorqueatis ab
eo spiritum.")

Ant. Cumque Sanctus Domini gravissime torqueretur voce
magna clamavit, Tu nosti, Deus omnipotens, quia haec
supplicia pro tuo sancto nomine libentissime sustineo.

(Mombritius 1: 354, lines 3–4: "Cumque duodecim milites
eum vicissim prolixius et exquisita crudelitate gravissime
torqueretur, adeo ut eius intestina durissima flagel-
lorum torsione, disrupto corpore, paterent, clamavit.")

Ant. Videntes autem milites intestina sancti viri profusa in
terram, caecati sunt, et Gallerius cum suis idolis repente
consumptus est.

(Mombritius 1: 354, lines 9–11: "Videntes milites qui eum
torquebant intestina eius in terram perfusa caecati sunt.
Gallerius quoque cum omnibus idolis suis est repente
consumptus.")

Ant. Gloriosus Cucuphas, visceribus in alvum ad oram
receptis, citius est divina operatione sanatus.

(Mombritius 1: 354, lines 11–12: "Sanctus vero martyr
visceribus in alvum receptis: citius est divina operatione
sanatus.")

Ant. Beatus Cucuphas, expansis ad caelum manibus, ait:
gratias tibi ago omnipotens Salvator mundi, qui me

---

primo plasmasti modo, iterum quasi a novo tua gratia
reformasti.

fol. 77r   Ant. Tunc omnes populi laudem dederunt Domino,
dicentes: Tu es Deus verus qui facis mirabilia haec.

(Mombritius 1: 354, lines 12–13: "Quo gratias agente,
omnes quoque populi laudaverunt Deum, dicentes: Tu
es verus Deus, quem Sanctus Cucufatus colit.")

Ant. Adloquens (?) autem Christi ad populum ait: videtis
quanta mirabilia fecit Deus verus, quem praedico vobis,
credere vos oportet in eum et ipsum adorare.

Ant. Magnus es Deus Cucuphatis ac potentissimus
liberator.

(Mombritius 1: 354, line 41: "Magnus est Deus
christianorum et potentissimus liberator eorum.")

RESPONSORIA UNDE SUPRA

Resp. Beatissimus Cucuphas Scillitana civitate nobilissimis
exstitit natalibus oriundus, fide Christi praepotens,
clarissimus fulsit in populis.

(Mombritius 1: 353, lines 28–29)

V. Daemones quoque solo verbo [ex]pellebat et a
credentium finibus perturbabat fide.

(Mombritius 1: 353, lines 44–45: "Daemones solo verbo
expellebat: et virtutem Domini confitentes etiam a
credentium finibus perturbabat.")

Resp. Eximius Cucuphas agonista divinus coepit
prodigiorum resplendere miraculis in nomine Domini et
virtute Christi.

(Mombritius 1: 353, lines 42–44)

V. Ita namque in gratiam curationum excrevit, ut nemo ab
eo salutem exposceret, qui non sine mora perciperet. In
nomine.

(Mombritius 1: 353, lines 44–46)

fol. 77v   Resp. Cumque Sanctus Domini gravissime torqueretur, ita
ut disrupto corpore interanea apparerent, voce magna
clamavit: Tu nosti, Deus omnipotens, quia haec
supplicia pro tuo sancto nomine libentissime sustineo.

(Mombritius 1: 354, lines 3–4)

V. Domine Iesu Christe qui omnia tuo praecepto fundasti
et me de fragilissimo limi pulvere formasti. Tu [nosti].

Resp. Domine Iesu Christe, qui cuncta prospicis, ostende

virtutem tuam incredulis, qui nomen tuum per-
sequuntur, ut videntes mirabilia tua credant et
convertantur.

V. Illumina faciem tuam super servos tuos et salvifica eos in
tua misericordia. Ut v[identes].

Resp. Iussit tyrannus Sanctum Domini et craticula assari et
abustum sinape et aceto perfundi, et sic in flammam
ferventem mitti.

(Mombritius 1: 354, lines 23–24: "Tunc praeses insaniens
in craticula iussit eum assari: et combustum sinapi et
aceto perfundi.")

V. Iratus autem praeses praecepit triumphantem Domini
bellatorem ferro vinctum suis tribunalibus praesentari.
Et abustum.

(Mombritius 1: 354, lines 29–31: "Tunc praeses iussit eum
ferro vinctum in custodiam reduci.")

Resp. Puer meus. V. Liberate de manu pessimorum.

fol 78r   Resp. In medio flammarum Christi hostia extendens
palmas cum alacritate cordis ait: Adesto mihi nunc
Domine Iesu Christe, qui in fornace ignea fidelibus tuis
tribus pueris adfuisti.

V. Invictissime Cucuphas martyr Christi psallebat, dicens.
Adesto.

(Mombritius 1: 354, lines 24–25: "Miles autem Christi
psallebat dicens.")

Resp. Retruditur Sanctus Domini catenarum pondere
pressus orans et dicens: satia, Christe, animas
esurientium te et sitientium sanguinis tui
consecrationem.

V. Tantum autem splendor ibidem refulsit, ut custodes
carceris crederent Christo; unde Sanctus gavisus ait:
Satia, Christe.

Resp. Confessor Domini, caesus chordis ferreis, suspiciens
[in] caelum cum magna voce dixit: Ago tibi gratias,
omnipotens Deus Iesu Christe, quia adpropinquavit
mihi gratia tua.

V. Dixit praeses militibus: Tormenta adhibete, ut
exterminetur caro eius, et hostia Domini ad haec agebat.

Resp. Famulo Christi in praecibus commorante salutaris
vox de caelis ruit, dicens: Quodcumque petieris dabitur
tibi secundum fidem tuam.

V. Corrobora cor meum, Christe, et da virtutem servo tuo qui mihi pollicitus es modo. Quodcumque.

fol. 78v   Resp. Cucuphas praedicator sanctissimus, adplaudente populo credentium fide, ita exorsus ait: Tibi laus Domine Iesu Christe; tibi omnis debetur honor et adoratio, qui incredulos destruis et te diligentes glorificas.

V. Quoniam magnus es tu et faciens mirabilia; tu es Deus solus. Ti[bi laus].

Resp. Deus omnipotens Domine Iesu Christe, qui fecisti omnia in virtute tua, fac misericordiam mihi servo tuo in hoc agone novissimo, ut gaudens in exultationem sanctorum introire merear.

V. Suspice nunc, Iesu benigne, animam meam in pace, sciens quia te desideravi ex toto corde. Ut gaudens.

ANTIPHONAE IN MATUTINIS LAUDIBUS

Ant. Sanctus autem Cucuphas ad praesidem dixit: Ego Deum alium nescio praeter Dominum, qui est Deus verus quem corde credo [et] ore confiteor et omni studio praedico.

Ant. Repletus iracundia iudex dixit: Si verus Deus est ille tuus quem dicis, modo veniat et eripiat te de manibus meis et de praeparatis tormentis.

Ant. Iussit tyrannus Sanctum Domini et craticula assari et abustum sinape et aceto perfundi, et sic in flammam ferventem mitti. (M 1, 354, lines 23–24)

Ant. Hostia Christi Cucuphas in mediis ignibus dans laudis praeconia ab omni vapore flammae inlaesus intractusque apparuit.

Ant. Tibi laus, Domine meus Iesu Christe; gloria tibi Deus omnipotens gratiarum actiones persolvo, qui incredulos destruis et te diligentes glorificas.

Ant. Deus omnipotens Domine Iesu Christe, qui fecisti omnia in virtute tua, fac misericordiam mihi servo tuo, et suscipe animam meam in pace, sciens quia te desideravi ex toto corde. Alleluia.

CHAPTER TWO

GREEK LETTER NOTATION IN THE *SPECULUM MUSICAE*: ELEMENTS OF A MUSICAL GAME

F. Joseph Smith

Chicago

Greek letter notation in a medieval treatise may sound like an elitist topic, because on the surface it is not immediately useful to the musician or the general reader. Yet in a lively and pertinent way the subject was basic to the whole rationale of that medieval Master of the Game, Jacques de Liège, a fundamental part of his musical game-plan in compiling his encyclopedia of musical knowledge in what Apel has called the most exhaustive treatise on music in the Middle Ages, a work that can hardly be ignored by the conscientious medievalist. Historically, Greek notation involves the first attempt in Western music to distill musical experience and performance into signs and symbols that constituted the *Glasperlenspiel* over which the Magister Ludi presided.[1] If we regard Jacques de Liège in this light, he becomes considerably more than even the author and compiler of the largest musical work of

---

[1] Hermann Hesse's classic work, *The Glass Bead Game*, a well-known masterpiece of twentieth century literature, describes the modern form of the speculative game played by Jacques de Liège in his encyclopedic medieval opus. Hesse redefines musicology's task in the light of this larger Game, something called for in his own masterful manner by Curt Sachs, who encouraged us to relate musicology to other arts and to general culture.

the late Middle Ages. He becomes a figure important in the eyes of such a virtuoso literateur and writer as Hermann Hesse, a matter not only of scientific musicology but potentially also of world literature and culture. For, though Hesse never knew of the *Speculum Musicae*, his Glass Bead Game began with the musical abacus, and his invoking of a larger and literary definition of musicology itself can hardly be ignored. In this view the musicologist is the player par excellence of this intriguing Game and is a prime candidate for Master of the Game, the Magister Ludi.

I

With Greek letter notation we catch the Game at but one primitive point, in its very origins, involving such masters as Boethius, Isidore and Guido. Jacques himself presents the medieval materials of the Game, as well as essential ground rules and structures, particularly his fundamental theory of musical proportionality, the key to all musical consonances and thus to any musical composition, whether (in his mind) of the Ars Antiqua or of the Ars Nova. Jacques abets the effort by giving what amounts to a *parvus prologus*, in which he maps out his procedure and intent: to describe the Greek alphabet and special notational signs interspersed within it; to show which letters and which notes go with what monochordal strings; to adapt this to the three musical genders (diatonic, chromatic, and enharmonic); and to show in detail the notational and modal implications thereof.[2]

---

[2] *Speculum Musicae*, VI ("Corpus Scriptorum de Musica," III, ed. Roger Bragard [Rome: American Institute of Musicology, 1973]), cap. 5, p. 19. In his book, *Homo Ludens*, J. Huizinga described in great detail the play mentality of the Middle Ages. The general idea is doubtless applicable to the *Speculum Musicae*. But, reference to actual *playing* is restricted to the playing of musical instruments. Thus, in Liber I, cap. 3, p. 18, the author states: ". . . ut bene et perfecte *ludere* sciant in suis artificialibus instrumentis vel cantare instrumentis naturalibus mediantibus" (emphasis mine); cap. 15, p. 55, "Unde potest esse bonus musicus, qui nescit *ludere* in instrumentis . . ."; cap. 19, p. 64, ". . . vel instrumentorum talium vel talium *lusorem*, ut buccinatorem, organizatorem, citharoedam . . ." However, there is little doubt that in the large sense envisioned by both Huizinga and Hesse, the "speculation" of the *Speculum Musicae* is an intellectual playing with the multifaceted mirror of the mind, making use of all the elements of music discussed above. The complete *musicus* is one who commands both practical and theoretical music. *Cf.* Liber I, cap. 3, p. 19, "Si quis autem musicam theoricam simul et practicam possideret, perfectior esset musicus eo qui solum haberet alteram, dum tamen perfecte ambas possideret, ut alteram alter possidet."

While girding himself for this formidable task, Jacques also frankly admits to his deficiencies in the knowledge of Greek, asking the reader to forgive him for being able only to depict the letters and notation as they lay before him in his available sources. It is not our purpose here to reduplicate the excellent graphs ready at hand for the diligent reader to inspect. But we can aid him or her in pointing out the differences between the classic Greek alphabet and that given by Jacques. The first thing that strikes someone familiar with Greek is that Jacques puts the Greek musical notation within the alphabet itself. And we can at once identify these *notae*: the episimon, ς; the cophe in both forms, ∇ or ⅃; the ennacos in either form, ↑ or Υ; and the chyle, ⋔ or Φ. Two of these letters are called number notes (*nota numeri*), the cophe and the ennacos, indicating already that the Game will involve number theory and proportionality, Jacques's contribution to what would otherwise only be a curiosity or a lexicographical entity. As to the letters themselves, one can note what appear to be Cyrillic forms not available in the classic alphabet, thus: lambda (sic!), Ⱡ, in addition to the classic Λ; and sigma, ⊂. Other variants, appearing perhaps only in music theory are ⊶₀ as additional M; ⊱ as an extra N; 3 as variant for ⅂ (usually Ξ); T in addition to ⅂ (usually Π); I as extra for T; and Υ as variant for Ψ. The ʋ (vi) is problematic also for Jacques, as he explicitly states.[3] All of this is of more immediate interest and concern to the linguistic scientist specializing in forms of the Greek alphabet. But for the musicologist, at least in Hermann Hesse's enhanced meaning, it is all part of the Game. It constitutes, in fact, the primary musical abacus.

In Liber VI, cap. 7 this becomes evident enough; for, relying on Isidore of Seville, the author tells us that letters have the power to become the signs and symbols of things and words, becoming the vehicles of memory concepts and the embodiment of facts themselves. The letters thus invite the reader on a veritable musical journey, he writes; and we might add, into the Game itself. This *iter legentis* can hardly be anything else, if it is to be more than a dead item in our encyclopedic musical knowledge.[4] The reader is asked to master the magic letters that will allow him to share the process of eventual epistemic achievement.

In Liber VI, cap. 7, we are treated to a literally colorful chapter on the Greek letters, being informed that the Phoenicians were the first to invent and use them, introducing also initial letters in red, the Phoeni-

---

[3] *Speculum Musicae*, VI, chart on p. 20 with photostat of MS P₁ (Parisinus Latinus 7207) facing; p. 28 on "vi."

[4] *Ibid.*, cap. 7, p. 21.

cian color taken from the people themselves, here described as being of
ruddy complexion![5] Among the letters certain ones stand out as symbo-
lically important. Thus, according to Pythagoras of Samos the letter Y
stands for human life itself. At the top the letter is bifurcated, the cross-
roads dividing the right from the left, i.e., according to our theorist, the
arduous path of righteous beatitude from the easy path that leads to sin
and corruption, a quaint notion that overlooks the fact that the path of
sinful and corrupt righteousness is equally arduous. One already gets a
good hint at what the Game is for this particular Magister Ludi. The
letter Θ stands for death (thanatos); and, of course, the T stands for the
cross, along with A and Ω, as the beginning and the end of things, a
crucial consideration.

Greek letters likewise functioned as numbers, moreso than Latin
letters still do. But the letter notation, more importantly, is adapted to
the musical genders and modes as well. But what is the function of these
notulae? Isidore has given us the expanded notion of these letter-notes.
They fit into the larger category of popular, juridical, military, and
confidential *notulae sententiarum*.[6] More pertinent of our purposes is
the musical notation itself, which expressed the vocables of strings,
genders, modes, and tonal divisions, rhythmic constitution and the
melody itself. The letters thus indicated just about everything one
needed to know about the rendition of music. The purpose was to
preserve the music for posterity; but it is up to "posterity" to play the
musical Game, now that all these musical elements have been supplied.

To exemplify the above, Jacques selects the lydian mode as characteristic, all of this explicitly adapted to the monochord. In so doing
Jacques makes a remark crucial to his critique of the musicians of the
Ars Nova, namely, that if Boethius could thus defer to the ancients, it
was a pity that the moderns, both singers and notators or scribes, could
not show similar respect for the opinions of the musical theorists of the
Ars Antiqua. Boethius was not Greek but Latin, and yet he gave a
systematic presentation of the ancient monochord and of the ancient
notational system.[7] Jacques avers that this example deserved imitation
on the part of the new musicians. Whatever the case may be, he
describes the lydian mode in Greek letter notation from the proslambanomenos (notated by a partial zeta over a sideways tau) through to
the nete hyperboleon (characterized by an iota and a sideways lambda

[5] *Ibid.*, p. 22.
[6] *Ibid.*, cap. 13, p. 40.
[7] *Ibid.*, cap. 8, p. 25.

plus appropriate strokes). Thanks to the incredible endurance of Roger Bragard, the editor of the Urtext, the chapter is there for the reader personally to admire and decipher.

Philologists will doubtless also note the explanation of the digamma, with help from Isidore's *Etymologia*. It has to do with the voiceless non-consonant, V, as in the word, *quis*. However, it is not simply nothing, because it can sometimes enhance the sound of the consonant, Q, with which it fuses. Another digammon is F, made up, he states, of two gammas, one above the other! In presenting this material without comment, one merely provides material for someone else more versed in the significance of such things. It is important for musicology only as part of the letter-notation alphabet.

In a further chapter and graph Jacques shows with Latin letters how the Greek voices match the modal genders, "repeating the names of the chords or strings." The whole apparatus is thus directly linked to the monochord. But he writes of chords and strings. Hence one wonders whether he is actually speaking of the monochord or of the tetrachord, described elsewhere as the practical instrument. Or he could be writing of the natural tetrachords obtainable on the one-stringed instrument, the monochord. One can only conjecture at this confusion. In practice, one has to work with the theoretical tetrachord on the monochord, it seems to me. The excellent graph shows clearly enough what Latin letters can be matched with what Greek letters, thus F with Z/T of the proslambanomenos, G with the regular and converse gamma of the hypate hypaton, forming a tonus, A with the R and L forming a semitone with the parhypate hypaton, etc., thus TST in all. (The R is, of course, a mutated B.)

The pertinent chapters (cap. 5 through 14) are loaded with musicological nuggets, as well, providing materials for the Game. Thus, letters and numbers are brought together in identical symbols, as alpha signifies one, beta two, gamma three, delta four, and so on. For the proportional game that Jacques already plays so well, without any reference to Hesse's Game, the conjunction of letters with numbers is of potential import. But as ordinary musicologist, I simply note it in passing. A more colorful historical nugget is proferred us in one declarative sentence, namely, that the nymph, Carmentis, Capitoline prophetess, as we can identify her, was the first to bring Latin lettering into Italy. We know from other sources that she was the mother of Evander, founder of the town of Pallantium at the foot of the Palatine hill within the present site of Rome. Carmentis supposedly came to Latium with Evander, bringing with her Latin letters, according to this one-liner. Perhaps she also had an abacus along with her to start up the Game. But all this is just so much quaint archaic knowledge, except that it provides a real link between medieval latinity and classic sources. This opens up the field of studious interest beyond mere nuggetry. The fact that latinity was introduced by a musical prophetess is also significant, joining word and song in her very name. The historically amusing find, which ordinarily would serve only to bring seraphic smiles of contentment to classicist or musicologist of the tradition, now has possibilities that could be developed in the Game.

Going beyond the lydian mode, Jacques demonstrates the use of Greek lettering in the other modes, but concentrates only on the diatonic gender, providing once more an excellent chart for our use, lining up the eight modes with the Greek strings, from proslambanomenos through nete hyperboleon. "secundum directum ordinem."[8] Every mode is paired with each string with a set of two Greek letters each, and the diagonal *notae similes* are opposed to and contrast with the *dissimiles* in a cross-reference of modalities that was a delight to the medieval mind and eye, but is mostly a curiosity to us. But this, too, is exquisite material for the Game. As the greatest medieval compiler of facts, numbers, notes, modes, and even of musical examples (cf. Libri VI and VII, as well as IIb), Jacques de Liège at least provides a prolegomenon to any truly musicological game-plan, as we shall see below, in synoptic view.

An additional and perhaps the most important graph now details the differences between the individual tones, with the *intercapedo* or interstitial blank space denoting the tonus (T), and the *tractus linealis* or simply the line/stroke that separates each space and denoting the minor semitone (S).[9] Again, this has to do only with the diatonic version of the eight modes and contains "the order and distinction" of the modes, insofar as one is higher than the other in its modal incipit (in suo principio), higher by a tone or semitone, as e.g., the hypophrygian compared with the hypodorian modes, or mixolydian relative to the lydian modes. The tonal distances from tonus through diapason are closely related, and tones become the building blocks of modes. In this context, obviously, tonus is not interchangeable with modus, though elsewhere in the *Speculum Musicae* they more often are. In the first chart Latin proportional numbers, derived from Boethius, are annotated in four places, the first number, 9216, being four times the least,

[8] *Ibid.*, cap. 10, p. 31; cap. 11, p. 34.
[9] *Ibid.*, cap. 13, p. 40.

1152, eventually to compute in terms of a ter diapason founded in an octuple proportion. As arcane as this might seem to the non-mathematician of our time or of those times, the important thing is that musical proportionality, the very basis of medieval music, is here introduced into the letter system which already has exemplified the modes on the monochord. What coordinates everything and is the link between mathematics and music is precisely musical proportionality. It is the lynchpin of the Game itself. From the musicological viewpoint, we note the compactness of a presentation that provides us with letters, numbers, modes, tones, and now with musical proportions. Even without the Game this is more than just a quaint account of Greek letter notation.

In the second of these final letter-graphs the strings of the single modes are named along with the voices and letters of "our monochord", i.e., the diatonic medieval monochord, as opposed to the trigender Greek one. Jacques details and explains that the chart 1.) matches the monochordal voices, i.e. Are, Bmi, etc. with the key letters, F, G, A, etc.; 2.) places beneath these voices the Greek equivalent, thus the proslambanomenos underneath Are, hypate hypaton beneath Bmi, and so on; 3.) stresses the existence of the diapason between Latin letters starting from F to g, at the juncture of the trite synemmenon, thus between F and f but not between G and g hypate hypaton, rather G at the paramese; 4.) the numbers are posited in which musical proportions of consonants pair with keys and voices, and 5.) placement of the Greek letters and notes, as already explained.[10] Now, although the eight modes differ in ascending scale, they agree in sharing an equal number of strings and voices, bridging a double diapason in their range, from proslambanomenos to nete hyperboleon. Thus the ancient monochord as described by Boethius and subsumed into the medieval system of Jacques de Liège!

Pursuing this further, Jacques states that the identical numbers obtain between the modes in accord with the unison formed lineally between them on the chart. Thus, the proslambanomenos of the eighth mode contains directly beneath it the hypate hypaton of the seventh mode, and so on through the rest of the modes. There occurs a continuous doubling of the numbers connected with each modal start, and at every modal intersection and in tetrachordal formation. Jacques assures us that through experimentation with the numbers he has

---

[10] *Ibid.*, cap. 12, p. 36.

correctly concluded there is an integral proportion between e.g., the numbers of the tetrachord of the hyperboleon of the eighth mode in chromatic gender, not just the diatonic, since 82944, the Boethian number, is divisible into nine equal parts, a ninth being the number 9216. Taken from the first number, 73728 results, and computing the tetrachordal numbers in sequence (82944 78732 73728 69984 62208) there results a sesquitertian proportion between the extremes, i.e., the major term contains the minor plus a third, 20736. The sesquioctave proportion is similarly computable. The chromatic gender is a little more complicated and consists in taking away the number closest to the minor term from the first five, leaving a diatessaron that computes integrally as chromatic. It is not merely a matter of abstract number theory but of number as applied to musical sound, anchored in the monochord. For, the numerical proportions are matched exactly within the system of the monochordal strings, i.e., divisions of the sole string. In this the tonal distance and the division of the semitone play an important role, and Jacques recalls what was already treated of in Liber III on the minor semitone.[11]

Without the intellectual number-game this is all senseless to the performing musician. But in the Middle Ages mental performance was also demanded, at least of the theorist; and with Jacques de Liège we find the conscious attempt to match theory with practice, in this case with the all important musical instrument, the monochord, the instrument fundamental to all musical consonances, and thus to plainchant and mensural music as constituted of them. It may be difficult for us to re-enter this special world, but we cannot ignore it. In these matters the modern musicologist sides automatically with the performer. In those days, in fact from Boethius on, the philosopher–mathematician was all-important. It was not to be until modern times that we tried more effectively to wed musical number with sounding number. But at least we ought to recognize the lead that Jacques gave us, however skewed by mathematical metaphysics. We have our own kind of mental warp today, too. Human subjectivity is always a kind of warp vis-a-vis "objective reality". And perhaps that is another way of saying the human subject is always creative when dealing with things. The element of fantasy always looms large in human arts and crafts; without it we would be lifeless computers. And for the modern musicologist and mathematician the figures involved here are in reality quite simple. They are hardly beyond our ken.

---

[11] *Ibid.*, p. 39; *cf.* Liber III, cap. 29, p. 57.

Although there was word of seven modes previously in his treatise, Jacques now explains why he describes eight. But before he answers objections to adding the hypermyxolydian mode, he leads us through a necessary lexical and proportional diversion. In reading this text in Latin — an indispensable task for the serious medievalist — a knowledge of some of the tricky-looking but essentially simple terms may be helpful, to abet the process of deciphering both the text and the musical proportionality it contains and illustrates with charts and graphs. First of all, the various figural terms connote different musical notation, the latter being a general term that embraces both notes and letters, as already discussed. But there are some *paginulae* that lack such notation. The word, *paginula*, is the same as *cellula*, or as *intercapedo*, i.e., what we would call a small box of whatever sort in a given chart. To the medievalist such a box, to be filled in or left blank, looked like a little page, a blank, literally an unfilled white space. But to the medieval thinker the space, even when blank or white, was not negative but positive, thus a page for writing something in or leaving open in terms of the system, here musical, being described. This seems like an almost vacuous stretching of a point, until we realize that materially a page of parchment or of sheepskin or even of paper in those days was a precious commodity, unlike today. A good *pagina* was in itself an object of wonder, appraisement, like canvas on which one could project imaginative visions long before the space was ever filled with illuminations or writing. The *tabula rasa* or blank tabulative space was even used later on by Descartes to describe the human mind, not in a negative but in a positive sense, as ready to be receptive of impressions from reality. Today, we wait before a blank screen for a television movie to be shown. The comparison is not untoward. The human mind is ever staring into space.

Paginula is further opposed to *versus* or *tractus linealis*, i.e., not a filled or unfilled blank space or box but interstitial stroke or line. This, too, would be an empty consideration, except for the fact that the *pagina* represents the distance of a tone (T), and the *versus* or *tractus* that of a semitone (S), essential to the build-up of the various modes, distinguishing them from one another. Now the hypermixolydian mode has, like other modes, interstitial spaces, lacking notation of any sort. Where the Greek letters are separated by a *paginula* there is an interval of one tonus; where the letters are separated by only a *versus* or *tractus linealis*, there is the distance of a minor semitone. Thus between Ω the proslambanomenos and Φ hypate hypaton there obtains a tonal distance, between Φ and Υ a semitone, as between hypate hypaton and parhypate hypaton. Along with the distances go also proportionalities, directly related to the monochordal strings.

From these monochordal proportionalities and letters come the modal intervals themselves. The whole is a coherent system, but it must be dug out of a careful reading and study of the text. Thus also, to lead back to the main point with regard to the eighth mode, there is a diapente between the mese of the doric mode and the hypomyxolydian. An *integra pagina* distinguishes the various meses, and in this case the mese of the doric is the lichanos hypaton in the hypermyxolydian mode, as easily scanned on the graph. All the tonal intervals are indicated on the strings in distances of from semitone through fourth and further consonances. If studied with the chart, the text is actually quite simple. Once the vocabulary and ambivalent wording are mastered, the rest simply follows. The task of the commentator, a time-honored role, is to ferret this all out and to clarify muddied waters, so that the reader can the more easily get into and through the text itself.

In the concluding chapter to this section Jacques shows how the eighth mode is added to the other seven.[12] He does this by pointing out the bis diapason obtaining between A and P of that segment of the Latin alphabet. Eight voices are contained between A and H, the first species of diapason, and then consecutively between B and I, C and K, D and L, and so forth. Traditionally, the diapason between H and P was excluded, but the integrity of the string-letters needs to be kept, as Ptolomey correctly pointed out, to complete the whole ancient monochord in the range of a double diapason. To us, at this end of history, this all seems like so much scholarly slight-of-hand or even as vacuous bombast of some medieval Music Man. But apparently at the time it was a matter of serious and considerable controversy, and one of the things they liked to sharpen their minds on. The authority of Boethius is invoked to settle the matter. In any case, by adding the eighth mode the entire ancient monochord is conjoined in one system from proslambanomenos to nete hyperboleon.

II

This may all be well and good, but what does it have to say even to the musicological medievalist? Let it suffice to say that Libri VI and VII

---

[12] Liber VI, cap. 14, pp. 44–55.

pretty well answer that question,[13] and one must bear in mind that Boethian monochordal theory is the basis of the whole Jacobean system, foundational to the production of musical consonances, and thus basic musical materials for composition of whatever sort, as well as for intellectual play. More importantly perhaps, and something Jacques de Liège would not have fully envisioned, musical and mathematical materials are provided for a larger Game, if we wish to take off from the virtuoso prose of Hermann Hesse's *Glasperlenspiel*. In this view Jacques would be the greatest medieval Magister Ludi or the only one, someone who did not stop with compiling musical materials but built them into a fascinating Game of musical proportionality and consonance production. The Game-player looks for patterns and emerging figurations, not just for isolated items. And the Game itself is described as summing up all the knowledge of the time symmetrically and synoptically around a central idea. But Hesse starts out the vaster cultural Game with the musical abacus, thus not just as a synoptic synthesis or summation in a Hegelian sense, but rather audially, as it were, synaesthetically, i.e., with all our various aesthetic faculties conjointedly. The "compilation" achieved by Jacques de Liège foreshadows the encyclopedists and dialectical synthesis not only in building a circle-of-knowledge (*paideía en kyklō*) but in subsuming Boethian and Guidonian principles into a new system, defining the monochord as distinctly medieval, and setting consonantal principles as foundational to all musical production.

Yet in a real sense, Jacques could not become a true Magister Ludi, because his otherwise enviable opus lacked the developed rhythmical element crucial to Hesse's Game. Instead, the medieval Game is brought to an intellectual stasis by its underlying metaphysics, though it still provides a cornucopia of musical materials for playing the Game afresh. Hesse envisions the musicological Game as embracing the whole of both physical and mental life as a dynamic phenomenon, which the Glass Bead Game comprehends aesthetically and rhythmically. (One recalls another such fundamental book, Huizinga's *Homo ludens*.) But the problem of the medieval Game is its elitism. The intellectual Game progressively abandoned experience and concrete praxis in favor of rarefied and abstract symbolization. And the Magister Ludi left Castalia precisely because it was apart from the real world. The Glass Bead Game itself was in a state of crisis according to the Magister's petition

---

[13] See F.J. Smith, *Jacobi Leodiensis Speculum Musicae, A Commentary*, III (Binningen: Institute of Mediaeval Music, 1983), pass.

of release from the Order. Small wonder, if it became a matter of abstracting music into a set of hieroglyphs that could then be generalized even further, reducing live sound to mentalistic symbols. Traditional music analysis has done this, too, but in pedantic manner without really having played the larger Game.

The idea of the Game, to which this might serve as a kind of prolegomenon, needs to be updated today and better fleshed out in terms of sound experience, rather than only of abstract symbol. For, music does indeed need to be subsumed into a general game plan and culture, of which musicologists feel it is an integral part. But what is the proper vehicle of an authentic subsumption of musical sound, beyond the mathematical and proportional metaphysics of the *Speculum Musicae*, or beyond our tentative contemporary philosophies? It would seem that a radical restructuring of the Game is called for today in terms of our musical experience. We would no longer want to write an encyclopedic compilation like that of Jacques de Liège, or attempt rationalistic systems like Rameau's; but the Game remains to be played and we are uneasy without it, wondering where we go with all this musicological information and prowess. Perhaps the tools are to be found in a phenomenology of sound, at least as a priming agent. But that, too, would undergo considerable change under the influence of musicians and musicologists intent on both art and science. Meanwhile, Hermann Hesse's masterpiece is a work that should be studied by every progressive musicologist and student intent on wedding his/her craft and knowledge with contemporary culture and critique. What Hesse asks of the contemporary musicologist, and does so explicitly, goes considerably beyond the necessary and requisite historical research skills of musicology and philosophy as we know them. And it guarantees both a future and a convincing present to musicological studies. Jacques de Liège writes that a musician is one who has music within himself ("Musicus est qui musicam in se habet.").[14] In his novel, *Damian*, Hesse wrote, "I felt that the music was in me." Only the *musicus*, who continually experiences music can think and write about it convincingly — or perform it properly. And only in this live context do the formidable and significant musicological and philosophical skills we must develop gain perspective and meaning for the whole.

Jacques de Liège's *Speculum Musicae* represents perhaps the most significant medieval attempt to play the Game, by assembling and developing systematically all the elements of music, including Greek

---

[14] Liber I, cap. 3, p. 17.

monochordal notation. It does not take a medievalist, aware of the vast range of artistic and intellectual endeavor of those times, to appreciate the insights of a virtuoso writer like Hermann Hesse. Rather, every musician is a player in a larger sense, as Jacques himself writes, in that he not only plays an instrument or sings but delights in the proportional interplay of the consonances that make music possible. And today in an earthier sense we can learn to play the Game, as musicology becomes "speculative" in some developed sense of the *Speculum Musicae*, broadening out to take in all human culture and finding its place under the direction of the Muse and the Magister Ludi that is within every good musician, however he may define himself otherwise. In this the musicologist makes passage from self-involvement toward community and social consciousness, as even Jacques de Liège, for all his intellectualism, already spelled it out: "It is a better and more perfect good that profits the entire city and community rather than just one member of it. And though it is admirable for a good thing to be of value to a single person, it is better and ordained by deity for it to redound to the good of the race and of the city; inasmuch as we grant good to be more divine the more it is held in common." "I have attempted in accord with my humble powers in this Mirror of Music so to conform myself to the natural genius of music that I might be of service to the range of the human condition."[15]

---

[15] Liber VI, cap. 1, p. 7.

CHAPTER THREE

THE LIVES AND LOVES OF ROBIN AND MARION: SUBJECTS JUXTAPOSED IN THE LATE THIRTEENTH-CENTURY FRENCH MOTET*

Linda Speck

Wayne State University

By the late thirteenth century, the French motet had abandoned its original liturgical function as a kind of trope and had taken on a life of its own. Composers' treatment of the genre increasingly reflected its secularized function as well as its role as a proving ground for the rhythmic innovations of the time. The typical French motet in the late thirteenth century consisted of three rhythmically and melodically distinct layers of sound, in which the top layer moved quite rapidly in relation to the other two, displaying both the breaking of the rhythmic modes into smaller time values and the division of the breve into more than three semibreves. An intricate complex of subjects, patterns of melodic repetition, rhyme schemes, phrase lengths, and rhythmic patterns exists within each work.[1]

---

* A version of this article was presented at the 15th International Congress on Medieval Studies in Kalamazoo, MI, in May 1979.

[1] For a study of these structures, see Linda Speck, "Relationships between Music and Text in the Late Thirteenth-Century French Motet" (Ph.D. diss., The University of Michigan, 1977).

The stock characters Robin and Marion, amid frequent misunderstandings and quarrels, find their way into a number of the motets, in
which their treatment provides a rather entertaining glimpse of the
compositional process as a whole. Their presence in one or more texts
of a motet is part of the distinctive array of similar and dissimilar
elements making up that particular work.

Of the 118 French motets in the repertory of the late thirteenth century, thirteen contain a reference to Robin, to Marion, or to both, in
one or more of their texts.[2] In some cases, the lovers are mentioned only
in borrowed refrains; in others, they are the subjects of extensive narratives, commentaries, or both. *Ba* 80 and *Mo* 291[3] mention the pair in the
former manner, and in only one voice part of each. In *Ba* 80, both texts
set forth the general topic of love. The upper voice parts share an
unusually large amount of musical and textual material, both in imitative passages (meas. 5-8)[4] and in voice exchange (meas. 1-4 and 21-24).
But only the triplum, which is a request for love, mentions Robin and
Marion. The motetus offers a philosophical commentary on the importance of love, going so far as to say that anyone who does not love does
not live at all. In spite of extensive similarities between the melodies of
the triplum and motetus, the subjects contrast to some degree, and the
mention of Robin and Marion is part of that contrast. In both upper

---

[2] The repertory under consideration consists of all motets in the following
manuscripts having at least one French text: Montpellier, Faculté de Médecine,
MS H 196 (*Mo*), fasc. 7 and 8; Bamberg, Staatsbibliothek, Lit. 115 (*Ba*); and
Turin, MS vari 42 (*Tu*). *Mo* has been edited by Yvonne Rokseth, *Polyphonies
du XIIIᵉ siècle: Le Manuscript H 196 de la Faculté de Médicine de Montpellier*,
in 4 vols. (Paris, 1939), and by Hans Tischler, *The Montpellier Codex* ("Recent
Researches in the Music of the Middle Ages and Early Renaissance," II-VII
[Madison, WI, 1978]). *Ba* has been edited by Pierre Aubry, *Cent Motets du
XIIIᵉ siècle publiés d'après le Manuscrit Ed.IV.6 de Bamberg*, in 3 vols. (Paris,
1908), and by Gordon Anderson, *Compositions of the Bamberg Manuscript,
Bamberg, Staatsbibliothek, Lit. 115 (olim Ed.IV.6.)* ("Corpus mensurabilis
musicae," LXXV [Neuhausen-Stuttgart, 1977]). *Tu* has been edited by Antoine
Auda, *Les "motets Wallons" du manuscrit de Turin: vari 42*, in 2 vols.
(Brussels, 1953).

[3] Motets are cited as follows: those occurring only in *Mo*, fasc. 7 and 8, or
both there and in *Ba*, are according to their location in *Mo*, with Rokseth's and
Tischler's numeration; those in *Ba*, in both *Ba* and *Tu*, or *Ba* and an earlier
fascicle of *Mo*, are according to Aubry's and Anderson's numeration. The
single *Tu* unicum is as it appears in Auda's edition.

[4] Measure numbers are those of Anderson's edition. Though Marion's name
often appears in a diminutive form such as Marot or Marotele, here it will
always be referred to as Marion.

voice parts of *Mo* 291, a man pours out his misery over a bad case of lovesickness. The motetus contains the standard pleas for a woman's love, crowned with dire predictions of the man's death should his love remain unrequited. The triplum, which has considerably more small note values than does the motetus, has a more eloquent and detailed text as well. Part of the lover's anguished plea is, as in *Ba* 80, a borrowed refrain; here only Marion is mentioned. In this motet, then, the patter-like character of the triplum contrasts with the motetus not only in the nature of its rhythm, but also in the degree of detail in its verbal content.

Five of the motets in the repertory present a narrative including Robin, Marion, or both in one of the upper voices, and closely-related ideas in the other. In fact, each pair of texts may be connected to the same incident, but in a different fashion. One voice part each of *Ba* 18 and *Mo* 336 relates to an amorous encounter between Robin and a woman. In *Ba* 18 (triplum), she is not Marion, but, rather, Amelot;[5] in *Mo* 336 (motetus), she is Marion. The other upper voices of each composition set forth the longings of a man for the woman he loves. Each of these motets, then, juxtaposes a request for love with an account of that request's fulfillment.

Both upper voice parts of *Ba* 34 and *Ba* 82 seem to address the same incident, though in contrasting ways. In the former, both parts describe Robin's and Marion's playing the game of love, but in one she is apparently a willing partner (triplum), and in the other, she protests Robin's advances, though in vain (motetus). In the latter motet, the motetus recounts Robin's foolishly refusing to give his sweetheart a kiss she requested, while in the triplum, someone (Marion?) lashes out at Robin for his hesitation.

The connection between the two upper voice parts of *Mo* 274 is a complaint over wrongdoing. The triplum, a narrative, describes a woman's lamenting over Robin's choosing Marion rather than herself; she says she saw Robin leading Marion off to the woods to play. Yet she plans to buy gifts for him and thus win him back.[6] Meanwhile, the

---

[5] Amelet may refer to the character by that name in Adam de la Halle's *Le Jeu de Robin et de Marion*; see Édmond de Coussemaker (ed.), *Les oeuvres complètes du trouvère Adam de la Halle* (Paris, 1872, rep. 1965), 345–412. According to Rokseth, *op. cit.*, IV, 289–290, Adam drew upon pre-existing material for the play. Though similarities between characters and incidents in the play and in the motets warrant consideration, it cannot be inferred that the composers of motets were, in turn, drawing their material from the play.

[6] In the version of the triplum in *Ba*, no. 69 (see also Aubry, *op. cit.*, I, ff. 44r–45r), it is the shepherd who is found lamenting over Robin's leading

speaker in the motetus comments on the sorry state of human affairs, in which all kinds of evil are held in esteem and there is no more courtesy or gracious talk. Further, people do bad enough things in public, but even worse ones in private. Here then, as in *Ba* 18, *Mo* 336, and *Ba* 34, the composer portrays an incident in one upper voice part and what may be considered a commentary on that incident in the other.

The six remaining motets demonstrate some type of contrast between the subjects of their upper voice parts. In some, Robin, Marion, or both of them are mentioned in all the texted parts; in others, they are mentioned in only one. The triplum of *Ba* 12 depicts a man riding around, who finds a shepherdess all alone. He offers to be her lover, but she declines, declaring her loyalty to Robin. The speaker in the motetus describes a shepherd's dance, during which Robin (perhaps showing off for Marion?) does the *estampie* so energetically that his jealous companions threaten to see that his flageolet is broken before nightfall. Even though both voice parts relate incidents reminiscent of scenes in *Le Jeu de Robin et de Marion*, there is no explicit link between the two in this composition.[7]

We meet a lonely and forlorn Marion in the *tripla* of both *Mo* 259 and 269. The speaker, who claims he is just looking around outdoors, happens upon Marion, who is lamenting over Robin's absence. (In *Mo* 269, she complains that he has left her for one Margot, daughter of Tierri.) Fortunately, Robin hears Marion, comes running to her playing his flageolet, and invites her to go into the woods to play. The motetus in each of the two above motets contrasts with the triplum to some extent. The motetus of *Mo* 259 describes a shepherd's dance in which each shepherdess (Marion and Amelot are named here) is dancing with her sweetheart. Apparently Robin, dancing with Marion, is remaining loyal to her, although Amelot's partner is not named. The motetus of *Mo* 269 presents a contrasting incident: Robin frets over not being able

---

Marion away and who vows to win her back by buying her gifts. Both Aubry and Anderson have treated the turnabout as an error and have corrected their editions to read as the version in *Mo*. The pertinent part of *Ba* reads as follows: Il me respont tout maintenant dolent sui quant je vif tant/bien croi qu'autre vuelt amer Marot car je li vi Robin mener. . . . Mais samedi se je la puis encontrer droit a la ville a li voudrai parler, courroie et gans blans et bourse a li donner. . . .

[7] The companions are Rogier, Guios, and Gautier; the last two are companions of Robin in *Le Jeu de Robin et de Marion*. Also, Robin's playing his "flagol d'argent" and Marion's hearing him are significant parts of the plot. Perhaps the similarity here with scenes in the play may be construed as a link between these otherwise separate incidents.

to find Marion. She hears his complaint, comes running to him, and declares her love for him. The lovers' joyful reunion, occurring in both upper voices, is reassuring in view of the tenor, in which Robin is warned to wake up, for someone is taking Marion away.[8]

Mo 261 offers a curious pair of incidents. In the triplum, the speaker says he met a lonely shepherdess, whom he asked for her love. She turns him away, out of loyalty to Robin. In the motetus, on the other hand, the narrator, also wooing a solitary shepherdess, persists in his advances despite her initial refusal (again, on account of Robin). He wins her favor, and she says that she loves him more than Robin. The shepherdess is not named; we cannot know whether she is the same one in both accounts or, indeed, whether either one is Marion.

The other motets with contrasting subjects present the general topic of love, but otherwise the subjects of the upper voice parts seem unrelated. In *Tu* 26, the motetus recounts the tale of one unfortunate Garin, whose wife has disappeared. The triplum depicts a pastoral scene in which an adventurer on horseback finds Robin with Marion, Joffroi with Fresen, and Gautier with Peronelle, all enjoying a rousing good time together.[9] Unless Garin is the adventurer on horseback, or his wife is one of the merrymakers, there appears to be no connection between the two narratives. *Mo* 265 also contains apparently opposite situations. The overall structure of the composition is based on that of the motetus, which is Marion's lighthearted *Robin m'aime, Robin m'a*.[10] She sings of her love for Robin, who has bought gifts for her. But in the triplum, a man grieves over the departure of his beloved, a beautiful woman whose striking physical attributes he enumerates. Here, then, as in *Ba* 12, *Mo* 259, *Mo* 269, and *Mo* 261, the subjects that are juxtaposed differ from one another.

The pastoral scenes, complaints, amorous longings, and philosophical comments in the thirteen motets chosen for this study all represent some aspect of love. Yet the subjects treated in a given composition always complement or contrast with one another; never do they coincide exactly. Just as a medieval painting shows a scene from the points of view an artist considers significant, so a motet offers, simultaneously, more than one aspect of a particular subject or else

---

[8] The tenor is a refrain which also appears in *Le Jeu de Robin et de Marion*, sung by Gautier; see Coussemaker, *op. cit.*, p. 377.

[9] Gautier and Peronelle are characters in *Le Jeu de Robin et de Marion*.

[10] This song opens *Le Jeu de Robin et de Marion*; see Coussemaker, *op. cit.*, pp. 347–348.

juxtaposes different subjects. The combination of subjects in a given composition forms but one facet of the entire array of similar and dissimilar elements making up a motet in late thirteenth-century France.

APPENDIX

Concordances for the Motets described in this study

Mo	Ba	Tu
259	56	
261	40	
265	81	
269		
274	69	
291		
336		
	12	
119	18	7
75	34	
104	80	
165	82	
		26

CHAPTER FOUR

A REAPPRAISAL OF THE ROLE OF MUSIC IN ADAM DE LA HALLE'S *JEU DE ROBIN ET DE MARION**

Matthew C. Steel

Western Michigan University

In his article on medieval drama in the *New Grove Dictionary*, the eminent scholar, John Stevens, seems to challenge the sanctity of one of the monuments of music history, Adam de la Halle's *Jeu de Robin et de Marion*, with the following statement: "One must not make heavy weather of the musical side of this delightful and essentially traditional entertainment."[1] Although such a caveat may appear iconoclastic to

---

* A form of this paper was originally presented at the Eighteenth International Congress on Medieval Studies at Kalamazoo, Michigan in May 1983.

[1] "Medieval Drama," *The New Grove Dictionary* (London: MacMillan Co., 1980), XII, 43. Among the possible interpretations of Stevens' admonition is one directed at editors who would distort Adam's original intent with elaborate and anachronous polyphonic arrangements of the simple tunes. A similar warning was issued in the "Introduction" to Jean Beck's and J. Murray Gibbons' *The Play of Robin and Marion: Medieval Folk Comedy Opera* (New York: G. Schirmer, Inc., 1928). Nonetheless, in a professed show of erudition, Beck provided the tunes with elaborate piano accompaniments that he claimed were "according to medieval custom." He justified such tampering by noting the appearance of the opening refrain of *Robin and Marion*, "Robins

the many early music enthusiasts who revere *Robin and Marion* as the oldest extant secular play with any appreciable amount of music, it does reflect a longstanding attitude toward the music that has generally precluded its serious scholarly examination. Indeed, the simple tunes in *Robin and Marion* seem to pale in comparison with most of Adam's oeuvre. However, the tunes are more than pitches and rhythms; as products of the medieval intellect, they are inextricably bound to a lyric. The result is a conceptual unit whose components tend to operate together on the same semantic level. Adam's insertion of several songs into a secular drama, although unprecedented, was no more capricious an act than was the established practice of inserting music into liturgical dramas. In each case, the selection of the music and its placement in the work were done in the hermeneutical spirit of the day, i.e., to help elucidate and intensify the drama. So, an evaluation of the music in Adam's Play should not ignore its importance to the drama.

Adam's *Jeu de Robin et de Marion* has been a source of scholarly pursuit for more than a century and a half.[2] Such scholarship has generated enough interest in staging the work that, since an early documented modern revival in Adam's home town of Arras in 1896,[3] numerous productions have been mounted on both sides of the Atlantic. The enduring appeal of the Play seems to be Adam's inspired dramaturgy in which a number of simple, common elements were worked into a deceivingly complex whole. Rarely, though, has the musical element been seen as a contributor to the dramatic complexity. After all, fewer than ten percent of the total number of verses in the

---

m'aime," in the *motetus* of a three-voice motet attributed to Adam. With deference to Jean Beck, would it not seem logical that Adam would have used motets in his drama if he had wanted them there? For modern editions of the motet, see Gordon Anderson (ed.), *Compositions of the Bamberg Manuscript* ("Corpus Mensurabilis Musicae," ed. Armen Carpetian, Vol. LXXV [Neuhausen-Stuttgart: Hanssler Verlag, 1977]), p. 113, and Hans Tischler (ed.), *The Montpellier Codex, part III: fasc. 6–8* ("Recent Researches in the Music of the Middle Ages and Early Renaissance," Vol. VI & VII [Madison, WI: A-R Editions, Inc., 1978]), p. 88.

[2] Among the earliest published studies is that of L.J.N. Monmerqué, *Li Gieus de Robin et de Marion* (Paris: Firmin-Didot, 1822). For a comprehensive list of editions and translations of the work, see Kenneth Varty, *Le Jeu de Robin et de Marion* (London: George G. Harrap & Co., Ltd.), 24–27.

[3] Beck and Gibbons, *op. cit.*, "Translators Preface." Now often performed indoors, some productions have sought to revive the medieval practice of outdoor staging. For one such revival done with real sheep, see Joel Kasow, "Holland Spans the Centuries," *Opera*, XXXI (1980), 100.

Play are set with musical notation. Moreover, until recently standard music history texts have forgone any analysis of the music, and many have offered up a perfunctory statement on the supposed lineal connection between Adam's Play and *opéra comique*.[4] Such an observation is artificial, and it tends to dismiss the music by making it seem important only in retrospect.

No published study of Adam's Play has done more to establish the validity of its music on medieval criteria than that of Jacques Chailley.[5] He confronted a major modern prejudice against the importance of the music: *viz.*, the nearly unanimous rejection of Adam as the original composer. Although Chailley would not categorically deny Adam's authorship in some of the songs, he was willing to accept the traditional opinion of scholars who had concluded that Adam had merely followed the conventional practice of inserting familiar sung refrains into a larger literary work.[6] This traditional hypothesis is difficult to substantiate in Adam's Play because concordances for most of the so-called refrains have not been located.[7] However, refrain borrowing for certain literary genre, including that of Adam's Play, had become so pervasive in Adam's day as to be, very nearly, obligatory.[8]

Chailley made clear the distinction between the modern literary definition of refrain and the type of refrain that Adam and his contemporaries inserted into their poetic works. The former type is stylistically suited to a particular poem and is identical in text and melody for each strophe; whereas, the latter type of refrain has the character of a musical quotation inserted into a strophe with little regard for an existing melody and poetic meter. Chailley labelled this type a *refrain-centon*.[9] Such "refrain-centos" were drawn from the vast supply of round-dance songs, called *rondets de carole*, which were extremely

---

[4] Although such a statement is avoided in more recent scholarship, it appears in sources as widely respected as Gustave Reese's *Music in the Middle Ages* (New York: W.W. Norton & Co., Inc., 1940), 213, and P.H. Lang's *Music in Western Civilization* (New York: W.W. Norton & Co., Inc., 1941), 108.

[5] "La nature musicale du Jeu de Robin et de Marion," *Melange d'histoire offert a Gustave Cohen* (Paris, 1950), 111–117.

[6] *Ibid.*, 111.

[7] See Friedrich Gennrich (ed.), *Adam de la Halle: Le Jeu de Robin et de Marion, Li Rondel Adam* ("Musikwissenschaftliche Studien-Bibliothek," Vol. XX [Langen, 1962]), pp. 7 & 36. Also see Gennrich, *Bibliographisches Verzeichnis der französischen Refrains des 12. und 13. Jahrhunderts* ("Summa Musicae Medii Aevi," Vol. XIV [Langen, 1964]).

[8] Chailley, *op. cit.*, 112.

[9] *Ibid.*, 112.

popular in thirteenth-century northern France.[10] The *rondet de carole* consists of a refrain sung chorally and a strophe sung to the same tune by the dance leader. As such, it served as a model for the later *formes fixes*.[11] The opening lines of *Robin and Marion* appear to be a *rondet de carole* complete in form (ABaabAB, where upper case letters represent repeated music and text, i.e., the refrain), an incipient stage of the later *rondeau*. (See Example 1)

Example 1. Adam de la Halle. *Jeu de Robin et de Marion*: "Robins m'aime."

---

[10] *Ibid.*, 115. For a comprehensive etymology of "carole," see Y. Lacroix-Novaro, "La carole," *Revue de Musicologie*, XVI (1935), 1–26, and Chailley, "La danse religieuse au moyen âge," *Arts Liberaux et Philosophie au Moyen Âge* ("Actes du Quatrième Congrès International de Philosophie Mediéval" [Montreal: Institut d'Études Mediévales, 1969]), 357–380.

[11] Pierre Bec, *La lyrique française au moyen âge (XIIe–XIIIe siècles)*, Vol. I: *Études* (Paris: Éditions A. & J. Picard, 1977), 12.

The repertory of *rondet de carole* was only sporadically preserved; in most cases, the choral refrain is the only surviving remnant.[12] Chailley hypothesized that the refrain-cento evolved from a shorthand method of notating complete *rondet de carole* in the romance. Scribes, whether lazy or just confident in the memories of their readers, inserted only the *rondet* incipit, i.e., its refrain. Seeing the refrain, a reader would recall the remaining verses from memory. Eventually, such notated refrains may have outlasted the memory of their unnotated *rondet* couplets and have taken on a separate existence.[13] The popularity of *rondets de carole* led to the reciprocal borrowing of *carole* refrains among thirteenth-century authors. As the same refrain may have appeared in several different sources, it would accumulate the literary associations of those sources.[14] An audience of Adam's day would have recognized a *carole* refrain by its dance character, and they would have been invited to recall its past associations while viewing it in its new context.[15] To the modern audience, on which the many associations are lost, refrain-centos, such as those in Adam's Play, are likely to be viewed as just so many randomly placed ditties.

Adam's *Jeu de Robin et de Marion* is a dramatization of two forms of the traditional medieval narrative lyric known as the *pastourelle*. The first half of the Play is based on the classic *pastourelle* in which a knight on horseback encounters a lone shepherdess (Marion), whom he energetically, if not violently, woos often to the dismay of the shepherdess' lover (Robin). The last half of the Play has as its matrix the *bergerie*, a type of *pastourelle* in which the knight is a passive observer of scenes of peasants playing games and dancing.[16]

The authentic remnants of the traditional *pastourelle-bergerie* genre in *Robin and Marion* are the inserted *carole* refrains. The remaining text is Adam's own achievement. Here, Adam defied tradition by presenting his text as spoken dialogue rather than as sung narrative. By design, the contrast created between the sung refrain-centos, i.e., *carole* refrains, and the spoken dialogue in *Robin and Marion* serves to

---

[12] Jean Maillard, *Adam de la Halle: Perspective Musicale* (Paris: Éditions Honore Champion, 1982), 151.

[13] Chailley, "La nature musicale," 116.

[14] *Ibid.*, 115.·

[15] Maillard, *op. cit.*

[16] Joseph Dane, "Parody and Satire in the Literature of Thirteenth-Century Arras, Part I," *Studies in Philology*, LXXXI, no. 1 (Winter 1984), 15 and "Part II," in LXXXI, no. 2 (Spring 1984), 141. Chailley had already used *bergerie* as a label in "La nature musicale," 112.

heighten the contrast between traditional *pastourelle* elements and Adam's characterizations. For the first time, the poet yielded some of the total control he had held through the narrative device and allowed the characters to speak for themselves. A comparison of the spoken with the sung text produces a rather discordant image of the peasants in *Robin and Marion.*[17]

A couple of examples may serve to demonstrate the irony that is created when the courtly ideal of bucolic life as presented in the sung refrain-centos is juxtaposed with the greater realism of Adam's spoken text. In the opening sung refrain (Example 1, vv. 3–5), Marion lists the following three gifts that Robin allegedly bought her: *cotele d'escarlate* (an elegant robe), *souskanie* (cloak), and *chainturele* (sash). Later, in an almost parallel construction in direct discourse (vv. 23–24),[18] she shows the knight, Aubert, three much more mundane gifts from Robin: a basket, a staff, and a knife.[19] In another instance (vv. 319–320), Marion, pestered by Aubert, sings that she hears Robin playing his *flajol d'argent* (silver flute). Here, the musical image of a silver flute hardly seems compatible with Marion's earlier, proud spoken description (vv. 55–56) of how Robin raises such a noise in their village with his raucous *musete* (bagpipes).[20]

---

[17] Jean Dufournet, "Complexité et ambiguïté du *jeu de Robin et Marion*. L'ouverture de la pièce et la portrait des paysans," *Études de Philologie Romane et d'Histoire Litteraire offertes à Jules Horrent* (Liege: Jean Marie d'Heur & Nicoletta Cherubini, 1980), 141.

[18] All verses cited are according to the exemplary edition of Ernest Langlois, *Adam le Bossu, Trouvère Artesien du XIIIe Siècle: Le Jeu de Robin et Marion suivi du Jeu du Pelerin (Les Classiques Français du Moyen Âge*, Vol. XXXVI [Paris: Librarie Honoré Champion, Éditeur, 1965]). A very satisfactory English translation of the Play is provided by Richard Axton and John Stevens in *Medieval French Plays* (New York: Barnes and Noble, 1971), 263–301.

[19] Dufournet, *op. cit.*, 145.

[20] Verses 55–56:

> A no vile esmuet tout le bruit
> Quant il jue de se musete.

One cannot discount the notion that Robin's *flajol* and his *musete* are one and the same instrument. According to Anthony Baines, *Woodwind Instruments and their History* (New York: W.W. Norton & Co., Inc., 1957), 227, the terms musette and flageolet have been used interchangeably at various times in France. David Munrow, *Instruments of the Middle Ages and Renaissance* (London: Oxford University Press, 1976), 10, noted that although the word *muse* implied the presence of a bag, the medieval French designation, *muse d'ausay*, actually denotes a flute.

The image of the silver flute was probably intended to evoke more than a mere musical irony. Robin was often depicted with a *musete* or a *flajol* in other *pastourelles*, but never was his instrument of the silver variety.[21] Marion seems to have created the silver flute image to boost Robin's stature in the eyes of the knight, i.e. to give Robin an aura of social parity with him. Indeed, an insight into the prestige associated with the *flajol* can be found in a passage from *Du métier profitable* by the fourteenth-century poet Eustache Deschamps.[22] Here, a gentleman, after acquiring the usual social trappings, is advised to take up the *flajol* because princes like to hear it. The irony created by the discrepancies between sung texts and spoken dialogue is, at once, humorous, but upon reflection the contrast that Adam established between Robin's lowly life as a *vilain* as portrayed in the spoken dialogue and Deschamps' vision of the courtly gentleman represented in the sung texts is so great that it evokes pathos.[23]

By inserting refrain-centos into *Robin and Marion*, Adam was able to work with great economy. He did not supply rubrics for stage directions and scene settings, and he did not resort to any artificial means of implying time or space. Such elements can be inferred from the refrain-cento texts. The *locus amoenus*, topos of the traditional *pastourelle*, is virtually assured from the outset of the Play with the opening *rondeau*, "Robins m'aime," and the subsequent appearance of the knight singing his refrain, "Je me repairoie." In addition to setting the scene, these sung texts introduce the principal characters of the drama and the literary genre on which it is based. Adam relied on the familiarity of his audience with this genre as he challenged them to recall the various literary associations that the sung texts bring with them from other *pastourelles*.[24]

---

[21] Repertory examined in Karl Bartsch, *Romances et Pastourelles Françaises des XIIe et XIIIe Siècles* (Darmstadt: Wissenschaftliche Buchgesellschaft, 1967).

[22] Edmund Bowles, "La hiérarchie des instruments de musique dans l'Europe féodale," *Revue de Musicologie*, XLII (1958), 166.

[23] It would indeed play into the irony if Robin's instrument were, in fact, a bagpipe because Deschamps deplored the instrument calling it an "instrument des hommes bestiaulx." (See Bowles, *Ibid.*, 169).

[24] Although the "Je me repairoie" appears to be unique to the *Robin and Marion* manuscripts, the brief, two-verse refrain does contain the standard opening for most *pastourelles*; so, it draws on the associations of nearly an entire genre or, at least, the substantial number of *pastourelles* in which Marion (dim. Marote) is named.

The texts of certain refrain-centos imply offstage action and there-fore, they extend the focus of the Play beyond the confines of the stage; they create a sense of space. The already-mentioned refrain, "J'oi Robin flajoler" (vv. 319–320), in which Marion hears Robin playing his "silver" flute, is sung in Robin's absence from the stage. Adam cleverly inserted the refrain so as to interject a sense of urgency in the midst of Marion's rejection of the knight's advances. The audience could predict the imminence of a confrontation between Robin and the knight by judging how quickly the sound of this offstage instrument draws closer. In the next refrain, "He resvielle toi, Robin" (vv. 358–360), Adam was able to work in a sense of time and space by implying that Robin had fallen asleep alone on stage and then, was abruptly awakened by companions singing from offstage. As if there is no one in sight, a startled Robin calls out in the next spoken line, "are you there, Gautier?"[25] Earlier, in the refrain, "He! Robechon" (vv. 101–114), Marion calls to Robin who calls back to her. One must assume that Robin had been offstage when Marion says, "Robin, I recognized you well in singing just as you came along."[26]

Adam utilized the three opening refrain-centos to establish the plot of the Play. In "Robins m'aime," Adam preempted the traditional *pastourelle* beginning with a touching vow of love and devotion from Marion to Robin.[27] The *pastourelle* plot is introduced next with "Je me repairoie." Then in the third refrain, "He, Robin" (vv. 11–12), before any spoken dialogue has occurred, the rescue of Marion from the knight by Robin is anticipated.

It has been suggested, from time to time, that Adam's Play is princi-pally concerned with the marriage of Robin and Marion;[28] the frame-

---

[25] Verse 361: Aimi gautier estes vous la.
[26] Verses 120–121:

> Robin, je te connuc trop bien
> au canter si con tu venoies . . .

[27] For a comment on this song in another context, see Linda Speck, "The Lives and Loves of Robin and Marion," in this book. The refrain-cento in the *motetus* of *Mo* 265 preserves a version similar to that in *Robin and Marion* except in verse five where Marion asks, rather mercenarily: "Why then would I not love him?"
[28] A convincing case is made by Kenneth Varty, "Le Mariage, la Courtoisie et l'Ironie comique dans le 'Jeu de Robin et de Marion' " in *Mélanges Charles Foulon*, Vol. II: *Marche Romane* (Liege: Universite de Liege, 1980). Of the three manuscripts that contain the Play, the one that is considered least reliable, MS A, has the title, "Mariage de Robin & de Marote," written in a latter hand.

work of the *pastourelle-bergerie* that serves as a vehicle for the Play was merely a convenient literary genre for Adam to parody.[29] The notion of the marriage plot is based, in part, on the theory that Adam's work is crammed with allusions to sexual desires and pleasures even to the point of the consummation of a marriage.[30] The premise seems tenable and can find support in the music. The first song, "Robins a m'aime," suggests Marion's betrothal to Robin. When Marion sings, "Robin has me, Robin asked me if he could have me," she is probably referring to the sexual possession that she would pledge to Robin in a betrothal. In the refrain, "He! Robechon," Marion begs Robin, as Robin begs Marion in the repeat of the refrain, to come to her so that they can "play" (*jeuer*). In the context of a marriage plot, it is likely that the word takes on its other traditional meaning, *viz.*, "to give in to pleasure."[31]

It is not difficult to discern in the elements of the *bergerie*, in the second half of the Play, a kind of peasant imitation of a courtly wedding celebration. The refrain, "Avoec tel compaignie," signals the beginning of the revelry of the impending nuptials. At first, the peasants play a rather witless game that is eventually brought to a close by Marion's protests. Then, they replace the first game with their version of a courtly parlor game for which they know neither the rules nor the correct name (v. 496).[32] Next, they lay out the wedding feast which seems to mainly consist of stale food kept stored in their bodices, pouches, or elsewhere. This feast of leftovers is made complete by Robin who describes his contributions in the refrain, "J'ai encore un tel paste."[33]

---

[29] Dane, *op. cit.*, 142. He points out that Adam's *Robin and Marion* is the last work resembling the traditional *pastourelle*, a literary genre that had become meaningless with the decline of courtly and high bourgeois culture.

[30] Varty, "Le Mariage," 287. According to Dane, *op. cit.*, 143, it is precisely the obscenity in *Robin and Marion* that separates it from the realm of the traditional lyric *pastourelle*.

[31] Varty, "Le Mariage," 288. Here Varty relies on the MS A reading which transforms what appears in the other MSS to be the nonsense syllables, "dou leura, leura," into the word "doleur," giving the phrase, "jouer doleur va," a euphemism for "faire l'amour."

[32] See Gennrich, *Adam de la Halle*, 36.

[33] Dane, *op. cit.*, "Part I," 7. Foods stored in the clothes can be metaphors for parts of the human sexual anatomy. Among many intimations is Marion's comment to Robin (v. 147) that she has cheese for him "en mon sein." On the other hand, Robin offers Marion (vv. 669-672) his "pois rotis" and "pommes" as if in substitution for real food.

A proper courtly wedding should be complemented with appropriate entertainment such as that described in the thirteenth-century Provencal romance, *Flamenca*, where hundreds of jongleurs performed every sort of heroic *lai* and *chanson de geste*.[34] In keeping with the satirical nature of the scene, Robin and Marion are serenaded by a single minstrel, the ever-vulgar Gautier, who chants one verse of the scatological *chanson de geste, Audigier*.[35] The absurdity of the situation is heightened by Gautier's confusion of the character Raimberge, Audigier's mother, with Grinberge, his enemy. The wedding celebration comes to a close with the final refrain-cento, "Venes apres moi," in which Robin leads the company in a dance into the woods, presumably offstage, that same venue where the knight had carried off Marion for the purpose of sex.

In addition to their apparent dramatic suitability, the refrain-centos also seem to display a purely musical suitability. Evidence suggests that Adam selected and arranged them according to a preconceived musical plan. On a large scale, Adam's formal plan neatly enframes the drama with musical settings at the very beginning ("Robins m'aime"), the very end ("Venes apres moi"), and at the exact dramatic midpoint (vv. 438–439, "Avoec tel compaignie"). This midpoint separates the *pastourelle*-oriented first part from the *bergerie*-like second part of the drama. The bipartite nature of the work is further highlighted by a striking shift in refrain finals from a preponderance of f finals in the *pastourelle* to a concentration on c finals in the *bergerie*. (See Table 1)

In the first five refrains in which only Marion and the knight are on stage, the melodies have a distinct lydian modal character.[36] Here

---

[34] *Flamenca*, vv. 583–731. For an account of the affair in English, see Peter Dronke, *The Medieval Lyric*, 2nd ed. (London: Cambridge University Press, 1977), 25–26.

[35] *Audigier*, verse 746:

> Audiger dist Raimberge bouse vous di . . .
> ("Audigier," said Raimberge, "dung on you").

Since no other melodic example from the sizable *chanson de geste* repertory has survived, some scholars have wondered whether this one is indicative of the entire genre. Given Gautier's insecure knowledge of the story and the fact that *Audigier* is only a parody of the true *chanson de geste*, any conjecture on the authenticity of the melody seems unfounded.

[36] Given the scant melodic material available, detailed analysis is virtually impossible. However, the reduced range and lower tessitura of Marion's refrains, "He! Robin" and "Bergeronette," may suggest the hypolydian mode.

TABLE I. Synoptic chart of refrains in Adam de la Halle's
Jeu de Robin et de Marion

	Refrain	Verse	Singer	Range	Initial–final
PASTOURELLE	Robins m'aime	1–8	Marion	6th: e–c′	f–f
	Je me repairoie	9–10	Knight	6th: e–c′	c′–e
	He! Robin, se tu m'aimes	11–12	Marion	4th: e–a	g–f
	Vous perdes vo paine	83–84	Marion	6th: e–c′	c′–f
	Bergeronnete sui	90–91	Marion	4th: e–a	a–f
	Trairire deluriau	95–100	Marion & Knight	6th: f–d′ +	c′–f
			Knight	8th: f–f′ +	c′–f
	He! Robechon, leura leura va	101–114	Marion & Robin	4th: f–b^{b+}	a–f
	Vous l'orres bien dire	164–65	Robin	5th: e–b^{b+}	g–g
	Bergeronnete, douche	176–91	Robin & Marion	6th: e–c′ +	b^{b}–f
	Robin, par l'ame ten pere	196–225	Marion & Robin	6th: e–c′ +	a–g
	J'oi Robin flajoler	319–20	Marion	5th: f–c′ +	f–f
	He! resveille toi, Robin	357–60	Gautier	5th: f–c′ +	g–g
BERGERIE	Avoec tel compaignie	438–39	The Company	5th: b–f′	f′–c′
	J'ai encore un tel paste	675–80 683–88	Robin	6th: b–g′	b–c′
	Audigier dit Raimberge*	746	Gautier	4th: g–c′	a–a
	(Implied Dance)	767			
	Venes apres moi (and Dance)	779–80	Robin	8th: c–c′	g–c

+ B flat signature.
* Not a refrain.

Adam, the trouvère, comes closest to the traditional *pastourelle* with a courtly emulation of the ecclesiastical modes. Then, a b-flat signature is introduced in the sixth refrain, "Trairire deluriau," the final musical passage of the knight. This modal alteration coincides with the temporary departure of the knight and the initial appearance of Robin. Robin's presence through the remainder of the *pastourelle* section of the Play is suggested by the consistent use of b-flat signatures in the refrains. The transformation of the lydian mode through the use of b flats appears to be a deliberate move away from ecclesiastical tradition and a move from the learned courtly practice, represented by the knight, to the unlearned folksiness of Robin and the *bergerie* elements that he represents.[37] In the first refrain given solely to Robin, "Vous

---

[37] Despite the fact that b flat in lydian mode gives the appearence of the modern "major" mode which was an anomaly in medieval theory, one must

l'orres bien dire" (v. 164), he not only introduces the first cadence on g, but also sings a melody outlining the forbidden tritone interval (b flat to e). Robin's association, here, with the *diabolus in musica*, i.e. tritone, could conjure up connections with the pagan past.[38]

The arrival of the *bergerie* section of the Play is clearly proclaimed by the disappearance of b-flat signatures beginning with the refrain "Avoec tel compaignie." It and the next refrain take on a modern c major-like quality with finals on c'. The only melody in the *bergerie* section that does not cadence on c (or c') is the fragment from *Audigier* which, in fact, is not a *carole* refrain but a *chanson de geste* verse. The gradual shift from a lydian mode in the beginning of the Play to a c "major" mode, coinciding with the shift in drama from a courtly *pastourelle* to a rustic *bergerie*, seems to reflect a conscious manipulation of musical elements.

Character identification through musical elements also seems possible to some extent. Marion always cadences on f with the descending cadential figure a-g-f except in the refrain "Robin par l'ame ten pere" (v. 196) which she shares with Robin. The greatest amount of her melodic material is confined to the interval of a fourth between e and a. In the *pastourelle*, Robin is identified with the b-flat signature and cadence on g. His musical character changes with the shift to the *bergerie*. There, his expanded range and higher tessitura recall, somewhat, the departed knight. In the three times that the knight sings, he has one consistent characteristic: he always begins on c'. He has the highest tessitura in the *pastourelle* section. Also, the knight can be associated with the grand courtly art of singing chansons *ex omnibus longis et perfectis*[39] in the refrain, "Hui main je chevauchoie" (v. 95). Can it be doubted that Adam deliberately chose such a static vehicle as a foil to the other lively, less aristocratic, rhythmic *carole* refrains? (See Example 2).

In two instances, different refrain texts are related by the same, or

---

take into account the evolution of modal theory that, in Adam's day, readily accepted b flats in lydian mode. Moreover, the use of b flats in refrains "He! Robechon" and "Vous l'orres" may be justified on the basis of the understood principle of *fa supra la* or modal commixture. See Frederick Andrews, "Mediaeval Modal Theory" (Ph.D. dissertation, Cornell University, 1935), Chapter V.

[38] See Y. Lacroix-Novaro, *op. cit.* Here Robin may have been projected into the role of *caragus*, the ancient musician–sorcerer and leader of the dance.

[39] See Ernst Rohloff, *Die Quellenhandschriften zum Musiktratat des Johannes de Grocheio* (Leipzig: VEB Deutscher Verlag für Musik, 1972), 130.

Example 2. Adam de la Halle. *Jeu de Robin et de Marion*: "Trairire deluriau."

very similar, musical material. The more striking of the two is the relationship between Robin's "Vous l'orres bien dire" and the nearly identical third melodic phrase of "Robin par l'ame ten pere" (See Example 3). There also seems to be a textual connection between the

Example 3. Adam de la Halle. *Jeu de Robin et de Marion*: "Vous l'orres bien dire," and "Robin par l'ami ten pere."

vv. 9-10

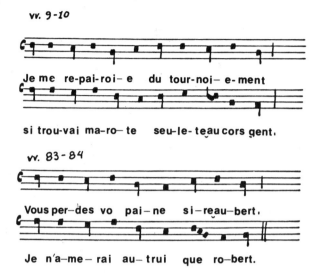

Je me re-pai-roi- e   du tour-noi- e- ment

si trou-vai ma-ro- te   seu-le- teau cors gent.

vv. 83-84

Vous per-des vo   pai- ne   si-reau-bert.

Je n'a-me- rai au-trui   que ro-bert.

Example 4. Adam de la Halle. *Jeu de Robin et de Marion*: "Je me repairoie," and "Vous perdes vo paine."

refrains. In the first refrain, Robin responds to Marion's remarks of surprise when he boasts of his athletic involvement. He tells her that she will hear the truth about it in time. A score of verses later, in the second refrain, he actually demonstrates his athletic prowess in a dance.[40] The second instance of musical similarity occurs between the knight's refrain, "Je me repairoie," and Marion's refrain, "Vous perdes vo paine" (See Example 4). They differ where Marion's musical phrase is compressed to accommodate a shorter verse length. In the first refrain, the knight ends his lydian tune, uncharacteristically, on an *e* as if he had reached some sort of medial cadence. Later, when Marion sings her similar tune in the second refrain, she seems to resolve the matter by cadencing on the anticipated *f*. Curiously, the two refrains mark the

---

[40] In this refrain, Adam provides the names of four dances: *aler du piet, tour dou chief, tour des bras*, and *baler au seriaus*. He included scant information on the steps of these dances which are, presumably, of a courtly provenance. What little that Adam did provide here should be considered in context before it is given any authority. For, it would be in character with Robin's ignorance of courtly culture for him to comically stumble through the dances having no idea of what he is doing. Nonetheless, if the dances mentioned in this refrain are suited to the tune, would they necessarily belong to the *carole* from which this refrain is extracted? Would Adam's audience have been aware of such a relationship? If so, would each refrain potentially require some sort of traditional choreography?

only point where Aubert (the knight) and Marion refer to each other by name. So, the musical similarity of refrains seems to be a consciously applied technique to lend cohesiveness to the drama, a kind of primitive *leitmotiv*.

The participation of musical instruments in *Robin and Marion* is supported by the text. An already-cited instance is Marion's refrain in which she hears Robin playing the *flajol*. In another passage near the end of the Play (v. 755), Peronnele asks Robin to lead the *treske*,[41] a line dance traditionally led by a player of the pipe and tabor. She adds that Huar will play the bagpipe (*musera*), and two others will play horns (*corneront*). Despite the absence of any musical notation at this point in the manuscripts, Robin soon asks (v. 768), "Est che bien bale marotele" (Was that a good dance, Marion?). Here, the inference is that the specified instrumental ensemble performed (improvised) a dance accompaniment. Then, it is likely that the same instruments would have been present to accompany the subsequent final refrain, "Venes apres moi," which is Robin's invitation to the company to join him in another dance.

The concept of musical timbre, in any era, is dependent upon the instruments known by a composer. As a trouvère of the first order, Adam belonged to a courtly tradition of poet-musicians whose principal performance medium, judging by manuscript miniatures, was the lute and fiddle. Thus, the use of such instrument types in *Robin and Marion* may be implicit and expected by his aristocratic audience.[42] On the other hand, Adam found it necessary to carefully point out in the text instruments of the peasants as if his audience would not have had a realistic notion of bucolic life. Whether the peasant instruments were meant merely as stage props or as functioning members of an otherwise courtly ensemble cannot be inferred with any assurance.[43]

In contrast to the trouvère's apollonian preference for stringed instruments, the peasants in *Robin and Marion* play, exclusively, wind and percussion instruments. When first asked to lead the *treske*

---

[41] Very little can be gleaned about the *treske* dance. In one of the earliest grammars of Old Provencal, the *donatz Proensals* of Uc Faidit (c. 1240 A.D.), it is simply described as "coream intricatam facere." See J.H. Marshall (ed.), *The Donatz Proensals of Uc Faidit* (London: Oxford University Press, 1969), 169. Editors have equated the *treske* with the *farandole*, a documented type of chain dance.

[42] Among the wealth of miniatures accompanying *Robin and Marion* in MS A, there is, indeed, a picture of a fiddle player.

[43] Axton and Stevens, *op. cit.*, 260, deny with great assurance the participation of instruments in the refrain-centos.

(v. 226), Robin says that he must get a *tabour* (drum) and a *muse au gros bourdons* (bagpipe with a large drone).[44] Could Robin's *flajol* then be a one-handed, three-holed pipe that was traditionally used in combination with the tabor by the dance leader? In verse 433, Huar is said to play a *kevrete* (cf. *chevrette* = small goat), probably a rustic version of the bagpipe (*muse*) that resembles some aspect of a goat either in the air bag (a goat skin) or in the visage carved on the chanter. The *kevrete* becomes a likely synonym for Robin's previously-mentioned *musete* when Gautier proclaims Huar the greatest player of the *musete* (vv. 637–638). The horns in the *treske* orchestra are described (v. 715) as *deus gran cornes* (two large horns). In some modern editions, they are curiously labelled *cornetti*, i.e., "little horns."[45] Despite the confusion arising from the plethora of names for wind instruments in Adam's time, it seems apparent that he chose the instruments for his Play with the same care that he chose the refrain-centos. The instruments all seem to fulfill a functional or symbolic role in the drama.

Is it not evident, then, that there is much more to the musical element of Adam de la Halle's *Jeu de Robin et de Marion* than most scholars have been willing to concede? The few verses set to music compared to the amount of spoken dialogue in the Play would seem to justify the scant attention the music has received over the years. However, in a performance, the concern for the proper execution of the music focusses a disproportionate amount of attention on the sung text. So, more than a mere diversion from the spoken dialogue, the sung texts, i.e., refrain-centos, were chosen for their precise suitability to the drama. Therefore, an appreciation of Adam's particular genius comes from an examination of his clever choice of pre-existing music and its careful placement in the drama. The more one delves into the nature of such music, the more John Stevens' comment seems untenable.

---

[44] According to Sibyl Marcuse, *A Survey of Musical Instruments* (New York: Harper & Row, 1975), 675, the first reference to the drone pipe occurs in French literature, and she cites *Robin and Marion* as the source. If she is correct on the first account, the second seems arbitrary; for, a *bergerie* by Jehans Erars, "Au tems pascor," mentions a "muse au grant forel."

[45] Even Axton and Stevens, *op. cit.*, 262, call them *cornetts*, "instruments . . . often used to double the boy-trebles in choir." They suggest that in modern performance recorders be used as substitutes! A miniature in MS A shows two men playing curved horns of, approximately, the size of the Renaissance *cornetto*. The horn players are the only unnamed characters in the Play; they have no dramatic role other than to be present in the dance orchestra. Could it be that these anonymous musicians were actual players of the long metal trumpets of the Artesian military with which Adam travelled in the service of Robert II, Count of Artois, during his campaign in southern Italy.

CHAPTER FIVE

THE LYRIC LAI BEFORE MACHAUT

Hans Tischler

Indiana University, Bloomington

In Jean Maillard's 1963 dissertation it is shown that the term "lai" has several distinct meanings.[1] Its etymology goes back to the Latin root *"laud"* whose derivatives can be traced through the early Middle Ages until the final form appeared around 1155 in Wace's *Roman de Brut*.[2] The term seems to have been first used in Celtic poems such as *Tristan* to designate instrumental melodies; but it also was applied to several literary types: to Irish lyrics of several stanza-like sections;[3] to short, single-stanza insertions in Arthurian epics;[4] to the long, versified stories of Marie de France in the late 12th century;[5] and also, like "chanson" and "lied," to middle-sized epics; finally, in the late 12th century there emerged the independent lyric, sung lai, usually treating love or religious subjects.

The lyric lai represents one of the types of medieval songs; it is characterized by two features, viz. (1) several stanza-like sections of differing length and versification and (2) musical repetition in most or all sections. Historically the lyric lais went through three stages: first the

---

[1] See Jean Maillard, "Évolution et esthétique du *lai* lyrique des origines à la fin du XIVe siecle" (Doctorate d'Université, Paris, 1963).

[2] *Ibid.*, p. 24ff.

[3] *Ibid.*, p. 43ff.

[4] *Ibid.*, p. 85.

[5] *Ibid.*, p. 66.

lais from the late 12th century to those from the *Roman de Fauvel* of the early 14th century, greatly varied in form and content; secondly the respective works of Machaut of the mid-14th century, which assume a standardized form of twelve sections, all in double versicles, the final section resuming the melody and rhymes of the opening one; and thirdly the post-Machaut rhetorical lais and complaints of the late 14th to the 15th century, which are purely literary and no longer sung.[6]

Little has been published about the pre-Machaut lais. Maillard's dissertation and the 1901 edition of thirty *Lais et descorts* by Jeanroy, Brandin, and Aubry[7] are the only extensive editions and studies of the genre as a literary-musical repertory. The pieces offered in the latter work are discussed in a long article by Hans Spanke,[8] and Friedrich Gennrich added a detailed study of two of these lais.[9] Maillard followed up his dissertation with a study in the Schrade memorial volume and an article in the *New Grove Dictionary*.[10] Gilbert Reaney introduced an analysis of Machaut's lais with general remarks on the earlier repertory.[11] This scholar is also preparing an edition of Machaut's monophonic works, which of course have already been edited,[12] including the lais. To these publications, this writer recently added two articles on the lais of the *Roman de Fauvel*.[13]

The pre-Machaut lyric lais divide into three groups or layers: first, those edited in JBA; secondly, the remaining lais of the 13th century; and finally, the pieces from the *Roman de Fauvel*. The first group

---

[6] *Ibid.*, p. 68ff. Maillard's account differs by including the *Fauvel* lais with Machaut's.

[7] *Lais et descort francaise du XIIIe siècle* (Paris, 1901). Herafter, this source will be called JBA in the text.

[8] "Sequenz und Lai," *Studi medievali*, XI (1938), 12–68.

[9] "Zwei altfranzösische Lais," *Studi medievali*, XV (1942), 1–68.

[10] "Lai, Leich," *Gattungen der Musik in Einzeldarstellungen: Gedenkschrift Leo Schrade* (Bern and München, 1973), 323–45; "Lai," *The New Grove Dictionary* (London: Macmillan, 1980), X, 364–376.

[11] "The Lais of Guillaume de Machaut and Their Background," *Proceedings of the Royal Music Association*, LXXXII (1955–56), 15–32.

[12] *Viz.*, Fr. Ludwig and H. Besseler, *Guillaume de Machaut: Musikalische Werk* (Leipzig, 1943), IV; Sylvette and Jacques Leguy, *Guillaume de Machaut 1300–1377: Oeuvres complètes* (Paris: Le Droict Chemin de Musique, 1977), IV.

[13] Hans Tischler, "A Lai from the *Roman de Fauvel*," *Essays on the Music of J.S. Bach and Other Divers Subjects: a Tribute to Gerhard Herz* (Louisville, 1981), 145–55; "Die Lais im *Roman de Fauvel*," *Die Musikforschung*, XXXIV (1981), 161–79.

includes 25 complete melodies (and one partial one) and 37 complete texts plus 3 fragmentary ones. The second layer falls into two distinct subgroups, the genuine lais and the strophic lais, so called by Gennrich. The latter are songs which stand midway between the genuine lais and the shorter trouvère lyrics. They have, like the lais, several musical sections, most or all repeated, but all of these together serve as the music for the first stanza of a multi-stanzaic song. The 29 lais offer 26½ melodies with 33 complete texts and one partial text; the 23 strophic lais include 24 melodies with 31 lyrics. The *Roman* contains ten lai melodies and texts, two of which already appear within the first two layers.

Two points need to be clarified at the start. As the title of JBA indicates, two terms often appear with songs formulated so that they fall into several sections, most or all of whose melodies are heard more than once; the terms are "lai" and "descort." No discernible difference can be assigned to them. In fact, one of the works included in the *Roman de Fauvel* is introduced as a lai but calls itself within the poem a descort.[14] In another song which is structurally not a lai, the two terms are also used as equivalent.[15] A few other labels are at times given to some of these songs, *viz.* "note," "notula," "estampie," and "chançonete." It must, however, be pointed out that not a single strophic lai is designated as a lai or descort. Indeed, only two of them are labelled in the sources, viz. as "chançonete" and "estampie."[16] But of the lais of the second layer also only two are typed, one as "note" and the other as "notula."[17] On the other hand, the term "lai" is applied as a nonspecific song designation to two of three pieces which do not belong to the type.[18]

---

[14] See "En ce dous tens" in Paris, Bibliothèque Nationale, MS f. fr. 146, fol. 34v.

[15] See "Bella donna cara" in MS M, fol. 117. Manuscript sigla taken from H. Spanke, *G. Raynauds, Bibliographie des altfranzösischen Liedes* (Leiden, 1955), are the following:

M = Paris, Bibl. Nat., fr. 844
N = Paris, Bibl. Nat., fr. 845
T = Paris, Bibl. Nat., fr. 12615

[16] Moniot de Paris's "Quant j'oi chanter" in MS N, fol. 94v, and Raimbaut de Vaqueiras's famous "Kalenda maya" in Paris, Bibl. Nat., MS f. fr. 22543, fol. 62, respectively.

[17] The *Note Martinet* in MS N, fol. 187v, and Adam de la Bassée's "Olim in armonia" in Lille, Bibliothèque municipale, MS 397, fol. 29, respectively.

[18] Thibaut of Navarre's "Comencerai a fere un lai" and "Bella donna cara" in MS M, fols. 99 and 117, respectively.

The second point concerns the language of the lyrics. Some scholars consider the term "lai" as applying exclusively to Old French and Old Provençal poems. But several of these are, in fact, contrafacta of, or models for, Latin texts; and there are a few Provençal and English texts which also parallel Latin ones. There are, in addition, a considerable number of Latin lyrics, many of them called *conductus*, whose musical form in no way differs from that of French lais. Some scholars, including Maillard, speak of such pieces as "secular sequences;" but this is hardly an appropriate term, indeed a contradictory one, for sequences are liturgical by definition and structurally are normally given to double versicles in the late 12th and 13th centuries. To be sure, some of these Latin lais are sermons or treat other religious subjects, but they are never liturgical: on the other hand, there are several French lais which are translations or paraphrases of well-known sequences, such as *Ave gloriosa virginum regina*, *Laetabundus*, and *Missus Gabriel de celis*, which are thus more closely related to liturgy than those Latin lais.

Several musical problems are presented by the edition of this repertory;[19] some are shared with the trouvère repertory in general, others are particular to the lais. In what follows, only four of them shall be discussed. The two related to other trouvère songs concern the rhythmic rendering and the modal analysis of the music which determines the approach to accidentals; the others concern the structural aspects of these works and their texts.

As to the first problem, the musical rhythm, twenty-one or nearly one-quarter of the melodies exist in mensural notation, at least in part or at least in one manuscript;[20] among them are seven pieces in the *Roman de Fauvel*. The mensural versions prove two things: firstly that the poetic rhythm parallels the musical one, and secondly that the lyrics are metrically conceived. But the rhythm follows by no means inflexibly any of the rhythmic modes of the contemporary Notre-Dame polyphony, though it is closely related to them. Thus the pervasive iambs, trochees, dactyls, anapests, spondees, and tribrachs of the lyrics correspond to the six modal patterns; and as the poetic meters often combine to form various kinds of lines with from one to eight ictus, the modal patterns likewise frequently intermingle. A transcription in

---

[19] A complete comparative edition of trouvère lyrics with melodies, and lais by this writer is in preparation.

[20] *I.e.*, mostly mensural notation in its early form, where only longs and breves are differentiated.

modern note values and with bar lines naturally emerges; and it easily transfers to the pieces which survive only in premensural notation, or what is variously called square, cum-littera, or motet notation. The first mode is by far most frequent. But whereas in more than half of the songs the basic mode continues throughout, in others it changes from section to section and at times within a section.

The recognition that metric rhythm prevails in this repertory by no means furnishes ready-made solutions for the rendition of particular verses. A trochee, e.g., may be rendered as an ordo of the 1st, 2nd, or 5th mode, i.e. as ♩♪ , ♪♩ , or ♩.♩. . The pattern chosen will usually depend on the placement of ornaments, i.e. on where in the modal pattern most ornaments occur, signifying its longer note values. Similarly an anacrusis may be either short or long, or it may be absorbed into the next verse foot, rendered respectively as ♪♩ ♪♩ , as ♩.♪♩ ♪♩ , or as ♩♪♪♩ ♪♩ ; and feminine endings may appear as ♩♩ ♪♩ ♪♩ ♪♩ ♪♩, as ♩♩ ♪♩ ♪♩.♩⹁♩ or as ♩♩ ♪♪♪♩♩ ♪♪♪. Thus a great flexibility in interpretation emerges. Indeed, fexibility is characteristic of every aspect of the entire trouvère repertory, whether in connection with the text, the melody, the accidentals, the ornaments, or the instrumentation. Therefore, every solution is, within certain limits, one of several possible and viable solutions. This fact is forcefully brought out by a parallel transcription of the several extant versions of many of these songs.

Turning to the second problem, modality, one finds that the behavior of the lais with regard to the scalar modes is quite complex. Sometimes a mode is maintained through several sections, as judged by finals and accidentals, but elsewhere it may change from phrase to phrase or be entirely unrecognizable. Accidentals are not consistently applied and often differ among the versions of a melody. Sometimes transpositions are indicated by accidentals, mostly transpositions by a 4th or 5th up or down, but here and there by other intervals. The most complex work in this respect comes from the *Roman de Fauvel*; it involves all twelve pitches of the octave and juxtaposes G ˙ and B♭ in the same phrase.[21] It is one of two works for which modal analysis seems inappropriate. But, there are others in which parts yield very unclear results. Overall, the modern major feeling prevails.

As to the structural features of this repertory, the third problem, the most important defining elements have already been mentioned, *viz.*

---

[21] See "En ce dous tens," (see fn. 14); Tischler, "A Lai from the *Roman de Fauvel*" (see fn. 13).

multi-sectionality and melodic repetition. Two scholars have tried to arrive at general distinctions among types of lais. In the 1901 edition, Aubry divided the lais into two groups using three elements as guidelines: one type is more elaborately ornamented by ligatures on single syllables, appears with author ascriptions, and is fully notated; the other type is melodically simple, syllabic, lacks ascriptions, and is only partially notated, *i.e.* omits music where repetition is implied. This division, based on the limited repertory surveyed, does not give a clear picture of lais, however. In fact, Spanke's discussion, based on the same repertory,[22] distinguishes four types, taking structure as the chief criterion: type 1 employs strict twofold melodic parallelism in all sections, except possibly the last one; type 2 comprises pieces in which some sections are heard more than twice, others only once; type 3 is that of lais which use freer repetitive arrangements based on short subsections and their variants; type 4 includes works without sectional repeats but with multiple phrase repeats and recurrences. To these types Gennrich added as a fifth type the strophic lai. A sixth type may be discerned in rondo-like pieces in which one or several section melodies are periodically repeated like refrains or ritornellos.

The number of sections within the various lais differs greatly, in fact from 2 to 22. Often the sections of a lai are melodically related. This is particularly so in Spanke's third and fourth types which use either short subsections or multiple phrase repetitions. Thus, in one lai which comprises 11 sections, sections 1, 2, 3, and 11 are interconnected as well as sections 6 through 10.[23] In the pieces subsumed under type 6, rondo-like repetitions of whole section melodies, with the same or new text, serve a similar purpose. The lai with the largest number of sections may serve as an illustration.[24] Its 22 sections divide into two parts of eleven sections each. In either part, the melodies of four sections serve all eleven: in the first part, sections 1, 3, 6, and 11 present the same melody as do, essentially, sections 2, 5, 8, and 10, and sections 4, 7, and 9; in the second part, sections 12 and 14; 13 and 15; 16, 18, 20, and 22; and 17, 19 and 21 correspond. This is, to be sure, the most unusual piece in this regard. On the other hand, the return in the final section to the melody of the opening one, so standard in Machaut's lais, is very infrequent in the earlier lais.

---

[22] Spanke, (see fn. 8).

[23] See "Par cortoisie despuel" in MS T, fol. 66.

[24] See "Psallat concors symphonia" in München, Bayerische Staatsbibliothek, MS lat. 5539, fol. 114v.

So much for the music. The texts of the pre-Machaut lais treat the same subjects as other trouvère lyrics, but their greater length and the large proportion of Latin texts skew the curve in favor of religious and other serious themes, particularly in the last two of the three layers. In the first layer, the lais of JBA, two-thirds of the poems deal with love and one-quarter with Mary; only four of the 37-plus texts deal with other subjects. Among the lais of the second layer, on the other hand, 20 texts are religious, leaving only 13 to deal with love, music, or other themes. The many strophic lais of this layer show their mid-position between lais and other trouvère songs not only in their strophic structure but also in their lyrics. The 31 poems divide rather evenly among love texts, *pastourelles* and social songs, and religious and related lyrics, most of them in Latin. A similar division emerges among the pieces from the *Roman de Fauvel*: the four French songs all deal with love, the six Latin ones include five sermons and a New Year's song, the latter being part of a strophic lai present in the second layer.

As to versification and rhyme schemes, the greatest possible variety obtains. Although syllable count is upheld by most linguists as a guide for versification in Old French, three factors show that it is not the deciding element. The correspondence between musical rhythm and poetic meter has already been discussed. Secondly, there are a good number of Latin-French contrafacta, and for Latin poetry meter, as a main aspect, is generally accepted. Finally, there is the correspondence of repeated musical phrases to which lines of different syllable count are often underlaid, proving their metric equivalence. It is true, however, that some metric accents fall on normally unaccented syllables, as is true of all metric poetry. One illustration will suffice: the opening lines of a lai by Adam de Givenci and its Latin contrafactum whose rhythm is clarified by mensural notation in two of three versions:[25]

Lá doce	á-	cor-dán-cē
Iám mun-	dús	or-ná-tūr
d'á-mors	sáns	de-scórt
mí-ra	gló-	ri-á

It is easily seen that in the French text *La doce* and *amors* are "misaccented," as is the Latin word *mundus*; *i.e.*, these words differ in enunciation from their prose stresses. But, of course, the majority of accents fall where expected.

In most instances, parallel verses will have an identical scansion. But quite often a regular heptasyllabic trochaic dimeter, *e.g.*, will correspond to a line of six or eight syllables with the same four ictus.

[25] In MS M, fols. 77 and 158v and MS T, fol. 82.

Elsewhere, one of the lines may have an anacrusis or a feminine ending omitted in the other. The same is true of corresponding verses in contrafacta, but there are interesting exceptions. A most striking one occurs in the following opening:[26]

Mís-sus	Gá-bri-	él de
No-stré	Sei-gnór	la-sús
cé- lís		
del ciél		

Not only verse 1 but the entire first Latin quatrain runs in trochees throughout, whereas the French version of this first part of the first double versicle reads iambically. Similarly in double and triple versicles the rhyme scheme, rhyme syllables, and even the versification may differ in the lines set to corresponding music.

Once more flexibility emerges as a prime element in this repertory. How much of this flexibility is due to oral tradition, to scribes' and collectors' individuality, or to memory failure remains a moot question. To this writer this flexibility seems rather to reflect a basic mindset characteristic of the period. This mindset affected music, literature, visual arts, architecture, philosophy, science, society — in other words everything; it tended to arrange individual, separable and replaceable elements within a frame establishing a certain overall, external order, without reaching for internal coherence or relatedness. For Gothic man value resided in the single element — the felicitous expression of a thought, a turn of phrase, a short tune, a single figure in sculpture or painting, a single problem in grammar or scriptural exegesis, a physical fact or an action — without considering the temporal, spatial, social, or psychological context as important. Thus the text or the melody of a song could be altered or replaced, or a line of either, a word or phrase or section.

Thus the lais all fall into individual sections and were appreciated as such rather than for any elusive inner unity. They were primarily enjoyed by the actual or potential performer, though they, or at least many of them, were also at times performed before larger company. When a lai was performed by a single person, usually the poet–musician himself, a lute or a harp probably would have been the most usual instrument heard. If he or she also had one or more minstrels to help, a vielle may have been used and perhaps some percussion instruments. Flexibility pertained to the performance practice as well as to all other aspects of this repertory.

---

[26] The Latin text is extant in Cambridge, University Library, MS Add. 270 (Dublin Troper), fol. 51; the French is in London, British Museum, MS Royal 16. E. viii (lost).

CHAPTER SIX

COMPOSITIONAL PROCESS IN MACHAUT'S BALLADES

Theodore Karp

Northwestern University

Processes of musical creativity are of no less concern to medievalists than to those who deal with more recent music. However, the lack of sketch materials and verbal documentation comparable to that available for music composed after 1700 necessitates special approaches to the topic. Normally our point of departure is furnished by the theorists, who describe a technique whereby the individual voices are created successively. If indeed these descriptions are accurate with regard to Machaut's oeuvre, the initial step to a better understanding of his compositional processes is to establish the order in which the voices were composed. To state this is not to imply that Machaut always created an entire voice part at a time. His canonic works alone would invalidate any such hypothesis. Nor does one need to posit that Machaut left the initial part unchanged when completing the polyphony. There are occasions when I believe the reverse to be true.

To be sure, not all composers straitly follow theoretical prescriptions. These undoubtedly had greater influence among young composers and fellow theorists than among mature masters. Moreover, the concept of the successive creation of voice-parts in Machaut's refrain forms has been questioned by Wolfgang Dömling.[1] This scholar obser-

---

[1] *Die mehrstimmigen Balladen, Rondeaux und Virelais von Guillaume de Machaut,* (*Münchner Veröffentlichungen zur Musikgeschichte,* XVI; Munich, 1970), 67–88.

ves that in certain works one may find recurrent successions of basic harmonic intervals. Such series are apparently not to be found among Machaut's motets, even though the repetitive nature of the tenors affords numerous opportunities for them to arise. Dömling is inclined to attribute this contrast in structure to a difference in compositional technique. Whereas the motets are obviously the product of successive composition, he concludes that the cantus and tenor of the polyphonic refrain forms may have been conceived simultaneously.

One could, of course, greatly extend the contrast between the styles of Machaut's motets and his refrain forms. Differences in melodic style, rhythmic detail, and harmonic underpinning are numerous and fundamental. They cannot be passed over with the bland observation that one genre employs a *cantus prius factus* and the other does not. Were it true that the technique of successive composition produced only one basic style, with no more than surface differences, one could conclude without further ado that Machaut employed different compositional processes when creating motets and ballades. However, our experience with compositions of the 10th–13th centuries shows that the technique is capable of producing markedly different styles. For example, both the melodic ductus and the harmonic microstructure of Notre Dame conductus vary significantly from that of the contemporary organa despite the underlying traits that link the two. Yet both are products of the same compositional technique. Furthermore, the two genres are contemporaneous with each other, so that the differences between them are not attributable to the changed tastes of a different age. In some instances the conductus and organum may be the work of the same musician. Thus, the mere presence of stylistic differences between motets and ballades does not establish that they were created in different fashions. If we are to provide a sound basis for the postulate that Machaut composed a structural pair of voices simultaneously, we must show why certain style traits are incompatible with the technique of successive composition. It is this step that is missing in Dömling's argument. To be sure, we are not obliged to dismiss Dömling's conclusion because of this weakness. Our evidence is neither so explicit or complete that it would be wise to ignore the instinctive reactions of a scholar well versed in Machaut's music for the reason that his argument has not been proven. By remaining alert to Dömling's reactions in this matter, we may perhaps discover evidence that would put his argument on a sounder footing. For the present, however, I suggest strongly that we are obliged to conduct our analyses in terms of known theoretical evidence. While such analyses may be supplemented by others of more intuitive character, we would be unwise to dismiss the evidence of the theorists on grounds of personal preference. Thus the following analyses will be couched on the assumption of the technique of successive composition.

While the temporal precedence of the tenor is a given with regard to the motet and related genres, matters are not quite so clear with regard to the polyphonic refrain forms. On the one hand, Gilbert Reaney has pointed to a passage in the *Ars Discantus secundum Johannem de Muris* that suggests the precedence of the tenor, even among song forms.[2] Not only is the tenor listed first (*"scilicet cum tenore carmine et contratenore"*), but the discussion of harmonic intervals proceeds on the basis of relationships formed with that voice. On the other hand, in letter 31 of the *Voir Dit*, Machaut writes that he had supplied a tenor and contratenor to an already existent rondeau melody. ("Je vous envoie un rondel noté, dont je fis pieca le chant et le dit. Sy y ay fait nouvellement teneure et contrateneure."[3])

Several eminent Machaut scholars have suggested that in his song forms the composer created the cantus first. Statements to this effect have been made by Friedrich Ludwig,[4] Gilbert Reaney,[5] Ursula Günther,[6] and Richard Hoppin.[7] Ernst Apfel, on the other hand,

---

[2] "Fourteenth Century Harmony and the Ballades, Rondeaux and Virelais of Guillaume de Machaut," *Musica Disciplina*, VI (1953), 136. The treatise is published in Edmond de Coussemaker, *Scriptorum de musica medii aevi nova series*, III (Paris, 1869; repr. 1931, 1963), 68–113. See *De compositione carminum*, 93f. The attribution of the treatise to Jehan has been rejected. (Cf. Lawrence Gushee, "Jehan de Murs," *The New Grove Dictionary of Music and Musicians*, ed. by S. Sadie, IX, 588.)

[3] Cited in Friedrich Ludwig, *Guillaume de Machaut: Musikalische Werke*, II (Leipzig, 1928; repr. 1954), 56.

[4] "Die mehrstimmige Musik des 14. Jahrhunderts," *Sammelbände der internationalen Musikgesellschaft*, IV (1902), 35; ". . . zum ersten Mal das Prinzip durchgeführt, umgekehrt zu dem Aufbau einer Komposition über einem gegebenen cantus prius factus die mehrstimmige Komposition aus einer frei erfundenen Oberstimme und einer einfach begleitenden Unterstimme . . . zu bilden."

[5] *New Oxford History of Music*, III: *Ars Nova and Renaissance, 1300–1540*, ed. by Dom A. Hughes and G. Abraham (London, 1960), 28. "Counterpoint is successive, i.e. the *cantus* will be composed first, the tenor second, *triplum* or contratenor third in three-part songs, and *triplum* or contratenor in four-part works. Contratenor and *triplum* are harmonized with the tenor rather than with the *cantus*. . . ."

[6] *Der musikalische Stilwandel der französischen Liedkunst in der zweiten Hälfte des 14. Jahrhunderts, dargestellt an Virelais, Balladen und Rondeaux*

strongly believes in the priority of the tenor voice.[8] None of these passages appeared in a context that permitted extended discussion. Although the rules-of-thumb have the surface appearance of universals, the various authors may not have intended them as such. Certainly a review of such works as *Je puis trop bien, Honte, paour, doubtance*, the isorhythmic *S'Amours ne fait*, the canonic *Sanz cuer m'en vois*, and the triple-texted *De triste cuer* reveals sufficient stylistic diversity that one may well question whether Machaut limited himself to any single compositional order. Through joint discussion we need to establish what criteria may permit us to discern the compositional order followed in a given piece. The purpose of this essay is to stimulate such dialogue by examining a series of pieces and setting forth certain interim conclusions. I suggest first that if the voice parts of a work differ considerably with regard to tonal stability, it is more likely than not that the part possessing greater tonal cogency was the one created first. Secondly, I suggest that if the voice parts differ considerably in the degree of medium-scale thematic interrelationship, it is more likely than not that the part possessing the greater thematic unity was created

---

von Machaut, sowie datierbaren Kantilensätzen seiner Zeitgenossen und direkter Nachfolger (dissertation, Hamburg, 1951); ". . . von der Oberstimme her konzipierten Liedkompositionen. . . ." This work was not available to me and the citation has thus been taken from Dömling, *Mehrstimmigen Balladen*, 88. The intended meaning of Professor Günther's remark is perhaps open to question and the interpretation given above seems not to be in keeping with her present views, expressed in conversation.

[7] *Medieval Music* (New York, 1978). ". . . Machaut not only created a new style but also developed a new process of composition. Instead of beginning with the tenor, as for a motet, he apparently composed the melody of the cantus and then added one or more other parts, as he said he had done for one of the rondeaux in the *Voir Dit*. In the early stages of his search for an appropriate polyphonic setting, Machaut added only a tenor part, perhaps in the way a skilled instrumentalist might have improvised an accompaniment to a trouvère chanson."

[8] "Zur Entstehung des realen vierstimmigen Satzes in England," *Archiv für Musikwissenschaft*, XVII (1960), 93. "Die geschilderten Zusammenhänge zwischen Motette und Chanson (Ballade und Rondeau) lassen darauf schliessen, dass letztere aus der (weltlichen) Motette entstanden ist. Der Unterschied zwischen den beiden Gattungen stört nur, wenn man die Chanson unter dem Aspekt der 'begleiteten Monodie' betrachtet, während die Motette auf c.f. im Tenor beruht. Die Chanson dürfte jedoch noch im 15. Jahrhundert vom Tenor aus komponiert worden sein, wie die Motette, nur dass der Tenor in der Chanson erst für den geplanten Satz geschaffen (cantus prius factus) . . . wurde. Dass in der Chanson die Oberstimme im Sinne einer Melodies besonders ausgearbeitet wurde, hat damit wenig zu tun."

first. A few secondary criteria will be mentioned in passing. While no one criterion seems to be consistently reliable, we may hope that a combination of evidence may lead to valid conclusions regarding compositional order.

Honte, paour, doubtance (Ballade 25) provides a particularly apt illustration of the first of our main criteria. The cantus of this work exhibits a diffuse tonal organization. Following an initial ascent of a second, the cantus descends a seventh, leaps a minor ninth, descends another seventh, ascends a fourth plus a decorative half-step, leaps down a sixth, leaps back up a sixth, descends a diminished seventh, and closes with an ascent of a minor third. Only two of the skeletal melodic intervals in the *pedes* may be described as stable. Although the concluding tones of the first two text lines are the same, the movement towards these tones is so variable that the outward impression belies the degree of control exercised by Machaut. The conduct of the tenor, on the other hand, is neatly organized. In the *pedes* we find that the tones are grouped into a lower tetrachord and upper pentachord that fill the octave, d-d'. The opening gesture outlines the tetrachord. The pentachord is then defined by means of an upward leap of a fifth and a subsequent conjunct descent that pauses on the tone a second above the pivot. From the pivot, the tenor ascends a fourth and then descends in conjunct fashion until the extreme of the lower tetrachord is reached. This motion is followed by a return to the pivot. There is a further ascent to the upper limit of the pentachord, still another segment that outlines the lower tetrachord, and finally a descent that takes us from the upper limit to the tone f, the goal of the first ending. In the second ending, this tone, situated a step below the pivot, forms the upper boundary of a new pentachord leading eventually to B flat.

In the *cauda*, the conduct of the tenor exhibits a similar clarity, although greater variety obtains there. The cantus again appears to be of diffuse nature. Beginning on c', the early movement neatly fills the octave, g-g', but there is tonal tension that is generated by the oscillation in the quality of the upper pentachord. The first major point of rhythmic repose is on e', while the second is on e' flat. The use of the former in the final cadential area does not accord well with the goal tone, b flat.

It seems unlikely to me that after having created a texted melody possessing very little tonal focus, Machaut discovered that he could support this with a tenor that would not only form appropriate counterpoint, but would also display a highly centralized tonal cogency. Nor is it likely that the rigorous tonal structure is the product of chance. If we postulate that Machaut conceived the tenor and cantus simultaneously, we need to explain why there should be so little reflection in the cantus of the strong tonal shape of the tenor. This seems difficult to accomplish. On the other hand, if we continue to think in terms of successive composition of voice parts, we may postulate that the rigorous ordering of the tenor serves a function comparable to that of a *cantus prius factus*. The latter governs shape in a different manner and does not necessarily have a strong tonal focus.

In this ballade I judge the temporal precedence of the tenor to be nearly certain. Even the contratenor possesses a higher degree of tonal organization than the cantus. And it generally forms a more stable intervallic counterpoint to the tenor than does the cantus. Nevertheless, the fact that the overall tonal direction of the piece points to b flat, while the contratenor ends on f, and the fact that at the two most important cadences the cantus is more stable than the contratenor prompt the conclusion that the contra was the last voice-part to be created.

The contrasting tonal organization of the various parts indicates that Machaut began the creative process by calculating the amount of musical space that would be required by his poem. He apparently designed the tenor with this in mind, clothed the structure with a decorative cantus, and completed the sonority with the contratenor.

Similar evidence — not all of it equally strong — suggests the temporal precedence of the tenor in a sizable group of ballades of different textures. We may proceed by considering some in two parts. In *Doulz amis* (Ballade 6), the cantus opens with a preliminary descent of a diminished fifth, this tone resolving upwards by half-step. There follows a further descent of a fourth, plus a decorative whole step. The melody for the first text-line thus forms the outline of a minor seventh. There follows an upward leap of a diminished fifth and a conjunct descent of a minor sixth. We have now reached a stable point, an octave below the opening tone. Machaut has the cantus leap up an octave and descend a major sixth. The first ending concludes on the fifth degree of the basic d-d' octave, while the second ending descends to the third degree. Again the underlying tonal organization is somewhat obscured by the decorative overlay. The tonal structure of the tenor, on the other hand, is far clearer. The initial d furnishes the point of departure for an ascent and return of a third, then a fourth, and finally a fifth. An implied intermediate cadence occurs on the intermediate third. (I describe the cadence as implied because the goal tone does not occur at the beginning of the breve; it is, however, anticipated at the end of the preceding breve and enters immediately after an intervening semibreve rest.) This f then acts as a momentary pivot, acquiring an upper pentachord of its own, before returning to the initial d. The first ending terminates on that tone, while the second leads to f, whose importance had previously been made clear.

Similar observations may be made concerning the treatment of the *cauda*. At the outset, the cantus leaps a major seventh to e', which resolves upward to f', only to descend a diminished seventh to g sharp. There is an ascent to b flat, followed by a resolution to a. Between the sixth and seventh lines of text there is an upward leap of a major sixth. The first ending concludes on d', and the second on c'. The entire cantus is imbued with a certain nervous tonal tension. In the tenor, the opening g of the *cauda* is but a step higher than the previous cadence tone. This g is clearly established as the main upper boundary first of a tetrachord leading eventually to d, and then of a pentachord with final resolution on c.

We may note that Machaut's monophonic works demonstrate his awareness of the purely melodic function of half-step motion. Especially in the lais, written accidentals may be employed in order that the resultant pitch provides a stronger sense of motion to the primary pitch that follows. In part this is true also for *Doulz amis*. Yet in the lais, the decorative function of the inflected pitches is normally underscored by rhythmic brevity. They are most often semibreves or minims although they may occur as breves. In *Doulz amis*, the initial g sharp is an imperfect long. The tone thus acquires limited stability even though it enters in the middle of a perfection and the text requires a sense of ongoing motion. The initial phrase is organized rhythmically into groups of 1, 1, and 2 longs, and the g sharp marks the halfway point. I find the tension between this tone and the initial d' and c' to be more intense than tensions in comparable monophonic passages, where the framing tones are more consonant. I would attribute the g sharp in large part to Machaut's desire to reach the succeeding harmonic fifth by route of a major third. (Had the composer begun with the cantus and with a consonant framework, he could have attained a comparable harmonic progression by having the tenor perform e flat.) The later leap of a diminished fifth may likewise be attributed to a wish to reach the harmonic fifth that follows by means of the closest available imperfect interval.

A slightly more complex tonal organization prevails in *N'en fait n'en dit* (Ballade 11). Here the skeletal foundation of the tenor arises from the interaction of the tetrachord, f-b flat, and the pentachord with infix, g-c'-d'. The tetrachord provides the overall sense of tonal movement. It is outlined at the opening, and both the final cadence and the second ending of the *pedes* conclude with b flat. The interior portions, however, emphasize the outer boundaries of the g-d' pentachord. The infix is prominent chiefly in the setting of the penultimate line of text. The cantus does not possess an equal sense of unity. There is an initial descent of a diminished fourth — or more specifically of a diminished fifth, if one includes the decorative upper neighbor to the opening f'. There are further descents from d'-g and d'-a, the first line of text thus concluding a minor sixth below the opening. The b natural that follows provides a sense of tonal tension with the surrounding context and most especially with the b flat that constitutes the second ending. Following this ending there is a leap of a major sixth to the opening g' of the cauda. After an extended upper neighbor there is a descent of a diminished fifth to c' sharp. Neither this phrase, nor the one following — which emphasizes e' in its interior — contribute much to the cogency of the overall movement towards b flat.

The last of the two-part works to be examined here is *De desconfort* (Ballade 8). Again the tenor exhibits a very clear tonal structure whose overall outline ranges down from the opening g to the d of the first ending, the c of the second, and the B flat of the final cadence. These tones each appear as the main internal points of reference. In the *pedes* the only unstable element is the f sharp appearing at breve 17. The cadence of the first phrase of the *cauda* leads to the interior third of the c-g pentachord. Machaut then leads the tenor through the tetrachord and pentachord above this e flat, emphasizing f in the process. (Cf. breves 32–34, 39, and 43–45). This f in turn forms the upper boundary of the pentachord leading to B flat. The last gesture in the tenor covers the octave, b flat-B flat, with the f acting as the principal intermediate tone.

Although one can perceive a cogent order among the main skeletal tones of the cantus, our attention is distracted from this organization by the way in which Machaut handles the details of the melodic movement. The five important upward leaps of a sixth impart a sense of restlessness to the tonal movement, even though they are each dead intervals. This sense of wandering is reinforced by several profiles that encompass unstable intervals. The f' in the middle of breve 13 leads eventually down a seventh to g. The following tone, probably to be understood as e' flat, leads to a. In the *cauda*, the g' of breve 30 leads down a seventh to a, and the peak tone of breve 44, probably to be understood as a' flat, leads down a seventh to b flat.

Turning to work for cantus, triplum, and tenor, we may consider *Amours me fait desirer* (Ballade 19). This work further illustrates points previously made, though in the context of a different texture. Again the chief elements of tonal stability are provided by the tenor. This voice opens on b flat, an octave above the final cadence, which duplicates that of the second ending of the *pedes*. The initial movement oscillates between b flat and the g a third lower. There is then a brief motion up a third to d', which is established as an intermediate center. An oscillation between d' and a follows, and the a then leads down — by way of g — to the d of the first ending. One may discern an arch to the overall tonal construction of the *pedes*: the basic opening movement by third is contrasted by a tetrachordal-pentachordal structure, which is followed by a further movement by third for the close of the second ending. The *cauda* divides the six brief verses into groups of threes, set to repeated music with alternative endings. Each of the cadential areas parallels its counterpart in the *pedes*. The opening of the *cauda* in the tenor prominently uses the skeletal tones, B flat, f and b flat. The only point of restlessness is provided by the dead interval of a major sixth between the eighth and ninth (and therefore the tenth and eleventh) verses.

The overall tonal arch present in the tenor is lacking in the cantus of *Amours me fait desirer*. This voice opens with the striking leap of a tritone, g-c#', and proceeds to focus on the g-d'-g' pentachord and tetrachord. This results in a strong sense of unity for the first half of the *pedes*, but this centricity only strengthens the contrast between the early use of c'# and f# and the ultimate conclusion on b flat. The final cadence of both sections is a curious one. While the tenor has a simple conjunct descent of a third, the cantus employs a contour and rhythmic pattern characteristic of many under-third cadences. The interval pattern, however, is distinctive in that the final is not reached from the third below, but from the fourth below. It would be unusual for such a cadence to arise as part of the initial voice of a polyphonic complex.

The previous examples suggest that the use of awkward skips and written accidentals belonging to the realm of ficta may serve as subsidiary criteria when attempting to determine the temporal priority of the various voice parts. The importance of these style traits is suggested by our experience with other facets of Machaut's work. In the Gloria of the Mass, for example, the tenor voice is distinguished not only in terms of tonal organization and rhythmic simplicity, but also in its use of conjunct motion and the avoidance of written chromaticism. I would therefore conclude that the tenor of this movement was shaped first, just as in the isorhythmic movements employing chant tenors. Among the rondeaux, awkward leaps and the use of ficta in the tenor voice of such works as *Puisqu'en oubli* (Rondeau 15) and *Cinc, un, treze* (Rondeau 6) seem to indicate that in these instances Machaut had created the cantus first. Nevertheless, it is my impression that these criteria are subsidiary and that, if treated in isolation, they are less reliable indicators of compositional procedure than the broader aspect of tonal cogency.

It is not possible to treat each of the Machaut Ballades within the framework of this essay. Since I have already indicated my belief that the composer worked in more than one fashion, I shall now turn to a group of pieces exhibiting structures that contrast with those discussed above. *Phyton, le mervilleus serpent* (Ballade 38) is a highly symmetrical work from the standpoint of repetition structure. The repeat characteristic of the *pedes* is matched by a comparable one within the *cauda*. Furthermore, the musical rhyme that relates the two main sections to each other is extraordinarily long, amounting to slightly more than half of each section. If one merely examines the tonal structures of the tenor and cantus in terms of the salient cadential tones and phrase openings, one might conclude that the relative stability of the two voices is approximately equal. In part this is a function of the repetitive nature of the piece. When, however, one examines the contours of the individual phrases, one notes a lack of stability in the tenor that contrasts strongly with examples cited previously. The opening d' forms an octave with the last tone of each of the first endings. But the part plunges quickly down from this opening tone to the c a ninth below. Immediately after this pitch has been reached, there is an upward leap of a major seventh. Machaut then leads the tenor back to d', only to descend a minor seventh to the cadence marking the end of the first line of text. The restless nature of the part is further emphasized by leaps of a major ninth in breves 18 (= 42) and 34, as well as a similar leap between the first ending and the ensuing repeat. There is also a dead interval leap of a major seventh between the end of the *pedes* and the opening of the *cauda*. Finally, there is an upward leap of a sixth between the first ending of the *cauda* and the following repeat. Even consonant leaps of a fourth or fifth seem to be used much more liberally than in the examples discussed previously. The restless nature of the voice part is further underscored by its rhythmic activity. The opening pattern of four minims and semibreve recurs with identical pitches in breves 19 (= 43) and 28. On numerous occasions Machaut employs a minim rest at the beginning of the breve, and there are several small passages of syncopation.

The cantus of *Phyton* is none too stable from the standpoint of pitch contour. However, it seems to be more cohesive than the tenor. The skeletal structure devolves about the octave f-c'-f', with final cadences on c'. However, one's attention is temporarily distracted from this stable foundation on various occasions. For example, after moving from the opening f to a sustained c', the cantus moves back and forth between e' and c' before descending to a cadence on g. (The gesture of breve 5 recurs in similar context in breve 16 [= 40].) The e' may be regarded as a member of a chain of thirds (as outlined by Curt Sachs). Such chains are to be found among trouvère chansons and elsewhere within Machaut's oeuvre. But the tertial nature of the present melody is not as obvious as it might be. There is a dead interval upward leap of a minor seventh in the cantus between breves 8 and 9, and a somewhat more surprising downward leap of the same distance between breves 32 and 33. The latter is within the context of ongoing motion. A further dead interval leap of an upward major sixth occurs in breve 35. Nevertheless, the leaps present in the tenor at the principal junctures are not matched in the cantus. The interval between the first ending of the *pedes* and the repeat is a moderately stable third. The interval between the second ending and the *cauda* is a second, and the interval between the first ending of the *cauda* and the following repeat is a unison. Thus the overall impression of the cantus is one of greater stability and I believe that in this ballade the cantus was conceived first.

Je puis trop bien (Ballade 28) is more cohesive tonally than *Phyton*. The focal role of the octave c-c' and of the subsidiary centers, g and e' is clearly established in the tenor. The low c is employed not only at the conclusion of the *cauda* and the second ending of the *pedes*, but at the lesser cadences marking the caesurae of lines 1–4. It appears also at the beginnings of the two endings of the *pedes* and at the opening of the *cauda*. The subsidiary centers make their presence felt by length, rhythmic position, or by being reached or left by leap. (Cf. the leaps from g-c and g-d in breves 3–4 and 7, as well as the succession, e'-c'-g in breves 25–26.) Nevertheless, the part is more disjunct than those in the ballades examined first. In order to be able to return to the opening a for the repeat of the *pedes*, Machaut finds it necessary to employ an octave leap, c-c' as part of the first ending. At the beginning of the setting of the sixth line of text there is a further octave leap, d-d', which is followed by the e'–c'–g descent mentioned previously.

The cantus possesses an even stronger tonal focus. The importance of c' is defined not only by the final cadences of the *pedes* and *cauda*, and the interior cadences of text lines 1–4, but by its prominent position at the caesura of line 7. The subsidiary centers, g', e', a/g, are also strongly defined. Furthermore, the part is unified motivically while the tenor is not. The minim pattern of breves 1–2 of the cantus recurs in breves 9–10 and 29–30. The latter two occurrences compensate for the absence of any strict musical rhyme. Moreover, the gesture that opens the setting of the second line of text is transformed rhythmically to serve at the *clos* cadence and is further transformed for the final cadence. The conjunct descent that opens the *cauda* recurs following the caesura of line 7, while the leap of a fifth that concludes line 5 forms the basis for the setting of most of the following line. The combination of greater tonal cohesiveness and tighter motivic structure suggest that here, too, Machaut created the cantus first.

In each of the past two examples the main criterion suggested for the determination of compositional order was tonal centricity. Motivic cohesiveness was treated as a secondary criterion. Yet this trait may also serve as a primary determinant, as in *Biaute qui toutes autres pere* (Ballade 4). Here we are primarily concerned with elements one or more stages larger than the small motive. In this work the conclusion of each *pes* is marked by an extended symmetrically constructed flourish on the final stressed syllable. This passage is then duplicated largely or entirely at the end of the *cauda*. Two points seem noteworthy. The major portion of the cantus consists of a three-fold sequence. However, Machaut does not employ similar construction in either the tenor or the contratenor. These voices develop in ongoing fashion. There are innumerable examples to demonstrate that Machaut is greatly concerned with the motivic unity of his refrain forms. And it is possible for a gifted composer having such concerns to create a sequential construction over an evolving line. Nevertheless, it seems more likely than not that the sequential line was composed first, that it afforded the degree of unity sought by Machaut, and that he thus felt free to vary the contrapuntal support of the remaining two voices. When the musical rhyme begins in the *cauda*, one finds that the return occurs first in the cantus and only later in the two supporting voices. Again it is simpler to posit that Machaut created the cantus first rather than superimposing a more symmetrical structure on a less regular foundation. That Machaut was able to accomplish the latter task seems to be demonstrated by the famous double ballade, *Quant Theseus/Ne quier veoir* (Ballade 34.) Here the extended musical rhyme begins considerably earlier in the second cantus than in the remaining parts. Yet the construction of this part leads one to doubt that this voice was composed first. I mention only the leap of a tritone near the opening of the second cantus. The sensitive tone is not concerned with half-step motion to a succeeding goal. Instead, it is followed by a decorated descent of a third and a downward leap of a fifth, producing the outline of a major seventh. In sum, the criterion of motivic cohesiveness needs to be employed with caution.

There are further contradictory elements within our evidence concerning this ballade. One finds a leap of a minor seventh in the cantus between the end of the penultimate line and the opening of the final phrase. The important sequence in the cantus devolves about the conjunct descent of a diminished fifth. Furthermore, the cantus contains several written accidentals, including f sharp and c sharp, as well as e flat in at least one MS source. On the other hand, the tenor also contains e flat and f sharp, and employs both b flat and b natural. In my opinion, the cantus, which displays a unified arch from the initial d' to the final d', displays an overall tonal cogency at least equal to that of the tenor. Thus it is the symmetrical construction of the cantus that provides the most important clue regarding the probable temporal priority of that voice part.

Mes esperis se combat (Ballade 39) shows a comparable solicitude in the handling of thematic detail. In breve 8 of the cantus, Machaut enlarges one of his most familiar motives, and after a breve that I shall describe as "free," moves to a cadence for the caesura. There then follows in breves 11–13 a syncopated passage leading to a cadence on d' in breve 14. The combined passage recurs in conjunction with the second ending of the *pedes*, although the single "free" breve is varied and expanded into two. This return occurs above a tenor that is basically non-repetitive. In the *cauda*, breves 30–31 of the cantus recur in breves 36–37, and the extensive musical rhyme begins one measure earlier in the cantus than in the tenor. Although the tenor emphasizes the final to a greater degree than the cantus in its various interior cadences and phrase openings, the cantus seems to achieve slightly greater overall cohesiveness in tonal structure. Both voice parts use the same palette of tones outside the Guidonian gamut, and both employ one large, non-consonant leap. In the tenor, the leap is emphasized inasmuch as it appears in perfect breves. In the cantus, on the other hand, it is part of a decorative figure that rapidly resolves to the octave. Again the interrelationships within the cantus furnish the main clue to the temporal priority of that voice.

Interrelationships unifying a voice part do not necessarily involve series of identical pitches. In *Ma chiere dame* (Ballade 40), the profile of breves 2–4 in the cantus recurs a fifth higher in breves 6–8. Musical rhyme is not present in the strict sense in this work. However, one may note that the rhythms of breves 11–15 of the cantus recur in breves 28–32, making the end of the *pedes* and the first ending of the *cauda* parallel. The first portion of this pattern is found additionally in breves 24–25. Furthermore, the repeated-note figure opening the second phrase of the cantus is reused for the opening of the fifth phrase. The repetitive elements in the tenor — such as the rhythmic identity of breves 26–27 and 29–30 — are of lesser scope and import for the total structure.

When voice-parts differ noticeably in the reuse of melodic or rhythmic patterns, it is generally the cantus that is the more tightly organized of the two. However, one may find mild exceptions, as in the repeat of the tenor opening of *Ne penses pas* (Ballade 10) in varied rhythm at m. 11. The importance of this constructive element is emphasized because both passage occur at the openings of text-lines. On the other hand, when the structural parts differ considerably in terms of tonal cogency, it is generally the tenor that is the more cohesive. Stable tonal construction in the cantus is normally mirrored to some extent in the tenor. Yet a restless and diffuse cantus may occur above a neatly formed tenor. It is of interest to note that in those instances in which I have suggested that the tenor was the first to have been created, the rhythm of that part is quite placid. On the other hand, in those instances in which I have suggested that the cantus was created first, the tenor tends to be more active. Thus rhythmic construction may afford still other clues bearing on the order of composition.

If we can clarify the alternative lines of evidence and reasoning that are open to us with regard to the very broad question of priority of conception for the voice parts, we shall be better able to deal with other issues, such as the size of the constructional unit. Certainly the canonic *Sanz cuer m'en vois/Amis, dolens/Dame, par vous* (Ballade 17) demonstrates Machaut's ability to shift attention from one part to another within a small time framework. (The canonic time intervals are more spacious in the *Lay de la fonteinne and the Lay de confort*.) However, I do not believe that this exceptional ballade provides either a model for his normal compositional procedure or evidence that substantiates the simultaneous conception of non-canonic voice pairs. I suspect that internal musical evidence bearing on this question will be difficult to find in quantity. It may be that we shall need to approach this topic in another manner.

We may benefit by clarifying our views on the possible interaction between the creative process and writing in Machaut's oeuvre. While musical creativity during the early Middle Ages was independent of the act of writing, the situation seems to change during the High Middle Ages. It appears to me that the more complex compositions of the 14th century depended upon the composers' ability of work out their thoughts by means of writing. I believe this to be true for many compositions by Machaut, including his isorhythmic motets. I suspect also that the longer and more complex refrain forms (i.e., most ballades) were also worked out in writing. If this be the case, then the normal writing techniques of the period would have had an effect on the compositional process. It is highly unlikely that the composer of that day would have employed a large quantity of parchment or paper for sketching purposes. The standard medium would have been either the wax tablet or a slate. Neither of these would have encouraged a composer to create a large amount of material at a time. This may perhaps be reflected in the rather sharp divisions that occur between the taleae of certain motets. In terms of the ballades, I suspect that Machaut subdivided the compositional procedure at least into the two main segments of that form, and that he may even have on occasion worked in terms of the individual text lines. Nevertheless, I believe that once a compositional order had been established for the structural pair of voices, that order was maintained throughout the piece.

Obviously, the conclusions reached in this essay are subjective and not susceptible of proof. My sense of commitment is more to the importance of the topic than to the validity of any of the arguments presented. The questions dealt with here are of vital importance to a full understanding of the music of one of the foremost masters of the late Middle Ages. The very act of coming to grips with these questions promises to provide insights into Machaut's music that are not likely to be obtainable in any other way. Differences of opinion among scholars will undoubtedly result from such attempts. This is not to be mourned, for complete unanimity often discourages further investigation. The provisional conclusions reached in this essay reinforce what is doubtless the basic conviction of most: that the genius of Machaut rests on a multifaceted versatility of imagination and technique.

RENAISSANCE MUSIC

CHAPTER SEVEN

GUILLAUME DUFAY, HELLENISM, AND HUMANISM[1]

David Crawford

University of Michigan

As is often remarked, Dufay is the earliest composer for whom a relatively thorough biography can be written. However, it appears that a fundamental question still invites attention: his most recent biographer speaks of him as a composer of the Middle Ages[2] while other scholars interpret some of Dufay's works in the light of Renaissance humanism.[3] Since one aspect of humanism is its interest in a non-Latin culture — Greek — this article brings together the information about his involvement with Greece and also adds new thoughts about that question.

The earliest sign of Dufay's involvement with Graeco–Latin relations is his earliest datable piece, *Vasilissa ergo gaude* (1420). This motet

---

[1] A shortened form of this article was presented to *Musica Antiqua Europae Orientalis* at Bydogoszcz in September, 1985.

[2] David Fallows, *Dufay* (London, 1982), p. 6 for example, mentions studying Dufay's music as "the rediscovery of medieval music." The question also received recent attention in Irving Godt, "Style Periods of Music History Considered Analytically," *College Music Society Symposium* XXIV (1984), 33–48.

[3] See, for example, Willem Elders, "Humanism and Early-Renaissance Music: a Study of the Ceremonial Music by Ciconia and Dufay," *Tijdschrift van de Vereniging voor Nederlandse Muziekgeschiedenis* XXVII (1977), 65–101 or Stanley Boorman, "The Early Renaissance and Dufay," *The Musical Times* CXV no. 1577 (July, 1974), 560–65.

celebrates the marriage of the Italian princess, Cleofe Malatesta, and the Greek prince, Theodore Paleologus II, and the background for that marriage goes back several years. Manuel II of Constantinople, acting upon an invitation from Sigismund of Hungary (titled King of the Romans), had sent representatives to the Council of Constance. Those representatives discussed reunion with Pope Martin V, and the result was a papal letter of 8 April, 1418, issued at Constance, arranging marriages between Roman Catholic princesses and men from the Byzantine emperor's family. One of the marriages was that of Cleofe Malatesta and Theodore Paleologus.[4] How Dufay got involved in that marriage is unclear;[5] however, *Vasilissa ergo* resulted from official Roman and Byzantine moves toward reunification.

In 1426 Graeco–Latin relations crop up again in a motet, *Apostoloso glorioso*, evidently composed for the rededication of a church of St. Andrew in Patras. The archbishop there was a member of the Italian Malatesta family, and that family was probably Dufay's connection to Patras, the only Roman Catholic area in the Peloponnese at that time.[6] Three lines of Dufay's texts read as follows:

Mo é prolasso in errore et facto tristo,	Now [Greece] has fallen again into error and has become sad.
Si che rempetraglie gracia si forte	
Che recognoscano dio vero et vivo.	May it receive such strong grace that it may recognize the true and living God.

Here Dufay expresses hope that Greeks will convert to Roman authority, and he sees the issues as ecclesiastical rather than humanistic or intellectual.

One other motet, *Balsamus et munda*, may deserve mention here. Thanks to Guillaume de Van's work on this text,[7] we learn that these rather well-known Leonine hexameters formed part of the liturgy for Saturday of Easter Week (April 7), 1431; they were associated with the papal blessing of certain waxen figures (*agnus dei*). The poetry was believed to have been written by Pope Urban V (r. 1362–1370), who sent the poem, along with an *agnus dei*, to Emperor John V Paleologus.

---

[4] Joseph Gill, S.J., *The Council of Florence* (Cambridge, 1959), p. 124. It should be noted, though, that the papal letter itself neither specifies the number of marriages nor the personages to be wedded. The text of the letter is given in *Epistolae pontificiae ad Concilium Florentinum spectantes*, ed. Georg Hofmann (Rome, 1940–46), vol. I, part I, 3–4.

[5] The biographical information is recounted in Fallows, *Dufay*, pp. 18–31.

[6] Fallows, *Dufay*, p. 23.

[7] Guillaume de Van, *Guglielmi Dufay: Opera Omnia* II (Rome, 1948), xi-xiii.

Later, in 1369, the Emperor visited Urban V, and they agreed upon a reunion of the Byzantine and Roman churches. Whether Dufay or his patron (Pope Eugene IV) understood the early history of this poem is a matter for speculation.

Now let us turn to *Ecclesie militantis*, an awesome and exceptional motet that praises Pope Eugene IV. It is Dufay's only isorhythmic motet composed for five parts. The bottom two parts sing different chants and this is his only motet built upon two different chants. The piece is also unique among Dufay's motets because the top three parts sing three different texts simultaneously.

Dating this motet had been problematic. It is frequently suggested that *Ecclesie militantis* celebrated the coronation of Eugene IV in 1431, but Charles Hamm found notational practices that support Haberl's theory dating the motet 1436.[8]

Here is the evidence for the coronation theory: 1) one *cantus firmus* gives the pope's original name (Gabriel); and 2) lines 19–21 of the *triplum* relate that God's will has pleased the Venetians (Eugene IV was Venetian).[9] The *triplum*, lines 7–12, states that Gabriel's name changed to Eugene when he took office. Significantly, though, the sentence is cast in the past tense.

I think it safe to abandon the coronation theory. The coronation occurred on 11 March, and the election had taken place only eight days earlier, 3 March. During those eight days Dufay would have had to obtain the three texts made especially for the occasion. Then he would have had to compose the music, and this is Dufay's most complex isorhythmic motet, all the more complicated if Dufay was interested in involved mathematical calculations.[10] The score, far from showing signs of haste, shows that Dufay was making the most opulent motet he could imagine. In addition to the exceptional features enumerated above, this work sometimes offers generous textless *caudae* between stanzas of poetry, a long introductory duet before the isorhythm

---

[8] Charles Hamm, *A Chronology of the Works of Guillaume Dufay Based on a Study of Mensural Practice* (Princeton, 1964), p. 67.

[9] Limitations of space prevent quoting all the poetry in full. Somewhat faulty readings of the complete texts can be studied in *Guillaume Dufay: Opera Omnia*, ed. Heinrich Besseler in *Corpus Mensurabilis Musicae* I (1966), 46. I am indebted to Ann Moyer of the History Department and Professor Don Cameron of the Classics Department, University of Michigan, for help with the texts.

[10] Newman W. Powell, "Fibonacci and the Golden Mean: Rabbits, Rumbas, and Rondeaux," *Journal of Music Theory* XXIII (1979), 258–67.

begins, and extravagant melismatic flourishes on the concluding *Amen*. The necessary rehearsals also would have required patience because of some atypically difficult combinations of mensurations.[11] Rather than trying to imagine all this work taking place within the eight days marking a change in the Vatican's administration, it is easier to believe that Dufay composed the piece for some later occasion.

Curiously, the text of *Ecclesie militantis*, although praising Eugene, is also filled with impatience, despair, and complaints of economic hardship. These texts would be quite inappropriate for the celebration of a papal coronation. So far as I know, no one has put forth a convincing explanation for these sentiments; to do so requires us to trace the careers of Dufay and Pope Eugene for the next few years.

Dufay worked for the Vatican from 1428 until August of 1433, then returned to Savoy and then Cambrai. By June of 1435 he was back in papal offices, but now the pope's residences were in Florence and Bologna. These years heard Dufay's famous *Nuper rosarum flores* for consecrating the Cathedral of Florence, 25 March, 1436, a ceremony celebrated by the pope himself. Between 1435 and 1440 Eugene demonstrated his interest in music by issuing bulls founding six cathedral schools in Italy for teaching singing.[12] Dufay's stay in Florence (1436–37) exposed him to the leading humanistic movements of the day, and as Fallows points out, three of Dufay's motets between 1436 and 1438 contain humanistic references to Greek history or mythology.[13]

Sometime in 1437 Dufay returned to Savoy, although newly-found documents designate him a singer and chaplain in the papal chapel on 6 July and 18 August of 1437 and also on 3 January of 1438.[14] By April of 1438 the Cathedral of Cambrai had appointed him a representative to the Council of Basel. Although that responsibility may have taken him to Ferrara when Eugene transferred the Council to Italy,[15] on 16 October we find Dufay setting out from Le Bourget to spend the winter

---

[11] Discussed in Hamm, *A Chronology*, pp. 67–70.

[12] See Giulio Cattin, "Church Patronage in Fifteenth-Century Italy," *Music in Medieval and Early Modern Europe: Patronage, Sources, and Texts*, ed. Iain Fenlon (Cambridge, Great Britain, 1981), p. 23.

[13] Fallows, *Dufay*, pp. 46–47.

[14] Alejandro Planchart, "Guillaume Du Fay's Benefices and his Relationship to the Burgundian Chapel," paper presented to the American Musicological Society, national meeting, Philadelphia, October 25, 1984.

[15] See Ann Scott, "English Music in Modena, Biblioteca Estense Alpha X.1.11," *Musica Disciplina* XXVI (1972), 155–56.

with Louis and Anne of Savoy at Pinerolo.[16] This Savoyard episode does not preclude Dufay from attending the Council of Ferrara-Florence. Since Pinerolo is near Turin, Dufay could easily have spent some time at the Council, serving either the Cathedral of Cambrai or Eugene. In fact, we have no proof about the length of Dufay's stay at Pinerolo or that he even arrived there at all. The next thing we know for sure is that Dufay appears at Bruges in early July.[17]

Clues in the texts suggest that *Ecclesie militantis* was composed for some ceremonial event of the ecumenical council of 1438-39. That council began due to disputes between Eugene and the Council of Basel. The pope, trying to dissolve that council, transferred it to Ferrara in a bull dated 18 September, 1437. Seeking unification with the Greek Church, he also invited the Byzantine emperor, the Patriarch of the Greek Church, and other Greeks (prelates, monks, and lay scholars). They accepted. Eugene arrived at Ferrara on 24 January 1438, but the inaugural public session was delayed until 9 April. Thereupon Greek delegates insisted upon a recess to wait for additional European princes to arrive. Serious discussion finally began on 8 October, but agreements seemed far away. Plague and financial difficulties prompted the pope to move the Council to Florence in January, 1439. Meetings resumed in mid-February, no progress having been made after a year of hoping, waiting, and quarrelling. The next three months were similarly discouraging, but the tide suddenly changed in June and on 5 July the Greeks and Latins signed their agreement to reunite.

Numerous ceremonies during the Council could have prompted Dufay's motet, such as 3 March 1439, when the eighth anniversary of Eugene's election was celebrated with some extravagance[18] or 11 March, 1439, described by one chronicler as a "great festivity because it was the day of the coronation of Pope Eugenius IV."[19] Unfortunately, we have no more information about either celebration. Although other occasions might have inspired the motet, the textual features that led previous scholars to the coronation theory also render the motet appropriate for an anniversary of Eugene's election or coronation.

Many heretofore puzzling lines in the poetry describe perfectly the

---

[16] Stanislav Cordero di Pomparato, "Guglielmo Dufay alla corte di Savoia," *Santa Cecilia — Torino* XXVII/3, no. 273 (1925), 34.

[17] Planchart, "Guillaume Du Fay's Benefices."

[18] Joseph Gill, S.J., *Eugenius IV; Pope of Christian Union* (London, 1961), p. 119.

[19] Gill, *Council*, p. 205.

state of the Council during the late winter of 1439. Let us now consider those passages, beginning with the complete text of the contratenor.

Bella canunt gentes, querimur, pater optime, tempus. Expediet multos, si cupis, una dies. Nummus et hora fluunt magnumque iter orbis agendum nec suus in toto noscitur orbe deus.[20]

The nations sing of war. We complain, most excellent Father, about the time. A single day, if you wish, would free many people. Money and time flow away; a great journey of the world must be done. Not all people of the world recognize their God.

I suggest that sentences 1 and 3 of the Latin refer to the Turkish advance toward Constantinople, a threat that helped motivate the Greek Church to ally with the Latin one. Those sentences also show the Roman willingness to launch a crusade against non-Christians. But alas, time is slipping away (sentences 1, 2, and 3); the Council procrastinates, even though everything could be solved by the actions of a single day (sentence 2), agreement to reunite. The complaint about lost money (sentence 3) refers to Eugene's serious financial difficulties, problems partly due to the fact that he personally paid the expenses for hosting all the Greeks, evidently about 700 people.[21] It cannot be determined whether the people to be freed (sentence 2) are the Christians living in lands occupied by Turks or the discouraged and tired fathers of the Council.

The first six lines of the *motetus* also can be interpreted as referring to the Council:

Sanctorum arbitrio
Clericorum proprio
Cordo meditanti
Neguam genus atrio
Recedat ludibrio
Umbre petulanti.

By virtue of the will of the saints operating in the thoughtful heart of each clergyman, let the worthless tribe with its mockeries retire outside to the troublesome darkness.

This brings to mind a theological premise shared by Latins and Greeks: the teachings of the saints represent a unified doctrine; otherwise the Holy Spirit, working through the saints, would contradict itself.[22] Perhaps the final three lines call for expelling unconstructive speakers or repelling the Turks.

---

[20] Our editorial policy resolves abbreviations and adds punctuation and capitalization, but retains original spellings. The spellings, symptomatic of the texts in general, are uninfluenced by humanistic practices.

[21] Joseph Gill, *Personalities of the Council of Florence* (Oxford, 1964), p. 4.

[22] Gill, *Council*, p. 255.

The next two stanzas (lines 7–18) praise Eugene's skill in law, his contempt for laziness or ignorance (*inertia*), his desire for peace for all, and his dislike for appeasement. All of these could refer to qualities deemed important for the negotiations.

The penultimate stanza (lines 25–30) reads as follows:

Eja [Te], pulcherrime,	Alas, most beautiful one,
Querimur, tenerrime,	we bewail, most tender one,
Moram longi temporis	the delay of a long time.
Ducimur asperrime,	We are most cruelly led,
Nescio quo, ferrime	I know not where, wildly,
Ad fulmentum corporis.[23]	to the destruction of the body.

Hardly the sentiments to celebrate a papal coronation! The final line may refer to waning hopes to reunite the two churches into one body; perhaps *corporis* also plays upon the idea of one communion within that body. (Communion was at issue during the Council because the Roman Church used unleavened bread, the Greek Church leavened.)

Turning now to the *triplum*, stanza 3 also seems to allude to a current event.

Quod consulta contio,	Since the consulted
Qua nam sancta ratio	assembly, sacred reason,
Sic deliberavit,	deliberated,
Ut sola devotio	so one devotion
Regnet in palatio	rules in the palace
Quod deus beavit.	which God blessed.

This text, praising the past deliberations of an assembly for having established a single devotion, may refer to earlier efforts by the Council of Ferrara-Florence to foil the conciliarism of the Council of Basel.

As is well known, one of the major theological issues dividing Greeks and Latins involved the Creed, for the Latin version read *Ex patre filioque*, thus stating that the Holy Spirit descended from both the Father and the Son.[24] Both the *motetus* and the *triplum* end with

---

[23] Besseler misread the first word of the second line as *Querimus*, an interpretation contradicted by the way *querimur* is written twice in the contratenor. Some other textual and musical details also call for revision, so Professor Cameron and I are planning a new critical edition of the piece.

[24] For information on how this issue may have influenced some Mass composers of the day, see Jeffrey Chew, "The Early cyclic Mass as an Expression of Royal and Papal Supremacy," *Music & Letters* LIII (1972), 254–69 and the sources cited therein.

something like a doxology, so we have two opportunities to see how this poetry handles the concept of the Trinity. In the *triplum* the lines read *Pater herens filio Spiritus confinio* (May the Father, joined with the Son, together with the Holy Spirit). This phrasing is non-committal, the kind of language that could satisfy either side. The possibility that this ambiguity is coincidental is reduced by the conclusion of the *motetus* (lines 31–36). There the wording is even more cautious, mentioning a single Trinity but not even naming the Holy Spirit:

Una tibi trinitas	May the single Trinity,
Vera deus unitas	God the true unity,
Det celi fulgorem,	grant the splendor of Heaven
Quem linea bonitas,	to you whom straightforward
Argentea castitas	and silver chastity
Sectavit in morem.	has pursued customarily.

The second line implies an eloquent appeal: if God is the true unity, then whose cause is served by disunity?

Perhaps the Trinity played a role in Dufay's musical plan for the motet. In laying out the piece, Dufay played heavily upon the number three: three different texts, six different mensurations, the threefold singing of the contratenor, the fact that the Tenor II rests one-third of the time (thus the proportions of rests to singing to total length is 1:2:3), and blocking out the six taleas of the tenors to form the proportion 6:3:4:2:6:3 while the contratenor's simultaneous proportions are 9:6:9. A multiple of three, 24, launches the whole piece; the introduction totals 24 *maxima* and so does the first talea.

If we redate *Ecclesie militantis* as 1439 rather than 1431, what are the consequences for other musicological information concerning that decade? First, this new proposal strengthens the possibility that Dufay attended the Council of Ferrara-Florence in early 1439, but it does not require us to accept that theory. Since Dufay had worked for Eugene in earlier years, the pope could have commissioned the work even if the composer resided elsewhere. Redating the motet poses no difficulties regarding the biography of Dufay.

Recent scholarship on the manuscript containing this motet (copied in Part I of Trent 87) surmises that the copying took place between about 1430 and about 1440, perhaps in the area of Basel-Strasbourg.[25]

---

[25] Trent, Museo Provinciale d'Arte, Castello del Buon Consiglio, MS 87. Concerning the provenance, see *Census-Catalogue of Manuscript Sources of Polyphonic Music 1400–1550*, (eds. Charles Hamm and Herbert Kellman; *Renaissance Manuscript Studies* I, vol. III [1984]) and Peter Wright, "The Compilation of Trent 87_1 and 92_2," *Early Music History* II (1982), 237–71.

If Dufay was in Savoy in 1439, then he was in the region where the copying perhaps took place. If, however, he spent some time at the Council, he could have brought the motet to Savoy while enroute to Bruges later in the year.

How does this redating change our picture of Dufay's evolving style? *Ecclesie militantis* is an exceptional work no matter when it was composed, but 1439 makes more sense musically than does 1431. This follows from briefly comparing it to Dufay's ten isorhythmic motets that can be dated between 1420 and 1442.

Various traits in *Ecclesie militantis* are shared with other isorhythmic motets composed in 1433 or later, but are absent from his motets composed between 1420 and 1431. First, the motet is based upon six talea, a scheme Dufay used three other times, once in 1433 and twice in 1442. The notation includes colored semiminims and the mensuration ¢; he first turned to those practices with *Salve flos* (1435–36). Colored semiminims obtain in every isorhythmic motet thereafter, and ¢ appears in all later isorhythmic motets except *Fulgens iubar*. The notation also includes ¢3, first used in *Supremum est mortalibus* (1433). Only three other motets sing different poems in the upper parts: *Salve flos* (1435–36), *Magnanime gentis* (1438), and *Fulgens iubar* (1442). Only one other motet quotes chant in a contratenor, *Nuper rosarum* (1436). As Fallows notes,[26] all the isorhythmic motets from 1435–6 on are scored for four parts but also include some *divisi* passages. *Ecclesie militantis* fits into that repertory because it is scored for five parts, but rarely do they all sound simultaneously. Finally, *Ecclesie militantis* uses the mensuration C, a characteristic of his late motets. It first occurs in *Salve flos* (1435–36), and then in all his isorhythmic motets of 1438 or later.

Moving the date of the motet to early 1439 enables us to understand all the otherwise confusing thoughts in the poetry. Also, stylistic traits in *Ecclesie militantis*, make no sense in a piece dated 1431, but conform to his practices later in that decade. Furthermore, this redating is compatible with all pertinent facts about source provenance and Dufay's biography.

Dufay's isorhythmic motets celebrated a variety of events, both worldly and sacred, between 1420 and 1442. These included a royal wedding, the dedication and rededication of churches and other liturgical events, two peace treaties, and encomiums to several of his host cities. Appropriately, *Ecclesie militantis*, his exceptionally complex and grand isorhythmic motet, seems to have been created in response to the

---

[26] Fallows, *Dufay*, p. 118.

most complex and grand dream of his era — unity between East and West.

When that dream collapsed with the fall of Constantinople in 1453, Dufay's eventual reaction was a set of four laments on texts sent to him from Naples. This information comes to us from a letter by Dufay at Geneva on 22 February, probably 1456, and addressed to Pierro and Giovanni de' Medici at Florence.[27] Probably *O très piteulx* is the one survivor of the four laments.

Dufay's reaction to the fall of Constantinople seems to have been quite atypical; at least we know of no other musical laments for that occasion. Humanists, however, used the event to parade their skilled rhetoric and their love for rare manuscripts and antiquity. For several generations popes urged royalty to organize a crusade to Constantinople, but the princes usually accomplished little more than some banquets and sabre-rattling. In short, except for some humanists and the Roman Curia, remorse seems to have been rare in Western Europe.[28]

Dufay's lament reflects the ecclesiastical more than the humanistic attitude, as we can see from these first six lines:

O très piteulx de tout espoir fontaine,	Fountain of all hope, Father of the
Pere du filz dont suis mere esploree,	Son, I, his mother, come to your sove-
Plaindre me viens a ta court souveraine	reign court to weep about your power and also mankind for allowing my
De ta puissance et de nature humaine,	son, who was such an honor to me, to
Qui ont souffert telle durté villaine	suffer such dire pain.
Faire a mon filz, qui tant m'a hounouree.	

This poem, then, is from the viewpoint of the Mother Church[29] and addressed to God the Father regarding the suffering Son. This approach brings to mind the decree of union signed at Florence on 6 July, 1439: the third paragraph speaks metaphorically of the Mother Church and her two dissident sons now being peacefully united.[30]

---

[27] For further, see Fallows, *Dufay*, p. 287, footnotes 37 and 38. He gives a facsimile of the letter at Plate 18.

[28] See Deno Geanakoplos, "The Council of Florence (1438-1439) and the Problem of Union Between the Greek and Latin Churches," *Church History* XXIV (1955), 336, 346, and Myron Gilmore, *The World of Humanism 1453-1517* (New York, 1952).

[29] The early history of the concept "Mother Church" is explained in Ferdinand Cabrol and Henri Leclercq, *Dictionnaire d'Archéologie Chrétienne et de Liturgie*, vol. IV (Paris, 1921), cols. 2230-2238.

[30] The full text is given in Gill, *Council*, pp. 412-415.

Motherhood also commonly being represented by the Virgin Mary, the metaphor associating the sack of Constantinople with the crucifixion of Jesus is obvious.

Views that *O très piteulx* was performed at a banquet in Lille in 1454 have been rejected,[31] but no alternate theory has yet been suggested. Since the text sings the prayer of the Mother Church in the first person, the most fitting place for performance is Rome. Furthermore, Dufay's letter states that the laments were composed during the past year, and also that he worked at the court of Rome during the past year. If we accept 1456 as the date for the letter, then the Roman sojourn had to take place between 1 January 1455 and 8 November, those being dates when his presence in Savoy is documented.[32] Significant, I believe, is the absence of his name from a list of Savoy's chapel members made on 1 May; that list permits us to hypothesize that Dufay was not in Savoy for all of 1455.

Pope Nicholas IV died 24 March of that year following more than a year's illness. Calixtus III (elected 8 April) deemphasized building programs and literary pursuits,[33] and immediately devoted all his energy and the wealth of the Church to promoting a crusade against the Turks. Dufay was probably at the papal court, and no more fitting project than the four laments can be imagined. Although *O très piteulx* is a lament rather than a call to battle, perhaps its premiere was related to the occasions of 15 May, the pronouncement of a Papal Bull planning a campaign against the Turks to begin 1 March, 1456.[34]

The thought that *O très piteulx* was composed at Rome may help resolve one other problem: Dufay's letter states he got the texts from Naples, and we have no other indications of Dufay connected to that city. Pope Calixtus (originally Alfonso Borgia) was born and educated in Spain, and in 1455 King Alfonso of Naples was one of his close friends. That they exchange literary materials is illustrated by Calixtus; just before his coronation he sent several Vatican books to Alfonso as a gift.[35] Perhaps Alfonso, knowing how passionately Calixtus cared

[31] Fallows, *Dufay*, p. 287, note 38, and Massimo Mila, *Guillaume Dufay* (Turin, 1972–3), I, 126.

[32] Fallows, *Dufay*, pp. 69, 224.

[33] Some evidence obtains, though, that Calixtus was interested in promoting church music. See G. Hofmann, "Papst Kalixt III. und die Frage der Kircheneinheit," *Miscellanea Giovanni Mercati*, vol. III (Vatican, 1956), *Studi e Testi* 123, 232.

[34] Ludwig Pastor, *The History of the Popes from the Close of the Middle Ages* (London, 1891), vol. II, 349.

[35] Pastor, *The History*, vol. II, 336.

about Constantinople, arranged for the poems to be sent to Calixtus at Rome.

* * * * * * *

Perhaps this concludes the list of Dufay's works with subject matter pertaining to Graeco–Latin relations. Those works span a time period of 35 years, from the beginning of his career to the 1450's. No other composer of his generation seems to have been so occupied with Greek culture. At first glance this seems to suggest that his interests were exceptionally humanistic, but we must ask if his pieces relating to contemporary Byzantium have anything to do with humanistic attitudes toward ancient Greece. During the Renaissance, "most Westerners continued to draw a gratuitous distinction between the ancient Hellenes and the contemporary Greeks."[36] Here we can only suggest that Dufay probably comprehended, particularly due to his associations with Florence and the Medicis, that some of the modern Greek minds were among the day's leading authorities on ancient Greek philosophy. For example, two Greek delegates to the Council of Ferrara-Florence, the eminent thinkers George Gemistus and Johannes Bessarion, were guests at some of Cosimo de' Medici's private banquets in 1439.[37] It is intriguing to recall that Dufay's letter to Piero and Giovanni de' Medici was addressed to Cosimo's two sons, and the letter is a warm one, indicating some kind of previous personal acquaintanceship.

Much of another task still lies before us: to what extent did Greek thought, whether ancient or modern, influence Dufay's music? Answers are elusive because we have no documentation to help us; we must analyze musical scores interpretively. Willem Elders has pointed out rhetorical devices and other humanistic traits in some Dufay works,[38] and Margaret Sandresky has discussed Platonic-Pythagorean proportions in some of Dufay's pieces.[39] Another path was implied by Mila, who wrote that a melisma near the end of *O très piteulx* resembled a Persian slave song in Musorgsky's *Kovanscina*, and that melodic devices in Dufay's piece recalled free variations over a fixed theme in

---

[36] Geanakoplos, *Interaction*, p. 284.

[37] Deno Geanakoplos, *Interaction of the "Sibling" Byzantine and Western Cultures in the Middle Ages and Italian Renaissance (300–1600)* (New Haven, 1976), p. 219.

[38] Elders, "Humanism."

[39] Margaret Sandresky, "The Continuing Concept of the Platonic-Pythagorean System and its Application to the Analysis of Fifteenth-century Music," *Music Theory Spectrum* I (1979), 107–20.

the manner of an Indian *raga* or an Arabian *maqam*.[40] The meaningfulness of such observations is yet to be developed.

Another approach might also be worthwhile, one looking toward aesthetics. Stanley Boorman draws an attractive analogy between Dufay's development of goal-oriented forms and painters' development of perspective.[41] He describes *Nuper rosarum flores* as "one of the first musical compositions with an organic shape." What needs to be added here is that the first theoretical description of perspective was written by the brilliant architect and humanist, Leone Battista Alberti. Alberti and Dufay happen to have been colleagues; Alberti joined the court of Eugene IV in 1431 and remained in papal service for many years. The remarkably influential version of his treatise that worked at analyzing perspective, *Della pittura*, was, like *Nuper rosarum flores*, released to the world at Florence in 1436. The treatise was dedicated to Brunelleschi and, at least in a figurative sense, so was Dufay's famous motet, since its plan was determined by the proportions of Brunelleschi's dome at Florence.[42]

Alberti's treatise reflects his belief in the metaphysical significance of numbers, and it plays heavily upon the interplay between mathematics and dramatic content — the kind of interplay also working in *Nuper rosarum flores*. While discussing these issues Alberti often demonstrates his humanistic orientation by citing ancient authors, both Roman and Greek. Renaissance architects needed to rely upon musical proportions and, observing an attitude that goes back to Vitruvius, formal musical training was thought to be an asset.[43] Alberti needed to understand music, and *Nuper rosarum flores* shows Dufay's interest in contemporary architecture; it is difficult to imagine the two masters failing to exchange ideas. We have no aesthetics written by Dufay, but studying his music with Alberti's aesthetics in mind would provide another approach for considering Dufay's relationship to humanistic thought and its concern for ancient Rome and Greece.

---

[40] Mila, *Dufay*, I, 126, 128.

[41] Boorman, "The Early Renaissance," pp. 560–61.

[42] Charles Warren, "Brunelleschi's Dome and Dufay's Motet," *The Musical Quarterly* LIX (1973), 92–105.

[43] Rudolf Wittkower, *Architectural Principles in the Age of Humanism* (New York, 1962), p. 117.

CHAPTER EIGHT

NOTES ON "UNA NOTA SUPER LA"

Bruce R. Carvell

St. Louis, Missouri

Perhaps the most ambitious challenge facing the research musicologist is the recovery of performance practices previously transmitted as part of an oral tradition. Approaching the music of successively more remote periods, this task becomes increasingly more formidable. It is particularly so for the music before 1600 since, for the most part, tradition inclined authors toward the speculative and philosophical aspects of music rather than matters of practical performance. The distinction between the true musician and the mere performer, drawn by Boethius in the sixth century, was repeated with great frequency in the music treatises of the fourteenth, fifteenth, and sixteenth centuries. During this period, most writers on music addressed themselves only to theory and composition. In this context, composition meant the study of discant and counterpoint, while theory included the discussion of proportions, both harmonic and rhythmic, the classification of modes, and the theoretical justification of *musica ficta*. Unfortunately, many matters of pressing interest to the modern performer of Renaissance music, such as tempo, ornamentation, and the actual application of *musica ficta*, apparently were considered to be beneath the dignity of the proper speculative musician and, as such, were only rarely mentioned. Most often, any practical information is only found as a passing remark or in the form of criticism of some practice made by "ignorant" performers which flies in the face of speculative tradition. However, by gathering and examining the existing evidence, one can deduce the performance conventions of the practicing Renaissance musician.

One of the most commonly invoked rules of *musica ficta* application is that of "una nota super la" which decrees that the note a whole step above *la* is to be lowered by a semitone and sung as *fa*. Universally regarded as a convention of Renaissance performance practice, this rule has received very little direct examination in the literature. Even the familiar formula "una nota super la semper est canendum fa" is not found before the seventeenth century, as Andrew Hughes has shown.[1] However, several explicit statements concerning this rule are to be found in treatises pre-dating 1600 as this passage from the *Practica Musica* (1556) of Hermann Finck shows:

> For a note ascending above *la*, do not make a mutation, instead *fa* is always sung in this case, unless this ♮, or this ✖ may be marked.[2]

The meaning of this is quite clear: when a melody goes one note beyond the upper limit of a hexachord, the interval sung should be a semitone instead of the written whole tone. Since this rule is expressed in terms of solmization syllables, it applies equally to the *b-flat* above the natural hexachord, the *e-flat* above the soft hexachord, and the *a-flat* above a transposed hexachord beginning on *b-flat*.

The modern orthodox explanation of this rule is that the note above *la* is flatted to avoid the linear tritone, as in the case of *F* and *B-flat* in the natural hexachord.[3] This explanation seems to be based mainly on a passage from Johannes Tinctoris' *De natura et proprietate tonorum* (1476) where, in the eighth chapter, the great Renaissance theorist and composer offers the following comment:

> It must be noted too that the tritone must be avoided not only in these two tones, but also in all the others. Hence, this rule is generally observed, that, in any tone, if after an ascent to *B fa* ♮ *mi* acute there is a more rapid descent to *F fa ut* grave than there is an ascent to *C sol fa ut*, it is sung uniformly by soft *b*, as is seen here:[4]

---

[1] Andrew Hughes, *Manuscript Accidentals: Ficta in Focus 1350–1450*, Musicological Studies and Documents No. 27 (American Institute of Musicology, 1972), p. 63.

[2] "Propter unam notam ascendentum super la, non fit mutatio, sed semper fa in ea est cantandum, nisi hoc ♮, vel hoc # assignatum sit." Hermann Finck, *Practica Musica*, Biblioteca Musica Bononiensis, Sezione II, No. 21 (Bologna: Forni Editore, 1969), f. F,ii. Unless otherwise indicated, all translations are the present author's.

[3] Edward Lowinsky, "Introduction" to *Musica Nova accommodata per Cantar et Sonar Organi*, (ed. C. Slim; "Monuments of Renaissance Music" I, (Chicago: University of Chicago Press, 1964), p. ix.

[4] Albert Seay, trans., Johannes Tinctoris, *Concerning the Nature and*

At this point, Tinctoris gives a series of examples (see Example 1) in which he demonstrates the use of *b molle* in each of the eight modes.

Example 1. Johannes Tinctoris. *De natura et proprietate tonorum.*

Propriety of Tones, ("Colorado College Music Press Translations:" No. 2 Colorado Springs: Colorado College Music Press, 1967), pp. 12-13.
    "Notandum autem quod non solum in hiis doubus tonis tritonis est evitandus, sed etiam in omnibus aliis. Unde regula haec generaliter traditur, quod in quolibet tono si post ascensum ad♭fa ♮ mi acutum citius in Fa fa ut gravem descendatur quam ad C sol fa ut ascendatur, indistinctive per *b* molle canetur, ut hic patet:" *Corpus Scriptorum de Musica* 22/1 (American Institute of Musicology, 1975), pp. 74-75.

That this convention was already known in the fourteenth century is demonstrated in this passage from the anonymous *Tractatus de musica plana* (CS II):

> Also it is known that the third tone is commonly sung with ♮ *durum*, uncommonly however with *b molle*; and on the other hand, the fifth tone is commonly sung with *b molle*, uncommonly with ♮ *durum*. And even the eighth tone is commonly sung with ♮ *durum*, uncommonly with *b molle*. Of course, in all of the other tones, this is to be observed according to the rule: that whenever the melody in the first, second, fourth, sixth, and seventh (tones), does not ascend to *c* acute or above, instead it comes to *b* acute, it is always to be sung and solmized with *b molle*, and never with ♮ *durum*. But if the melody reaches *c* acute while ascending, or above it and a mutation is made, then it is always to be sung with ♮ *durum*, and not with *b molle*. But if nature or the force of ♮ *durum* is renounced, once more it is to be solmized with *b molle*.[5]

Comparing these two passages, one is struck by the observation that this special use of *b molle* may occur in any appropriate circumstance regardless of mode. Of particular interest is the similarity between the two explanations despite the hundred-year difference. This suggests a certain continuity of practice that is sometimes ignored in discussions of *musica ficta*. Furthermore, the lack of any attempt to justify this practice in the second passage is noteworthy, which suggests that the author felt that no further explanation was necessary for such a familiar practice.

The search for further references to the rule of *"una nota super la"* yields an additional explanation for the use of *b molle* given in an anonymous fifteenth-century *Tractatus de musica figurata et de contrapuncto* (CS IV).[6] (See Example 2.)

---

[5] "Item sciendum est quod tertius tonus regulariter cantatus per ♮ durum; irregulariter autem per b molle; et per oppositum quintus tonus regulariter cantatur per b molle; irregulariter per ♮ durum. Octavus etiam tonus regulariter cantatur per ♮ durum; irregulariter per b molle. In omnibus quippe aliis tonis hoc observandum est pro regula: quod quandocumque cantus ejus scilicet primi, secundi, quarti, sexti, septimi, non ascendit ad c acutum aut super ipsam, sed venit ad b acutam, semper cantandum et solmizandum est per b molle, et numquam per ♮ durum. Sed si contingit cantum ad c acutam ascendere, vel supra eam et mutationem in c acutam facere, tunc semper per ♮ durum est cantandum, et non per b molle; sed dimissa natura seu vi de ♮ duro, iterum est per b molle solmizandum." Anon., *Tractatus de Musica Plana*, CS II, p. 449.

[6] "Item b. mol inventum est propter." CS IV, p. 447.

Example 2
Anon., *Tractatus de musica figurata et de contrapuncto.*

Also *b mol* was invented
on account of: tritonum

suavitatem

mutationem

mobilitatem

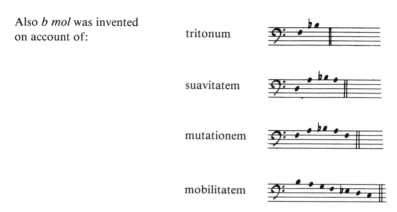

Of these reasons given for the invention of *b molle*, the first, the avoidance of the tritone, is the most familiar. The third reason, mutation, is also quite common since the *b rotundum* (flat) was used to indicate the syllable *fa* in the hexachordal system of solmization and, as such, was used to designate the soft hexachord. The fourth reason, *mobilitatem*, would appear to be best understood as "transposition" since the appearance of *b rotundum* on any note other than *B* indicates that *fa* is sung on a note where it is not ordinarily found; thus, the appearance of a flat on *E* indicates a transposed hexachord.[7] The remaining reason, *suavitatem*, is the one most relevant to the present discussion.

Suavitas, meaning sweetness or pleasantness, brings to mind one of the two traditional reasons for the addition of *musica ficta, causa pulchritudinis* (for the sake of beauty).[8] The melodic example presents a figure in which the "nota super la" (*b-flat*) appears in the context of the natural hexachord, clearly outlined by the skip from *re* to *la* and the return to *la*, and in which no tritone appears to otherwise account for the presence of the *b-flat*. This figure is often found in plainsong, particularly in those chants classified as being in the first mode. Furthermore, it brings to mind the description of the "una nota super la" rule given by Ornithoparcus (c. 1485–c. 1535) in his *Musicae activae micrologus* (1517):

---

[7] Following this reasoning, the *B* in the example should be understood to be b-flat.

[8] The other traditional reason is *causa necessitatis* (for the sake of necessity).

Whensoever a Song ascends from *D sol re* to *A la mi re* by a fifth, mediately or immediately, and further onely to a second, you must sing *fa* in *b fa* ♮ *mi* in every Tone, till a song do againe touch *D sol re*, whether it be marked or no. But this rule failes, when a Song doth not straitways fall to *F fa ut*, as in the Hymne, ave maris stella, you may see.[9]

The implication is quite clear; as long as one remains within the limits of a single hexachord, only going beyond the upper note *la* to a second, the rule of *"una nota super la"* applies. Ornithoparcus' second statement, however, offers an exception to the rule, i.e., if the melody does not return downwards to *F*, the rule does not apply. Seemingly, this raises the issue of the tritone once again, but there is another aspect that must be considered.

Stephano Vanneo (b. 1493–d. ?), in his *Recanetum de Musica Aurea* (1533), describes the rule in this manner: "Whenever a note will be one tone above La, it shall be called by the name of Fa, and then there is not any necessity for a mutation."[10] Returning for a moment to the fourteenth-century *Tractatus de musica plana*, consider this statement:

. . . whenever the melody . . . does not ascend to *c* acute or above, instead it comes to *b* acute, it is always to be sung and solmized with ♮ *molle*, and never with ♮ *durum*. But if the melody reaches *c* acute or above it and a mutation is made, then it is always to be sung with ♮ *durum*, and not with *b molle*.[11]

The key phrase here is "and a mutation is made." While there is a lack of agreement among scholars concerning specific solmization practices during the fourteenth, fifteenth, and sixteenth centuries, it is possible to see clearly the process involved in this particular instance. The example

---

[9] John Dowland, trans., *A Compendium of Musical Practice* (New York: Dover Publications, Inc., 1973), p. 135.

"Quoties cantus ascendit ex Dsolre ad alamire per quintam mediate vel immediate, et ultra tantum ad secundam, cantandum est fa in bfa ♮ mi in omnis tono, quo ad cantus iterum dsolre tetrigerit, sive signatus sive non casoetur aunt hec regula quotiens cantus ad ffaut mor non reciderit ut in hymno Ave maris stella licet videre." *Ibid.*, p. 21.

[10] Stephano Vanneo, *Recanetum de Musica Aurea*, ("Documenta Musicologica," Series I, No. 28, Kassel: Bärenreiter, 1969), fol. 16ʳ.

"Ubi uö una tm̄ supra La erit notula, cognoĩe Fa nūcupabitur, nec tūc ulla op' est mutatiõe."

[11] See above for full text.

mentioned, but not given, by Ornithoparcus, the hymn *ave maris stella**, provides an excellent demonstration piece.[12]

Example 3
"*Ave maris stella*"

re   la:
re   mi   ut   re   mi   sol   fa   mi   re   ut   re

The most cursory glance through the material dealing with solmization and mutation in the fourteenth, fifteenth, and sixteenth centuries sufficiently discloses two fundamental rules: a mutation should be made only when necessary, and that the two most frequently-used syllables in mutation are *re* and *la*. Analyzing the opening phrase of *ave maris stella*, it is obvious that, with the exception of the initial *D*, the melody falls entirely within the hard hexachord. Thus, the melody is solmized in the following manner: the first two notes are sung as *re-la* in the natural hexachord and a mutation (*la:re*) to the hard hexachord is made on the second note *A*. If, on the other hand, the melody did go down to *F* before ascending, the situation would be quite different. (See Example 4.)

Example 4
"*Ave maris stella*" — opening phrase modified.

re   la   fa   sol   fa   sol   la:
re   mi   sol   fa   re

Since the melody in Example 4 descends to *F*, one must remain in the natural hexachord longer, with the mutation being made on the seventh

---

[12] *Liber Usualis* (Tournai: Desclée & Co, 1950), p. 1259.

* Please note that the solmization syllables found in this and subsequent examples have been added by the author and are not found in the original unless otherwise indicated. In this context, a colon (:) indicates a mutation (*re:la*) while a dash (—) indicates a melodic interval (*re-la*).

note. While the descent to *F* certainly does provide a tritone to be avoided, the effect would be the same if the note were an *E* or *D* where no tritone is involved. In the examples given by Tinctoris in the passage from *De natura et proprietate tonorum* cited above, one finds this excerpt (see Example 5) from his example of the use of *b molle* in the fourth tone.[13]

Example 5
Tinctoris. *De natura et proprietate tonorum,*

mi fa mi sol la   fa la sol   la mi fa sol   la fa mi

By regarding the *b-flat* as the "nota super la," the entire melody may be sung in the natural hexachord without requiring a mutation. This excerpt is particularly revealing since Tinctoris has explained the appearance of *b molle* in terms of avoiding the tritone and, in this particular example, obviously there is no tritone present. Since the point of the series of examples from which this excerpt was taken was to illustrate the use of *b molle* in each of the modes to avoid the tritone, clearly Tinctoris intends the *B* to be flatted.

While the examples cited heretofore have dealt with a single melodic line, certain evidence indicates that the rule of "una nota super la" also fulfilled an important function in polyphony. In his discussion of the proper progression from imperfect harmonic intervals to perfect harmonic intervals in the *Ars discantus* (c. 1330), Jehan de Murs makes the following comment:

> Whenever a perfect third, which is full of tones, ascending only one note, has a fifth or some other perfect species immediately after it, this perfect third must be imperfected by *b molle*.[14]

Example 6 gives the examples he provides to illustrate his point.

---

13 See Example # 1 for complete example.

14 "Quandocumque tertia perfecta, id est plena de tonis, immediate post se habet quintam sive aliam quamcumque perfectam speciem ascendo solam notulam, illa tertia perfecta debet imperfici b molli. (example) tertia habens quintam post se. tertia habens octavam post se." CS III, p. 73.

Example 6
Jehan de Murs. *Ars discantus.*

third having a
fifth after it.

third having an
octave after it.

In the subsequent discussion, Jehan de Murs supplies further examples of the same procedure involving the intervals of a tenth, a sixth, and a twelfth, each resolving downwards to a perfect or a compound perfect interval. This is all in accordance with the principle of propinquity — the basis of all Renaissance counterpoint and voice-leading — which decrees that imperfect consonances resolve to the nearest perfect consonance. A clear example of this principle at work is that given by Prosdocimus de Beldemandis in his *Contrapunctus* (1412).[15]

Example 7
Prosdocimus de Beldemandis. *Contrapunctus.*

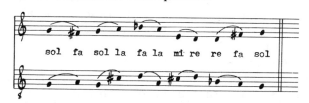

sol   fa   sol   la   fa   la   mi   re   re   fa   sol

Once again, by regarding the *b-flat* as *"una nota super la,"* the entire melody may be solmized in the natural hexachord without making any unnecessary mutations.[16] In addition, flatting the *B* creates the minor sixth that resolves to an octave in accordance with the directions of Jehan de Murs cited above. Above all, this example illustrates the

---

[15] Prosdocimo de' Beldomandi, *Contrapunctus*, Jan Herlinger, ed. and trans., (Lincoln and London: University of Nebraska Press, 1984), p. 84.

[16] The relationship between *musica ficta* and the actual solmization of a particular passage is the subject of some debate. However, it is clear from the context of Prosdocimo's comments that he is demonstrating those notes that would be supplied by the singer and, for that reason, would not have to be notated by the composer. In this light, it would seem that the sharps would have no effect on the solmization of this melody.

importance of taking into consideration both the horizontal and vertical circumstances of a particular situation when playing *musica ficta*.

Perhaps the most explicit discussion of the *"una nota super la"* rule is that offered by Lodovico Zacconi (1557–1627) in the first book of his *Prattica di Musica* (1592). While Zacconi's qualifications as a speculative musician may have been suspect (Zarlino certainly thought so), there can be no doubt concerning his accomplishments as a performing musician.[17] Taken in this light, one can assume that his remarks reflect actual practice and, as such, raise several points of considerable interest.

In the chapter "On the use of *b molle* and *b quadro*," Zacconi discusses the practical application of this rule at some length. In addition, he includes several examples in which he indicates the flatted or natural state of E, not with flat or natural signs, but by showing the appropriate syllable, either *mi* or *fa*. Here then is the relevant passage.

> Wherefore when the song is formed by *b molle* with the clef of *C sol fa ut*, the figure that passes beyond *D la sol re* is not always sung properly; by this I alert singers that though the degree that follows after *D la sol re* is the degree of *E la mi*, and that one does not find *fa* in *E la mi*, because of this he must not always say *mi*: but some times and in some instances yet *fa*: notwithstanding whether the *b molle* is absent, since the figure passing only a step beyond *D la sol re* is put in this song: by reason that the scale of music of *ut, re, mi, fa, sol, la* allows a *fa* above it: by this also in such a case *fa* must be said in *E la mi* although it might not be there as the intention is better shown with the example written below.

fa

But when the figure passes from *D la sol re* to *F fa ut*, in that case it is sung according to its nature, that this concession is made only when it passes one step above the ordinary scale. And therefore one sees that of the degree of *E la mi*, without any sign placed before it, there are some times when one says *mi*, and some other times *fa*, as one may see here.

---

[17] *The New Groves Dictionary of Music and Musicians*, 6th ed. (1980), S.v. "Zacconi, Lodovico," by Gerhard Sunger.

This I say, since many singers not seeing the flat and not knowing that one finds *fa* in the degree of *E la mi*, by saying *mi* when it is not needed make dissonances such that more may not be said: rather that presuming those composers that the figures not passing more beyond the degree of *E la mi*, they might wish without setting the *b quadro* which figure would be said as *mi*, and they do not remember the jurisdiction of the scale that is able to obtain the *fa* by a step, without taking aid or making a change with another scale: and that he understand never to say *mi*; though not in the case of a fifth, as one sees here;

Since the singers walk according to the university of the rules and by the more common streets leaving the particulars to he who wishes it: and therefore the composers are obligated every time that the songs do not attain the second *F fa ut*, as in the example, and they wish that the figure in *E la mi* is sung by nature, to place there the *b quadro*, otherwise this error they will make against the rules of the ancients which are very well heeded (this error not being a supportable error), as their works show and bear witness. And this I say of the degree of *E la mi*; I mean to say, as much of the first, so much that of the second, by the low clef, and in which other cases one wishes.[18]

---

[18] "Onde perche quando il canto è per b molle formato con la chiave di C sol fa ut, le figure che passano oltra a D la sol, re, non tutte le volte sono pronuntiate bene; per questo avertisco i cantori, che se bene la corda che seguita dopo D la, sol, re, à la corda de E la mi, & che in E la mi non si trova *fa*; non per questo sempre gli si deve dir *mi*: ma alcune volte, & in alcune occasione ancora *fa*: (non ostante che vi sia l'absenza del b molle, perche passando le figure poste in esso canto solamente un grado oltra la corda di D la, sol, re; per ragione che nelle scale Musicali di ut, re, mi, fa, sol, la; se il concede un *fa* di sopra: per questo anco in E la mi in tal caso si doverà dir *fa* quantunque non vi sia come per darlo meglio ad intendere con l'essempio infrascritto il si dimostra.
Ma quando che le figure passano da D la sol, re, in Fa fa ut, alhora le si

Despite Zacconi's rambling prose and tortuous syntax, he is clearly describing the rule of "una nota super la" in the same terms as those authors of the fourteenth, fifteenth, and sixteenth centuries whose descriptions have been cited above. When the gist of Zacconi's description is restated in a more straight-forward manner, this similarity becomes even more striking:

> Whenever a melody, occuring in the soft hexachord, passes a step beyond *D la sol re* to *E la mi, fa* is sung in *E la mi* although it does not appear there naturally.

What is most unusual about Zacconi's directions is his choice of an example in the soft hexachord, rather than the more usual natural hexachord. Perhaps he felt that, while it was common knowledge that this rule was applied in the natural hexachord where the note above *la* is *B*, in which both *mi* and *fa* occur naturally, there was some confusion when applied in the soft hexachord where the note above *la*, *E la mi*, did not normally contain *fa*. Whatever his reason, the example demonstrates his intention quite clearly. (See Example 8.)

---

cantano secondo la loro natura, che qoesta concessione è fatta solamente per quando le passano un grado solo oltra l'ordinaria scala. E però si vede che nella detta corda di E la mi, senza che vi sia posto alcun segno alcune volte si li dice *mi*, & alcune altre volte *fa*, come qui si può vedere.

Questo io lo dico, perche molti cantori non vedendoci il b & sapendo che nella corda di E la mi non vi si trova *fa*, col dirci *mi* quando non bisogna fanno dissonanza tale che piu non si può dire: Anzi che si riprendano ancora quei compositori che non passando le figuri piu su della corda di E la mi, vogliano che senza porvi il b quadro quella figura sia pronuntiata in *mi*, & non si ricordano della iurisdittione delle scale che possano per un grado sevirisi del *fa*, senza pigliar aiuto ò far cambio con altre scale: & che non s'intende mai di dirci *mi*; se non in occasion di quinta, come qui si vede;

Perche il cantore camina per l'universita della regole, & per le vie piu commune lasciando le particulare a chi le vuole: e però essi compositori sono obligati ogni volta che i canti non arrivano per essempio in F fa ut secondo, et vogliano che in E la mi si canti la figura per natura, di porci il b quadro, altrimente contrafaranno alle regole de gl'antichi i quali si sono molto ben guardati di commetter questo errore, non essendo errore supportabile, come l'opere loro ne lo dimostra, & fa fede. Et quello che io dico della corda di E la mi; intendo di dirlo, tanto di primo, quanto che del secondo, per la chiave grave, & in qual si voglia altra occasione."

Lodovico Zacconi, *Prattica di Musica, Libro Prima*, ("Biblioteca Musica," Sezione II. No. 1 Bologna: Forni Editore, N.D.), fol. 37v.

Example 8
Zacconi. *Prattica di Musica*.[19]

re la sol fa sol mi fa sol la fa la la re

Not surprisingly, the melody is one that may be solmized entirely in the soft hexachord without requiring a mutation when the highest note is regarded as "una nota super la." Furthermore, the melody begins and ends with the skip of a fifth (*re-la, la-re*) that outlines the hexachord and which has appeared in several previous discussions of the rule cited above.

Zacconi also offers the expected exception to the rule: "But when the figure passes from *D la sol re* to *F fa ut*, . . . it is sung according to its nature."[20] The accompanying example demonstrates this quite clearly. (See Example 9.)

Example 9
Zacconi. *Prattica di Musica*.[21]

la fa mi fa sol re mi fa re mi fa sol fa mi re: la la:

sol sol fa fa la fa sol sol mi re

Beginning in the soft hexachord, the melody mutates into the natural hexachord, which requires the *E* to be natural, before returning to the soft hexachord in which the *E* becomes the "nota super la" and is sung as *E-flat*.

---

[19] *Ibid.*

[20] "Ma quando che le figure passano da D la sol, re, in F fa ut, alhora le si cantano secondo la loro natura." *Ibid.*

[21] *Ibid.*

While Zacconi is just one of several authors to declare that it is the composer's responsibility to mark those instances where the note above *la* should be sung as *mi*, he is nearly unique in the attention he draws to the use of a skip of a fourth or a fifth to prevent the application of the rule of "una nota super la." He is unusually specific in his insistence on the purity of the melodic fourth and fifth.

And since I have made mention of the fifth from *A la mi re* to *E la mi*, I do not wish to allow it to be said that one can make a passage from *mi* to *fa* in a fifth at the time with a minim rest, or with a *sol* third in the middle, as this example shows.

g fa g fa

Otherwise, false relations, never allowed by the rule, would exist and fall between them.

By this many times one finds a figure that naturally must be sung *mi*; and because its following (note) is *fa* set at a fourth, one needs to raise it from its nature, and putting it in the Tone by chance in order to accompany the fifth without false relations, as one see here.

Though as much in this example as in the one above one wishes to put to the times in *b*. Whence though not to put it there is an error: this by the authority of the scale of music; thus also because *fa* in a fifth calls for another *fa*, thus as *mi* another *mi*: since *fa mi* between themselves are capital enemies, and everyone that finds them as companions seeks to destroy it, when therefore they meet in a fifth one following another, that in such cases, always the first deranges (*discaccia*) the second.

But that I find thus discrepancies in fifths, also in fourths I ever seek concords, by the true Tritone that of half one gathers there, as may be seen.

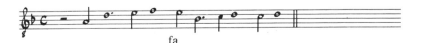

fa

If one can form a thousand of this sort of example, thus he will see clearly that they will never agree if both are not of the same species. Either then the singer is alerted in the case of the fifth as much as in the case of the fourth of accompanying *fa* with *fa*, and *mi* with *mi*, by recognizing these as what they are, since badly recognizing it by itself he may prevent the proper voices, and make discord in that case where he seeks and believes more resonant: and because their nature the composer has the liberty of placing the *b molle* or of allowing compositions to stand without it.[22]

The well-known injunction to avoid *mi contra fa* is generally regarded as referring to the perfect intervals — fourths, fifths, and octaves — in a harmonic context alone. Zacconi's rambling description and examples clearly imply that this rule extends to the perfect melodic intervals as well. In addition, he gives examples that illustrate this rule in specific circumstances. Of particular interest is his statement that fifths must be pure even if there is an intervening rest or third. (See Example 10.)

Example 10
Zacconi. *Prattica di Musica.*

---

[22] "Et poiche io ho fatta mentione della quinta di A la, mi, re, in E la mi, non voglio lasciar di dire che alle volte col mezzo delle pause, overo col mezza di una sol terza si può far passaggio da mi fa in quinta, come questo essempio dimostra.

Altrimente non si concede mai per le principale cattive relationi, che infra di loro si trovano essere, et caddere.

Per questo molte volte si trova una figura che naturalmente si doveria pronuntiar *mi*; e perche la sua sequente è *fa* posto in quarta bisogna levarla dal suo naturale, & porla in Tuono per accidente per accompagnar la quinta senza cattive relationi, come qui si vede.

Se bene tanto in questo essempio quanto che nel superiore vi si suol porre alle volte in b. onde se bene non vi si pone non è errore: sì per l'auttorità delle scale Musicali; sì anco perche *fa* in quinta chiama un'altro *fa*, si come *mi* un'altro *mi*: perche *fa mi* infra se stessi sono nemici capitali, & ogn'uno che trovana il

His example (Example 11) illustrates this.

Example 11
Zacconi, *Prattica di Musica.*

re   fa   mi   fa   sol   fa   sol   sol   re   sol

In this example, Zacconi presents a melody that may be solmized in the natural hexachord with the exception of the highest *b-flat* which would ordinarily be regarded as the "nota super la" even though the flat is included as a signature. However, since the *b-flat* is approached by the skip of a fifth from E-natural, the flat must be cancelled and the note sung as b-natural in order to insure the purity of the melodic fifth.

In Example 10, Zacconi has shown the error in singing the note above *la* as *fa* in these two specific circumstances despite the intervening rest or mediant third. In these situations when the E is sung as E-flat as he has indicated by marking each with the syllable *fa*, the singer would once again be transgressing against the injunction to avoid *mi contra fa* in a perfect fifth. Furthermore, he also provides a rule for determining which of the two notes forming the skip of a perfect fourth or fifth should be altered.

> Since *fa mi* between themselves are capital enemies, and everyone that finds them as compagnions seeks to destroy them, therefore when they meet in a fifth one after another, that in such cases, the first always chases away (*discaccia*) the second.[23]

---

compagno lo cercadi destruggere, quando però s'incontrano in quinta uno seguitar dopo l'altro, che in tale occasione sempre il primo discaccia il secondo.

Anzi che io il trovo si discrepanti in quinta, che anco in quarta non li trovo mai concordi, per il vero Trittono che di mezzo vi corre, come si può vedere.

Di questa sorte d'essempii se ne possano formar mille, che apertamente si vedra che non si possano mai accordare se non son tutti dua d'una istessa specie. Sia dunque il cantore avertito tanto nella quinta quanto che nella quarta d'accompagnar *fa* con *fa*, & *mi* con *mi*, per riconoscerli per quelli che sono, perche riconoscendoli male da se stesso si può torre della propria voce, & dissonare in quello ch'egli cerca, & si crede piu rissonare: e questo perche la natura loro mette in libertà il compositore di porci il b molle ò di lasciarle compositioni cosi senza."

Lodovico Zacconi, *Prattica di Musica, Libro Primo*, ("Biblioteca Musica," Sezione II, No. 1, Bologna: Forni Editore, N.D.), fols. 37v–38r.

23 "Perche *fa mi* infra se stessi sono nemici capitali, & ogn'uno che trovano il

In explaining why the note above *la* is sung as *fa*, Zacconi makes the statement that the "musical scale of *ut re mi fa sol la* allows a *fa* above it."[24] Further along in his discussion, Zacconi refers to "the jurisdiction of the scale that is able to obtain the *fa* by a step, without taking aid or making a change with another scale."[25] This certainly suggests that the rule of "una nota super la" was well-known to singers of Zacconi's generation and that it had been so for a long enough time that any further explanation was not required.

In the course of this investigation, passages from several fourteenth- and fifteenth-century authors have been cited demonstrating that this rule was consistently applied in both plainsong and polyphony. While some authors declare that the rule is necessary to avoid the linear tritone, others state that it is applied to make either the melody or harmony more elegant, and still others offer no explanation of any kind. Zacconi's reference to the "jurisidiction of the scale of music" seems to imply yet another reason — a scaler pattern occurring naturally in the gamut. This situation arises when the natural hexa-chord overlaps the hard hexachord. (See Example 12.)

Example 12
Hard hexachord overlapped by the natural hexachord.

Assessing the evidence set forth in this article concerning the rule of "una nota super la," several salient points emerge. While the various authors in the fourteenth, fifteenth, and sixteenth centuries explain and justify the rule in a variety of ways, it is clear that the convention was well-known throughout this period. Furthermore, although several authors explain the use of the rule to avoid the linear tritone, there are a number of other authors who understand the rule as an extension of

compagno lo cercadi destruggere, quando però s'incontrano in quinta uno seguitar dopo l'altro, che in tali occasione sempre il primo discaccia il secondo." Zacconi, *op. cit.*, f. 37v.

[24] "per ragione che nelle scale Musicali di ut, re, mi, fa, sol, la; se il concede un *fa* di sopra:" Zacconi, *op. cit.*, fol. 37v.

[25] "Della iurisdittione delle scale che possano per un grado sevirsi del *fa*, senza pigliar aiuto ò far cambio con altre scale:" *Ibid.*

solmization practices — that is, a way to extend each hexachord by a semitone in order to avoid extra mutations. In addition, it appears that, while the rule of "una nota super la" was generally regarded as primarily a melodic rule, it also had an important function in a harmonic context. Thus, it is necessary for the modern musician, whether scholar or performer, to consider all of these elements when applying the rule of "una nota super la." For only in this way, can he develop an awareness of the various situations in which a Renaissance performer would have applied this convention.

CHAPTER NINE

ST. MARY MAGDALEN — A PAINTING, A POEM, AND A MADRIGAL

Margaret Rorke

University of Utah

In 1619 Giambattista Marino (1569–1625) published *La Galeria*. He was then at the French court enjoying his reputation as Europe's leading literary figure, a reputation that rested firmly on the enthusiastic reception of his previous works: *Le Rime* (1602), *La Strage degl'Innocenti* (written 1605, but published 1632), *La Lira* (1614), and *Dicerie sacre* (1614). Only *La Sampogna* (1620) and *L'Adone* (1623) were yet to be issued.

Since the early years of the seventeenth century, Marino had been attached to several brilliant courts: the household of Cardinal Pietro Aldobrandini in Rome and Ravenna (1604–1609), the court of Duke Carlo Emanuele of Savoy in Turin (1610–1615), and the court of the French King Henry IV and Marie de' Medici in Paris (1615–1623). At these places and on his travels, he developed a love for the visual arts, and he formed friendships with many of the foremost artists of his day: Cesare d'Arpino, Bernardo Castello, Pietro da Cortona, Michelangelo Caravaggio, and Nicolas Poussin. While in Rome he began his own art collection, one he hope would rival those he had seen in the palaces of Europe. The contents of this collection are unknown now.[1] However,

---

[1] Jean H. Hagstrum, *The Sister Arts* (Chicago, 1958), p. 102.

Marino's *Galeria* remains as a testimony of the poet's love of art and his admiration for artists.

Marino's *Galeria* is a collection of madrigals, sonnets, and a few larger poems all based on works of art, real or imagined. It includes six hundred-old poems divided into two groups — Painting and Sculpture. Among the works of art treated are the *Apollo Belvedere*, Michelangelo's *Pietà*, *Moses*, *Night*, and *Day*, Caravaggio's *Head of Medusa*, and Guido Reni's *Massacre of the Innocents*.[2]

Also rendered is the famous *St. Mary Magdalen in Penitence* by Titian (ca. 1488-1576). Marino's poem on this painting in *La Galeria* was one of his most popular creations, and it was so celebrated in the early seventeenth century that some of its stanzas were set to music by the prominent Roman composer, Antonio Cifra (1584-1629). The lineage is clear. A painting by Titian became the subject of a renowned poem by Marino, portions of which in turn provided the texts of two spiritual madrigals by Cifra. As a phenomenon, such a transference from painting to poetry to music is novel in the literature on the arts and is interesting in itself. More importantly, it provides an opportunity to seek empirically the relationships between these three works of art, each in a different medium. Let us start at the beginning with Titian's painting.

Titian's *St. Mary Magdalen in Penitence*

Titian's *St. Mary Magdalen in Penitence*, now in the Pitti Palace, has for its subject the saint during her last years. Previously, she had been a sinner, a prostitute, but she sought and received forgiveness from Christ, washing His feet with her tears, drying them with her hair, and anointing them with ointment from her alabaster jar. Joining Christ's followers, she was the first to see Him after the Resurrection, whereupon Christ instructed her to tell the disciples to go to Galilee where they would see Him. Mary Magdalen spent her last years alone in the desert in southern France as a contemplative communing with God.

Titian's painting on this subject (see colorplate) was executed ca. 1530-1535 for Duke Francesco Maria I della Rovere of Urbino; the Duke's son, Guidobaldo II, received Titian's legendary *Venus of Urbino* in 1538. Titian's art reached maturity in the 1520s, and the

---

[2] *La Galleria* has recently been published in a modern edition: Giovanni Battista Marino, *La Galleria*, ed., Marzio Pieri (Padova, 1979).

Plate 1. Titian. *St. Mary Magdalen in Penitence.*

richness of color, the luminosity, and the rendering of texture for which Titian was the acknowledged sixteenth-century master is evident in *St. Mary Magdalen*. Note particularly the glowing alabaster flesh tones, the tear-reddened eyes, and the ruby lips. Most remarkable is the hair which, falling in waves, covers and reveals the reformed prostitute's body. The dark brown hill in the background, set off by the cloud-filled blue sky, adds to the warmth of the composition.

St. Mary Magdalen belongs to a genre that Titian originated, a religious image, overtly sensual, that evokes piety and delight. It is easy to see how Mary Magdalen, a repentant prostitute, would be ideal for such a painting. As interpreted by a recent Titian authority, David Rosand, "the modesty of her covering gesture reveals her sinful past, while the trembling passion of her communion with the divine is signified by the rippling patterns of her radiant hair, its febrile motions con-

veying a state of fervent hope and nervous exceptation.''[3] The covering
gesture itself derives from antique statues of the *Venus pudica* (modest
Venus) type.[4] Significantly, Titian's *St. Mary Magdalen* is cast as the
nude celestial Venus, who, according to Renaissance tradition, could
lead the viewer into the realm beyond sensory perception.

Notable sixteenth- and early seventeenth-century connoisseurs substantiate Rosand's assessment. Referring to a later version of *St. Mary
Magdalen* painted by Titian for Philip II of Spain, Giorgio Vasari
(1511–1574), artist and art historian, wrote in 1550:

> . . . all dishevelled; that is, with the hair falling over the shoulders, about
> the throat, and over the breast, the while that, raising the head with the
> eyes fixed on Heaven, she reveals remorse in the redness of the eyes, and
> in her tears repentance for her sins. Wherefore the picture moves mightily
> all who behold it; and, what is more, although she is very beautiful, it
> moves not to lust but to compassion.[5]

After purchasing a replica of *St. Mary Magdalen* (Pitti version) for the
Ambrosiana Gallery, Federico Borromeo, nephew of Carlo Borromeo
and Cardinal of Milan (1595–1631), defended the nude in 1625 by
saying that Titian "knew how to maintain its honesty."[6]

Marino's *Magdalen of Titian*[7]

1. Questa, che'n atto supplice e pentita
   Se stessa affligge in solitaria cella,
   E de la prima età fresca e fiorita
   Piagna le colpe, in un dolente e bella,
   Imago è di colei, che già gradita

   She, who with suppliant and peni-
   tent gesture
   Chastises herself in a solitary cell,
   And, at once beautiful and mournful,
   Weeps for the sins of her fresh and
   flowered youth,
   Is the image of that other one, who

---

[3] David Rosand, *Titian* (New York, 1978), p. 106.

[4] Ibid.

[5] Giorgio Vasari, *Lives of the Most Eminent Painters, Sculptors and
Architects*, trans. Gaston Du C. de Vere (New York, 1979), pp. 1982–83.

[6] Harold E. Wethey, *The Paintings of Titian*, 3 vols. (London, 1969), vol. 1:
The Religious Paintings, p. 144.

[7] In the interest of saving space, only six of the fourteen stanzas of *La
Maddalena di Tiziano* have been quoted here, and three more are cited later;
these are sufficient to establish the nature of the whole. The text and translation
derive from James V. Mirollo, *The Poet of the Marvelous: Giambattista
Marino* (New York, 1963), pp. 286–293, where the entire poem may be found.

Fu del Signor seguace e cara an-
  cella;
E quanto pria del folle mondo er-
  rante,
Tanto poscia di Cristo amata
  amante.

once,
Welcome and dear handmaiden,
  followed the Master;
And as much as she was earlier of the
  mad and sinful world,
So much was she later of Christ a
  beloved lover.

2. Ecco come con lui si lagna e come
  Del volto irriga il pallidetto aprile,
  E, deposte de cor l'antiche some,
  Geme in sembiante languido ed
    umile;
  E fanno inculte le cadenti chiome
  Agl'ingnudi alabstri aureo monile:
  Le chiome, ond'altrui già, se stessa
    or lega,
  Già col mondo, or col cielo; e
    piagne e prega.

Behold how she complains to him,
  and how
She irrigates the pallid April of her
  face,
And, the old burdens gone from her
  heart,
How she sighs in a languid and
  humble manner;
Her loose locks falling make
For her naked alabaster a golden
  necklace;
Her locks, once used to tie others,
  now tie herself;
Locks which once tied her to the
  world now tie her to heaven; and
  she weeps and prays.

3. Felice donna e fortunata a pieno,
  Cui, di falso piacer già sazia e
    schiva,
  Di là, 've altrui lusinga amor ter-
    reno
  E più l'anime alletta esca lasciva,
  Qual tradito augelletto al ciel
    sereno,
  O qual cerva trafitta a l'onda viva,
  Umilemente al Redentore a lato
  Così per tempo ricovrar fu dato.

Happy and most fortunate of women,
To whom — already sated with and
  scornful of false pleasure —
From that place where earthly love
  entices others,
And where lascivious snares attract
  souls even more,
Like a little bird betrayed in a clear
  sky
Or a deer wounded in the fresh
  waters,
Humbly at the side of the Redeemer,
It is granted that she be rescued in
  time.

4. Tu, del senso sprezzando ingordo e
  vano
  I fugaci diletti e i lunghi affanni,
  Campar del mondo, adulator,
    insano,

You, scorning the fleeting delights
  and endless suffering
Of the insatiate and vain senses,
The life of this adulterous and insane
  world

Dall'insidie sapesti e dagl'inganni;
E 'n questo della vita ampio oceàno,
In sul fior giovenil de' più verd'anni,
Trovasti al fragil legno, e quasi absorto
Da l'umane tempeste, il polo e 'l porto.

Knew from its deceits and lies,
And in this wide ocean of life
You found in the youthful flower of your greenest years
A fragile bark and, when almost drowned
By the human tempest, and pole and the port.

8. Beato pianto, aventurose e belle
Lagrime, a lei cagion d'eterno riso,
Non così 'l mar di perle, il ciel di stelle,
S'orna come di voi s'orna il bel viso.
Perdon l'acque de l'Ermo e perdon quelle,
Appo voi, ch'hanno il fonte in paradiso;
Chè, tra 'l bel volto sparse e 'l crin celeste,
Rive di fiori e letto d'oro aveste.

Blessed weeping, lovely wandering
Tears, the cause of an eternal smile on her,
The sea is not adorned by pearls, the sky by stars,
As her face is adorned by you.
The waters of Hermus and those that have their source
In paradise cede to you;
For, scattered over her beautiful face and celestial hair,
You had streams of flowers and a bed of gold.

9. Fûr vivi specchi, in cui l'alma si scerse,
I vostri puri e flebili cristalli;
E vide, allor che 'n voi se stessa asperse,
De' suoi sì lunghi error gli obliqui calli;
Là dove quasi in pelago sommerse
I gravi troppo e vergognosi falli,
Quando a lavar que santi piè vi sciolse
E fûr le chiome il velo onde gli avolse.

Your pure and plaintive crystals
Were living mirrors in which the soul mirrored itself;
And the soul, when it liquefied itself in you,
Saw the jagged cliffs of its long wandering;
There, as though in the sea, she drowned
Sins too heavy and too shameful,
When she loosened you to bathe those saintly feet,
And her hair was the veil she used to swathe them.

Marino's *Magdalen of Titian* dates from the 1590s when the poet first saw a copy of Titian's *St. Mary Magdalen* in Naples at the gallery of one of his early patrons, Matteo di Capua, Prince of Conca. At that time, Marino subscribed to the current thought on the relationships between painting and poetry, affinities expressed in the sixteenth-century traditions of *ut pictura poesis* and the *paragoni*.[8] In fact, Marino's later writings, particularly *Dicerie sacre* and *La Galeria*, contain passages paraphrasing earlier critics on these subjects.[9] As stated at the outset of this article, observation will be the primary means of detecting the transmission of ideas and techniques from Titian's *St. Mary Magdalen* to Marino's *Magdalen of Titian*, from painting to poetry. However, by way of providing a scientific control (a standard of comparison for checking or verifying the results of an experiment), these observations will be made within the context of late sixteenth-century critical theory.

Sixteenth-century critics felt that it was in the pictorial vividness of representation — in the power to produce clear images of the external world in the mind's eye — that the poet primarily resembled the painter. To quote Lodovico Dolce, the first biographer of Titian and the author of an important humanistic treatise on painting, *Aretino* (1557):

> I add, then, that the painter is concerned to imitate, by dint of lines and colors (whether it be on a flat surface or panel, wall or canvas), everything that presents itself to the eye; while the poet, through the medium of words, characteristically imitates not only what presents itself to the eye, but also what presents itself to the intellect.[10]

And it is in the transfer of the pictorially vivid elements — the gestures and action, the setting and coloring of the painting to the imagery of the

---

[8] During the High Renaissance with the creations of Leonardo, Michelangelo, Raphael, and Titian, the visual arts enjoyed a prestige they had never known, and their practitioners and supporters sought for them the status of a liberal art, a status that poetry and music had possessed since antiquity. In *paragoni* (comparisons of the arts), the most famous of which was by Leonardo da Vinci, advocates for the visual arts attempted to prove the superiority of the visual arts over poetry and music. For Titian's view on the relative value of painting and music as interpreted in a fascinating group of paintings by and after Titian: *Venus and a Musician*, see Erwin Panofsky, *Problems in Titian, Mostly Iconographic* (New York, 1969), pp. 119-125.

The theories of *ut pictura poesis* evolved from a somewhat different premise. Here Renaissance enthusiasts seizing upon a phrase in Horace's *Ars poetica*, "ut pictura poesis" (as a painting, so a poem), imposed on painting the rules of poetry in the hope of elevating the position of the visual arts. Important information regarding Renaissance thought on the relationships among the arts can be derived from both traditions.

[9] Gerald Ackerman, "Gian Battista Marino's Contribution to Seicento Art Theory," *Art Bulletin*, XLIII (December 1961), pp. 330-35.

[10] Mark W. Roskill, *Dolce's "Aretino" and Venetian Art Theory of the Cinquecento* (New York, 1968), p. 97.

poetry — that one most readily notes the kinship between Titian's and Marino's works. Mary Magdalen "illuminating the shadows again with celestial rays and sweetly conversing with the highest Love," the "suppliant and penitent gesture," the "loose locks falling," the "pallid April of her face," the "deserted grotto," the "tearful eyes," the "ruby lips," the "candid hand," the "eternal smile," and the "pure alabastrum" are all present in Marino's poem to conjure up the vision in the mind's eye of Titian's *St. Mary Magdalen*.

In his classic study of literary pictorialism, *The Sister Arts*, Jean Hagstrum emphasizes one important development in the relationship between painting and poetry during the sixteenth century:

> Posture reveals grace, an eye expresses mental power, a lip suggests the power of mental conceiving. This too the poet can learn from the painter. Although his medium has greater range of expression than the painter's and goes beyond the use of sensuous detail and visible image, he can derive from the sister art the power of expressing meaning through *visibilia* alone. The *paragone* forced him to consider the claims of painting, an art that during the Renaissance had learned the full scope of its own peculiar genius. [11]

This was a lesson that Marino took very much to heart. In *L'Adone*, as he prepares to recount the death of Adonis, Marino remembers Morrazzone's painting of the scene, and he implores (XVIII, 99): "Insegni a la mia penna il tuo pennello" (Let your brush be the teacher of my pen). [12]

Sixteenth-century criticism establishes another point of contact between the two arts. In its pages, one is cautioned repeatedly to adhere to Horace's dictum that painting, like poetry, should instruct as well as delight. [13] Marino in *Dicerie sacra* reiterated this same truth, but colored it with a Counter-Reformation tinge:

> They are both of them aimed at one same goal, that is, to delightfully feed human souls and to console them with the highest pleasure. [14]

As we have seen, Titian's *St. Mary Magdalen*, a religious image, was created to "feed human souls" and to delight. On examination, these are also certainly two of the intentions behind Marino's *Magdalen of*

---

[11] Hagstrum, *The Sister Arts*, p. 70.

[12] Mirollo, *The Poet of the Marvelous: Giambattista Marino*, p. 199.

[13] Rensselaer W. Lee, "Ut Pictura Poesis: The Humanistic Theory of Painting," *Art Bulletin*, XXII (December 1940), p. 226.

[14] Mirollo, *The Poet of the Marvelous: Giambattista Marino*, p. 201.

Titian. In both the poem and the painting, the same episodes of Mary Magdalen's life are clearly delineated — her sinfulness, her redemption, and her last days on earth spent in prayer. Paramount is the moral that a repentant sinner may possess life everlasting through the compassion of God. To cite only one of several references to this lesson in Marino's poem: "Locks which once tied her to the world now tie her to heaven." This message, in fact, is delivered with more urgency by Marino than by Titian, being present in nearly every stanza of the poem. As a loyal son of the Counter-Reformation, Marino was giving the appropriate proselytizing treatment to Mary Magdalen, the Catholic Church's leading symbol for conversion and grace.

Delight in sensuousness present in Titian's painting is also a dominant feature in Marino's rendering of Mary Magdalen. The appeal to the senses was commonplace in Counter-Reformation art, and it was a particular specialty of Marino. In part, the sensual aura of his work is due to Marino's descriptive powers, but as with his famous predecessor, Torquato Tasso, it is also the result of choosing word rhythms and sounds appropriate to his subjects. The liquidity of sound of the repeated vowels in the following line from the *Magdalen of Titian*, for instance, makes more vivid and sensuous the image of Mary Magdalen's luxuriant locks.

Chiome, che sciolte in preziosa pioggia

Sixteenth-century criticism offers no other clue to perceiving transference from painting to poetry. It is noticeably silent on the subject of form, and observation discloses that the design of the painting has not influenced that of the poem. In this context, it is interesting to note that literary historians have traced the transfer of pictorial form to poetry at a later date, among the English Neoclassicists, John Dryden, James Thomson, and Thomas Gray.[15]

There is a certain quality about Marino's poem, however, that is not attributable to Titian's painting, and Marino's writings aid in identifying this. In the preface to *La Galleria*, Marino states that "his principal intention" in creating this poetry was "to let the mind play about certain few (works of art) in accordance with the poetic ideas which are produced in the fancy."[16] This point is clarified by a passage in *Dicerie sacre* where Marino asserts that a painting can produce phan-

---

[15] Hagstrum, *The Sister Arts*, pp. 181–82, 256–61, 301–14.
[16] Marino, *La Galleria*, ed. Pieri, p. 3.

tasms in the mind of the beholder, can excite the wit with artifice, and can re-create remembrances of things past.[17]

The mental and imaginative activity to which Marino's mind was stimulated was primarily a display of wit. For Marino, the most important ingredient of poetry was wit. This provides the reader with insights into previously unsuspected aspects of reality and the pleasure of instantaneous and vivid impressions. The main tools of wit are the figures and tropes of rhetoric. Of these, the metaphor reigns supreme because it is most capable of achieving, through analogy, *meraviglia*, i.e., wonderment.[18]

As can be seen from a comparison of Titian's painting and Marino's poem, Marino added, often by means of metaphor, ingenuous images of his own that do indeed induce 'wonder' in the reader's mind. Note, for instance, the effect of the chain of metaphors on the tears in Stanza 8 and the phastasm of the drowning of the sins in the tears in Stanza 9. Less spectacular use of metaphor abounds, "Eye/The emissary of flames and sparks only," "Candid hand/the unchaste mistress of artifice and impure stratagems," and so on.

Present also are a number of other rhetorical devices that astound. In fact, the rhetorical ornaments of poetry constitute, at times, an end in themselves. Plentiful are instances of oxymoron (the juxtaposition of words of opposing meaning) and antithesis (the balancing of parallel word groups conveying opposing ideas): "Bathed on *earth* (oh, marvel!) the *sky*" and "the *fleeting delights* and *endless suffering*," for example. Moreover, many of the stanzas are divided into two sections dealing with the contrary personalities of Mary Magdalen, one the sinner and the other the saint. Less frequent is *adnominatio* (the use of words from the same grammatical family or from the same stem, or words in various degrees homophonic, but not related), its most prominent occurrence being at the end of the first stanza, "di Cristo amata amante" (of Christ a beloved lover).

Associations with earlier literature are also evoked for Marino by Titian's *St. Mary Magdalen*. Most striking are the references to the ancient Hermus River with its gold-bearing sands and to the locks of Berenice, wife of Ptolemy III, who promised to sacrifice her hair to the gods, if her husband returned home the conqueror of Asia. Curious is

[17] Giambattista Marino, *Dicerie sacre e La Strage degl'Innocenti*, ed. Giovanni Pozzi (Turin, 1960), p. 81.

[18] On the poetics of *meraviglia*, see Mirollo, *The Poet of the Marvelous: Giambattista Marino*, pp. 115–20.

the fact that Titian's overt reference to the celestial Venus is not transferred to Marino's poem. Here the poet may very well have been
heeding the directives of Counter-Reformers that the pagan must be
eliminated from religious art.[19] Marino relies heavily not only on
devices of rhetoric, but also upon past poetic conventions, specifically
the conventions of the amatory lyric going back to Petrarch. The tropes
of the white hand, the pearls, the rubies, the roses, and the ice, to name
only a few, are all staples of Petrarch's *Canzoniere*. In addition, one of
the images, that of the fragile bark almost drowned by the human
tempest while seeking a safe port, derives from the same source.[20] It was
Marino's belief that the art of poetry lay in novel reworkings of a
received body of motifs, with Petrarch's poems providing a central
corpus.

Before leaving the role of "fancy" in Marino's *Magdalen of Titian*, it
is interesting to note that literary historians consider *La Galleria* a mile-
stone in literary pictorialism. As Jean Hagstrum puts it:

> The example of Marino is important. He conceived of the icon as a kind
> of objective correlative for the emotion he was expressing poetically. The
> poem should never be allowed to become subservient to description. It
> should be autonomous, held together by the bone of its own meaning and
> the sinew of its own wit.[21]

In the often quoted final stanza of Marino's *Magdalen of Titian*, the
poet draws not on the art work itself, but on popular tenets of current
art theory:

14. Ma ceda la natura e ceda il vero
    A quel che dotto artefice ne finse,
    Che, qual l'avea ne l'alma e nel pensiero,
    Tal bella e viva ancor qui la dipinse.
    Oh celeste sembianza, oh magistero,
    Ove ne l'opra sua se stesso ei vinse;
    Fregio eterno de' lini e de le carte,
    Meraviglia del mondo, onor de l'arte!

But nature and truth cede
To that which the learned artificer has imaged,
For he painted her here, as beautiful and alive
As he conceived her in his soul and thought.
Oh, celestial semblance, oh, masterly craft,
For in his work he outdoes himself;
Eternal ornament of cloth and paper,
Marvel of the world, honor of art!

---

[19] See Anthony Blunt, *Artistic Theory in Italy, 1450–1600* (Oxford, 1940), pp. 113–17.

[20] The image is from the sonnet "Passa la nava mia colma d' oblio."

[21] Hagstrum, *The Sister Arts*, p. 104.

The first two lines allude to the belief that, now possessing the new tools of perspective and anatomy, the Renaissance artist can surpass nature, the ideal of Renaissance man. Titian's personal emblem was, in fact, the image of a she-bear licking her cub into shape captioned with the motto, NATURA POTENTIOR ARS (Art more powerful than nature). The next two lines refer to the Counter-Reformation theory that the idea for a work of art is conceived in the artist's soul and mind and not according to the doctrine of the 'imitation of nature' as espoused in the High Renaissance.

Cifra's "O come bella" and "Chiome, che sciolte"

Antonio Cifra published in his *Scherzi sacri, libro primo* (1616) and *Scherzi sacri, libro secondo* (1618) musical settings of two of Marino's key stanzas, the sixth, "O come bella a la solinga grotta," which describes the entire scene presented by Titian, and the tenth, "Chiome, che sciolte in preziosa pioggia," which concentrates on the central element in the iconography of the painting, Mary Magdalen's hair.

6. Oh come bella a la solinga grotta,
   Pastorella romita, entro ti stai!
   Oh come chiara, ove più quivi annotta,
   L'ombra rallumi co'celesti rai!
   Oh come dolce in flebil voce e rotta
   A ragionar col sommo Amor ti stai!
   Si vivi espressi son gli atti e i lamenti,
   Ch'io vi scorgo i pensier, n'odo gli accenti.

   Oh, how beautifully, solitary shepherdess,
   You inhabit that deserted grotto!
   Oh, how brightly you illuminate the shadows
   Again with celestial rays, there where it grows darkest!
   Oh, how sweetly you converse with the highest Love
   In a weak and broken voice!
   So vividly expressed are the gestures and laments
   That I perceive your thoughts and hear their sounds.

10. Chiome, che, sciolte in preziosa pioggia,
    Su le rose ondeggiate e su le brine,
    Beate o voi, che 'n disusata foggia,
    Incomposte e neglette e sparse e chine,
    Quell'altezza appressaste ove non poggia
    Di Berenice il favoloso crine!

    Tresses which, let loose in a luxuriant cascade,
    Wave your way through roses and frost,
    Blessed are you, for in unusual array,
    Loose and neglected, disheveled and falling,
    You approach that height where even the fabulous locks
    Of Berenice do not contend with you!
    Darkness and gold defer to you be-

| Ceda a voi l'ombra e l'or, poscia che sole Quel piè toccaste a cui soggiace il sole. | cause you merely Touched that foot to which the sun pays homage. |

Cifra, who was an important figure in Roman musical life, had held the prominent posts of *maestro di cappella* at both the Roman Seminary (1605–1607) and at the Collegium Germanicum (1608–1609). He was then engaged at his principal appointment as *maestro di cappella* at Santa Casa di Loreto, a position he retained from 1609 to 1622 and from 1626 until his death in 1629. Because it was the chief Marian sanctuary in the Counter-Reformation and a major center of pilgrimage, enshrining as it did the home of the Blessed Virgin in Nazareth, Santa Casa di Loreto maintained strong ties with Rome, and its directorship was normally reserved for a Roman. The monodic madrigals and *scherzi* and the polyphonic madrigals and strophic variations in Cifra's two books of *scherzi sacri* may have been first performed in the Oratorio della Compagnia del Giesù in Loreto.[22]

The relationship between text and music was clear to a *seconda prattica* composer like Cifra. It was the duty of music to provide a suitable setting for the words. Cifra achieved this end chiefly through employing the repertoire of visual and aural figures then current. Generally in his *scherzi sacri*, Cifra used dissonance and melodic intervals in the style of Palestrina. His melodic lines were extremely lyrical, and his chromaticism did not exceed the chromatic third-relation with single degree-inflection. Over this fundamental structure, Cifra overlaid a number of musical-rhetorical ornaments, the most prominent of which was *hypotyposis*, a figure illustrative of words or poetic ideas that frequently emphasizes the pictorial nature of words. This is best illustrated in "Chiome, che sciolte," where the words that convey the image of the waves of hair ("sciolte," "pioggia," "ondeggiate," "foggia," and "sparse") are underlaid with undulating and sometimes lengthy melismas (Ex. 1). Thus the gestures and action of the painting are expressed through music's *visibilia*.

In this context, it is valuable to recall an observation by Alfred Einstein on the aesthetics of the Italian madrigal:

. . . the madrigal was chiefly meant not for the listener but for the singer.

---

[22] For more information on Cifra's *scherzi sacri*, see Margaret Ann Rorke, *The Spiritual Madrigals of Paolo Quagliati and Antonio Cifra* (Ph.D. diss., University of Michigan, 1980). Both "O come bella" and "Chiome, che sciolte" are transcribed in the appendix of this dissertation.

Example 1. Antonio Cifra. "Chiome, che sciolte."

. . . Furthermore, in the normal madrigal (for there are other varieties) everything is done to convey to each of the singers the imaginative conception, even through the eye, so that each may feel himself an equal part of the whole, that each may sing as a soloist within the frame of the whole.[23]

With this new emphasis on musical notation, it seems likely that the sixteenth- and early seventeenth-century composer, as well as poet, had learned in part from the painter the power of expressing meaning through the visible.

Another important feature of Marino's *Magdalen of Titian*, its play of rhetorical devices, was also not lost on Cifra. For a number of these ornaments, the composer has provided the equivalent musical–rhetorical figure. The beginnings of Lines 1, 3, and 5 of "O come bella," for instance, start with the same two words, *anaphora*, as it is termed in rhetoric. In the Cifra setting, the motive that initiates Line 3 (Ex. 2b) is the inversion of that which commences Line 1 (Ex. 2a), and the motive that begins Line 5 (Ex. 2c) is a variation of the one that starts Line 3. The *antithesis*, "ombra" and "celesti rai," ("O come bella," Line 4) is adorned by *antitheton*, a musical contrast to express opposing ideas. Here it is an opposition of texture, "ombra" set imitatively at first and "celesti rai" homophonically (Ex. 3).[24]

---

[23] Alfred Einstein, *The Italian Madrigal* (Princeton, 1949), p. 243.

[24] To what extent the musical-rhetorical figures defined primarily in German treatises of the early seventeenth century are also found in contemporary Italian music is yet to be determined; however, several of these figures are indeed present in Cifra's "O come bella" and "Chiome, che sciolte." The definition of *hypotyposis* employed here derives from Joachim Burmeister's *Musica*

Example 2. Antonio Cifra. "O come bella."

Example 3. Antonio Cifra. "O come bella."

As might be expected, Cifra carefully observed word rhythms and syntax in his settings. He acknowledged the mosaic-like, two-to-three-word units in Marino's verse by fitting each with a musical motive. Marino's *Magdalen of Titian* is cast in *ottave*, and "O come bella' is set to the *Aria di Gazella* and "Chiome, che sciolte" to the *Aria di Romanesca*. In this Cifra was following the century-old practice of singing *ottave* to pre-existent musical formulas including these very *arias*.

It is possible to contend that the soprano duets in parallel thirds and sixths throughout produce a sensual sheen comparable to that created by Titian and Marino, but is there any correspondence of the general tone that can be discussed more objectively? Some of the theories of Nicolas Poussin (1594–1665), master painter and a friend of Marino during the poet's last years, shed some light on this. Poussin, who lived primarily in Rome after 1624, associated with artists interested in music, and by 1647, he had transposed the classical Greek modes of music as he had read about them in Gioseffo Zarlino's *Le Istituzioni harmoniche* into his theory of modes for painting.[25] According to this theory, different subjects should have different dispositions and colors. Poussin retained the designations for the modes present in the *Istituzioni* as well as their qualities of ethos. Thus, the Phrygian mode was for furious scenes, such as battles; the Lydian for mournful subjects; the Ionic for cheerful scenes, particularly festivals and

---

poetica (Rostock, 1606) and the definition of *antitheton* from Johannes Nucius's *Musices practicae* (Neisse, 1613). For an excellent discussion of music and rhetoric, see *The New Grove Dictionary of Music and Musicians*, 6th ed. (1980), s.v. "Rhetoric and Music," by George J. Buelow.

[25] As early as the 1630s when Poussin was beginning to formulate his theory of the modes, he was in the studio of Domenichino. Domenichino, according to Giovanni Pietro Bellori, had made a special study of music and was a friend of the music theorist, Giovanni Battista Doni.

bacchanals; and the Dorian for serious subjects that might induce wisdom and virtue in the observer.

We need not explore Poussin's theory of the modes further to see that it raises some intriguing questions. Today, the degree to which Renaissance and early Baroque composers concerned themselves with the expressive possibilities of modal ethos is still unknown.[26] But does it seem likely that Poussin, who was informed in the theory of music, would derive a theory of painting from a theory of music totally ignored by composers? With recent research in musicology uncovering new ways in which music of this period was dependent on antique thought, modal ethos is indeed an issue that needs re-examination. Suffice it to say here that the mode of Cifra's "O come bella" and "Chiome, che sciolte" is the one most appropriate, Dorian on G.[27]

Although Titian's *St. Mary Magdalen* had many descendants in the world of painting, we are now at the end of this rather unique branch of her family tree. In the course of this examination of Titian's, Marino's, and Cifra's renderings of St. Mary Magdalen, we have attempted to seek empirically the relationships among these three art works. We have seen transferred from the painting to the poem and the spiritual madrigal, the painting's pictorial vividness, sensuous quality, pious mood, and intentions to instruct and delight, albeit in terms of the individual arts involved. Also present in the poem was the painter's artistic philosophy.

Equally informative were the elements that did not transfer or those that were added anew. Both the painting and the poem employed the Renaissance tradition of making telling references to the antique, and all three works involved the novel reworking of past conventions within their respective arts. At times the political-religious climate or simply the artist's desires influenced decisions not to transfer elements, as with Marino's omission of Titian's *Venus pudica* allusion; at other times, the artist's imagination, "fancy" as Marino called it, was responsible for portions of the derived work.

This study introduces a new methodology. In contrast to the more general 'Zeitgeist' approach of the past, it proceeds by investigating empirically within the framework of contemporary artistic theory

---

[26] See *The New Grove Dictionary of Music and Musicians*, 6th ed. (1980), s.v. "Mode," by Harold S. Powers.

[27] Sometimes different theorists of this period attributed different qualities to a given mode. However, in the case of the Dorian mode, most influential theorists (Nicola Vicentino and Heinrich Glarean, for instance) described its ethos in the same terms as did Zarlino.

works of art known to be intimately connected. It does not pretend to be the definitive statement on the relationships of the arts in the sixteenth and early seventeenth centuries. Had we begun, for instance, with a more rhetorically conceived painting, possibly one by Poussin, we might have discovered a transfer of rhetorical devices from painting to poetry to music. Instead, the study suggests that a number of empirical investigations of its kind involving numerous different artistic personalities might lead to more cogent statements on the relationship of the arts for the period indicated or for any other period. Moreover, as found with Poussin's theory of the modes, they might cause us to reassess some of our fundamental notions about the music itself.

CHAPTER TEN

CARL LUYTHON AT THE COURT OF EMPEROR RUDOLF II: BIOGRAPHY AND HIS POLYPHONIC SETTINGS OF THE MASS

Carmelo Peter Comberiati

Manhattanville College

Carl Luython was born at Antwerp in either 1557 or 1558 and died at Prague in 1620.[1] He worked in the Habsburg imperial chapel from 1566 until the death of Rudolf II in 1612; his only departure was for a short period of study in Italy. Luython's work is of interest as it represents the work of a conservative late-Renaissance musician at the end of the era. Luython looks backwards, with respect, to the work of Rudolf's more famous chapel master, Philippe de Monte, as well as reflecting some forward-looking ideas of his contemporaries.

Few documents survive concerning Luython's life; the principal sources have been collected in his only biographical monograph by De Burbure.[2] These include his will, the record of its execution and the list

---

[1] The family name appears as Luthon, Luycthon, Luiton, Luyton, Luitton, Luythonius, and Luython. The latter has been the accepted form and has been chosen for this study because it appears as a signature to his *Liber Missarum* of 1609.

[2] Leon Marie de Burbure de Wesembeek, Chevalier, *Charles Luython Compositeur de Musique de la Cour Imperiale (1550–1620)* (Brussels:

of relevant notices in the court records at Vienna. To these can be added the dedications from his five published works and the notices compiled by Smijers in his study of the imperial music chapels of the Habsburg Emperors.[3]

These sources draw a picture of Luython as a loyal servant of the court. He appears not to have been an outstanding member of the chapel either in terms of his creative output or musical accomplishments, but rather because of his longevity. Luython's association with the court spanned forty-five years. These years traverse a critical period in music history, the intersection of the Renaissance and Baroque eras. This study presents the background for musical patronage at the imperial court of Rudolf II, in regard to one genre, the polyphonic Mass Ordinary, and one composer, Carl Luython.

De Burbure settled the dispute over Luython's birthplace by discovering Luython's father, Claude, as rector of the Latin school in Antwerp beginning in 1532.[4] Born in Valenciennes, Claude Luython was author of two books: *La merveilleuse et joyeuse vie d'Esope, avec quelques Fables* (Antwerp, 1548) and *Dictionnaire en Français et Flamend ou bis allemand* (Antwerp, 1552). The latter lists the author as "C. Luython, schoolmaster living in Antwerp at the Church of Saint Andruskerk [Sint Andruskerk]."[5] Claude had both a son and grandson of the same name who followed him in this position, therefore a Claude

---

L'Academie Royal de Belgique, 1880), pp. 17–20.

[3] Luython's five published works include: *Il primo libro de Madrigali a cinque voci* (Venice: Angelo Gardano, 1582); *Popularis Anni iubilus . . . sex vocibus illustratus* (Prague: Georg Nigrinus, 1587); *Selectissimarum sacrarum cantionum . . . sex vocibus, fasciculus primus* (Prague: Georg Nigrinus, 1603); *Opus musicum . . . in lamentationes Hieremiae prophetae* (Prague: Georg Nigrinus, 1604); and *Liber I Missarum* (Prague: N. Strauss, 1609). The most comprehensive study of the sources for the Habsburg music chapels is now dated, but still a valuable reference guide for contemporary documents: Albert Smijers, "Die kaiserliche Hof-Musikkapelle in Wien von 1543–1619," [hereafter Smijers, "Hofmusik-kapelle"] *Studien zur Musikwissenschaft: Beihefte der Denkmäler der Tonkunst in Österreich* [hereafter *StMW*] IX (1922): 43–81.

[4] De Burbure, *Charles Luython*, pp. 4–5, presents the evidence for Antwerp. Fetis had suggested Germany as Luython's birthplace, and Köchel France. A.G. Ritter claimed Luython's parents were English, but apparently without any evidence. See A.G. Ritter, *Zur Geschichte des Orgelspiels, vornehmlich des deutschen im 14. bis zum Anfange des 18. Jahrhunderts*, vol. 1 (Leipzig: M. Hesse, 1884), pp. 50–1.

[5] "C. Luython, maistre d'école demourant en Anvers chez l'église de St. Andrieu." See Rene Vannes, "Luython," in *Dictionnaire des Musiciens (Composituers)* (Brussels: Maison Larcier, 1951), p. 255.

Luython was schoolmaster at St. Andrews from 1532 until 1638, and Carl was the youngest son of the first Claude.

Albert Smijers refined De Burbure's estimated birthdate of 1550 by establishing the date of Luython's recruitment into the imperial chapel.[6] Johann Huis was sent to Antwerp by Maximilian II in 1566 in order to recruit choirboys for the chapel; it appears that he brought Carl to Vienna. According to Smijers, the recruited boys were usually between eight and ten years of age, thus Carl's birthyear probably lies between 1556 and 1558. However, Carl's oldest brother, Claude, the second schoolmaster at St. Andrews, was born in 1555, and he was followed by a sister, Sibilla. Therefore, the earliest Carol could have been born is 1557. Smijers thus was able to place Luython's birth between 1557 and 1558.[7]

That Carl was born in Antwerp is established by a document written 1–2 October, 1620, and submitted by Carl's brother, Claude, to the City Notary of Antwerp on 20 October concerning the estate of the composer at his death.[8] Claude states that his brother was organist at the courts of Maximilian II and Rudolf II, that he was born in Antwerp, and that he died in Prague in August, 1620. Claude refers to his brother's will, written 7 April, 1618, and read (gepubliceert) 29 August, 1620, but this document has not been preserved.

Luython probably received his early musical education at his father's Latin school. De Burbure describes the education typical of a school at this time and draws specifically on an act passed by the ecclesiastical and communal authorities in Antwerp in 1521 that called for the institution of classical education.[9] The Latin school at the parish of St. Andrews was responsible for the singing of the Office at the church and for general processions in the village. Carl would have learned the rudiments of music and probably the singing of Gregorian chant. Bergmans

---

[6] Albert Smijers, "Karl Luython als Motet Komponisten," (Ph.D. dissertation, University of Vienna, 1923).

[7] Johann Huis appears as Johan Huyssens, Johannesen Huissenns, and Johann Huissens in the court records, and has been recently misidentified as Jean Louys (Jhan de Loys), see *The New Groves Dictionary of Music and Musicians*, (London, 1980), S.v. "Louys," by Howard Slenk. Walter Pass sides with Slenk and also favors 1557 as Luython's birthyear, see *Op. cit.*, S.v., "Luython." Jhan de Loys was a singer in the chapel of Ferdinand I and died 15 October, 1563; he could not have been in Antwerp in 1566. See Smijers, "Hofmusik-Kapelle," *StMW* VI (1919): 143–5.

[8] The original document is in Latin, but is translated into Dutch by De Burbure, *Charles Luython*, pp. 17–8, and partially into French on pp. 5–6.

[9] De Burbure, *Charles Luython*, pp. 8–9.

maintains that Carl also sang in the Antwerp Cathedral School, but this has not been confirmed.[10]

The first record of Luython in the imperial archives appears in 1571, stating that his voice had changed and that he had been paid the usual stipend for his services.[11]

Juli, 1571	July 1571
Die Kay[serliche] M[ajestä]t haben derselben gwesen vier singer-khnaben, so mutirn, als Anthonio Merre, Carolo Luiton, Joanni Planchon und Andreen Plazer, für das gwöndlich stipendium jedem 50 cronen und ain claidt wie gebreuchig aus gnaden zu raichen gnedigist bewilligt.	The Imperial Majesty etc. graciously has granted to the four former choirboys, Anthonio Merre, Carolo Luiton, Joanni Planchon and Andreen Plazer, on their change of voice, the usual stipend of 50 crowns and one suit of clothing as is the custom.

It was customary for the boys' names not to appear in the financial record books before this time because either the chapel master or the preceptor of the choirboys would have been paid for their care. The only direct payment would be for their eventual dismissal. Therefore, we may assume that Luython had been in the chapel for a time.

Smijers has uncovered documents that support 1566 as the year of Luython's arrival at the court. Johann Huis, a bass in the court chapel, brought four boys back from Antwerp in 1566. Luython was probably among them. The same document has been used to suggest Luython's birthdate as well. Although Luython is not mentioned by name, no other record describing the recruitment of boys in Antwerp at about this time exists, so the following most likely refers to him.[12]

1566	1566
Johann Huissens sonst Grand Juan genanndt, Römischer Kay. Mt. etc. cappellbassisten und pfarrherrn in der kayserlichen burg alhie zu Wienn, haben Ir Kay. Mt. etc. jüngstlichen ins Niderlanndt zu herbringung etlicher singer und khnaben genedigist abgefertigt; und dieweil er kann auf zerung und uncosten von Irer Mt.	Johann Huissens, already named Grand Juan, chapel bass and priest to the Imperial Roman Emperor etc. at the imperial court in Vienna, has been dispatched by your Imperial Majesty etc. recently to the Netherlands to bring back some singers and boys; and for that purpose, he can withdraw from Christof Friesinger, your

---

[10] Paul Bergmans, S.v., "Luython," in *Biographie Nationale . . . de Belgique*, vol. 12, cols. 629–33.

[11] Smijers, "Hofmusik-Kapelle," *StMW* VIII (1921): 196. E. 295, f. 289v.

[12] Smijers, "Hofmusik-Kapelle," *StMW* VII (1920): 104.

etc. diener und factor zu Antorf, Christoffen Friesinger funfundsibenzig gulden reinisch . . . entnomen.

Imperial Majesty's etc. official and agent in Antwerp, 75 guilders towards expenses.

As a choirboy, Luython probably continued his education under the chapel masters, Jacob Vaet and Philippe de Monte, or the assistant chapel master, Alard du Gaucquier. Organ instruction might have been with the court organist, Wilhelm Formellis, or one of his assistant, Wilhelm van Mülin or Paul von Winde. No payment records establishing any one of these as Luython's organ instructor have been found, although two notices from 1570 confirm that at least Formellis did have organ students. His pupils were Queen Anne of Spain and her daughter. Also, in 1575 he received thirty florins for "instructing a young boy organist for one year." However, this would have been too late for Luython.[13]

Luython received fifty crowns upon his dismissal, and then apparently traveled to Italy in order to continue his education. He did not return to the imperial court for five years. The following two notices from the court payment records of 1575 and 1576 refer to him, and help establish the date of his return to Vienna.

The first of these notices mentions that Luython, still designated a "choirboy", was in Italy. Philippe de Monte, as chapel master, received payment in his place.[14] According to the second notice, dated 26 February, 1576, Luython received payment himself, and he is referred to as a "singer," no longer a boy. At this point he might have been back at Vienna since he, rather than de Monte, is held accountable.[15]

Mehr nachdem die Röm. Khay. Mt. etc. derselben capellnsingerkhnaben, Carln Luython, welicher Jhr Mt. etc. ain componierte mess, als er in Italiam verraist, uunderthänigist verehrt, auss gnaden zwanzig gulden rh. zu bezallen genedigist verordnet. Unnd weill auch solliche obgedachter Jrer Mt. etc. capellmaister Philipp de

More concerning the same Roman Imperial Majesty's etc. chapel singer Carl Luython. Your Majesty etc. graciously has ordered twenty guilders to be paid to him for a Mass setting, but he is away in Italy, and because your Majesty's chapel master Philipp de Monte had brought Luython here, thus I have thought to pay de Monte

---

[13] Smijers, "Hofmusik-Kapelle," *StMW* VII (1920): 137, H.Z.A.R. 1575, f. 827v.

[14] Smijers, "Hofmusik-Kapelle," *StMW* VIII (1921): 196, H.Z.A.R. 1575, f. 841v.

[15] Smijers, "Hofmusik-Kapelle," *StMW* VIII (1921): 196, H.Z.A.R. 1576, f. 587.

Monte ime Luÿthon hievor erlegt. Demnach so hab ich gedachtem de Monte die angezaigten zwanzig gulden reinisch lauts particular bevelchs unnd seiner quittung der datum am dreissigisten Juli diz jars weiderumben vergnuegt.

the abovementioned twenty guilders in return for a receipt on 30 July of this year [1575].

Carolo Luithon, singer, hab ich benenntlichen zweinzig gulden rein-ish, so Jr Mt. etc. ime vonweegen das er Jrer Mt. etc. ein componierte mess dediciert, aus gnaden zue geben gene-digist verordnet haben, laut particular bevelchs und quittung, am sechs- und-zweinzigisten tag Februari dis jars bezalt.

To Carl Luython, the singer, I have paid, on 26 February of this year, 1576, the already mentioned twenty guilders, which your Imperial Majesty etc. graciously had granted by oral command and receipt on account of a Mass setting dedicated to your Majesty.

The identification of the Masses to which these notices refer is uncertain and a suggestion will be made below; however, it is possible that only one Mass is the subject of the two notices. Both payments are for twenty guilders, the first for the composition of a Mass, and the second for the dedication. Furthermore, the circumstances of Luython's return could account for the second entry. He could have accepted the money only after his return, cashing the receipts taken from de Monte.

Luython's official re-entry into the imperial court was recorded 18 May, 1576, when he was issued a salary of ten guilders per month.[16] In December of that year he is listed as a chamber musician (camer musicus), and it is made clear in later entries that his position was that of an organist.[17]

Retained in the chapel after Maximilian II's death, Luython followed Rudolf's court to Prague. There he was assigned the duties of the assistant cloakroom attendant (unndergwardaroba) from 25 February, 1580, to 28 February, 1581.[18] He was promoted to the position of third court organist in 1582 upon the death of Wilhelm Formellis. His salary was retroactive to 1 January, 1577, which suggests that he might have

---

[16] Smijers lists all the recorded payments to Luython; the details of his salary can be found there. The same information is summarized by Robert Eitner in his *Biographisch-Bibliographisches Quellen-Lexicon*, vol. 6. (Leipzig: Breitkopf und Härtel, 1899–1904; reprint ed., Graz: Akademische Druck, 1954), pp. 257–58.

[17] Smijers. "Hofmusik-Kapelle," *StMW* VIII (1921): 197.

[18] Smijers. "Hofmusik-Kapelle," *StMW* VIII (1921): 197.

been fulfilling the duties of that office for about a year while Formellis was ailing.[19] Later, after Paul Van Winde's death in 1596, Luython became the first court organist under similar circumstances. Luython probably had filled that post since 1594 since Van Winde left for the Netherlands in that year.[20]

In 1582 Luython accompanied Rudolf to the parliament at Augsburg, as second organist, and in the same year published his first book of madrigals with Angelo Gardano at Venice.[21] The book is dedicated to Johann Fugger, Barone di Kirchberg at Weissenhorn,[22] whom Luython met at the parliament. Out of the eleven madrigals contained in this, his only madrigal collection, ten use texts by Petrarch. Philippe de Monte was also fond of Petrarch texts at this time, which perhaps underlines the older composer's influence. However, a clear connection to de Monte is found in the sixth composition, the two-part "Sacro monte mio dolce — Sio giusto bel disco," which pays homage to the chapel master.[23] Einstein suggests that Luython may have written the text himself.

Luython's fame and position increased after 1582. He attended the parliament in Regensburg in 1594,[24] and shortly after that time became first court organist. His motet book, *Popularis Anni Jubilus*, was published at Prague in 1587 and dedicated to Rudolf's brother, the Archduke Ernst, upon the occasion of his becoming a bishop.[25]

---

[19] Smijers. "Hofmusik-Kapelle," *StMW* VIII (1921): 198.

[20] Not 1593, as stated by Jozef Robijns in his article "Luython," in *MGG*, vol. 8, col. 1353. Paul Van Winde received his pension beginning in 1594, after accompanying Rudolf to the Parliament in Regensburg. See Georges van Doorslaer, "La Chapelle musicale de l'empereur Rudolphe II, en 1594 sous la direction de Philippe de Monte," *Acta Musicologica* V (1933): 150.

[21] *Il Primo Libro de Madrigali a cinque voci novamente composto, et date in luce* (Venice: Angelo Gardano, 1582).

[22] Not Rudolf, see Rene Vannes. *Dictionnaire des Musiciens* (Brussels: Larcier, 1951), p. 256. Gioan Fugger is Hanna Fugger, with whom Rudolf stayed at the Regensburg Parliament of 1594.

[23] For information on this dedication piece, see Alfred Einstein, "Italienische Musik und italienische Musiker am Kaiserhof und an den erzherzoglichen Höfen in Innsbruck und Graz," *StMW* XXI (1934): 27-9. The dedication madrigals from these courts are edited by Einstein in *DTÖ*, vol. 77 (1934), including two of Luython's pieces, pp. 40-3. The piece in honor of de Monte is listed incorrectly as two separate pieces in *Il Nuovo Vogel*, vol. 1, p. 955.

[24] Georges van Doorslaer, "La Chapelle musicale de l'empereur Rudolphe II, en 1594 sous la direction de Philippe de Monte," *Acta Musicologica* V (1930): 150.

[25] *Popularis Anni Jubilus . . . sex vocibus illustratus* (Prague: Georg Nigrinus, 1587).

Luython was given the title of court composer with an increase in salary after de Monte's death in 1603.[26] Thereafter followed two further publications: a book of sacred songs for six voices in 1603, and a book of lamentations in 1604.[27]

Like others in Rudolf's employ, Luython had trouble collecting his salary. Smijers presents the letters from 1591 that detail Luython's efforts to obtain sixteen hundred guilders in arrears pay, the same kind of problem he was to face upon his retirement.[28] As a loyal employee, Luython worked conscientiously on the reconstruction of the Prague castle organ with the organ builder, Albrecht Rudner. The two disagreed upon several matters, and Luython recorded his grievances in great detail. Their conflict lasted ten years and is documented in the court records from 17 April, 1581, to 22 December, 1590.[29]

Luython left the service of the court when the chapel was disbanded upon Rudolf's death in 1612. He had never married, but there is no evidence that he had taken holy orders. However, since that information is conspicuously lacking in his will, he probably was not a priest. In view of the hostility between Rudolf and his brother Matthias, the next emperor, it is not surprising that Rudolf's former chapel members ran into difficulties collecting their due. Such was the case with Luython, who had been awarded a yearly pension of two hundred guilders for life on 16 May, 1611, for his 35 years of loyal service, as the following notice shows.[30]

An die frl. Drh. etc. Erzherzog Maximilian zu Oesterreich, wassmassen Jhre Mt. etc. die järigen 200 fl. järliche provision, welche weilandt Warmundt Jgl aus dem salzmayrambt zu Haal im Ynthal zue genissen gehabt, von eingang nechstkünfftigen monatts Junij deroselben componisten und organisten Carll Luiton umb gelaister 35 järiger continuirter

To the baronial canon etc. Archduke Maximilian of Austria. Your Majesty etc. has proclaimed that the same composer and organist Carl Luython receive, for as long as he shall live, a yearly pension of 200 fl., which Warmundt Igl has recovered from the Salzmaier Office in Innthall of Hall, beginning next 5 June, for his 35 years of continued, conscientious service.

---

[26] Not in 1596, as Pass suggests in *The New Grove*, vol. 11, p. 378; cf. Smijers. "Hofmusik-Kapelle," *StMW* VI (1919): 149.

[27] *Selectissimarum sacrarum cantionum sex vocibus compositarum, nunc primum in lucem aeditarum: Fasciculus primus* (Prague: George Nigrinus, 1603); *Opus musicum . . . in lamentationes Hieremiae prophetae* (Prague: Georg Nigrinus, 1604).

[28] Smijers, "Hofmusik-Kapelle," *StMW* VIII (1921): 198–200.

[29] Smijers, "Hofmusik-Kapelle," *StMW* VII (1920): 110–8.

[30] Smijers, "Hofmusik-Kapelle," *StMW* VIII (1921): 203, R. 637, f. 86v.

vleissigen dienst willen auf sein leben-
lang reichen und ervolgen zu lassen
bewilligt.

Luython's severe financial problems began with Rudolf's abdica-
tion. He was hard pressed to collect his yearly pension before Rudolf's
death, and he never succeeded in collecting payment afterwards. He
died a pauper, forced to sell his especially-built archicembalo, in 1613,
to Duke Karl, the brother of Emperor Ferdinand II, who was at that
time Bishop of Breslau. This instrument has a history of its own, described by Michael Praetorius with a special term, "Clavicimbalum uni-
versale seu perfectum"; Luython sold it for one hundred guilders.[31] In
his will, Luython left two thousand four hundred guilders in uncol-
lected arrears pay to his brother Claude and two sisters Clara and
Sibella, but the will was never honored.

Luython is known to have written eleven Masses, one of which,
Missa Elselein liebstes Elselein, is missing, as is an unidentified fragment of a six-voice Kyrie. Nine of the remaining Masses are contained
in his *Liber primus Missarum* of 1609. The *Missa Tytire tu patule* is
found in a choirbook from Graz, and is surely an earlier work.

Following is an alphabetical listing of Luython's Masses, including
bibliographical information.

Masses by Luython

1. *Missa Ad aequales*, a 4 (Quodlibetica).
   Luython, *Liber Missarum*, ff. 139v–146.[32]

---

[31] For the history of this interesting instrument, see Adolf Koczirz, "Zur
Geschichte des Luython'schen Klavizimbals," *Sammelbände der Internationalen Musikgesellschaft* IX (1908): 565–70.

[32] Liber I./Missarvm/Caroli Lvython/Sacrae Caesa: Maiest:/Organistae et
Com-/ponistae/cvm gratia et privilegio sac: Caesa: Maiest:/Prage,/
Imprimebatvr/APVD Nicolavm/Stravs./Anno Domini,/M.DC. [I]X. The
preface of this first edition is dated 1 October, 1608, and the I in the Roman
numeral MDCIX has been scratched out to read 1610 rather than 1609. The
reason for this is unknown. The copy used in this study is from the Österreichische Nationalbibliothek; RISM falsely lists two copies in their possession,
perhaps the scratched out numeral accounts for these two listing of 1609 and
1610. Later editions of the *Liber Missarum* appeared at Frankfurt by G.
Tempachius in 1611 and 1621. Modern editions of four of the Masses of the,
Liber Missarum are found in Franz Commer, *Musica Sacra: Sammlung der
besten Meisterwerke des 16t. und 17t. Jahrhunderts: Missa Quodlibetica, Ad
aequales*, in vol. 17 (Berlin: M. Bahn, 1876), pp. 76–85; *Missa Quodlibetica* a 4

2. *Missa Amorosi pensieri*, a 6.
   Model: Philippe de Monte, "Amorosi pensieri".
   Luython, *Liber Missarum*, ff. 41v–58; VienNB 15951, 56v–77;
   WroU 110 [missing].[33]
3. *Missa Basim: Caesar Vive*, a 7.
   Luython, *Liber Missarum*, ff. 1v–22; the Gesellschaft für Musik-
   forschung lists the Kyrie and Christe in its possession.[34]
4. *Missa Elselein liebstes Elselein*, a 6.
   WroU 100 [missing].
5. *Missa Filiae Hierusalem*, a 6.
   Model: Philippe de Monte, "Filiae Hierusalem".[35]
   Luython, *Liber Missarum*, ff. 23v–40; Prag KHC; VienNB 16194,
   ff. 55v–73; WroU 97 (without Christe), and WroU 100
   [missing], attributed to de Monte.
6. *Missa Ne timeas Maria*, a 5.
   Model: Philippe de Monte, "Ne timeas Maria".[36]
   Luython, *Liber Missarum*, ff. 80v–101.
7. *Missa Quodlibetica*, a 3.
   Luython, *Liber Missarum*, ff. 147v–158.
8. *Missa Quodlibetica*, a 4.
   Luython, *Liber Missarum*. ff. 121v–133.
9. *Missa Quodlibetica*, a 6.
   Luython, *Liber Missarum*, ff. 59v–79.
   Possibly in WroU 100 [missing].
10. *Missa Tirsi morir volea*, a 5.
    Model: Philippe de Monte, "Tirsi morir volea".
    Luython, *Liber Missarum*, ff. 102v–120.
11. Missa Tytire tu patule, a 5.
    Model: Orlando de Lasso, "Tityre tu patule."[37]
    GrazU 22, ff. 198v–222, and 82, ff. 199v–221.[38]

---

and *Missa Quodlibetica* a 3, in vol. 13, pp. 59–71 and 72–80; and *Missa super
Ne timeas Maria*, in vol. 19, pp. 24–42 (Regensburg: Georg Joseph Manz,
1877–1878).

[33] The abbreviations used for the manuscripts in which Luython's Masses
appear are realized in Appendix A.

[34] See "The Gesellschaft für Musikforschung," *Monatshefte für
Musikgeschichte* X (1878): 174–6.

[35] In the new edition of de Monte's *Complete Works*, R.B. Lenaerts, ed. Ser.
A, vol. 1, p. 95.

[36] Lenaerts, *De Monte: Complete Works*, Ser. A, vol. 2, p. 1.

[37] Franz X. Haverl, ed., *Orlando di Lasso Sämtliche Werke*, vol. 19 (Leipzig:
Breitkopf & Härtel, 1908), pp. 68–73.

[38] Anton Kern, *Die Handschriften der Universitätsbiliothek Graz*, vol. 1
(Leipzig: Breitkopf & Härtel, 1939), pp. 8 and 36.

12. Unidentified fragment, "Kyrie," a 6.
   WroU 103.

Four payments to Luython from the court in return for Mass dedications have been recorded. The two already mentioned helped establish the date of his return to Vienna. That these two notices might refer to one Mass has already been suggested. In any case, the *Missa Tytire tu patule* may have been written at that time. The model for this Mass is a motet by Lasso that was widely popular; perhaps significantly, it was also used as a model for a parody Mass by Luython's early teacher at Vienna, Jacob Vaet.[39]

Circumstances suggest that Luython might have met Lasso at Vienna during one of the Bavarian chapel master's visits to Maximilian II's court while Luython was a choirboy in the chapel. Lasso was at Prague in February, 1570, and at Vienna in October, 1573.[40] Close ties existed between the courts of Maximilian and Albert V, where Lasso was chapel master. Vaet based his own motet, "Vitam quae faciunt beatiorum", on Lasso's "Tityre tu patule", and then based a parody Mass on materials from both motets.[41] The motets by Lasso and Vaet appear in the Österreichische Nationalbibliothek ms. 18828, and the relationship between these pieces has been shown by Steinhardt.

Circumstantial evidence argues against a third notice in the payment records from the year 1578 referring to Luython's *Missa Tytire tu patule*.[42]

Carl Luithan camerorginistën supp. umb ein gnadengelt, vonwegen einer Jrer Mt. dedicierten mess, ist sambt der hofcamer relation da.	The petition of Carl Luython, the chamber organist, for a monetary gift on account of a Mass dedicated to your Majesty is here together with a report of the court chamber.

Lasso had not been to the imperial court during the two years between Luython's return from Italy and the date of this notice, 1578, thus reducing the possibility of a direct influence. De Monte had been installed as chapel master to the court, and three years had passed since

---

[39] Wolfgang Boetticher, *Orlando Lasso und seine Zeit* (Kassel and Basel: Bärenreiter, 1958), p. 853.

[40] Horst Leuchtmann, *Orlando di Lasso: Sein Leben*, vol. 1. (Wiesbaden: Breitkopf & Härtel, 1976), pp. 50-1.

[41] Milton Steinhardt, *Jacobus Vaet and his Motets* (East Lansing: Michigan State College Press, 1951), p. 10. Prof. Steinhardt quotes a letter from Dr. Seld, a Vice-Chancellor to Archduke Albert V of Bavaria, to his patron mentioning the hearing of Vaet's Mass, and its relationship to Lasso's motet, dated 23 December, 1559.

[42] Smijers, "Hofmusik-Kapelle," *StMW* VIII (1921): 197, E. 339, f. 164v.

Vaet's death. A piece possibly in homage to his early teacher could have been overdue by 1578, whereas it would have been especially fitting for 1575 or 1576, near the time of Vaet's death. Therefore, the *Missa Tytire tu patule* could probably have been a student work of Luython's, dating from 1575 or before, and might be the Mass mentioned in one or both of the early notices.

The largest gift Luython received was for the dedication of his *Liber Missarum* of 1609. The gift was presented to him through the paymaster's office in Silesia, the last large sum of money he was to obtain.[43]

Der hoffzallmaister [Joachimb] Hueber solle für Carl Luiton organisten und componisten seine quittung über 500 fl. für aines Jhrer Mt. etc. dedicirten buchs bewilligten recompens aine quittung auf dem renntmaister in Schlesien ferttigen und sich hergegen wieder quittiren lassen.	The court paymaster, Joachim Hueber, should draw up the receipt of Carl Luython, the organist and composer, for 500 florins, which he receives for the dedication of a [Mass]book, for payment from the treasurer in Silesia, and let him (the treasurer) sign the receipt.

The preface of the *Liber Missarum* is quoted and translated below. From the text, we see that Luython was forthright in his desire for reward, and clever in the execution of that aim. The first sentence is a clear reference to classicism in its use of the Greek word "Ethnicos" for nations, and within that context, the emperor is praised as a patron of a court gathered from "various parts of the world." Luython mentions his position at the court, and tantalizes us with the information that he has, at home, more music than is being published. Unfortunately, this body of music has not been found. Rudolf would have been pleased with having the better part dedicated to him in any case; and whether or not a great deal of other music actually did exist, only a few other Masses are available today.

Ad Sacratissimvm Atqve Avgvstissimvm Principem Ac Dominvm, Dominvm Rvdolphvm Romanorvm Imperatorem Eivs Nominis II. Dominvm Dominvm et Patronnum meum clementissunum.	To the most sacred and Holy Prince and Lord, Lord Rudolf, Emperor of Rome named the second, my most eminent Lord Master and Patron.
MUSICAM esse donum Dei inter reliqua non minimum, atq; apud	Music is a gift of God, not least among the others, and among the

---

[43] Smijers, "Hofmusik-Kapelle," *StMW* VIII (1921): 203, R. 628, f. 205v; see other notices on same page with similar contents.

Ethnicos in maiori apud Christianos, laudesq; innumeras promereri, & locum praecipuum semper in templis, diuinisq; officijs, itemq; in CAE-SARVM, REGVM, PRINCIPVM, & optimorum vivorum domibus obtinere, nemo est, qui nesciat.

Ethnicos [Greek = nations] greatly prized, greatest among Christians and worthy of numerous praises; and it obtains the chief place always in sanctuaries and services, in the Offices and likewise, in the home of the emperor, kings, princes, and of the greatest living men. There is no one who is ignorant of it.

Hanc M.V.S.C. more amicorum suoru, virtutum, acientiarumq; nobilissimaru Moecenas, ita semper sublimem fecit & gloriosam, ut selectiassimos quosq; Musicos, ex varijs mundi partibus, impensis honorificus conuocarit, sustenarit, promouerit.

Thus, Your Sacred Imperial Majesty [M.V.S.C.], and most noble patron, always made this Musicus sublime and glorious, in the custom of his great virtues and noble skills, in order to call together, maintain, and promote each one of the most select musicians, from various parts of the world with great honors.

In quorum collegio, ab ineunte aetate, usq; ad hunc diem vixi ego, per gradus semper promotus, vt nunc apud M.V.S.C. Organistam & Componistam agam, & seruitia mea non nisi cum morte, si DEVS concesserit, vbi cepi, finire constituam.

In the association of those [select musicians], I lived from youth up to today, step-by-step always having advanced so that now I may pass for organist and composer to Your Majesty, and as I have received my appointment, God willing, I shall set out to complete it until my death.

Itaq; in tam incyta aula, sub tanti CAESARIS patrocinio, sub tam, excellentibus Musicis, huic vni sacultati deditus, tàm sacras quam prophanas (quae tamen honori diuino non praeciudicant) Mutetas, vu vocant, tanto tempore modulari vel componere studui, ut earü partem aliquam, quamuis minima, in lucem emiserim, maiorem longè mecu domi habeam, omina tamen in gloriam DEI & M.V.S.C. honorem perptuum.

Thus, in so renowned a court, under such a great patron emperor, and among such excellent musicians dedicated to this one skill as much sacred as profane (which, however, they do not prejudge in the respect of the day), as they say, in such a time I have pursued performing or composing motets [in this sense, polyphony]. So that in any part of the same music, however small, may be brought into light [published], [I shall] hold the far greater part with me at home, all, however in the glory of God and the perpetual honor of Your Majesty.

Atq; ut aquae in mare redondent, unde fluxerunt, & pro beneficijs, gratiae, licet non condignae, tamen è

Thus, as waters overflow into the sea from whence they issue and for favors of esteem, although not very worthy,

grato humiliq; animo profectae, habeantur, atq;

ego lucrum vsuramq; tanti tamq; benè collati & accepti temporis communicem, OFFICIA VEL MISSAS plurium vocum, quaru multae coram M.V.S.C. saepè fuerunt decantatae, in unum congessi opus, illudq; nouis planè notis diligentia Typograohi, vt in lucem prodeat, ad laudem S.S. ECCLESIAE nec non ad vsum Reipublicae Christainae, curaui, quod ita concinnatum & elaboratum M.V.S.C. tanquam optimo & clementissimo CAESARI, Moecenati & benefactori meo,

cliens ego humillimus & perpetuus, offero, dedico, deuouco, omni animi submissione debita oblectans atq; obtestans, vt pro innata sua CLEMENTIA CAESAREA, vti hactenus seruitia mea qualia qualiacunq; fidelia, tamen & parata, ita & nunc eorum recordationem mentisq; meae subiectissimae gratitudinem, meq; ipsum complecti & fouere dignetur, DEVS OPTIMVS MAXIMVS M.V.S.C. omnem gratiam foelicitatemq; ad animi sui pientissimi vota & desideria concedat, quod vnicè oro.

PRAGAE, I. Octobris, Anno M.DC.VIII.
MAJEST: VEST: SA: CAE: HUMILLIMUS SERUUS CAROLUS LUYTHON.

nevertheless they are held truly in humble gratitude, and their source is kept in mind.

Thus, I share the opportunity for these polyphonic Offices or Masses, many of which often were sung in the presence of Your Majesty, to be collected in one work, printed in a new manner, and diligently typeset, so they are published. For praise from the most sacred church and also for the use of the Christian State, I have provided that these be put together and elaborated for Your Majesty as the best and most eminent Emperor, patron, and benefactor.

As a perpetual and humble vassal, I offer, dedicate, and devote [these works] with all submission of my indebted spirit, for the purpose of delighting and pleasing the emperor's own innate generosity. That thus far if my service possesses any quality, fidelity, or skill whatsoever, that thus and now the remembrance of these [works] and of their intention — namely, the gratitude of my most exposed and worthless self, I myself am honored and dignified to cherish, God on high, Your Majesty of all grace and fortune, so that your most pious spirit yields the promises and desires which I especially beg.

Prague, 1 October 1608.

Your Majesty's humble servant, Carolus Luython.

The *Liber Missarum* contains music written over the span of at least a decade, and Luython mentions that many of the pieces were often sung in the emperor's presence. It is unclear what constituted the new manner of printing, but the copy of the Liber now at the Österreichische Nationalbibliothek indeed is "diligently printed" and corrected. In several places within the print, small corrections have been pasted in over mistakes.

The overt request for "promises and desires which I especially beg" was reinforced by the dedication piece of the collection, the *Missa super Basim Caesar vive*, which was composed near the time of the publication. The superimposed text "Caesar vive" appears in the print each time the melody appears.

Caesar vive, faxit Deus noster. Omnes gentes clamant: Caesar vive, Caesar vive.	The Emperor live, may God grant it. All the people proclaim: The Emperor live, the Emperor live.

In 1608, Rudolf was alienated from his brother Matthias, and the Habsburg family had already begun plans to have Rudolf replaced as head of the House of Austria. The text, "the Emperor live", would have had special meaning for the now isolated emperor.

The models for the four parody Masses in the *Liber Missarum* are by Philippe de Monte. Luython drew upon two motets and two madrigals from the works of his previous chapel master. Two of Luython's Masses appear in earlier manuscripts, the *Missa Amorosi pensieri* in the Österreichische Nationalbibliothek, Ms. 15951. and the *Missa Filiae Hierusalem* in Ms. 16194, both dated before 1600. The appearance of the Masses in the manuscripts confirms that the composition of these two works predated the *Liber Missarum* by at least a decade, and suggests that these works might have been current in the court chapel's repertory for at least that time. As mentioned above, Luython states in the preface to the *Liber Missarum* that Rudolf often had heard the works contained therein.

There are no other known surviving copies of the remaining two parody Masses in Luython's print. The *Missa super Ne timeas Maria* and the *Missa super Tirsi morir volea* appear in no manuscript copy, and might have been written for the publication; however, de Monte died on 4 July, 1603, at least six years before the publication of Luython's work. These two Masses based on de Monte's pieces would seem more fittingly placed closer to the chapel master's lifetime. Like the other parody Masses, they probably predate the *Liber Missarum*. De Monte's madrigal "Tirsi morir volea" appears in his ninth book of five-voice madrigals of 1586, and the motet "Ne timeas Maria" in his second book of five-voice motets of 1573. Therefore, the composition of the two Masses by Luython must lie between the time of de Monte's compositions and probably before the time of his death in 1603.

The remaining four Masses of the *Liber Missarum* are each entitled *Missa Quodlibetica* (Quodlibet Mass), and have been a puzzle to scholars. The term "quodlibet" originated in the middle ages as the name of a scholastic exercise at the University of Paris. In the sixteenth century, the term was common in German lands referring to an improvised oral examination "disputatio de quolibet", but had taken on the connotation of being a foolish collection of loosely-related ideas linked by a topic used as a basis for poetry. These humorous catalogue poems apparently influenced Wolfgang Schmeltzl, who was the first to apply the term to music. Schmeltzl published a collection of musical quodlibets in 1544 with the title *Guter seltzamer, und künstreicher teutscher Gesang, sonderlich ettliche künstlicher Quodlibet.*[44] At the time of publication, Schmeltzl was a teacher at the Schotten Kirche in Vienna, which suggests that a connection between his works and Luython's Masses might exist; however, none is apparent. Neither does Jacob Vaet's five-voice *Missa Quodlibetica* show motivic relationships to pieces in either Schmeltzl's collection or Luython's, *Liber Missarum*.

Peter Wagner discusses three of Luython's Quodlibet Masses and defines the term as referring to "a Mass in a less pretentious vein which is meant for simple choral means, for the purpose of executing the liturgical text in a shorter way than a monophonic setting."[45] This definition applies to the three Masses for three and four voices, but is less appropriate if we also consider the six-voice setting which Wagner probably did not see. The polyphony in the latter Mass is not intended for simple choral means, and is at times quite complex. The Crucifixus contains a canon between the two upper voices, and throughout the Mass the polyphonic style is typical of Netherlands composition. Whereas the three Masses for fewer voices resort to sequential repetition of polyphonic

---

[44] Published by Jo. Petreium in Nuremberg, 1544; see Elsa Bienenfeld, "Wolfgang Schmeltzl, sein Liederbuch (1544) und das Quodlibet des XVI Jahrhunderts," *Sammelbände der Internationalen Musikgesellschaft* VI, no. 7 (Oct.–Dec. 1904): 80–135.

[45] Peter Wagner, *Geschichte der Messe*, vol. 1 (Leipzig: Breitkopf und Härtel, 1913). Wagner apparently did not see Luython's, *Liber Missarum*, but based his information upon Franz Commer's editions in *Musica Sacra*, vols. 17 (1877) and 19 (1878), which do not include the *Missa Quodlibetica* a 6.

complexes for text repetition, the six-voice Mass is mostly through-composed and more expansive with melodic materials.

The similarities between the four settings include a quick execution of the text and a remarkable thematic unity within each setting. The settings are mostly syllabic throughout, and the text of the Agnus Dei is given only once, with the Hosanna elided into a part of the Pleni sunt coeli. The thematic unity within each setting suggests a previous model, and perhaps the Quodlibet Masses are parody Masses; however, no models have been found.

APPENDIX A

Abbreviations for Manuscripts

GrazU 22	Graz, Austria. Universitätsbibliothek. Ms. 22.
GrazU 82	Graz, Austria. Universitätsbibliothek. Ms. 82.
Prag KHC	Prague, Czechoslovakia. Hudební oddelení Národniho musea [Music Division of the National Museum], Kutná Hora Codex, sign. 151/55.
VienNB 15951	Vienna, Austria. Österreichische Nationalbibliothek, Ms. 15951.
VienNB 16194	Vienna, Austria. Österreichische Nationalbibliothek, Ms. 16194.
WroU 97	Wrocław, Poland. Biblioteka Uniwersytecka, Ms. 97 [formerly Breslau, Stadtbibliothek].
WroU 100	Wrocław, Poland. Biblioteka Uniwersytecka, Ms. 100 [formerly Breslau, Stadtbibliothek].
WroU 103	Wrocław, Poland. Biblioteka Uniwersytecka, Ms. 103 [formerly Breslau, Stadtbibliothek].

BAROQUE AND CLASSICAL MUSIC

CHAPTER ELEVEN

THE FUNCTION OF MUSIC IN THE FORTY HOURS DEVOTION OF 17TH- AND 18TH-CENTURY ITALY

Howard E. Smither

University of North Carolina at Chapel Hill

The Forty Hours Devotion was a three-day period of continuous prayer by clergy and laymen before the Eucharist, exposed for approximately forty hours in a monstrance on the high altar of a church or an oratory. While the roots of this Devotion are found in the medieval ceremony of the *Depositio*, the modern form originated in sixteenth-century Italy and was practiced throughout the Roman Catholic Church until the 1960s.[1] Art historians have recognized the Devotion's importance to the visual arts, but musicologists have paid little attention to its music. The present study treats the function of music — including the relationship of music to visual decoration — in the Forty Hours

---

[1] The Devotion was virtually discontinued after the sweeping changes of the Second Vatican Council. According to Nathan Mitchell, O.S.B., *Cult and Controversy: The Worship of the Eucharist Outside Mass* (New York: Pueblo Publishing Company, 1982), p. 337, the Revised rites of 1973 "do not speak any longer of the Forty Hours Devotion, but only of 'Lengthy exposition' [of the Blessed Sacrament] on certain occasions approved by the local ordinary." I wish to thank the reverend Timothy O'Connor for his bibliographical assistance with reference to the Forty Hours Devotion.

Devotion.[2] The study is based largely on the printed librettos of cantatas and oratorios listed in the appendix to this article.[3]

*   *   *

In the medieval *Depositio*, on Good Friday after the Mass of the Presanctified and the Adoration of the Cross, the burial of Christ was symbolized by the placement of a cross, a consecrated Host, or both in a model of the holy sepulchre.[4] The faithful would then take turns watching before the sepulchre for forty hours, which symbolized the period of Christ's entombment. On Easter morning, at the ceremony of the *Elevatio*, the elements were removed from the sepulchre to symbolize the Resurrection. The watch before the sepulchre, already known in the thirteenth century as the *Oratio quadraginta horarum*, continued to be practiced at least through the fifteenth century.

The modern version of the Forty Hours Devotion began in 1527 in Milan, a city then devastated by the wars of Charles V.[5] In that year, at the initiative of the Augustinian Gian Antonio Bellotto, the Eucharist was exposed on an altar of the church of San Sepolcro for forty hours, not only in Holy Week but also in the periods of Pentecost, the Assumption, and Christmas. The members of the church's lay confraternity prayed continuously before the Eucharist for expiation and to alleviate the suffering of the city's populace. Soon the new version of the Forty Hours Devotion was adopted, both within and outside Holy Week, in other churches of Milan. In 1537 the Devotion was officially established in Milan — and approved by Pope Paul III — as a perpetual prayer, which would begin in one church as soon as it ended in another; and in 1567, Carlo Borromeo, the bishop of Milan, pre-

---

[2] I am grateful to Ann M. Woodward for her readings of this manuscript and her valuable suggestions.

[3] These librettos, often important for determining the function of a musical work within its context, are my primary sources. Musical scores, usually less useful for this purpose, were not consulted.

[4] On this ceremony, see Neil C. Brooks, "The Sepulchre of Christ in Art and Liturgy with Special Reference to the Liturgic Drama," *University of Illinois Studies in Language and Literature*, VII (1921), 145; Karl Young, *The Dramatic Associations of the Easter Sepulchre*, ("University of Wisconsin Studies in Language and Literature," no. 10 [Madison, 1920]), p. 7; and Anicetto Chiappini, "Quarant'ore," *Enciclopedia cattolica* (Florence: G.C. Sansoni, 1948–54), vol. 10 (1953), col. 376.

[5] This paragraph and the next are based on Chiappini, "Quarant'ore," cols. 376–78; and Angelo de Santi, *L'Orazione delle quarant'ore e i tempi di calamità e di guerra* (Rome: "Civiltà Cattolica," 1919), pp. 1–12.

scribed the Devotion for his entire diocese and regularized its rotation among the churches.

In Italy of the Counter Reformation — a time when the traditional doctrines of the Eucharist, among others, were under attack and the Church was swept by strong reaction — the Forty Hours Devotion became an immensely popular reaffirmation of the real presence of Christ in the Eucharist. By the turn of the seventeenth century, virtually every city of Italy was practicing the Devotion, which was actively promoted by certain religious orders — the Jesuits, Cappuchins, and Friars Minor, among others. Filippo Neri is credited with having introduced the practice in Rome in 1550 at the church of San Salvatore in Campo, where the Devotion began on the first Sunday of every month. In 1592 Pope Clement VIII prescribed the Devotion as a perpetual prayer in the churches of Rome, and other cities soon followed Rome's lead.

Of the various papal instructions for holding the Forty Hours Devotion, the most influential was the *Instructio Clementina*, published by Pope Clement XI in 1705 and republished, in Italian, by Clement XII in 1730–31.[6] Although binding only in Rome, the *Instructio* was widely adopted and remained standard until the Second Vatican Council. According to the *Instructio*, the Devotion begins with a votive High Mass of the Blessed Sacrament — called the Mass of Exposition. This is followed by a procession, during which the *Pange lingua* is sung. (The procession could be visually striking — candles and torches blazing, lay confraternities dressed in distinctive costumes, surpliced singers, cross bearer, canopy bearers, and the celebrant carrying the Sacrament in a monstrance under the canopy, preceded by the thurifers and their clouds of curling incense.) After the procession the Sacrament in its monstrance is placed on a throne (a kind of pyramid draped in white) located on the high altar. Litanies and prayers are recited, the *Tantum ergo* is sung, and the Forty Hours Devotion

---

6 The *Instructio Clementina*, which consists of thirty-seven articles, is printed in its entirety in Italian, together with extensive Latin commentary, in: *Decreta authentica congregationis sacrorum rituum*, 3d ed., edited by Aloisio Gardellini (Rome: S. Congregationis de propaganda fide, 1856–58), vol. 4, "Appendix." A summary of the *Instructio*, together with notes on subsequent modifications, is found in Adrian Fortescue, *The Ceremonies of the Roman Rite Described*, (7th ed.; further revised and augmented by J. O'Connell London: Burns, Oates and Washbourne, 1943), pp. 349–59. The summary of the Devotion in this paragraph is based on a combination of Gardellini's edition of the *Instructio* and Fortescue's summary.

begins. By taking hours or shorter periods by turn, the laymen and clergy watch continuously. On the second day a votive High Mass for peace is celebrated (no doubt a trace of the Devotion's early history in Milan). On the third day, another votive High Mass of the Blessed Sacrament — called the Mass of Deposition — is celebrated, while the Sacrament is still exposed. Litanies and prayers are then recited and the Sacrament is carried in a colorful procession like that of the first day, again accompanied by the *Pange lingua*. When the celebrant returns to the altar, he gives the Benediction of the Blessed Sacrament — which includes the singing of the *Tantum ergo* — and concludes the Forty Hours Devotion by placing the Host in the tabernacle.

It is of special interest that the *Instructio*'s rules for the Sacrament's visual context — paintings, statues, and lighting — during the exposition are rather severe:

> the exposition should be made at the High Altar of the church. If there is a picture over the altar it is to be covered with a red or white hanging. In the same way all pictures close to the altar are to be covered. No relics or statues of saints are to be placed on the altar. . . . Around the throne or place where the monstrance will stand, wax candles are to burn continually during the time of exposition. At least twenty such candles should burn all the time. Flowers may be placed on and around the altar (but they should not be too near the place where the monstrance will stand). . . . No light may be placed behind the monstrance, so as to shine through the Sanctissimum.[7]

Such austerity by no means corresponds to what was clearly a common practice for the Forty Hours Devotion in the seventeenth and eighteenth centuries. It would seem, in fact, that the *Instructio* was in part· an attempt to modify current procedures. Far from obscuring works of visual art near the Sacrament, the practice often emphasized the visual and pictorial element to enhance the Sacrament's meaning — and lights did, indeed, shine through the Sacrament from behind the monstrance. The reason for the elaborate visual display may relate to a characteristic timing of the Devotion within the church year. Beginning in the mid-sixteenth century, the Devotion was frequently held during the final week of carnival, and particularly the last three days — at the peak of the revelries. The Devotion would then serve as a spiritual counterbalance to the season's worldly excesses and a preparation for Lent. The sumptuous visual element — and at times the music

---

[7] As summarized in Fortescue, *Ceremonies*, p. 351, from the *Instructio*, articles 3, 4, and 6.

as well, as we shall see — clearly made the Devotion a favorable competitor of carnival's secular entertainments.

*   *   *

The Forty Hours Devotion is of considerable interest to the historian of the visual arts, for the manner of decorating the church and the high altar closely relates to the development of illusionist painting and shows remarkable change during the course of the Baroque period.[8] Such decoration is also of interest to the musicologist, for it provides a context which at times is indispensible to the interpretation of the musical works known to have been performed during the Devotion. Of particular importance in the decoration was the *teatro, macchina,* or *apparato,* which has been described as

> a temporary set decorating the high altar chapel in order to call attention to and glorify the Sacrament. At first such *apparati* were composed of candles in silver candlesticks, oil lamps, silver reliquaries, silver vases filled with flowers, and hangings of different sorts of precious material. During the first decade of the seventeenth century, the *apparati* developed into complex architectural settings. By the middle of the century they had changed into allegorical tableaux in which scenes of contemporary, historic, and Biblical salvation were used to illustrate the saving power of the Sacrament, which normally appeared in heaven surrounded by a glory.
>
> Mid-century *apparati,* like most seventeenth-century stage sets, were composed of painted flats arranged to give the illusion of a space different from that which actually existed. The *apparati* differed from normal stage sets in that they were complete in themselves rather than serving as back drops for dramatic action. All of the figures as well as the illusionistic settings were painted *a chiaroscuro* on flats and flat silhouettes, which were arranged to form a single scene. These sets were illuminated by thousands of oil lamps and candles placed behind the flats so that neither the lamps nor the workmen who tended them could be seen by the viewer. The further the flat from the front of the set, the more brightly it was lit. In the case of the Forty Hours Devotion, the monstrance containing the Eucharist was placed at the deepest point of the

---

[8] For a study of the visual aspect of the Devotion, see Mark S. Weil, "The Devotion of the Forty Hours and Roman Baroque Illusions," *Journal of the Warburg and Courtauld Institutes* XXXVII (1974), 218–48. Weil also presents, on pp. 220–24, a summary of the Forty Hours Devotion in general. I am grateful to Professor Weil, who, some years ago, first pointed out to me the importance of the Forty Hours Devotion and encouraged me to pursue its musical aspects.

theatre where it was bathed in the light of all the hidden lamps as well as others placed behind the monstrance. The Eucharist glowed as if it were the source of illumination for the entire scene.[9]

The earliest pictorial stage set associated with the Forty Hours Devotion is one by Giovanni Lorenzo Bernini (1598–1680), designed in 1628 for the annual Devotion which began on the first Sunday of Advent in the Pauline Chapel of the Vatican Palace.[10] The Bernini work was described in its time as "a most beautiful *apparato* representing the Glory of Paradise shining with tremendous brightness without one's seeing any light except that which emanated from more than two thousand lamps hidden behind the clouds [of the glory]."[11] The earliest known allegorical *apparato*, one which was clearly intended to serve as a "visual sermon," was designed in 1640 by Niccolò Menghini for the church of the Gesù in Rome. An engraving of it survives, as does a contemporary printed pamphlet describing it.[12] The *apparato* evidently occupied the entire area of the high altar and totally obscured it — as became characteristic of such sets. According to the pamphlet, the lower level of the work includes various Old Testament figures — King David, Elijah, Melchesidech, Samson, and Moses — and each is to be interpreted in relation to Christ and the Eucharist; the focal point of the upper level is the Eucharist, placed in the center of a mass of clouds on top of Mount Sinai and surrounded by the twenty-four elders (scattered among the clouds) of St. John's Apocalypse. A few other engravings and drawings of *apparati* for Forty Hours Devotions survive, as do numerous printed pamphlets describing them. The surviving pamphlets show that in Rome, at least, the tradition of erecting such *apparati* continued until 1825.[13]

* * *

Little is known about music in the Forty Hours Devotion. The types of pamphlets mentioned above focus on the *apparati* and rarely

[9] *Ibid.*, pp. 218–19.

[10] *Ibid.*, pp. 227.

[11] As translated in *ibid.*, p. 227, from I-Rvat: Urb. lat. 1098, pt. 2, fol. 701, *Avviso* of 6 December 1628.

[12] For a discussion of the engraving and its printed description, together with an argument that Bernini would have been consulted in the planning of this work, see Weil, "Forty Hours," pp. 231–34; Weil reprints the engraving as plate 52.

[13] For numerous reproductions of engravings, drawings, and paintings, see *ibid.*, in which the appendix (pp. 243–48) lists seventy-nine pamphlets from 1608 through 1825.

mention music. As noted, the *Instructio* specifies that the *Pange lingua* and the *Tantum ergo* are sung on the first and last days. At High Mass on each of the three days, not only would a mass and some motets be performed, but possibly church sonatas and concertos as well. In some churches and oratories, the function of music during the Devotion went beyond that at Mass. For instance, in a Florentine lay confraternity, the Compagnia dell'Arcangelo Raffaello — where the Devotion was practiced as early as 1558 — evening meetings during the Devotion included "sermons, prayers, *lauda* singing, and an *apparato* that resembled paradise."[14] In the same confraternity, in the 1580s and 1590s, the *apparati* for the Devotions during Holy Week and for All Saints Day were sepulchres, and during evening meetings solo motets and spiritual madrigals were sung (some by Giulio Caccini), apparently in a declammatory style and at times from within the sepulchre.[15]

In Rome of the late seventeenth and early eighteenth centuries, the Forty Hours Devotions sponsored by Cardinal Pietro Ottoboni — among the city's most munificent patrons of the arts — were held at the basilica of San Lorenzo in Damaso, which was attached to his palace, the Cancelleria.[16] Ottoboni's household account books show that these Devotions in the period of Archangelo Corelli's service to the cardinal were musically among the most elaborate occasions of the church year.[17] The Devotions, which included both instrumental and vocal music, were held annually near the end of carnival, beginning on Thursday in the week of Sexagesima and closing on Saturday — or at times on Quinquagesima Sunday.[18] The pope was often present for the opening of the Devotions, as he was on 2 February

---

[14] John Walter Hill, "Oratory Music in Florence I: *Recitar Cantando*, 1583–1685," *Acta Musicologica* LI (1979), 132, fn. 98.

[15] For full details, see *ibid.*, pp. 113–16 and pp. 133–34, documents 2–11. According to document 11 (pp. 116 and 134), on Easter morning of 1591 a kind of *visitatio sepulchri* was enacted before the sepulchre, with music, costumes, and acting — presumably the Sacrament would have been removed from the sepulchre, during an *Elevatio*, before that miniature drama took place.

[16] This is the same church as is sometimes erroneously referred to in documents of the time as that of Santi Lorenzo e Damaso.

[17] For details, see Hans Joachim Marx, "Die Musik am Hofe Pietro Kardinal Ottobonis unter Arcangelo Corelli," *Analecta musicologica* V "*Studien zur italienisch–deutschen Musikgeschichte*" 5, 1968), 107–9.

[18] Of. *ibid.*, p. 107; and pp. 139–40, document 64a–g, which suggests a closing on Sunday. A four-day schedule, rather than the usual three-day one, would imply that the Forty Hours Devotion was not continuous but interrupted, perhaps in the evenings, as was at times permitted and practiced. Cf. Fortescue, *Ceremonies*, p. 350.

1690, when the *apparato* represented Jacob's Ladder;[19] and the "concerto for His Holiness, attending the Forty Hours Devotion" was performed by "18 violini, 7 violette, 7 violoni, 7 contrabassi, 2 trombe, and 5 arcileuti."[20] On another occasion when the pope was present, 31 January 1704, the theme of the *apparato* was the Purification of the Virgin.[21] One chronicler of the time wrote that the Forty Hours Devotion opened after the midday meal (*doppo pranzo*) and that the Holy Father admired the grandness of the *macchina* which was "of the most noble ideas of the Signore Cardinale Ottoboni";[22] and another chronicler added that "the excellence of the music, the *sinfonie*, the *concerti*, and above all the sacred orators rivaled one another in these days."[23] That Devotion ended on Saturday, 2 February, with the *Te Deum* sung by a double chorus.[24] While none of the available records tell us what works, either vocal or instrumental, were heard on these occasions, the account books suggest that the repertoire included double-chorus masses and motets; and a note in the *Avvisi* of 1695 suggests that concerted masses and possibly spiritual cantatas were sung — indeed, Ottoboni presented one singer with a diamond-studded watch for his performance during the Devotion.[25] Whether the texts of such cantatas might have related to the themes of the Devotion's apparati (as do the texts of some of the cantatas and oratorios mentioned below) is not known.[26]

In previous musicological literature, no cantatas and only three oratorios have been identified as works sung during Forty Hours Devotions. The oratorios, all performed in Palermo, are Giovanni Conticini's *L'Abramo*, for carnival of 1650 at the church of the Gesù; Antonio Binitti's *L'eucharistiche lautezze*, for carnival of 1682, possi-

---

[19] For the full title of the printed pamphlet, date of the Devotion's beginning, and theme of the *apparato*, see Weil, "Forty Hours," p. 245, appendix no. 24.

[20] Marx, "Ottoboni," p. 124, document 5.

[21] Weil, "Forty Hours," p. 246, appendix no. 31.

[22] Translated from the *Avvisi di Roma* (I-Rvat: Cod. Ottob. lat. 37–32, fol. [22]) as quoted in Marx, "Ottoboni," p. 108.

[23] Translated from the *Breve Ragguaglio* (Rome, 1704), p. 6 (= I-Rvat: Cod. Urb. lat. 1699, fol. 173v), as quoted in Marx, "Ottoboni," p. 108.

[24] Marx, 'Ottoboni," p. 159, document 178.

[25] *Ibid.*, p. 109–10; the *Avviso* is in I-Rvat: Cod. Ottob. lat. 3359, fol. [34].

[26] In addition to the themes mentioned above, those sponsored by Ottoboni included a Vision of the Heavenly Jerusalem (1700), St. Francis Xavier Baptizing People on St. John Island off the Coast of China (1702), and Pentecost in a Hexagonal Temple (1706). Cf. Weil, "Forty Hours," pp. 245–46, appendix nos. 26, 29, and 34.

bly at the Gesù; and Bernardo Pasquini's *L'Abramo*, for the first three days of Holy week in 1688 at the church of the Congregazione dell'Oratorio.[27] The title pages of all three are given in the appendix, as numbers 1, 14, and 2, respectively. Pasquini's *L'Abramo* is briefly treated below, in relation to oratorios for Palermo.

* * *

Of all the librettos listed in the appendix, the nine printed for performances at the small Umbrian town of Foligno reveal the most about the music's function and its relationship to the *macchine* erected for the Forty Hours Devotions.[28] All nine works were performed at the Oratorio del Buon Gesù between 1742 and 1756 — at least eight at Devotions held during the last three days of carnival,[29] and these bear dedications to the bishop of Foligno, Mario Maffei, whom one might well assume had a special interest in the visual and musical elaboration of the Devotion.[30] The themes of the *macchine* for these Devotions include those of the triumph of Judith (no. 16, 1745), Daniel in the lions' den (no. 20, 1749), the judgement of King Solomon (no. 21, 1746), Moses and the burning bush (no. 22, 1756), the sacrifice of Abraham (no. 23, 1751; 24, 1757), and the serpent of bronze (no. 25, 1744).

The libretto of the oratorio *Giuditta* (no. 16, 1745), with an anonymous text based on Judith 13–16 and set to music by Giuseppe Carcani, affords an excellent opportunity to understand now a *macchina* and an oratorio could work together to provide complementary visual and musical sermons — which would surely have been joined by a spoken sermon as well. The libretto's title page (see plate 1) is here translated in full:

---

[27] Cf. Egils Ozolins, "The Oratorios of Bernardo Pasquini" (unpublished Ph.D. diss., University of California at Los Angeles, 1983), p. 169, fn. 72 and pp. 167–68, where Ozolins provides background information on the Forty Hours Devotion in general and on the practice in Palermo.

[28] See appendix, index 1, for the numbers and year of the Foligno librettos.

[29] Cf. appendix, index 2.

[30] The title-page citation given in Claudio Sartori, "Primo tentativo di catalogo unico dei libretti italiani a stampa fino all'anno 1800," might be incomplete in the case of no. 19, which may also have been performed during the last three days of carnival and may bear a dedication comparable to the others.

Plate 1. Title page of the printed libretto for *Giuditta*, by Giuseppe Carcani
(I-Bc: Lib. 8066).

JUDITH

FIGURE OF CHRIST, OF MARY,
AND OF THE CHURCH.

Sacred Composition, to be sung in the Venerable
Oratory of the Good Jesus of Foligno, for the occasion
on which, in the last three days of Carnival of the
year 1745, is exposed there, solemnly, for the
public adoration of the Faithful, the MOST HOLY
SACRAMENT, in a *macchina*,
representing the triumph of the same
Judith.

DEDICATED TO THE ILLUSTROUS AND REVEREND
MONSIGNOR
MARIO MAFFEI
EXCELLENT SHEPHERD OF THE SAID CITY
AND OF HIS DIOCESE
IN FOLIGNO; By Feliciano and Filippo Campitelli, Episcopal Printers.

The libretto's dedication, written by Sebastiano Branducci, rector of the Oratorio del Buon Gesù, elaborates on how Judith may be considered a figure of "the same Divine Redeemer, whom the Faithful adore under the veil of the Eucharistic Species," a figure of "Most Holy

Plate 2. Description of the *macchina* for Carcani's *Giuditta* (printed libretto, page [24]).

Mary, Mother of Compassion," and also a figure of the Church.[31]

The final page of the libretto consists of a description of the *macchina* (see plate 2), which is not only a work of visual art, but also incorporates written mottos selected from the *Psychomachia* of the fourth-century Aurelius Prudentius Clemmens. Essential to an understanding of the interdependence of music and visual art in this Devotion, the description of the *macchina* is translated in full:

Description of the Macchina

On an inclined plain, in perspective and to the left, one sees abandoned and ruined the camp of the Assyrians, who were besieging the city of Bethulia. At the mid-point of the plain, still on the left side, the city itself extends in profile, and between two pilasters[32] of the walls there rises a majestic gate, whence exit the virgins and the people to meet Judith. Dancing and playing, [the people] sing a song of victory:

She challenges the perils of furious warfare to overcome them.[33]

From the gate one notices several streets of the city, solemnly draped, and one sees the head of Holofernes, hanging above [the gate]. On the pediment are imprinted in marble the following words:

This woman brought back from the enemy a glorious trophy.[34]

At the right appears the beautiful and proud Judith magnificently and charmingly attired, in a posture of coming from the camp of the enemy. On the gold border of her dress one reads this embroidered motto:

Chastity shining in beauteous armor.[35]

In her right hand she holds the bloody sword, in her left the head of Holofernes, toward which she turns and says:

No longer will you venture to hurl deadly flames.[36]

Near Judith one sees Ozias, who hastily walks toward her from the city; his eyes fixed on the Most Holy Sacrament, and motioning toward the great lady with his right hand, he expresses himself in this manner:

For thee she fights, and for thee she conquers.[37]

---

[31] P. 3: "Giuditta, che figure fu di quello stesso Divin Redentore, ch'adorano i Fedeli sotto il velo delle specie Eucaristiche"; p. 4: "che parimente figura fu di Maria Santissima Madre di Miserazioni; p. 5: "Giuditta fu eziando figura della Chiesa . . ."

[32] Baloardi = Paloardi? Columns?

[33] Line 27. The line numbers are those of the *Psychomachia*, in vol. 1, pp. 274–343, of: *Prudentius*, edited and translated by H.J. Thomson, Loeb Classical Library (Cambridge, Mass.: Harvard University Press; London: William Heinemann, 1949). The present author's translations of the Latin mottos are based largely on Thomson.

[34] Line 64.

[35] Line 41.

[36] Line 55.

[37] Line 17.

Between and a step behind Ozias and Judith, Joachim is placed in an act of admiration, pointing at the Most Holy Sacrament and looking at the other priests, saying to them:

The lady prefigures Christ.[38]

Judith is encircled by victorious soldiers, who sing to her as a mark of jubilation and respect:

A defender with Heaven-inspired boldness.[39]

In the midst of the clouds, by which, on high, the Most Holy Sacrament is surrounded, there flies an angel, who bears the sword of Holofernes, offering it to the Lord; one reads these verses, which hang from it: .

At the altar of the Divine Fount,
she dedicates [the sword], there to shine and flash with
unfading light.

The mottos are all extracted from the *Psychomachia* of Prudentius. The invention and the painting of the *macchina* are by signor Niccola Epifani of Foligno.

END

This *macchina* would seem to be comparable in conception to the Roman ones described by Weil (see above, pp. 153–54). Whether Mario Maffei, as the bishop and patron, wished to imitate a Roman practice, or whether the practice was more widely disseminated, remains an open question.[40]

Following Baroque tradition, the oratorio is in two parts. While the parts are not so labelled, they are clearly evident by the action of the drama and the placement of the *sinfonie*, which function as overtures. The libretto provides no evidence that the tradition of preaching a sermon between the parts was or was not followed in this instance. The numbers of the oratorio (omitting connective recitatives) are, in part one, an opening *sinfonia* followed by two choruses and three arias; in part two, an opening *sinfonia*, a chorus, three arias, a duet, and a final aria with chorus.

That the oratorio libretto and the *macchina* were planned as two aspects of a single presentation is clear from the correspondences between them. The setting of both is the same: the entire oratorio takes

---

[38] Lines 66–67.

[39] Line 65.

[40] A Roman connection is clear with no. 25, of 1744, for the librettist, Gregorio Giacomo Terribilini is described in the libretto as "romano, beneficato di San Lorenzo in Damaso"; and the composer, Antonio Bencini, as "romano, maestro di capp. nella detta basilica [San Lorenzo in Damaso] e in S. Giacomo degl'Incurabili di Roma."

place before the gate of Bethulia. The personages are also the same — in the oratorio: Judith, the widow of Manasses; Ozias, the prince of Bethulia; Joachim, the high priest; and choruses of the Virgins of Bethulia, the People of Bethulia, the Soldiers of Ozias, and the High Priests. The narrative content of the oratorio, too, at times corresponds with that of the *macchina*. At the beginning, the Virgins sing a chorus of victory and of praise for Judith, and she is described as standing "at the gate of Bethulia, with the bloody sword in her right hand, and the head of Holofernes in her left";[41] Judith describes her deed, and, according to the "stage" directions, "gives the head of Holofernes to a soldier,"[42] to be hung up to frighten the enemy who are still encamped nearby. Through the comments of Ozias and the chorus, the libretto conveys the image of Judith as beautiful, chaste, noble, and heroic. In part one of the oratorio, she attributes the decapitation of Holofernes not to her own hand but to the Divine Hand.[43] She urges Ozias and his soldiers to attack the enemy, which they are about to do at the end of part one. Part two begins with the Soldiers' chorus of victory after their return. The libretto then turns to a recapitulation of Judith's noble deed and its relationship to the power of God; near the end, Judith has a vision which shows her to be inspired by God,[44] and the final number of the oratorio, an aria and chorus by Joachim and the priests, makes clear that she is a figure of Christ, of Mary, and of the Church.[45]

The Foligno *Giuditta* shows the extent to which music and visual art could complement each other in conveying a spiritual message in the Forty Hours Devotion. How widely practiced such interdependence of the arts in the Devotion might have been has yet to be determined. The

---

[41] Libretto, p. 8: "Giuditta sulla Porta di Betulia, con la Spada insanguinata nella destra, e la Testa d'Oloferne nella sinistra." It is curious that the hands are reversed in the libretto."

[42] Libretto, p. 9: "Consegna la testa d'Oloferne a un soldato." Descriptions of the appearances and even occasional actions of personages are found throughout the libretto, as they are with many others of the period; there no clear evidence that the oratorio was staged and acted, in the manner of an opera. Operatic presentation was becoming increasingly popular in the mid-century but was rarely used in oratories or churches. For details of the operatic presentation of oratorios in this period, see Howard E. Smither, "Oratorio and Sacred Opera, 1700–1825: Terminology and Genre Distinction," *Proceedings of the Royal Musical Association* CVI (1979–80), 88–104.

[43] Libretto, p. 9.

[44] Libretto, pp. 20–21.

[45] Libretto, pp. 22–23.

librettos printed for Forty Hours Devotions in cities other than Foligno are less explicit about the music's relationship to the visual decorations. Those printed for Milan, however, include some interesting details about function.

The information gathered thus far about Milan shows that only one church, Santa Maria presso San Celso, performed either cantatas or oratorios during Forty Hours Devotions. Of the eleven Milan librettos, the earliest in the appendix is dated 1689, and the latest 1757. Every libretto lists performance dates, which show that the performances always occured on the final Saturday through Monday of carnival. Each libretto includes the texts of three cantatas (nos. 5–12) or one three-part work, which might be considered an oratorio — nos. 3, 13, and 34; one cantata or one part of an oratorio was performed on each day. For instance, L'Abramo (no. 3, 1755) — with a text by Francesco Tosi based on Genesis 14–15 and with music by Antonio Negri — is a three-part work which includes three characters: Abramo; Sara, his wife; and Melchisedecco, king of Salem, great prophet, and priest of God; and portions of the text are marked coro. All characters sing — recitatives and arias — in each of the three parts. The music for each day is interrupted by a discorso, and the texts for the three days are similarly structured: three arias and a chorus, each preceded by a recitative; then the discorso; and finally two arias preceded by recitatives. The libretto names the priest who will deliver the discorso on each day and gives, in a few lines, his argomento. As one expects, the argomenti show that the discorsi focused on the Eucharist and on the need for penance by those who participate in carnival, but the argomenti do not mention Abraham. The libretto's introduction, "A chi legge," interprets the text in relation to the Eucharist; whether a macchina at the altar represented the oratorio's theme remains an open question.

As may be seen from index 1 in the appendix, the largest number of librettos — nineteen of the forty-one total — were printed for performances in Palermo and date from 1650 through 1754. Seven were performed in the Jesuit church, the Gesù (nos. 1, 4, 17, 27, 31, and 37); two in the church of the Congregazione del Oratorio (nos. 2 and 18); and each of the remaining nine in a different church, convent, or monastery. The title pages of the Palermo librettos mention several occasions for holding the Forty Hours Devotions: four during the carnival season, with no time specified within that season (nos. 1, 4, 14, and 17); one during the last three days of carnival (no. 41); one during the first three days of Holy Week (no. 2); two as part of the "circular" or "circulating" Forty Hours (nos. 29 and 35);[46] and one on the feast of San Francesco d'Assisi (no. 39).[47] On ten of the Palermo title pages, no information is given about the occasion of the Forty Hours Devotion.

As mentioned above, Pasquini's *L'Abramo* (no. 2, 1688), has been previously treated in the literature on oratorio.[48] Like eight of the other Palermo works, it is termed a *dialogo* on its title page.[49] In a performance of 1693 for the Congregazione dell'Oratorio in Florence, however, essentially the same work was called, on the title page of its printed libretto, *L'Ismaele, oratorio a cinque voci*.[50] The Florentine version is divided into two parts, as are most Italian oratorios of the period, while the Palermo version is in one part. Thus, the Palermo libretto offers no suggestion that in its Forty Hours version the oratorio (or "dialogue") was divided by a sermon, as it would have been in Florence. The two librettos include the same texts for fifteen arias and three duets — the differences between the librettos are minimal.

The two Florentine oratorios listed in the appendix allow for few conclusions. One of them (no. 30, 1739) does not specifically state that the oratorio is to be performed at a Forty Hours Devotion, but only at the exposition of the Sacrament — without further indication of an occasion — in the church of San Pier Maggiore; the other oratorio (no. 15 1780) was sponsored by a lay confraternity — the Compagnia di San Sebastiano — and was "to be sung in the church of the Reverend Fathers of the Scuole Pie on the final evening of the solemn *triduo* of the Most August Sacrament which is usually done on the last three days of carnival." The extent to which oratorios were performed on such an occasion in Florence has yet to be explored.

* * *

Of immense popularity in Counter Reformation Italy, the Forty Hours Devotion acquired a tradition of sumptuous visual decoration

---

[46] That is, the Forty Hours Devotion as it circulates from church to church, as a perpetual prayer.

[47] The wording of this title page ("per l'espositione delle quarant'ore, che corrono con la solennità di S. Francesco d'Assisi") might imply that the coincidence of the Forty Hours Devotion with the feast of San Francesco was accidental and that this was a "40 ore circolari" performance.

[48] See above, fn. 27.

[49] The other eight are nos. 14, 18, 27, 29, 38-41. In the appendix, the term *dialogo* in found only on these Palermo librettos.

[50] The remainder of this paragraph is based largely on Ozolins, "Pasquini," pp. 178-87.

intended to focus attenttion on, glorify and interpret the Sacrament. From the mid-seventeenth century until the early nineteenth, the decorations were at times allegorical scenes comparable to stage sets — called *teatri, macchine,* or *apparati* — displayed frequently near the end of carnival, when they would rival the season's secular entertainments and prepare the faithful for Lent. At times the degree of musical elaboration of the Forty Hours Devotion would seem to have matched the visual: declamatory solo madrigals in late sixteenth-century Florence; elaborate instrumental, choral, and solo vocal works in late seventeenth- and early eighteenth-century Rome; and cantatas and oratorios — as seen from the librettos listed in the appendix of this study — from the mid-seventeenth century to the late eighteenth in Foligno, Milan, Palermo, and Florence. A close and complementary relationship between the music and the *macchina* can be demonstrated in Foligno. Whether the performance of cantatas and oratorios at Forty Hours Devotions was a widespread practice in Italy of this period and whether the music and the *macchina* were characteristically interrelated as they were in Foligno remain questions for further investigation.

APPENDIX

Librettos for Cantatas and Oratorios Performed in Forty Hours Devotions

The appendix consists of an alphabetical list — together with three indexes — of the title pages of forty-one printed librettos for cantatas and oratorios performed during Forty Hours Devotions. An an informal byproduct of research done for the present author's *A History of the Oratorio* (vols. 1–2, Chapel Hill: University of North Carolina Press, 1977; vol. 3, 1987) the list is only a beginning — it should not be regarded as exhaustive. The chronological limits (1650–1780) and the five cities included (Florence, Foligno, Milan, and Palermo) were neither selected nor predetermined, but simply represent the materials as found in the sources searched — mainly Claudio Sartori, "Primo tentativo di catalogo unico dei libretti italiani a stampa fino all'anno 1800," a photocopy of the card catalogue in the Ufficio ricerca fondi musicali, now located at Milan, Conservatorio di musica Giuseppe Verdi. Also searched were various European libraries and the secondary literature on oratorio.

Unless otherwise indicated, the title pages and library locations are taken from Sartori, "Catalogo." The library locations use standard *RISM* sigla. The names of librettists (L) and composers (C), when given by Sartori, are supplied only if not named on the title pages. Only the librettos identified by library call numbers have been seen by the present author.

1. *L'Abramo. Attione in gran parte accresciuta da padri della Compagnia di Giesù di Palermo. In occasione delle quarant'ore di carnovale del 1650. Data in luce per commodita degli uditori dall'illustre signor Don Gregorio Castello, Conte di San Carlo* (Palermo: Coppola, 1650). (Cf. Ozolins, "Pasquini, p. 169, fn. 72.) I-PLcom, Rsc.

2. *L'Abramo. Dialogo a 5 voci con istromenti. Posto in musica dal signor Bernardo Pasquini. Per cantarsi nella chiesa della Congregatione dell'Oratorio di Palermo. Nella solenne espositione del SS. Sacramento per le quarant'hore della penitenza ne primi tre giorni della settimana santa 11. 12. 13. aprile dell'anno 1688* (Palermo: Giacomo Epiro, 1688). (Cf. Ozolins, "Pasquini," p. 167) I-PLcom.

3. *L'Abramo. Sacra azione a lode del Santissimo Sacramento esposto nell'insigne tempio della Beatissima Vergine de' Miracoli presso S. Celso, da recitarsi in occasione degli esercizi spirituali ne' giorni 8. 9. 10. febbrajo 1755. Poesia del sig. dottore Franco Tosi, fra gli Arcadi Merilgo. Musica del signor Antonio Negri, maestro di capella di detto insigne tempio ec.* (Milan: Giambattista Bianchi). I-Mb: Racc. Dramm. Corniani Algarotti 4003.

4. *Le avventurose nozze di Booz e Ruth. Azione sacro-drammatica a quattro voci, e più stromenti da cantarsi nel Gesù da Palermo per le quarantore del carnovale dell'anno 1750* (Palermo: Stefano Amato, 1750). C: Francesco Feo, maestro di capp. napolitano. I-PLcom.

5. *Cantate a gloria del Santissimo Sacramento esposto nell'insigne tempio della Beatissima Vergine de' Miracoli presso S. Celso, in occasione degli esercizj spirituali alli 19. 20. e 21. febraro 1689. Poste in musica dal sig. Francesco Rossi maestro di capella del detto tempio e de RR. PP. di S. Gio. in Conca e date alle stampe da un divoto della B.V.* (Milan: Carlo Antonio Savesi). I-Mb.

6. *Cantate a gloria del Santissimo Sacramento esposto nell'insigne tempio della Beata Vergine de' Miracoli presso S. Celso, in occasione degli esercizj spirituali alli 1. 2. 3. marzo 1710. Poste in*

musica dal M.R. sig. Dionigi Erba maestro di capella del detto insigne tempio, e date alle stampe da un divoto della Beata Vergine (Milan: heredi Camagni alla Rosa). I-Ma.

7. *Cantate a gloria del Santissimo Sacramento esposto nell'insigne tempio della B.ma Vergine de' Miracoli presso S. Celso, in occasione degli esercizj spirituali alli 26. 27. 28. febbraio 1718. Poste in musica dal M. rev. sig. Dionigi Erba maestro di capella del detto insigne tempio e date alle stampe da un divoto della Beata Vergine* (Milan: Giuseppe Pandolfo Malatesta). I-Ma, Mb.

8. *Cantate a gloria del Santissimo Sacramento esposto nell'insigne tempio della Beatissima Vergine de' Miracoli presso S. Celso, in occasione degli esercizj spirituali alli 10. 11. e 12 febrajo 1725. Poste in musica dal M.R. sig. Dionigi Erba maestro di capella di detto insigne tempio* (Milan: Carlo Giuseppe Quinto) I-Ma.

9. *Cantate a gloria del Santissimo Sacramento esposto nell'insigne tempio della Beatissima Vergine de' Miracoli presso S. Celso, in occasione·delgi esercizj spirituali alli 26. 27. e 28 febbrajo 1729. Poste in musica dal M. rev. sig. Dionigi Erba, maestro di cappella del detto insigne tempio, e date alle stampe da un divoto della Beata Vergine* (Milan: Carlo Giuseppe Quinto). I-Bc.

10. *Cantate a lode del Santissimo Sacramento esposto nell'insigne tempio della Beatissima Vergine de' Miracoli presso S. Celso, da recitarsi in occasione degli esercizj spirituali alli 11. 12. e 13 febbrajo 1741. Poste in musica dal sig. Antonio Negri, maestro di cappella del detto insigne tempio* (Milan: Carlo Giuseppe Quinto). I-Mb.

11. *Cantate a lode del Santissimo Sacramento esposto nell'insigne tempio della Beatissima Vergine de' Miracoli presso S. Celso, da recitarsi in occasione degli esercizj spirituali alli 3. 4. e 5 febbrajo 1742. Poesia del sig. dottore Francesco Tosi, musica del sig. Antonio Negri, maestro di cappella del detto insigne tempio* (Milan: Carlo Giuseppe Quinto). I-Ma.

12. *Cantate a lode del Santissimo Sacramento esposto nell'insigne tempio della Beatissima Vergine de' Miracoli presso S. Celso, da recitarsi in occasione degli esercizj spirituali alli 15. 16. e 17 febbrajo 1744. Musica dal sig. Antonio Negri, maestro di cappella del detto insigne tempio ec.* (Milan: Carlo Giuseppe Quinto). I-Ma.

13. *Il David. Cantate a lode del Santissimo Sacramento esposto nell'insigne santuario della Beatissima Vergine de'Miracoli presso S. Celso. Da recitarsi in occasione degli esercizj spirituali ne' giorni 28. 29. febbrajo e l marzo 1756. Musica del sig. Gio. Lorenzo*

Fasietti, maestro di cappella dello stesso insigne tempio (Milan: Giambattista Bianchi, 1756). I-Ma.

14. *L'eucharistiche lautezze compartite al peccatore in persona del prodigo penitente. Dialogo posto in musica dal signor D. Antonio Binitti maestro di cappella nel Gesù di Palermo. Per la sollenitta delle 40. hore di carnovale del 1682* (Palermo: Pietro dell'Isola, 1682). (Cf. Ozolins, "Pasquini," p. 169) I-PLcom.

15. *Il Giobbe. Oratorio sacro per musica da cantarsi nella chiesa de' RR. PP. delle Scuole Pie l'ultima sera del solenne triduo dell'augustiss. Sacramento che è solito farsi gl'ultimi tre giorni del carnevale dai fratelli e congregati della ven. Compagnia di S. Sebastiano. Dedicato al merito sublime dell'illustrissimo . . . Niccolò Goni patrizio fiorentino* (Florence: Francesco e Pietro Allegrini, 1780). L: P.C.D.S.P. Accad. Fior.; C: Gio. Marco Rutini, Accad. Filarmonico e maestro di capp. del duca di Modena. I-Fm, Vgc.

16. *Giuditta figura di Cristo, di Maria, e della Chiesa. Componimento sacro da cantarsi nel venerabil' Oratorio del Buon Giesù di Foligno, in occasione, che negl'ultimi tre giorni del carnovale dell'anno 1745., s'espone ivi, solennemente, alle pubblica adorazione de fedeli il Santissimo Sacramento, in una macchina, rappresentante il trionfo della stessa Giuditta. Dedicato all'illustr. e reverend. monsignore Mario Maffei ottomio pastore di detta città, e sua diocesi* (Foligno: Feliciano e Filippo Campitelli Stamp. Vescovili). C: Giuseppe Carcani. I-Bc: Lib. 8066; FOLc, PESo, Rvat (Casimiri).

17. *La morte d'Abel. Componimento sacro-drammatico del signor abbate Metastasio da cantarsi nelle quarantore del carnevale nella chiesa del Giesù di Palermo* (Palermo: Pietro Bentivegna, 1754). C: Girolamo Abbos. I-PLcom.

18. *La penitenza al soglio ovver il Manasse pentito in Babilonia. Dialogo a 5 voci composto dal sig. don Pietro Riccio, da cantarsi nella venerabile chiesa de' RR. PP. dell'Oratorio, nella esposizione del Santiss. Sacramento per la 40 ore della penitenza. Posto in note musicali dal sig. don Pietro Pizzolo Maestro di cappella di detta venerabile chiesa* (Palermo: Domenico Cortese, 1703). I-PLcom.

19. *Per la solenne esposizione del SS. Sagramento. Cantata a due voci per musica* (Foligno: Pompeo Campana, [1742]. C: Giuseppe Radicchi. I-FOLc.

20. *Per la solenne esposizione del SS. Sagramento in una machina rappresentante Daniele nel Lago de' Leoni nel venerabile Oratorio*

del Buon Gesù de Foligno ne' tre giorni antecedenti alla quaresima
dell' anno 1749. Drama sagro dedicato all' . . . Mons. Mario
Maffei, vescovo vigilantissimo . . . (Foligno: Pompeo Campana,
1749). L: Neralco, Pastore Arcade [Giuseppe Ercolani]; C:
Giuseppe Dol di Monaco di Baviera. I-FOLc.

21. *Per la solenne esposizione del SS. Sagramento in una machina*
rappresentante il giudizio del re Salomone nel venerabile oratorio
del Buon Gesù di Foligno nei tre giorni antecedenti alla quaresima
dell'anno 1746. Cantata a due voci dedicata all' illustrissimo . . .
monsignor Mario Maffei vescovo vigilantissimo di d. città . . .
(Foligno: Pompeo Campana). L: Neralco Pastore Arcade
[Giuseppe Ercolani]; C: Niccolò Sabbatino napolitano. I-Nc, PEc.

22. *Per la solenne esposizione della SS. Sagramento in una macchina*
rappresentante il Roveto di Mosè nel ven. oratorio del Buon Gesù
di Foligno negli ultimi tre giorni del carnevale dell'anno 1756.
Cantata a due voci per musica dedicata all'illustriss. . . . monsig.
Mario Maffei vescovo vigilantissimo di detta città . . . (Foligno:
Francesco Fofi e com.). L: Abate D. Gregorio Ciacomo Terribilini
romano, Pastore Arcade ed Accad. Infecondo; C: Antonio Bencini
romano, maestro di capp. nella basilica di S. Lorenzo in Damaso di
Roma. I-FOLc, PEc.

23. *Per la solenne esposizione del SS. Sagramento in una machina*
rappresentante il sagrificio d'Abramo nel ven. Oratorio del Buon
Gesù di Foligno ne' tre giorni antecedenti alla quaresima dell'anno
1751. Drama sagro dedicato all'ill.mo . . . Monsign. Mario Maffei
vescovo vigilantissimo di detta città (Foligno: Francesco Fofi,
1751). Invenzione e pittura della macchina di Niccola Epifani di
Foligno. L: Neralco Pastore Arcade [Giuseppe Ercolani]; C:
Niccola Vettori agostiniano di Firenze. I-FOLc.

24. *Per la solenne esposizione del SS. Sagramento in una machina*
rappresentante il sacrifizio d'Abramo nel venerabile oratorio del
Buon Gesù di Foligno ne' tre giorni antecedenti alla quaresima
dell'anno 1757. Componimento sacro dedicato all'ill.mo . . .
Mons. Mario Maffei, vescovo . . . (Foligno: Francesco Fofi e
compagno, 1757). C: Angelo Seaglies, maestro di capp. della
cattedrale di Camerino. FOLc.

25. *Pe la solenne esposizione del SS. Sacramento in una machina*
rappresentante il serpento di bronzo esaltato da Mosé nel deserto
nel venerabile oratorio del Buon Gesù di Foligno nei tre giorni
antecedenti alla quaresima dell'anno 1744. Cantata a due voci per
musica dedicata all'illustrissimo . . . monsignor Mario Maffei

vescovo vigilantissimo di detta città (Foligno: Feliciano e Filippo Campitelli). L: Abbate Don Gregorio Giacomo Terribilini romano, beneficiato di San Lorenzo in Damaso; C: Antonio Bencini romano, maestro di capp. nella detta basilica è in S. Giacomo degl'Incurabili di Roma. I-PEc.

26. *Per la solenne esposizione del SS. Sagramento nel venerable oratorio del Buon Gesù di Fuligno negli ultimi tre giorni del carnovale dell'anno 1770. Cantata a due voci per musica dedicata all' . . . mons. Mario Maffei vescovo vigilentissimo di detta città* (Foligno: Francesco Fofi, 1770). C: Giuseppe Radicchi, maestro di capp. della cattedrale di Spoleto. I-FOLc.

27. *Pharao erythraeo submersus. Sive Daemon ab Eucharistici sanguinis und triumphatus. Dialogus canoris concinnatus numeris a Petro Pizzolo Collegij Panormatani Soc. Jesu musices moderatore et in ejusdem templo pro solemni SS. Eucharistiae expositione emodulandus anno 1711* (Palermo: Franciscum Ciché). I-PLcom.

28. *Pharaonis naufragium. A virga Moysis suscitatum, sacratissimi Panis symbolum. A don Joseph Salina majoris panormitanae ecclesiae musices moderatore harmonicis expressus numeris. Pro SS. Eucharistiae expositione sub auspiciis a D.M. rev. matris sororis Luciae Mariae Termini in monasterio Sanctae Mariae virginum secundo abbatissae concinendus anno 1710* (Palermo: Domenico Cortese, 1710). I-PLcom.

29. *Il popolo ebreo guarito dal serpe di bronzo, appeso alla Croce. Figura dell'uman genre risanato e redento da Giesù crocifisso. Dialogo a 5 voci e più stromenti; da cantarsi nella chiesa del venerabile monistero di Santa Maria del Cancelliero, per la solenne sposizione del SS. Sagramento Eucaristico, nelle 40 ore circolari dell'anno 1706. Nel governo della R.M. abbadessa suor Giovanna Caterina Oddo. Consecrato all'illustre . . . D. Giuseppe Fernandez de Medrano, marchese di Mompiliero . . . protettore di detto venerabile monistero. Posto in note da D. Francesco Bajada, maestro di cappella di detta chiesa* (Palermo: Onofrio Gramignani, 1706). I-PLcom.

30. *Il prodigioso transito di S. Giuseppe. Oratorio per musica da cantarsi nell'insigne chiesa di San Pier Maggiore di Firenze nell'esposizione dell'august. Sagramento. Dedicato al merito singolare dell'illustriss . . . conte abb. Pandolfo de' Bardi de' conti di Vernio abbate di Prato ecc. Musica del sig. Bartolommeo Felici* (Florence: Pier Martini, 1739). L: Andrea Nati; C: Bart. Felici. I-La, Vgc.

31. *Il ritorno di Tobia. Dramma per musica da cantarsi nella ven. chiesa del Collegio Nuovo de' PP. Gesuiti per la solennità delle quarant'ore del 1753. Musica del sig. David Perez maestro di cappella napolitano* (Palermo: Pietro Bentivegna, 1753). I-PLcom.

32. *Sacre delitie dell'anima al convito dell'Eucharistico Pane. Componimento per musica a cinque voci con più strumenti da cantarsi nelle 40 hore esposte nella real Confraternita della SS. Nunciata vicino la Porta di San Giorgio. Posto in note da Nicolo Filomena dedicata alla grandezza delli signori D. Geronimo Carsia . . . D. Antonio Parisi . . . D. Paulo Riggio e Saladino . . . rettori di quella* (Palermo: Agostino Epiro, 1704). I-PLcom.

33. *Sacrae nuptiae in novo Paradiso Terrestri a divino amore celebratae. Melos in templo ven. M. Sanctae Rosaliae noviter erecto pro Sanctissimae Eucharistiae expositione, ejusdem gloriosae Virginis festivate emodulandum anno 1709. Patrocinium dicatum U.J. Petri Sartorio ejusdem monasterij protectoris. Harmonicis distinctum numeris a D. Joseph Spina monasterij praedicti cantus moderatore* (Palermo: Felicis Marino, 1709). I-PLcom.

34. *Salomone. Cantate in lode del Santissimo Sacramento esposto nell'insigne santuario della Beatissima Vergine de' Miracoli presso S. Celso. Da recitarsi in occasione degli essercizj spirituali ne' giorni 19. 20. 21 febbrajo 1757. Musica del sig. Gio. Lorenzo Fascetti, maestro di cappella dello stesso insigne tempio* (Milan: Giambattista Bianchi). I-Ma.

35. *Gli sforzi della splendidezza e della pietà. Oratorio a 5 voci a più stromenti da cantarsi nella chiesa della ven. Compagnia di San Francesco sotto titolo di San Lorenzo in occasione del riaprimento della medesima chiesa magnificamente rinovata et rabbellita e nell'esposizione della Sacratiss. Eucaristia per le 40 ore circolari nell'anno 1707. Musica del signor Francesco Mancini* (Palermo: Felice Marino, 1707). I-Vgc.

36. *Susanna. Oratorio del signor D. Giachino Bona e Fardella da cantarsi nella congregazione delle dame sotto titolo di S. Maria della Raccomandata, per la sponsizione del Sacramento nelle 40 hore dell'anno 1705. Sotto il governo della signora D. Thomasa Branciforti e Guerrero, contessa di S. Antonio ec. Posto in note da Bartolomeo Matraja* (Palermo: Delice Marino, 1705). I-PLcom.

37. *La temporale generatione del Verbo da madre senza padre non dissimile al l'eterna generatione da padre senza madre rende Maria*

sempre Vergine privileggiata quasi dea nella sua purissima Annunciatione. Poesia sagra di don Giovanni Zito e Riggio ornata di note armoniche da D. Arcangelo Corello Foggino per cantarsi nel triduo delle 40 hore che si celebrano nell'Oratorio de'Nobili nella Casa Professa del Giesù di Palermo per la sollennità di detta signora nell'anno 1700 sotto il governo del signor D. Balsco Impellizzeri (Palermo: Agostino Epiro, 1700). I-PLcom.

38. *Trionfante passaggio da questa vita al Paradisco del gran patriarca S. Benedetto. Dialogo da cantarsi nella chiesa dello Spirito Santo de' PP. Cosinensi nell'esposizione del Santissimo Sagramento per l'orazione delle 40 ore nell'anno 1703* (Palermo: Agostine Epiro, 1703). I-PLcom.

39. *Il trionfo delle virtù sopra la nava mistica della Chiesa. Dialogo a 5 voci da cantarsi nella chiesa de ven. monistero di S. Maria del Monte Oliveto sotto vocabolo della Badia Nuova, per l'espositione delle quarant'ore, che corrono con la solennità di s. Francesco d'Assisi, in questo anno 1707. Sotto il governo della rev.a sig.a madre suora Stefana Francesca Spatafora, la terza volta abbadessa. Posto in note dal sig. don Francesco Bajada, maestro di cappella nella Casa Professo di Palermo* (Palermo: Domenico Cortese, 1707). I-PLcom.

40. *L'umanità in ossequio del sacramentato suo Redentore. Dialogo a tre voci e più stromenti da cantarsi nella venerabile chiesa di S. Lucai del Monte della Pietà, per la solennità delle quarant'ore delli signori Giuseppe Monreale . . . Pietro Filingeri . . . Bernardo Giusino . . . Girolamo Oliveri e Pilo, Gio. Battista marchese Bargellini . . . Mario Bocca di Foco, Ludovico Alliata Spatafora . . . Giulio Pollastra ed Algaria, Gio. Battista Caspinta* (Palermo: Antonio Epiro, 1715). I-PLcom.

41. *La verga mosaica a' danni di Faraone, simbolo del Cattolico agonizante, che passa libero da Luciffero alla celeste Terra di Promissione, sotto la potentissima Verga della protezione della Gran Madre di Dio degl'Agonizanti. Dialogo a quattro voci e stromenti dèdicato alla grandezza del signor Don Girolamo Graffeo e Filinceri, principe di Partanna, duca di Ciminna, signore delle Terre di Tripi, ecc. Poste in note dal signor Don Vincenzo Naro maestro di cappella della detta città di Partanna. Per le 40 ore si solennizano nel ven. chiesa degl'Agonizanti di essa città ne tre giorni ultimi di carnevale dell'anno 1703* (Palermo: Domenico Cortese, 1703) I-PLn.

INDEXES TO APPENDIX

Index 1: Cities

Florence	15 (1780), 30 (1739)
Foligno	16 (1745), 19 (1742), 20 (1749), 21 (1746), 22 (1756), 23 (1751), 24 (1757), 25 (1744), 26 (1770)
Milan	3 (1755), 5 (1689), 6 (1710), 7(1718), 8 (1725), 9 (1729), 10 (1741), 11 (1742), 12 (1744), 13 (1756), 34 (1757)
Palermo	1 (1650), 2 (1688), 4 (1750), 14 (1682), 17 (1754), 18 (1703), 27 (1711), 28 (1710), 29 (1706), 31 (1753), 32 (1704), 33 (1709), 35 (1707), 36 (1705), 37 (1700), 38 (1703), 39 (1707), 40 (1715), 41 (1703)

Index 2: Occasions

Carnival (dates unspecified)	1 (Palermo, 1650), 4 (Palermo, 1750), 14 (Palermo, 1682), 17 (Palermo, 1745)
Carnival, last Sat.–Mon. of	3 (Milan, 1755), 5 (Milan, 1689), 6 (Milan, 1710), 7 (Milan, 1718), 8 (Milan, 1725), 9 (Milan, 1729), 10 (Milan, 1741), 11 (Milan, 1742), 12 (Milan, 1744), 13 (Milan, 1756), 34 (Milan, 1757)
Carnival, last three days of	15 (Florence, 1780), 16 (Foligno, 1745), 20 (Foligno, 1749), 21 (Foligno, 1746), 22 (Foligno, 1756), 23 (Foligno, 1751), 24 (Foligno, 1757), 25 (Foligno, 1744), 26 (Foligno, 1770), 41 (Palermo, 1703)
Circolari	29 (Palermo, 1706), 35 (Palermo, 1707)
Feast of S. Francesco d'Assisi	39 (Palermo, 1707) (& *circolari?*)
Holy Week, first three days of	2 (Pelermo, 1688)
No information (*circolari?*)	18 (Palermo, 1703) 19 (Foligno, 1742), 27 (Palermo, 1711) 28 (Palermo, 1710), 30 (Florence, 1739), 31 (Palermo, 1753),

32 (Palermo, 1704), 33 (Palermo, 1709),
36 (Palermo, 1705), 37 (Palermo, 1700),
38 (Palermo, 1703), 40 (Palermo, 1715)

Index 3: Years

1650	1 (Palermo)
1682	14 (Palermo)
1688	2 (Palermo)
1689	5 (Milan)
1700	37 (Palermo)
1703	18 (Palermo), 38 (Palermo), 41 (Palermo)
1704	32 (Palermo)
1705	36 (Palermo)
1706	29 (Palermo)
1707	35 (Palermo), 39 (Palermo)
1709	33 (Palermo)
1710	6 (Milan), 28 (Palermo)
1711	27 (Palermo)
1715	40 (Palermo)
1718	7 (Milan)
1725	8 (Milan)
1729	9 (Milan)
1739	30 (Florence)
1741	10 (Milan)
1742	11 (Milan), 19 (Foligno)
1744	12 (Milan), 25 (Foligno)
1745	16 (Foligno)
1746	21 (Foligno)
1749	20 (Foligno)
1750	4 (Palermo)
1751	23 (Foligno)
1753	31 (Palermo)
1754	17 (Palermo)
1755	3 (Milan)
1756	13 (Milan), 22 (Foligno)
1757	24 (Foligno), 34 (Milan)
1770	26 (Foligno)
1780	15 (Florence)

CHAPTER TWELVE

A BRIEF ANALYSIS OF THREE SERMONS PREACHED ON ST. CECILIA'S DAY IN LONDON DURING THE 1690'S

Charles H. Biklé

West Des Moines, Iowa

This article will examine the three surviving sermons which were preached in London on the occasion of St. Cecilia's Day celebrations. The sermons were delivered by three different clergymen and deal with the subject of the place of music in worship. A series of festivities honoring St. Cecilia, the patron saint of music and song, was held almost annually from 1683 to 1703, producing a large body of music, much of it of excellent quality. The celebrations nearly always took place on the saint's day, November 22. The sermons in question were delivered during the latter part of the series. Investigation of the sermons will reveal prevailing attitudes of the Anglican Church regarding music in its services, especially elaborate vocal and instrumental music.

A brief review of the origins and distinct character of the London celebrations is necessary, however, before considering the sermons themselves. The London festivities honoring music's patron saint were characterized by their secular as opposed to ecclesiastical sources. The celebrations developed as a result of financial needs of musicians residing in London since the restoration of the Monarchy. They were, in effect, public concerts, providing a showcase for displaying the talents of noted poets and composers.

Arrangements for the festivities were entrusted to a group of musicians and music lovers, called the Musical Society. From the group's membership, stewards were appointed each year for the task of selecting a poet to write an appropriate ode text, and a composer to set the words. A number of poets, including John Dryden and Thomas D'Urfey, lent their skills, as did composers John Blow, Henry and Daniel Purcell, and Giovanni Battista Draghi. Most of the secular events of the festivals were held at Stationers' Hall, near St. Paul's Cathedral.

For the initial ten years of the celebrations, only a secular entertainment, including a dinner, was provided. During the second decade, however, a liturgical service was added. St. Bride's Church, Fleet Street, was the site of most of the services. Not as much information has survived regarding the ecclesiastical aspects of the Musical Society's celebrations as has for the secular entertainment. Besides the three sermons, two settings of the *Te Deum Laudamus and Jubilate Deo* are extant, one by Henry Purcell (1694) and the other by John Blow (1695). In addition, a setting of Psalm 21, *The King Shall Rejoice*, composed by William Turner for the celebration of 1697, is preserved. All three of the compositions are for voices and instruments, with trumpets and, most likely, timpani having prominent parts. According to Thomas Tudway (d. 1726), composer, editor, and compiler of *English Cathedral Music*, Purcell's composition was the first setting of its kind in England.

Although the festivities were never under ecclesiastical control, the Musical Society enlisted at least three eminent clergymen to speak at the liturgical services. The names of the speakers, whose sermons survive, are as follows:

Ralph Battell (1649–1713)
Charles D. Hickman (1648–1713)
William Sherlock (c. 1641–1707)

Battell, himself the son of a clergyman, was educated at Peterhouse, Cambridge. He obtained a M.A. in 1673 and his D.D. in 1705. He was Rector of St. Peter's Church, Canterbury, and of Edworth, Bedfordshire. He then became Sub-Dean of the Chapel-Royal and Sub-Almoner to Queen Anne. Hickman was a Kings Scholar at Westminster School in 1665. He attended Christ Church, Oxford, beginning in 1667. In 1685, he earned his Doctor of Divinity. Hickman was chaplain to

Laurence Hyde, the Earl of Rochester; and chaplain to William and Mary, later to Queen Anne. He became Bishop of Derry, Ireland, in 1703, although he lived chiefly in England after the appointment. Sherlock, also educated at Peterhouse, Cambridge, obtained a M.A. in 1663. He went to St. George's near Lower Thames Street in 1669. In 1681, he assumed the Prebend of St. Pancras in St. Paul's Cathedral. He became Dean of St. Paul's in 1691.

The central theme of the three sermons under scrutiny is the role of music in public worship services. The theme befits the occasion, and reflects on the attitudes of the rulers during the Commonwealth. Thirty-three years prior to 1693, the year of the first surviving sermon, England was emerging from Puritan rule, which had lasted from the death of Charles I (1649). During the Commonwealth, the Calvinists, who constituted the ruling majority, imposed their own viewpoints concerning the place of music in church services. It is a mistake to assume that, because the Puritans were strict regarding the application of music in church, they abhorred music in general. The opposite is true. Cromwell himself was an ardent music lover. Under his direction, secular music flourished. The regime also established a committee to support the arts. Dispossessed church musicians were compensated in some cases. However, the Puritans felt that elaborate and accompanied music would interfere in worship services. Thus, their basic position was not that they loved music less, but religion more.

The attitude adopted by the Puritans was not unique to them. It existed almost from the beginnings of the Christian Church. The question posed by those with stances similar to the Puritans was: does music provide a means to an end, or is it an end in itself? That is, does it assist the worshiper in his devotions, or does the hearer become overwhelmed by the music? St. Augustine addressed the problem in his *Confessions*. Criticisms of a similar kind were directed at the use of organum and the introduction of musical instruments in services during the eleventh and twelfth centuries. Erasmus also complained about the complexity of music in services, as well as the use of a language (Latin) that no one understood. He furthermore attacked the idea of spending lavish sums to support elaborate musical activities, while the poor could have been fed from the funds.

The Eastern Orthodox Church, which claims direct descendancy from the early Christians, generally permits no instruments in its services. Tradition seems to side with Puritan thought. The early Protestant Church in England also considered musical instruments to be worldly. A resolution calling for the removal of all organs in churches missed being passed by only one vote in 1563.[1]

Memories of Puritan restrictions on church music remained strong during the period under consideration. The sermons are a rebuttal, at least partially, to the philosophy espoused by Calvinist rule regarding music in worship services.

The preceding historical review gives a background for examination of the sermons in detail. Ralph Battell's sermon, preached on St. Cecilia's Day in 1693, is the first surviving discourse and the only one of the three having a title, that being: *The Lawfulness and Expediency of Church-Musick*. The biblical text for his sermon is the opening two verses of Psalm 100:

> O be joyful in the Lord all ye lands.
> Serve the Lord with gladness and come before
> His Presence with a song.

The text upon which he based his sermon is appropriate, since the entire psalm comprises the "Jubilate," the companion canticle to the "Te Deum." According to Battell, the text gives direction on how to "behave ourselves in the Publick Worship of God."[2] Psalm 100 and others, notably Psalm 150, justify the policy of the Anglican Church allowing elaborate music with both voices and instruments. The lawfulness and fitness of vocal and instrumental music in public worship needs to be asserted, "because some have been heretofore scandalized at it, and others may perhaps still remain scrupulous about it."[3] The reference here, of course, is to the Puritan attitude, enforced nationwide a generation earlier.

The sermon has two sections. The first is a discourse on how ancient peoples observed religious customs, including the Israelites. Scriptural recommendations are treated as well as practices in the early Christian Church. The section then summarizes how musical practices are lawful in spite of the opposing attitude espoused by the Calvinists. The second section derives from the first because it illustrates not only how music is lawful in church services, but also that it is a highly advantageous and

---

[1] Percy Scholes, *The Puritans and Music in England and New England* (London: Oxford University Press, 1934), pp. 220–221, 230.

[2] Ralph Battell, *The Lawfulness and Expediency of Church-Musick* (London: Printed by J. Heptinstall, for John Carr, at the Middle-Temple-Gate in Fleetstreet, 1694), p. 1. An Anthology containing the three sermons under scrutiny is located in the Durham Cathedral Library, Durham, England under *Twelve Sermons and Other Discourses on Musical Subjects*, File Number B 18.

[3] Battell, *op. cit.*, p. 2.

excellent aid toward a better worship of God.

The initial section commences with an assertion that music has a natural propriety to excite and heighten devotion. The concept is not new with Battell. He is stating the feeling of his time regarding music's power to arouse the passions of mankind. Offering proof, he refers to the heathen peoples, such as the Greeks praising their heroes with the harp, the Phrygians worshiping Cybelle with a drum, and the Egyptians playing timbrels at ceremonies honoring Isis. The third chapter of Daniel records Chaldean rites where people were required to fall down and worship the image Nebuchadnezzar had erected when they heard the sound of the cornet, sackbut, and psaltery.

> Even these [customs] had some Light, together with their Darkness and were in the Right concerning a Religious Worship to be paid somewhere, though in the Wrong as to its object. . . .[4]

Religious ceremonies involving instruments were observed by the Israelites, as many psalms attest. According to Battell, worship services with musical instruments, as practiced by the pagans, were not the result of corruption or delusion, "but a remnant of that natural Light and natural Religion, which was still left in them. . . ."[5]

Aside from the Psalms, the Old Testament contains other references to worship of Yahweh with instrumental accompaniment. Examples are: Miriam's playing the timbrel during the Song of Moses (Ex. 15:20 — this example refers to Egyptian worship rites); Saul's meeting with a group of prophets having a psaltery, tabret, pipe, and harp (I Sam. 10:5); the Psalm in the Book of Habbakuk, Chapter 3, appointed to the choirmaster with stringed instruments.

The New Testament has references to music as practiced by Jesus and the apostles. A hymn was sung at the Last Supper (Mt. 26:30). Paul and Silas sang while imprisoned (Acts 16:25). The Book of Revelation (15:3) declares that those in Heaven sang the Song of Moses and the Song of the Lamb. Furthermore, the Apocalypse refers to "the voice from heaven like the sound of many waters . . . and the voice I heard was like the sound of harpers playing on their harps" (Rev. 14:2).

Battell notes that both secular and religious authors confirm music as an integral part of early Christian worship. He cites such men as Pliny the Younger, Justin Martyr, Clemens Alexandrinus as documenting music-making among the early Christians. Vocal music, apparently,

---

[4] *Ibid.*, pp. 2–3.

[5] *Ibid.*, p. 4.

was the principal type reported. Battell raises the question concerning the validity of continuing only that method of church music nowadays. An analogy, he states, would be to meet still in caves and upper rooms. Because the early Christians were persecuted, they were forced to be economical in musical resources.

Evidently, Psalm 150 had come under a different interpretation by the Calvinists. Battell had an opportunity to examine a Geneva Bible, and he noted the following marginal inscription by the Psalm:

> David maketh mention of these instruments which by God's Commandment were appointed in the old law, but under Christ the use thereof is abolished in the Church.[6]

According to the interpretation, instrumental music was a part of the Ceremonial Law of Moses that disappeared with the coming of Christ. However, the New Testament does not state that the Law of Moses is to be abolished. Thus, Battell wondered where objections lie regarding church music with instruments. If the objections are for calling people to worship, maybe the church bells should be silenced. If musical instruments had the power to stir up joy in order to praise God better in David's time, Battell asked, can that power have changed since?

The clergyman summarizes the initial section of his sermon by asserting the lawfulness of elaborate church music with a compilation by a certain Mr. Baxter [probably Richard Baxter (1615–1691), a Presbyterian (!) Divine]. The principal items are as follows:

1. God set up instruments of music in His service according to the Ceremonial Laws of Moses.
2. Ceremonies are not only mere institutions, but also a natural help to the spirit of man. If spectacles can be used to aid in reading the Bible, so Music can help direct the soul toward God.
3. Jesus joined with the Jewish people who followed the Ceremonial Laws with respect to music and said nothing against it.
4. Scripture does not forbid the use of instruments.[7]

The second section, shorter than the first, asserts that "Musical Harmony by both voices and instruments is so pleasing and agreeable to that part of man which is most Divine."[8] If music is so agreeable, why

---

[6] *Ibid.*, p. 11.
[7] *Ibid.*, pp. 14–15.
[8] *Ibid.*, p. 15.

not take advantage of its qualities? The early church fathers endorsed music in Christian services, chiefly because it is

> apt to move the Mind to pious Dispositions, and raise it up to a pitch above itself. . . .[9]

Although Battell admits that music is not necessary for worship, the art is "an agreeable attendant and a suitable Ornament to Religious Services."

The conclusion of his sermon, however, hearkens to the reasons why the Puritans refrained from having all but the simplest music in their services. The minds of worshipers, Battell asserts, should not stray from their principal objective for being in church. The same concern was expressed by St. Augustine. "The Heart is the best Psalmist and the inward Affection of the Soul is the best Musick in God's ear. It is purely for the sake of this that the other is used."[10] Therefore, the text set must be understood by the listeners, and church music must be grave and solemn, befitting the House of God.

Ralph Battell favors a policy admitting instrumental and vocal music into worship services. He supports his opinion with scriptural and temporal evidence. At the same time, he agrees with the views of Augustine and Erasmus in their criticism of music interpreted as an end in itself, instead of as a means to an end. The church should ensure that music in services will aid the worshiper, and not be a hindrance.

Battell's sermon is the only composition of the 1693 festivities that has survived. Charles Hickman's discourse is not all that remains from the Cecilian celebrations for 1695. Besides Hickman's sermon, John Blow's *Te Deum and Jubilate* is extant. Furthermore, the ode, *Great Choir of Heaven*, also by Blow, survives. The latter composition is believed to have been the central work performed at Stationers' Hall that year.[11]

Charles Hickman, while not giving his discourse a title, precedes it with an apology to the stewards, who are named. Here, he states that he is sorry for not having much time to think about his sermon, much less having to publish it at their request. "But I know not how you can pardon me for exposing your Names before it: nor yet how you can

---

[9] *Ibid.*, p. 20.

[10] *Ibid.*, p. 24.

[11] Charles H. Biklé, "The Odes for St. Cecilia's Day in London (1683–1703)" (Ph.D. diss., University of Michigan, 1982), Vol. I, pp. 43–44.

pardon me for taking this innocent revenge."[12] He continues by declaring that if the sermon does not meet expectations after second thoughts, it is not a good one.

> That the excellent Musick which they heard worked upon their Affections, and raised their Good Nature above their Judgment, and made them approve that in the Pulpit which they now dislike in the Press: so that in truth, it was not the Sermon that commended the Musick, but the Musick set off the Sermon.[13]

The above assertion not only reveals Hickman as a child of his time regarding the power of music, but also it is a compliment to Blow's *Te Deum and Jubilate*. Since Hickman was asked to put his sermon to press, he says he feels somewhat like Orpheus without his harp; so he must expect to be pulled in pieces.

The clergyman also chooses the initial two verses of Psalm 100 for his text. He calls Joy, Gladness, and Song the three charming ingredients that make up the heavenly banquet.[14]

Some dichotomies exist between the text and religious tradition, he states. One is instructed to be "on guard," while the psalm bids people to indulge themselves. Devotions are taught to be a private affair, yet the verses draw individuals out and make them glad. As a rule, God's presence strikes terror, thus the thought of coming before Him as a proper subject for music is a very strange one. Hickman's objective is to try to resolve the paradoxes by, first, declaring what it means to be joyful in the Lord; second, revealing how necessary it is to serve the Lord with gladness; finally, commenting on how decent and convenient it is to express this joy and gladness with a song. What derives from the above is the direction behavior should take at religious festivities, the cheerfulness one should have approaching religious worship, and the appropriateness of music in services.

Since being joyful is commanded in the text, and is such an innate thing, Hickman contends, religion should not suppress the feeling. He supports the premise that being joyful is good in worship since religion is supposed to show mankind to the best advantage. The day of rest is designed for that purpose as well.

---

[12] Charles Hickman, "A Sermon Preached at St. Bride's Church on St. Cecilia's Day, Nov. 22. 1695." (London: Printed for Walther Kettlby, at the Bishops Head in St. Paul's Churchyard, 1696), no page number.

[13] *Ibid.*, no page number.

[14] *Ibid.*, p. 1.

If true religion is to bring out the best in man, then it should encourage the use and improvement of all faculties. Religious dictates, then, ought not extirpate those passions endowed by nature, but make the feelings spiritual. Thus, Hickman argues, because Christian beliefs and doctrine teach that God is the author of all that is good, and Heaven is the only seat of pleasure, one must be joyful in the Lord if that joy is to be real and lasting. True pleasures benefit both body and spirit. Religion and enjoyment cannot be separated.

True joy will not allow drudgery at worship services, Hickman asserts. The text itself states otherwise by saying, "Serve the Lord with gladness."

> When we come to this House of God, we come, as Jacob calls it, to the *Gate of Heaven*, to the very borders of Paradise, to take a Prospect of those Glories, and Beauties, which adorn the Seat of the Almighty Creator of the World. . . .[15]

This thought, he argues, is a source of genuine pleasure, as compared to sensual gratification only, which the world offers.

Since mankind is imperfect and strivings for this sort of joy fall short frequently, art must provide assistance. Both Battell and Hickman point to the ancient religious practices of the heathen and the Hebrews in which music had an important role. Hickman especially emphasizes the universal application, stating that Psalm 100 is directed to all lands. It was an instinctive practice, both clergymen assert. Music was supposed to "adorn their Religious Worship, and inspire them with pious, exalted, devout Affections; not to gratify their itching Ears; but to refine their Notions, abstract their Thoughts, and prepare their Souls for Heavenly Contemplations."[16] The argument is similar to Battell's, illustrating the power of music.

Hickman postulates that the act of worship itself must be out of the Affections and not out of Reason.

> 'Tis the workings of an exalted Love; the outgoings of an inflam'd Desire; the breathings of a pious Soul, in the extasies [sic] of his Joy and Admiration.[17]

Music, more than any other art form, has the capacity to inspire mankind to such exalted devotional levels, and that is why its practice

---

[15] *Ibid.*, pp. 8–9.

[16] *Ibid.*, p. 12.

[17] *Ibid.*, p. 15.

184 Charles H. Biklé

was retained in the early Christian Church.

The discouragement of instrumental music in churches, Hickman states, is based on the premise that musical instruments are played at secular entertainments. Thus, what is common, is profane. But feasts are to be consistent with religion. Therefore, music likewise is to be compatible. He argues, "Why is it more indecent to use the same instruments, than it is to wear Apparel in the Church as in the Dining Room?"[18]

Charles Hickman declares that he could list more examples endorsing his position regarding music in worship services. He realizes, however, that people are there also to hear the central religious composition for the occasion. The clergyman may have delivered his sermon before Blow's *Te Deum and Jubilate* was performed, for he says,

> I am sensible that 'tis Loss of time for me to speak longer in the Praise of Musick, which, when I have done, will speak much better for itself. . . . And therefore I shall only add (for a conclusion) that we must compose ourselves to hear it, with heavenly, abstracted, devoted minds: For there is something, in Religious Musick, so Divine, something so like the Joys of Heaven, that the Blessed above do not disdain to hold Communion with us, in these Exercises of our Devotion.[19]

The above is an admonition to the listeners; Hickman is speaking directly to the situation and not merely about musical practices in the church. The statement is the first of its kind in the surviving sermons, but not the last.

Charles Hickman has achieved his objective in his discourse and supported his opinion with Scriptural and secular references. Both Hickman and Battell approach the same text in similar ways. Hickman, however, stressed the joyful aspects of worship, whereas Battell dealt principally with vocal and instrumental music as an aid to the churchgoer. Perhaps Hickman emphasizes joy to the extent he does, being mindful that Henry Purcell had died the previous evening, a loss felt acutely, no doubt, by all present.

The last surviving sermon preached at the Musical Society's celebration of St. Cecilia's Day was delivered in the newly reopened St. Paul's Cathedral on November 22, 1699. The year is the only known one in the history of the festival, as sponsored by the Musical Society, that the liturgical service was not held in St. Bride's Church. William

---

[18] *Ibid.*, p. 19.
[19] *Ibid.*, p. 21.

Sherlock, Dean of the Cathedral, was the speaker. His sermon is the only composition for the festivities of 1699 to survive.

The text for his sermon is the opening two verses of Psalm 81:

> Sing aloud unto God our strength, make a joyful noise unto the God of Jacob. Take a Psalm, and bring hither the Timbrel, the pleasant Harp, with the Psaltery.

Sherlock begins his discourse by stating that the praising of God is acknowledged to be the most excellent part of divine worship.[20] Among the reasons why, such praise exercises the best passions of souls in the most perfect manner. Clarification is required, however, on what it means to praise the Almighty. Is it enough, he asks, to praise God by singing and making a joyful noise; or composing the best anthems, then performing them well; or when we feel ourselves transported and ravished with excellent music, performed by the best voices, the choicest instruments, and greatest masters?[21] Should the above be sufficient, he says, praising God would be easy. However, music itself would become the object of praise, or the composition, or the performance. The Dean of St. Paul's addresses the chief concern of the Puritans and others regarding music in church services.

Sherlock admits that he does not want to discourage the use of music in the worship of God, but he desires

> to persuade and direct you to turn the Delights and Charms of Musick into the Raptures of Devotion, which would the most effectually silence all the Enemies of Church-Musick, and Cathedral-Worship. . : .[22]

The statement outlines the objective of his sermon.

If the role of music in church services is to assist the worshiper, one must determine: first, what kind of music is acceptable to God; second, how to promote it; third, how to improve the art for worship purposes. The body of his discourse treats these three considerations.

The melody of the heart is what is pleasing to God, asserts Sherlock. Battell expressed similar thoughts six years earlier. True Christian worship is an application of both mind and spirit. Therefore, the best music consists of lifeless sounds until animated and inspired by

---

20 William Sherlock, "A Sermon Preach'd at St. Paul's Cathedral, November 22, 1699. Being the Anniversary Meeting of the Lovers of Musick." (London: Printed for W. Rogers, at the Sun against St. Dunstan's Church in Fleetstreet, 1699), p. 1.

21 *Ibid.*, p. 3.

22 *Ibid.*, pp. 3–4.

devotion of the heart.[23] If voices and instruments assist toward that end, they are of excellent help, but

> it is only their Subserviency to the Devotion of the Mind, which gives them any Value, or allows them any place in Religious Worship.[24]

Sherlock's second consideration is the promotion of music acceptable in ecclesiastical services. Music in the church has the task of exciting and quickening affections, thus giving a new life and spirit to devotion. Sherlock states that Man is a compound creature, consisting of body and soul. The concept was a dominating one in the Baroque Era. The souls of men, being vitally united to bodies, receive most of their strong feelings from them.

> Words and Sounds have powerful Charms, and give as quick a turn to our Thoughts and Passions, as Sight itself. . . .[25]

Music does have power to raise and calm passions of the mind, he concludes. If so, then devotional music will excite or heighten devotional feelings in the same manner that

> Wanton and Amorous Aires are apt to kindle Wanton Fires; for Nature will act like itself, whether you apply it to Good or Bad Purposes.[26]

While people may speak out against songs that might exert a bad influence, it appears incongruous to condemn church music which is capable of stimulating a devout mind.

The principal application of music in the Old Testament, according to Sherlock, was to assist in worship services. Although the Song of Moses was sung before the giving of the Law, many critics of music in Christian worship based their arguments on the premise that ceremonies with Jewish Law were fitted to the carnal state of the people at that time. The more perfect dispensation of the Gospel removed the need for such rites.[27] However, if singing had been a part of the Mosaic Directives, then

> The Gospel of our Saviour Abrogates nothing of that Law, but such Types as receive their Accomplishment in Christ. . . .[28]

---

[23] *Ibid.*, p. 5.
[24] *Ibid.*, p. 7.
[25] *Ibid.*, p. 7.
[26] *Ibid.*, pp. 8–9.
[27] *Ibid.*, p. 10.
[28] *Ibid.*, p. 11. See also: Mt. 5:17.

Similar reasoning could be applied to criticisms of church music in order to abolish vocal prayer in services, a practice also directed by Mosaic Law.

Echoing Battell, Sherlock states that the early Christian Church dispensed with elaborate music out of necessity. Moreover, the times of persecution did not allow permanent meeting places. When the Christian Church gained in stature, its rites became more elaborate.

The principal objection concerning music in church services, expressed by Erasmus, was to the singing in an unfamiliar language. Since the hearer could not understand what the music was about, his worship was hindered, not helped. The Reformation has solved the problem, says Sherlock. Anthems and prayers are in English.

The third section of the discourse is novel among the several sermons discussed, although Hickman anticipates it briefly. Sherlock proposes how music may and ought to be improved for the purposes of devotion. He addresses composers, performers, and listeners of church music.

Speaking to composers, the Dean admits his lack of musical skill. He wishes to clarify that all the rules which must be followed for excellent music may not apply and be proper for devotional purposes. One must consider notes which are most suitable

> to Excite or Quicken such Passions of Devotion as the Words of the Hymn or Anthem Express. . . . True Devotion is the best Director of that Skill [in music]; for a Devout Mind will judge of the Devotion, as a skilful Ear does of the Musick of Sounds.[29]

It follows that the composer must be inspired to a high level of devotion before putting the notes on paper.

> A Grave, Serious Mind, which is the true Temper of Devotion, is disturbed by Light and Airy Compositions, which disperse the Thoughts; and give a Gay and Frisky Motion to the Spirits, and call the Mind off from the Praises of God. . . .[30]

Sherlock's statement is an apparent contradiction of Hickman's premise of serving the Lord with gladness. Moreover, it appears to be a censure leveled at anthems interspersed with instrumental interludes, a practice begun during the Restoration. The Dean is thankful that the service is grave and solemn, well fitted for devotional purposes.

---

[29] *Ibid.*, p. 19.
[30] *Ibid.*, p. 20.

> And as for more Modern Compositions, the Governors of Churches ought to take care to receive nothing into the Worship of God, but what is fitted to serve Devotion; and this would Effectually Answer the greatest Objections against Church-Musick.[31]

Sherlock next addresses the performers. They must behave devoutly in their duties. Musical instruments, he states, have no life and sense, but they may minister to our devotion, though they are capable of none themselves.[32] The remark is the only one in the sermons elucidating exactly the role of instrumental music in the church. Musicians are called upon to set the example at all times. It is scandalous, he declares, to see those employed daily in the singing of God's praises showing no signs of devotion and exhibiting irreverent behavior. Musicians must be inspired themselves in order to assist worshipers achieve a higher level of devotion. Furthermore, it is offensive to be employed as a church musician, then sing wanton, atheistic songs in other places. Church musicians have consecrated themselves when they accepted ecclesiastical employment.[33]

Sherlock preaches to the listeners of sacred music by stating that their business at church is

> not meerly [sic] to be Entertained with Musick, but to Exercise their Devotions, which is the true end of Church-Musick; to Praise God with the more fervent Passion.[34]

Apparently, some people came to services only to hear the anthem, then departed upon its conclusion. A measure of good was derived from their departure, leaving more room for devout individuals. Sherlock summarizes his attitude on music as an aid to worship with these words:

> Those who find that Musick does not Assist, but Stifle their Devotion, and many such there may be, had much better keep to their Parish-Churches, and prefer Devotion before Musick. For to come to Church without any intention to worship God in His own House, or to pretend to worship Him without Devotion, are great Affronts to the Divine Majesty.[35]

Finally, Sherlock speaks to the gathering before him. People who profess to be lovers of music should consider what the true end of music

---

[31] *Ibid.*, p. 21. Similar exhortations are heard in our own day.
[32] *Ibid.*, p. 21.
[33] *Ibid.*, pp. 22–23.
[34] *Ibid.*, p. 23.
[35] *Ibid.*, p. 25.

is, he declares, and to improve it to the noblest purposes. Music lovers ought to be devout men "if they love Musick for that which is most valuable in it, and its last and noblest End."[36]

In summary, all three sermons endorse both vocal and instrumental music in church services. The first and last, however, temper their endorsements by declaring that music is to be a means to an end and not an end in itself. Paradoxically, none of the discourses make mention of St. Cecilia by name, or allude to her legend. The sermons, at least by implication, appeal to an attitude of tolerance. Religious factions should not impose their views on everyone. Instead, each worshiper may determine for himself whether or not music assists him in his devotions. Thus, the "Lawfulness and Expediency" of church music rests with the individual.

The attitude favoring music in worship is not new, since its origins are in antiquity. A generation later, Johann Sebastian Bach would re-echo the sentiment expressed in the sermons, declaring:

> The aim and final reason, as of all music, . . . should be nothing else but the Glory of God and the recreation of the mind.[37]

---

[36] *Ibid.*, p. 26.

[37] Hans T. David and Arthur Mendel, eds., *The Bach Reader* (New York: W.W. Norton and Company, 1966), p. 33.

CHAPTER THIRTEEN

RANGE AS A STRUCTURAL DETERMINANT IN BEETHOVEN'S PIANO MUSIC*

William S. Newman

The University of North Carolina at Chapel Hill

One of the early signs of Beethoven's growing independence in his musical style is the increasing need to compromise with the traditional five-octave range (contra-F to f³) of the harpsichord and early piano. Already in the first of the three sonatas dedicated to Haydn (in 1796), Beethoven seems to have been thwarted by a ceiling that compelled him to transpose down instead of up (as in the initial idea of the finale in Op. 2. No. 1. which first repeats a 5th higher, mm. 2–4, but soon after must repeat a 4th lower, mm. 50–52 — Example 1).

Granted that Beethoven lived at a time of noteworthy advances in all aspects of piano construction, it still seems significant that no such champing at the bit manifests itself in the keyboard music of his main 18th-century predecessors. J.S. Bach, far from straining the five-octave limit — which may not have been available on all his harpsichords, anyway — confined himself with seeming ease to no more than four and a third octaves (contra A to c³) in a work as brilliant as his "Italian Concerto." Haydn did make use of the full five octaves in his keyboard

---

* This paper was originally read on October 31, 1975, during a panel discussion chaired by the late Edwin M. Ripin at a national meeting of the American Musicological Society in Los Angeles. It has been revised and updated for this publication.

Example 1. Op. 2/1/iv/2–4 and its altered transposition in mm. 50–52. This example and also Example 3. 4. and 5. all from Hans Schmidt's edition of the first volume of Beethoven's Thirty-Two Sonatas in *Beethoven Werke*, are reproduced with the kind permission of G. Henle Verlag in Munich.

music, yet showed only passing interest in exploiting the added high notes on the Broadwood piano that was lent to him during his second London visit, in 1794 to 1795. Thus, in the one oft-cited instance, the late Sonata in C (Hoboken XVI/50), those added notes appear only in a single recurring phrase, in the ebullient finale, which extends to g³ three times and a³ once. There they stand out like a sore thumb (Example 2).[1]

Example 2. From Haydn's single adventure into higher ranges, in his Sonata in C Hoboken XVI/50/iii/76–80, reproduced from G. Feder's complete edition of Haydn's Piano Sonatas Vol. III, with the kind permission of G. Henle Verlag in Munich.

As for Mozart, who probably never was exposed similarly to upper extensions of the five octaves, that master managed easily to stop at f³, occasionally accommodating the fixed limit with subtle adjustments of his thematic material, but not with bold transpositions. To be sure,

---

[1] Cf. Horst Walter in *Haydn-Studien* II, 268–70.

Mozart eventually had a pedal board made for his piano that permitted him to extend the bass line, or, more important, to reinforce it at the octave as far down as contra-C.[2] However, his purpose seems to have been not to extend or expand his ideas, but to enrich their sonorities. In any case, whatever he may have added below contra-F in actual performance, it left no trace in his autographs or early printed editions.[3]

Apart from a single curious extension upward by one half-step in Op.

Example 3. Treatment of a peak in the exposition and in the recapitulation of Op. 13/i/105–113 and 257–62.

---

[2] Cf. Eva and Paul Badura-Skoda. *Interpreting Mozart on the Keyboard* (New York, 1962), pp. 13–15.

[3] Badura-Skoda, *Interpreting Mozart*, pp. 204–205.

14/1/i/41,[4] Beethoven had to cope with the five-octave limit throughout his first twenty piano sonatas with opus numbers, or through Op.
49. For instance, in Example 3, when he reaches the recapitulation in
the first movement of *Sonate pathétique* (mm. 257–62), he has to forgo,
in the tonic key, the sense of peaking that he has been able to create, in
the relative major key, in the corresponding measures of the exposition
(105–113). On the other hand, by similar reasoning, Beethoven actually
seems to exploit the range limitation in the analogous measures (97–106
and 278–86) of the first movement in Op. 10, No. 3. This time he has to
interrupt the ascent, in the exposition's dominant conclusion, just short
of the ceiling, whereas, in the recapitulation's tonic conclusion, he can
find room ("upward mobility" in the arts?) to complete that ascent to
its peak (Example 4).

Example 4. Making the best of the limited range, in Op. 10/3/i/97–106 and
278–86.

Less frequent in those early sonatas is evidence that Beethoven found
the bass range inadequate. Thus, in measures 268 to 274 of that same
movement, he had to content himself by replacing four of the
descending octaves that he obviously intended (cf. mm. 90–91) with
single notes that would not exceed his lower limit of contra-F (Example
5). But as with Mozart, so with Beethoven the need to

Example 5. Early signs of range limitations in the bass, in Op.
10/3/i/268–74 (with the lowest notes added in parentheses by the modern
editor).

extend the bass range seems to have been more a matter of sonority than
of thematic integrity or fulfillment.

Throughout the composition of his first twenty sonatas, up to 1803,
Beethoven showed no awareness — at least none that I have been able
to document — of the high notes occasionally added to contemporary
English pianos, partly to accommodate a new interest in four-hand
playing. For that matter, he seems not yet to have responded to any
English pianos at all, although he surely must have learned about the
Broadwood and other makes, if in no other way, after Haydn's return
from London in 1795 and after his own visit to the court of King
Friedrich Wilhelm II in Berlin in 1796. By mid 1803 he had received his
French Erard piano, with its extension a 5th higher, up to c^4. That c^4 was
a 3d higher than he soon would be requiring in order to realize fully the
symphonic ideas in his "Waldstein Sonata" Op. 53. Furthermore, by
1803 the German pianos, including Beethoven's eventual favorite in
Vienna, the Streicher, were catching up with the English pianos in range
and even surpassing them.[5] Only four years later Beethoven could call
for an e^4, just short of a total six-octave range. The e^4 was needed to
provide a stunning top to the runs that climax the longer of the two
cadenzas he supplied for the "Rondo" in his piano transcription of his
Violin Concerto (Example 6).[6]

[5] Cf. William S. Newman, "Beethoven's Pianos Versus His Piano Ideals," in
the *Journal of the American Musicological Society XXIII* (1970), 484–504.
[6] See m. 15 in this cadenza, which is published in Willi Hess's *Beethoven:
Supplemente zur Gesamtausgabe* X (Wiesbaden, 1969), 73–74.

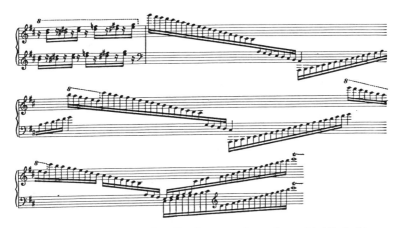

Example 6. Extended range in a Beethoven cadenza (mm. 14–15), in his transcription of his Violin Concerto, reproduced from Willy Hess's Supplement to the *Beethoven Gesamtausgabe,* Vol. X, with the kind permission of Breitkopf & Härtel in Wiesbaden.

Thereafter, Beethoven extended his ranges a little at a time, as the need arose and as it became possible on the pianos at his disposal. However, prior to the Viennese Graf lent to him in 1825, *no* piano is known to have been at his disposal that encompassed both extremes of his widest piano range, six and a half octaves from contra-C to f^4. That is the over-all range of his "Hammerklavier Sonata" Op. 106. Apparently he was disappointed, among other things, still to find a range of only six octaves on the new Broadwood piano he received in 1818, about the time he was completing Op. 106.[7]

The mention of contra-C in Op. 106 reminds us of an essential fact about how Beethoven dealt with his keyboard ranges. He called for no extension of the bass range before his last five piano sonatas, from 1816. That he realized how innovational such bass extensions would be then is suggested by his letter in January of 1817 requesting Tobias Haslinger to insert the letter names beside the new lower bass notes in the finale of Op. 101, in the original Steiner edition of that year.[8] The letter names still show up faintly in the autograph (on p. 24, mm. 223–28) and in the Steiner edition (reduced to only one "contra E," on p. 15). Now the low range was needed for a deeper melodic foundation as well as for a fuller sonority (Example 7). But unlike the higher and higher

---

[7] Cf. Newman, "Beethoven's Pianos," p. 493.

[8] Cf. Emily Anderson (ed. and trans.), *The Letters of Beethoven*, 3 vols. (London, 1961), II, p. 660.

Example 7. Low range and a deeper melodic foundation, in Op.
101/iv/223–28. This example and also Example 9 and 10 are reproduced
from B.A. Wallner's edition of Beethoven's Thirty-Two Piano Sonatas Vol.
III with the kind permission of G. Henle Verlag in Munich.

ranges that Beethoven, Cramer, Dussek, and other cultivators of the
new piano had been advocating,[9] the lower ranges — only a 4th lower
at most in Beethoven's time — had come into use more slowly, partly
because the composers had demonstrated less need and partly because
current piano makers found the lower ranges a little more difficult to
incorporate in their piano designs.[10]

It is important to our topic — to the influence of range on the very
structure or melodic shape of Beethoven's piano music — to observe at
this point how his compromises with range decreased as the available
ranges increased. In his later works there is little evidence of dissatisfac-
tion with the piano in this respect at least. Obviously, Beethoven did not
seek increased range for novelty's sake as, for exmaple, Dussek did in
his less serious moments. The few compromises that still appear are
concessions in details to different makes of pianos. Thus an *ossia* had to
be supplied for the early English editions of piano sonatas Opp. 106 and
111 wherever the range goes above c⁴ (as at Op. 106/i/46–47, in
Example 8).[11]

Example 8. An extreme range and an *ossia*. in Op. 106/i/46–47; after the
original edition of the Regent's Harmonic Institution, London, 1819.

---

[9] Cf. William S. Newman, *The Sonata Since Beethoven*, 3d ed. (New York,
1983), pp. 88–89; *Haydn Studien* II, pp. 269–70 (Horst Walter).

[10] Cf. Arthur Loesser, *Men, Women and Pianos* (New York, 1954),
pp. 226–67.

[11] The *ossia* in Op. 111/i/132 appears in both extant autographs as well as in
the original editions published by both Clementi and Schlesinger.

It is pertinent, too, at this point to observe that in his later years Beethoven considered as one reason for a new edition of his works the possibility of eliminating the compromises in his earlier sonatas by exploiting the increased ranges now available to him. But he never quite realized that edition. Perhaps, among other reasons, he may have decided against the range alterations, dismissing them as stylistic incongruities in music still oriented basically to the five-octave range.[12]

In summary, increases in the piano's range permitted Beethoven to arrive at the proper-size canvas for his composing. He was not primarily a miniaturist. As he expanded the scope of his musical thinking, or — if such an abrupt shift of metaphors can be pardoned — as he planned ever broader strategies, he required larger and larger fields for his battles. Color for its own sake does not seem to have interested him to the same extent, whether it was in the new higher tones that he called "too much piccolo" in Czerny's arrangements or in the new lower tones that were lending a quality of mysticism to the piano writing of young Romantics like Dussek and Schubert.

It is not merely that deafness blocked Beethoven from knowing adequately the newer sounds of the newer pianos. But even as the composer of the sensitively colorful "Sinfonia pastorale," he thought

Example 9 New depths of range, new freedom to roam, in Op. 101/iv/352–59.

---

[12] Cf. Otto Erich Deutsch, "Beethovens gesammelte Werke — des Meisters Plan und Haslingers Ausgabe," in *Zeitschrift für Musikwissenschaft* XIII (1930–31), pp. 60–79; also, Donald S. MacArdle (ed.), *Beethoven as I Knew Him . . . by Anton Felix Schindler* (Chapel Hill, 1966), pp. 402 and 444.

first and foremost in architectonic terms, with both color and chiarascuro serving him primarily as means to that end. To twist the metaphors still a bit more, Beethoven found in the new ranges the needed *Lebensraum* for his operations. When he ends his Piano Sonata in A Op. 101 on a slow trill in the bass over a pedal on contra-E (mm. 347–58), he is leaving room for the curiously wistful figure that leaps about in the right hand (Example 9). When he spreads the hands further and further apart, finally down to contra-G and up to b-flat[3], starting with the triple trill in the transcendental close of his Piano Sonata in C Minor Op. III (mm. 112–120), he is filling the space it takes to move us all the way from this mundane world to an ethereal, unknown world beyond (Example 10).

Example 10. Simultaneous descent and ascent into the extremes of range, in Op. 111/ii/112–120.

19TH- AND 20TH-CENTURY MUSIC

CHAPTER FOURTEEN

SEALING PUSHKIN TO HIS PLACE*

Robert William Oldani

Arizona State University

In the summer of 1868, three months before beginning work on Alexander Pushkin's *Boris Godunov*, Modest Mussorgsky set to music the first scene of Nikolai Gogol's prose comedy *The Marriage*. Imitating Alexander Dargomyzhsky's setting of Pushkin's tragedy in verse *The Stone Guest*, Mussorgsky attempted nearly a word-for-word setting of Gogol's text. After finishing the scene, he set forth, in a series of letters to friends, a philosophy of text setting to which he expressed allegiance for the rest of his life. He writes to Lyudmila Shestakova, for example, on 30 July, 1868:

> Here is what I would like. That my characters speak on stage as living people speak, but at the same time, that they speak so that the character and force of their intonation, underscored by the orchestra . . ., attain their goal directly, that is, my music must be an artistic reproduction of human speech in all its most subtle windings, that is, *the sounds of human speech*, as the outward manifestations of thought and feeling, must become, without exaggeration or coercion, truthful and accurate *music*, but artistic, highly artistic. . . .
>
> Now I am working on Gogol's *Marriage*. The success of Gogol's speech depends on the actor, on his correct intonation. Well, I want to seal Gogol to his place and to seal the actor to his, that is, to speak musically in such a way that you will not speak differently, and to speak as

* The author read a preliminary version of this paper at the annual meeting of the Midwest Slavic Conference, Chicago, 6–8 May 1983.

> Gogol's characters want to speak. . . . This is living prose in music . . ., a reproduction of simple human talk.[1]

Soon after he had written these lines, however, Mussorgsky abandoned *The Marriage* because of his growing interest in *Boris Godunov*. He had given up trying to seal Gogol to his place and would now try to seal Pushkin to his. My goal in this article is to show something of how he made the attempt.

But before turning to *Boris*, we must consider further its predecessor. Described on the manuscript's title page as an "experiment in dramatic music in prose,"[2] *The Marriage* demonstrates on page after page what we may call the composer's *empirical* manner, that is, that part of his harmonic, melodic, and rhythmic style which seems to derive from experimentation at the piano. Throughout the work, Mussorgsky attempts to suggest the prosody of the text in the rhythm of its vocal setting. Apparently preoccupied with creating a "speechlike" setting, he writes jagged vocal lines that are filled with tonally unstable intervals: tritones, augmented seconds, diminished fourths, and the like. He does not attempt to compose melodies having balanced phrases, but goes to great length to avoid them. He naively tries to depict phrases of text in the music. For example, when Podkolyosin, the comic hero, is told that after he is married he surely will have a little bird in his home, the bird's chirping is imitated in the piano. Perhaps in an attempt to maintain forward motion, Mussorgsky shuns conclusive cadences, both in the vocal parts and in the harmony. Indeed, the harmony is virtually an unbroken stream of dissonances; some of the most striking discords occur when the text suggests irritation, unpleasantness, or falsehood. Form depends primarily on the divisions and subdivisions of the text.

Few passages illustrate so many of the traits of *The Marriage* better than the closing measures of Scene 2, in which the matchmaker Fyokla tells Podkolyosin, to his horror, that he has gray hair. Metric and tonic accent reinforce in the vocal parts the accented syllables of the text, with unaccented syllables grouped in chains of short, equal note-values between the accented ones. Furthermore, in order to avoid introducing

---

[1] Modest Petrovich Musorgskii, *Literaturnoe nasledie* [Literary heritage], ed. by A.A. Orlova and M.S. Pekelis, 2 vols. (Moscow: Muzyka, 1971–72), I, 100. I have used the Library of Congress transliteration system, without diacritical marks, throughout the documentation.

[2] Modest Petrovich Musorgskii, *Zhenit'ba* [The Marriage], ed. by Pavel Lamm (Moscow: "Muzyka," 1965), p. 9.

a secondary accent, unknown in Russian, the composer never places an unaccented syllable at the beginning of a beat. Thus, in a measure of 4/4 meter, if an accented syllable falls on the first or third count, succeeding unaccented syllables are squeezed in "after the beat" on succeeding counts. The melodic contour of both vocal parts is jagged, with unstable augmented and diminished intervals in nearly every measure. Tonal ambiguity persists throughout the passage, and dissonance is used in the harmony to mirror Podkolyosin's distaste for the irritating words "gray hair." The scene ends with even stronger dissonances as the agitated Podkolyosin goes off to find a mirror in order to prove his hair is *not* gray (see Example 1).

The result of this experiment in dramatic music in prose is a disjointed work in which music, in the words of César Cui, "is so closely joined to the words . . . that, considered alone, without the words, it loses half its value and occasionally becomes incomprehensible."[3] As a piece of musical theater, *The Marriage* seems stillborn, and one suspects that Mussorgsky may have agreed. In a letter to Lyudmila Shestakova, he described the work as a cage in which he was imprisoned. He was even more explicit in a letter to his friend Vladimir Nikolsky, dated 15 August 1868:

> You don't cook a soup without preparation. This means in preparing oneself for work, even though it be Gogol's *Marriage*, a most capricious thing for music, wouldn't you be accomplishing a good deed, that is, wouldn't you be drawing nearer to your cherished and vital goal? It's possible to say to this: And why is everything only a preparation — it's about time to do something! The trifling little pieces were preparations; *The Marriage* is a preparation; whenever will something be ready? To this there is one answer: *the force of necessity*; perhaps someday it too will be ready.[4]

The Marriage turned out to be Mussorgsky's final preparation. When he began to compose *Boris*, only a few months after interrupting work on the Gogol text, he had retreated from the experimental extremes of the earlier work. Though one sees in *Boris* the influence of *The Marriage* in such features as the predominantly syllabic, *parlando* text setting and the many passages of empirically derived harmony, one nevertheless must acknowledge that these features are not injected with

---

[3] César Cui, *La musique en Russie* (Paris: G. Fischbacher, 1880), p. 109. In the passage quoted Cui is discussing Dargomyzhsky's *Stone Guest*, but the description applies equally to *The Marriage*.

[4] Musorgskii, *Literaturnoe nasledie*, I, 103.

Example 1. Modest Mussorgsky. *The Marriage*: closing measures of scene two.

the same grim determination as in *The Marriage*. By attempting to set a virtually unaltered prose comedy, Mussorgsky made the mistake of adding music to a literary work that was already self-contained. He may have believed that his music resulted in "an artistic reproduction of human speech," but in fact it was superfluous, serving merely to slow the pace of Gogol's humor without providing the degree of emotional intensification of which music is capable. In *Boris*, he avoids extremes of disjointed recitative, unresolved dissonance, and naive representation of text. He has discovered that while the sectionalization of the text may form the principal delineation in the musical form, this delineation can be reinforced by musical means so that the result, while remaining "closely joined to the words," no longer "loses half its value and occasionally becomes incomprehensible" without them. We shall attempt to confirm these points as we now turn to *Boris Godunov*.

Mussorgsky adapted his libretto for *Boris Godunov* primarily from Alexander Pushkin's tragedy of the same name. Because of circumstances that need not be detailed here, the composer completed two versions of the opera, an initial version finished in 1869 and a revision published in 1874.[5] We may summarize the main differences between the two versions as follows: the scene in front of St. Basil's Cathedral appears only in the initial version; the two Polish scenes and the scene in Kromy Forest appear only in the revision; the scene in the tsar's quarters is extensively rewritten in the revision; the remaining scenes exhibit various cuts and addition. Several details, moreover, are brought into the revision from Nikolai Karamzin's *History of the Russian State*, and the later text strays further from Pushkin than does the earlier. We shall center our examination of the opera in Boris's monologue "Dostig ya vyshei vlasti [I have attained the highest power]" from the scene in the tsar's quarters.

The composer's initial setting of this text already shows a retrenchment from the extremes of *The Marriage*. We scarcely see the unstable augmented and diminished intervals so prevalent in the vocal lines of *The Marriage*. A specific key, G-sharp minor, and clear tonal organization replace the ambiguity of *The Marriage*'s *ad hoc* harmony. Themes that return elsewhere in *Boris Godunov* — reminiscence themes — bring cohesiveness to this monologue. By contrast, in *The Marriage* recurring themes are treated clumsily, and they remain little more than calling cards for the various characters. The only feature brought unchanged into the initial *Boris* from *The Marriage* is Mussorgsky's consistent use of agogic, metric, and tonic accent to reinforce the prosody of the text. The text itself is not set word-for-word,

---

[5] For further information on this and related matters, see my articles "Mussorgsky's *Boris Godunov* and the Russian Imperial Theaters," *Liberal Arts Review*, no. 7 (Spring 1979), pp. 6–24, and "Editions of *Boris Godunov*," in *Musorgsky: In Memoriam, 1881–1981*, ed. by Malcolm H. Brown (Ann Arbor: UMI Research Press, 1982), pp. 179–213.

but is altered by many minor additions, deletions, transpositions, and paraphrases (see Example 2).[6]

In the revised version of this monologue, Mussorgsky deviates even further from Pushkin, as Example 3 reveals. From the changes he has made in the poet's text, one infers that the composer's work on *The Marriage* and on the initial *Boris* taught him that a good play is not necessarily by itself a good libretto. Since words cannot be sung as quickly as they can be spoken, compression and condensation are essential in a libretto. Conversely, since musical setting can distort words, the extensive development of ideas is out of place. In compensation for the loss of verbal subtlety, however, strong emotions can be given musical expression in opera. Thus a good libretto develops a tension between information and reflection and takes advantage of music's ability to convey what cannot be said in words.

Perhaps because of such considerations, Mussorgsky in this revision eliminates much of the information contained in Pushkin's text and writes instead a reflective monologue of increasing psychological tension, a "criminal arioso" for the "criminal Tsar Boris," as he puts it in one of his letters.[7] Nearly two-thirds of the monologue's text is by the composer. Only the first twelve lines are drawn from Pushkin, and they do not occur together but appear throughout the first three-quarters of the poet's text.[8]

Mussorgsky's Boris is a pitiable creature tormented by guilt and regarding the calamities that have befallen his country as punishments for his sin. Yet his concern for his daughter demonstrates the compassion, even tenderness, of which he is capable; her grief comes to mind before his own, and he speaks of her as his "pure dove." After the first third of this monologue (the part derived from Pushkin), Boris's mind becomes so excited that he sometimes fails to complete his thoughts. Fears and agonies are half-formed and then left suspended in mid-air as his mind races ahead to another thought, perhaps unrelated

---

[6] The changes that Mussorgsky introduced throughout Pushkin are discussed in detail in Caryl Geppert Emerson, "Boris Godunov and a Poetics of Transposition: Karamzin, Pushkin, Mussorgsky" (Ph.D. dissertation, The University of Texas at Austin, 1980), pp. 326–415.

[7] Musorgskii, *Literaturnoe nasledie*, I, 122–23.

[8] Mussorgsky's practice of freely combining passages of Pushkin with his own text is further illustrated in the text of the revision's hallucination scene, part of which is paraphrased from the last twelve lines of Pushkin's "Dostig ya vyshei vlasti," part of which is taken from an entirely different scene in the play, and part of which is by the composer himself.

Example 2. Texts by Pushkin and Mussorgsky (1869) of the monologue "I have attained the highest power" (Pushkin's text appears in Roman letters. Lines preserved by Mussorgsky are underscored; Mussorgsky's additions are shown in italics.)

tortured

I have attained the highest power. Six years
Have I reigned peacefully; but happiness
Dwells not within my soul. Even so in youth
We greedily desire the joys of love,
But scarce have quelled the hunger of the heart
With momentary pleasure, when we grow
Cold, weary, and oppressed. In vain the wizards
Promise me length of days, days of dominion
Untroubled and serene--not power, not life

Neither glory's seduction nor the shouts of crowds

Bring me happiness; I forebode the wrath of Heaven
and woe. For me there is no joy. I thought
To give my people glory and contentment,
To gain their loyal love by generous gifts,
But I have put away that empty hope;
The living power is hateful to the mob;
Only the dead they love.

vain
O, how We are but fools
When our heart shakes because the people clap
Or cry out fiercely. When our land was stricken
By God with famine, perishing in torments
The people uttered moan. I opened to them
The granaries, I scattered gold among them,
Found labor for them; yet for all my pains
They cursed me! A fire consumed their homes;

A storm scattered their wretched hovels--

I built for them new dwellings;

I provided for all their wants,
I watched over and protected them,

then
They blamed me for the fire! Such is the
Judgment of the mob! Seek its love, indeed!
I thought within my family to find solace;
I thought to make my daughter happy by wedlock.

I prepared a joyful wedding feast for my daughter,
For my tsarevna, my pure dove.
But God did not predestine this comfort for me.

Like a tempest, Death took off her bridegroom.
And at once a *stealthy* rumor *considered* me
Guilty of her grief--*righteous God--*
Me, me, her unhappy father!

Whoso dies, I am the secret murderer of all;
I hastened Fyodor's death,
I poisoned my sister-queen, the nun--

I killed the unhappy tsarevich, the baby--always I!

Ah! now I feel it; naught can give us peace
Mid worldly cares, nothing save only conscience!
When clear, she triumphs over wickedness,
Over dark slander; but if she be found
To have a single stain, then misery!
With what a deadly sore the soul doth smart;
The heart with venom filled, beats like a hammer
And dins reproach into the buzzing ears;

The head is spinning, nausea tortures one,
And bloody boys revolve before the eyes;
And one would flee, but refuge there is none!
Oh, pity him whose conscience is unclean!

SOURCE: *The Poems, Prose and Plays of Alexander Pushkin*, selected and edited with an introduction by Avrahm Yarmolinsky, translation of *Boris Godunov* by Alfred Hayes, The Modern Library (New York: Random House, 1936), pp. 352-53. I have made a few small changes in Hayes's text.

Example 3. Mussorgsky's revised text (1874) of the monologue "I have attained the highest power."

R

I have attained the highest power,
Six years have I reigned peacefully,
But happiness dwells not within my tortured soul.
In vain the wizards promise me
Length of days, days of dominion untroubled and serene.
Not life, not power, neither glory's
Seduction nor the shouts of crowds
Bring me happiness.
I thought within my family to find solace,
I prepared a joyful wedding feast for my daughter,
For my tsarevna, my pure dove.
Like a tempest, Death took off her bridegroom.

A_1

X
The hand of God, the awful Judge is on me,
The verdict on my sin-stained soul is spoken. . . .
Impenetrable darkness enwraps me;
Oh, could some ray of light flash comfort.

Y
My heart is filled with sorrow,
With grievous affliction my soul is weary,
Some kind of secret trembling. . . .
All awaiting something. . . .

X
With fervent prayers to the saints in the highest
I thought to subdue this fearful anguish.

Y
In brilliance of pomp and power, none to thwart me,
I, Russia's ruler, with bitter tears entreated pardon.

Z
Yet discontent: boyars revolting,
Lithuanian plots and secret intriguing,
Famine, plague, and perfidy beset me.
Like a prowling beast the folk roam the land, stricken with disease,
And destitute, hungering Russia groans! . . .

X
And in this fearful misery, sent down by God
In punishment on us the guilty
All lay reproach on me, and they call out,
They curse in all the squares the name of Boris!

A_2

Night brings no rest to me; there stands in the darkness
A bloody child before my sleepless eyes.
Hands clasped in anguish, eyes terror-stricken,
Begging for mercy and mercy was not granted!
Horribly gapes his wound,
His agonised shriek is never silenced. . . .
O God above, O my God!

SOURCE: M. P. Moussorgsky, *Boris Godounov*, vocal and piano score strictly according to the original version, English by M. C. H. Collet (London: J. & W. Chester, Ltd., 1926), pp. 124-30. I have made several changes in Collet's translation in order to show more clearly the relationship between the initial and revised forms of Mussorgsky's text.

to its predecessor. Then the image of the blood-stained child fills his mind. This most powerful and gripping image will not leave him; it possesses him and drains him of strength, leaving him exhausted and crying to God.

Pushkin's Boris, by contrast, is more restrained and rational. Cataloging everything that has gone wrong in his six-year reign, he senses that events have moved beyond his control. His own worries come to mind before his daughter's, and he refers to her simply as "my daughter." Complaining that the people have no reason to blame him for what fate has brought to Russia, he declares that he has done all that he could to alleviate their suffering only to find himself slandered for his pains. The tone seems almost bitter: he is annoyed that he is blamed for occurrences that he could not prevent and further annoyed that he is prevented from finding solace by his conscience and visions of "bloody boys."

The music of this revised monologue shows even further retrenchment from *The Marriage* than that of the initial version. The monologue is in three sections corresponding to the divisions in text marked in Example 3 with the sigla R, A_1, and A_2. The first section, marked R, incorporates text and music from the initial version of the monologue and is close in style to that version. Changes of meter appear in order to permit the composer to lay agogic stress on a few important accented syllables in the text (Example 4); there is no extensive repetition of musical phrases within the passage, although reminiscence motives that will return in the Death scene are introduced; and the passage modulates, beginning in iv/iv of the monologue's principal key, E-flat minor, then passing through its subdominant, finally cadencing on its dominant at the words "Death took off her bridegroom." The second part of the monologue, consisting of the text

Example 4. Modest Mussorgsky. *The Marriage*: excerpt from the Monologue "I Have Attained the Highest Power."

Example 5. Modest Mussorgsky. *The Marriage*: excerpt from the
Monologue, "I Have Attained the Highest Power."

marked A$_1$ in Example 3, is in E-flat minor and exhibits a design both
sectional and symmetric. If we mark the music beginning at the phrase
"The hand of God" with the letter X, the music at "My heart is filled
with sorrow" with the letter Y, and the music at the words "Yet discontent" with Z, then this central portion of the monologue emerges in
the sectional form X-Y-X-Y-Z-X. A throbbing undercurrent of triplets
in all but the first X section gives rhythmic unity to the passage and
provides a rhythmic link between this section and the monologue's final
part, consisting of the text marked A$_2$ in Example 3. The final section
also centers on E-flat, but the appearance of the highly chromatic
motive associated throughout the work with Boris's guilt (Example 5)
provides contrast and helps separate the A$_1$ section from the A$_2$ section.
In sum, Mussorgsky has written in this monologue a piece of music in
which a character at first relates circumstances and events in a relatively
free-flowing *parlando* and then expresses his emotions in more
melodious, lyrical, and symmetric music. If this sounds very much like
a recitative/aria pair from Italian opera, I believe it is no coincidence.[9]

As reference to the score will confirm, Mussorgsky has come a long
way from *The Marriage*. He has retained a style of vocal writing which
emphasizes musically the accented syllables of the text while passing
over the unaccented ones, and he still uses note values that are in
keeping with the pace of "simple human talk." But he has placed this
apparently naturalistic declamation in a musical setting that is more
closely in line with Western models than we sometimes think. Those

---

[9] Scholars only recently have begun to explore the connections between the
Mighty Handful and composers whom they professed to abhor. See, for
example, Roland John Wiley, "The Tribulations of Nationalist Composers: A
Speculation Concerning Borrowed Music in *Khovanshchina*," in *Musorgsky:
In Memoriam*, pp. 163–77.

models are apparent in small things, as we have just seen in Boris's monologue, and in large. Although I lack the space to discuss the structure of the entire opera, I can say that, in my view, reminiscence themes, tonal-dramatic associations, a comprehensive key scheme, and the division of the text into musico-dramatic periods all play significant roles in *Boris Godunov*, whereas they are negligible in *The Marriage*. In short, *Boris* represents a synthesis of the composer's empirical manner with elements rooted in the tradition of Western music. The composer neither falls into mere imitation of Western models nor founders in a sea of experimentation. Although it may be too presumptuous to maintain that Mussorgsky has sealed Pushkin to his place, perhaps we can agree that he has come as close to the goal as anyone else.

CHAPTER FIFTEEN

TONAL STRUCTURE AND FORMAL DESIGN IN JOHANNES BRAHMS'S OP. 118, NO. 6

Patrick Miller

Hartt School of Music
University of Hartford

Numerous descriptions have been written to capture the character and mood of Johannes Brahms's Intermezzo in E-flat minor, Op. 118, No. 6.[1] While acknowledging the work as "an outstanding masterpiece," James Friskin and Irwin Freundlich comment on "the mysterious color and atmosphere of the opening and the powerful central climax."[2] Karl Geiringer describes the piece as "nebulous" with a "wonderfully enhanced middle section."[3] Denis Mathews considers Op. 118, No. 6 a work of "high drama and pathos" and one that is

---

[1] The first edition of Op. 118 was published by N. Simrock (Berlin) in November, 1893, with the publication number 10054. Brahms's copy of the first edition of Op. 118 is located in the Gesellschaft der Musikfreunde (Vienna). An autograph of Op. 118, No. 6 is located in the Staatsbibliothek Preussischer Kulturbesitz Musikabteilung (West Berlin) and is catalogued at that institution within a collection of Brahms piano pieces designated as *Mus. ms. autogr. Brahms 12.*

[2] James Friskin and Irwin Freundlich, *Music for the Piano: A Handbook of Concert and Teaching Material from 1580 to 1952*, ("The Field of Music," vol. V [New York: Holt, Rinehart and Winston, 1954]), p. 98.

[3] Karl Geiringer, *Brahms: His Life and Work*, (2nd ed., rev. and enl. London: George Allen and Unwin Ltd., 1948), p. 221.

Plate 1. First page of Op. 118, No. 6 from Brahms's personal copy of the first edition of Op. 118. Reproduced by permission of Gesellschaft der Musikfreunde (Vienna).

Plate 2. Page of an autograph of Op. 118, No. 6 showing mm. 41–56 of Part II. Reproduced by permission of Staatsbibliothek Preussischer Kulturbesitz (West Berlin).

"profoundly tragic" and "secret-laden."[4] The Intermezzo conveys all of the aesthetic qualities the foregoing writers have ascribed to it. On a more concrete level, it is a piece that does not easily give up its secrets. Since the melodic, harmonic, and formal aspects of the piece are so skillfully wrought and integrated, the selection, identification, and description of individual musical elements often seem like elusive activities. Certain features seem clear and simple, other aspects reveal a nebulous complexity of associations. While not attempting to dispel the poetic beauty of the Intermezzo, an investigation of tonal and formal aspects does uncover unique and remarkable relationships. In the present study, tonal structure refers to both the large-scale functional association of keys and the local arrangement of individual chords. Formal design refers to the organization of melodic-rhythmic elements

---

[4] Denis Matthews, *Brahms Piano Music*, ("BBC Music Guides," no. 37 [Seattle: University of Washington Press, 1978]), pp. 49, 69.

into phrases and the harmonic relationships among phrases.

Perhaps the most unusual feature of the Intermezzo is its formal design of three parts which are organized within a tonal framework of two broad key areas. The Intermezzo consists of the following formal arrangement:

Part I (mm. 1–20),
Modified repetition of Part I (mm. 21–40),
Part II (mm. 41–62)
Part III (mm. 63–80),
Coda (mm. 81–86).

Mm. 1–54 are in the dominant key area of B-flat minor, mm. 55–86 are in the tonic key area of E-flat minor.[5] During Part I, the only discernible authentic cadence occurs in mm. 12–13 (mm. 32–33 of the modified repetition of Part I). The initial presentation of Part I concludes in mm. 20–21 with an apparent secondary dominant-seventh chord of an E^b minor triad. The absence of a D ♮ in the B^b seventh chord in m. 20, however, supports the interpretation that Part I can be heard in B-flat minor while the two chords in mm. 20–21 can be analyzed as a diatonic progression, b^b: i^7–iv. The modified repetition of Part I continues in B-flat minor while Part II commences with a G^b major chord, b^b: VI, in m. 41. During Part II, the key of E-flat minor is established with an authentic cadence in mm. 54–55.

Example 1 illustrates the formal arrangement of phrases within each part. The form of Part I, as well as the form of the modified repetition of Part I, is an enlarged period.[6] Phrases 1, 2, and 3 constitute a series of antecedent phrases. The elided authentic cadence in mm. 12–13 is followed by two consequent phrases, Phrases 4 and 5. Except for a change in the accompanimental figuration in mm. 23–24 and the omission of the diatonic progression of b^b: i^7–iv in mm. 40–41, the modified repetition of Part I conforms to the material in mm. 1–20. Part I commences with a period, Phrases 1 and 2, and continues with a single phrase (Phrase 3) that concludes with a perfect authentic cadence

---

[5] In Op. 118, No. 1, the opening ten measures of the Intermezzo are in the mediant key area of C major; an impression of the tonic key of A minor is not established until m. 11 with the occurrence of a: V^9. The presentation of the tonic key area may be heard at the outset of all pieces in Opus 118 except Nos. 1 and 6.

[6] A summary analysis of the phrase structure of the Intermezzo may be found in Percy Goetschius, *The Homophonic Forms of Musical Composition*, Issue 16 (New York: G. Schirmer, Inc., 1926), p. 97.

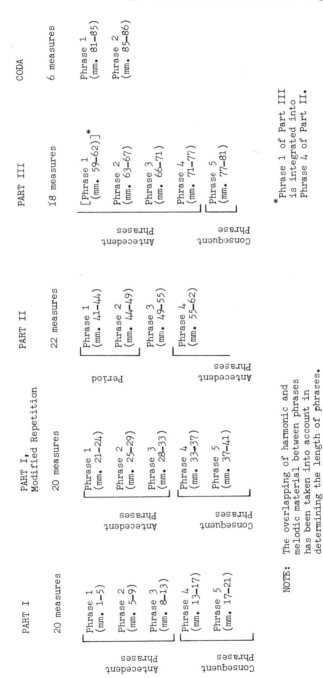

Example 1. Brahms. Opus 118, No. 6: Formal Arrangement of Phrases.

in E-flat minor. The fourth (final) phrase of Part II is remarkable in that it is not only a sequential repetition of the preceding third phrase, but is also tonally and formally linked to Part III by being the first of a series of antecedent phrases. Furthermore, Phrase 1 of Part III, which melodically conforms to Phrase 1 of Part I and its modified repetition, is integrated, with melodic and harmonic modification, into the final phrase of Part II. Part III, like Part I, is an enlarged period; however, whereas the enlarged period of Part I consists of three antecedent phrases and two consequent phrases, the enlarged period of Part III contains four antecedent phrases and one consequent phrase. Even with the contrasting formal arrangement of Part II and the overlapping formal and tonal elements of Parts II and III, the overall formal design of the Intermezzo is one of similar proportions: Part I (modified repetition of Part I), 20 measures; Part II, 22 measures; Part III, 18 measures. The Intermezzo concludes with a six-measure Coda in which the first phrase melodically conforms to Phrase 1 of Parts I and III.

The theme of the Intermezzo is presented during the opening phrase (mm. 1–5).[7] Example 2 contains an illustration of the twelve-note theme, commencing on g^{b2}, and a linear analysis of the theme. The basic linear structure of the theme consists of a descending third with an intervening descending passing note.[8] Throughout the Intermezzo, the

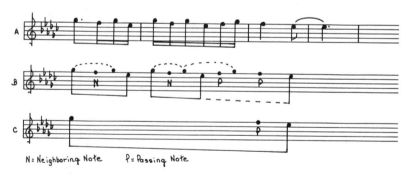

N = Neighboring Note   P = Passing Note

Example 2. Brahms. Opus 118, No. 6: Theme, Mm, 1–4.

---

[7] Melodic-rhythmic features have been primary factors in determining the musical content of phrases while harmonic characteristics of phrases have been determinants in perceiving formal relationships among phrases. As indicated in Example 1, the overlapping of harmonic and melodic material between phrases has been taken into account in identifying the length of phrases.

[8] A linear analysis of the theme is also given in Allen Forte and Steven E. Gilbert, *Introduction to Schenkerian Analysis* (New York: W. W. Norton & Company, 1982), p. 24.

Example 3. Brahms. Opus 118, No. 6: Linear Analysis, Mm. 7–9.

interval pattern of a descending third is a prominent and recurring musical element. The second phrase of the Intermezzo (mm. 5–9) not only contains a presentation of the theme, beginning on g^{b1}, but also consists of a series of descending thirds beginning with great B^b (m. 7, second beat). Example 3 contains an illustration of the music in mm. 7–9 and a linear analysis of the passage. A G^b–F–E^b linear pattern, the basic linear structure which was traced through the theme, may be observed within the series of descending thirds. Two significant features of the passage are the linear descent from G^b to C and the omission of an intervening passing note between B^b and G^b.

During the unfolding of the theme in mm. 1–4, a fully-diminished seventh chord (A ♮–C ♮–E^b–G^b) is presented and continued into the second phrase. The resolution of this seventh chord, which may be analyzed as b^b: vii°7, to an E^b minor chord (m. 7, second beat) seems to serve two harmonic purposes.[9] First, the deceptive resolution to an E^b minor harmony allows for a postponement in the arrival of a B^b minor tonic harmony (which occurs with the authentic cadence in mm. 12–13). Second, the durational emphasis upon E^b minor for five beats (in conjunction with descending thirds from B^b) not only fore-shadows the role of E^b minor as tonic harmony, but also suggests the momentary illusion of an apparent E^b minor tonic.

Within a broader perspective, the diminished seventh chord preced-ing the series of descending thirds beginning in m. 7 can be seen as a component of a large-scale harmonic complex for the Intermezzo which involves the linear successions of A ♮–A^b, C ♮–C^b, and F–F^b. The harmonic complex is illustrated in Example 4. The observation of harmonic relationships involving these linear successions, in

---

[9] For an analysis of Part I in which the opening ten measures are considered in the key of E-flat minor, see Douglas Green, *Form in Tonal Music: An Introduc-tion to Analysis*, (2nd ed.; New York: Holt, Rinehart and Winston, 1979), pp. 64–65.

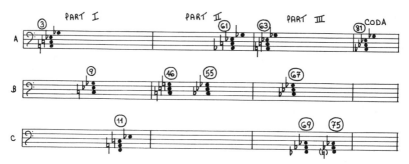

Example 4. Brahms. Opus 118, No. 6: Distinct Seventh Chords and Triods.

conjunction with observations of formal design and register, seems essential to a discussion of the unique tonal and formal aspects of the Intermezzo.

While an A ♮ fully-diminished seventh chord (b♭: vii°⁷) first appears during the initial phrase of Part I, an A♭ major-minor seventh chord (e♭: IV⁷) occurs in m. 61 during the final phrase of Part II which is integrated with Phrase 1 of Part III. An A ♮ fully-diminished seventh chord (e♭: vii°⁷/V) immediately follows in m. 63 which clearly establishes a sense of reprise. The linear succession of A♭ – A ♮ between the seventh chords in mm. 62–63 is the most dramatic instance of linear harmonic succession in the Intermezzo. During Phrase 1 of the Coda, an A♭ minor-minor seventh chord (e♭: iv⁷) may be observed briefly in m. 81. The seventh chord in m. 81 functions as a subdominant harmony and assists in the expansion of the tonic harmony during the opening measures of the Coda.[10]

The initial appearances of these three distinct seventh chords, as illustrated in Example 4a, are distributed throughout the Intermezzo at strategic locations: A ♮ fully diminished seventh chord (Part I), A♭ major-minor seventh chord (Part II), and A♭ minor-minor seventh chord (Coda). As illustrated in Example 4b, a similar, though more complex, distribution may be observed with regard to triads containing either C ♮ or C♭ as root. The unfolding of an E♭ minor triad (b♭: iv) in mm. 7–8 is followed by the initial presentation of a C ♮ diminished triad (b♭: ii°) in mm. 9–10.[11] While the occurrence of C major harmony (b♭: V/V) in mm. 46–47 of Part II does not correspond formally to the

---

[10] The idea of harmonic expansion refers to the elaboration of a chord through such procedures as repetition, arpeggiation, interpolation of diatonic and/or chromatic chords, and the interpolation of a non-modulating sequential passage.

occurrence of the C ♮ diminished triad in Part I (m. 9) or the C♭ major triad in Part III (m. 67), the C major harmony of Part II is preceded by E♭ minor harmony (b♭: iv). During Part II at the outset of the tonic key area (m. 55), an E♭ minor triad (e♭: i) is followed by a C♭ major triad (e♭: VI). The introduction of the singular and brief occurrence of C♭ major harmony at this point in Part II is an essential factor in establishing the tonic key area. The next presentation of C♭ major is more extensive and is located in mm. 67–68 (Part III, Phrase 3) and formally corresponds with the C ♮ diminished triad of mm. 9–10 (Part I, Phrase 3). As illustrated in Example 4b and 4c, the initial presentation of the C ♮ diminished triad in Part I and the singular occurrence of the C♭ major triad in Part III are directly and respectively related by fifth root movement to the F major-minor seventh chord (b♭: V^7) in mm. 11–12 (Part I) and the F♭ major triad (e♭: bII) in mm. 69–70 (Part III).

Large-scale linear harmonic relationships are demonstrated most explicitly with the pitch successions F-F♭, A ♮ –A♭, and C ♮ –C♭ associated with the occurrences of an F major-minor seventh chord (b♭ : V^7) and an F♭ major triad (e♭ : bII). These chords may be heard as harmonic and chromatic intensifications of the pitch-class F derived from the descending passing note F of the theme. Throughout the Intermezzo, the descending F of the theme is given emphasis through duration and metric accent. In the initial presentation of the theme (mm. 1–4), the descending passing F occurs as the eleventh note of the twelve-note melody. The initial occurrence of an F major-minor seventh chord in m. 11 commences with the eleventh notes (d♭^{2} –b♭^{1}) within a modified presentation of the theme beginning with durational extension on b♭^{2} –g♭^{2} in m. 8. The presentation of the F♭ major triad in mm. 69–70 formally corresponds to the F major-minor seventh chord of mm. 11–12.[12] A brief occurrence of an F diminished triad may be interpreted in m. 75 (third beat) within the expansion of an A♭ minor triad (e♭ : iv) beginning in m. 74 (third beat).

While the harmonic content of Phrase 3 of Part I clearly establishes B-flat minor with descending fifth root movement (b♭:ii°–V^7–i), Phrase 3 may be seen as consisting of two phrase members.[13] Melodically each

---

[11] A harmonic analysis of b♭: ii^{ø7} (C ♮-E♭-G♭-B♭) could be made for the harmonic content of mm. 9–10. An analysis of b♭: ii° is presented here on the basis of the left-hand figuration in mm. 9–10.

[12] As if to mitigate the harmonic intensity of the Neapolitan harmony, Brahms indicates *dolce* at the onset of the chord in m. 69.

[13] Phrase member is used to refer to a melodic-harmonic component within a phrase. An important factor in determining members within a phrase is the

Example 5. Brahms. Opus 118, No. 6: Linear Analysis, Mm. 8–12.

phrase member is an elaboration of a series of descending thirds which may be traced to the descending third introduced in Phrase 2. Example 5 is a linear analysis of the music in the right-hand part mm. 8(third beat)–12(second beat). The first phrase member may be seen as a melodic elaboration of B♭–G♭–E♭–C ♮, while the second member may be viewed as an elaboration of G♭–E♭–C ♮. Each of the two phrase members employs the rhythm of the theme with durational extension at the beginning of each member and durational curtailment at the end of the second member.[14] As illustrated in Example 5, the thematic linear pattern of a descending third with intervening passing note is now not only employed within a succession of descending thirds, but each succession of descending thirds is intensified with a texture of simultaneous thirds. A salient feature of the melodic elaborations is the introduction of appoggiaturas. In Example 5, the resolution of appoggiaturas is shown by arrows.

With the arrival of b♭: i in mm. 12–13, the first antecedent phrase of Part I harmonically consists of a series of triads with root movement in descending thirds, b♭: i–VI–iv–ii°. The musical impression of this phrase is one of a *harmonic magnification* of the descending third pattern B♭–G♭–E♭–C ♮. The harmonic rhythm of each triad is three beats in duration. An illustration of the harmonic and melodic descending third patterns of the phrase is given in Example 6. The phrase consists of three phrase members, the second and third members being

---

repetition, either exact or modified, of identifiable melodic-harmonic material.

[14] The G♭ major chord heard briefly at m. 8(third beat) is the first triadic simultaneity to be presented in the Intermezzo. This simultaneity could be regarded as a foreshadowing of G♭ major (b♭: VI) heard at the outset of Part II, m. 41. Likewise, the brief succession of g♭1–b♭1–d♭2 at the outset of the modified repetition of Part I (m. 23, second beat), which appears within the harmonic context of b♭: vii°7, could also be regarded as a foreshadowing of G♭ major at the beginning of Part II.

Example 6. Brahms. Opus 118, No. 6: Descending Third Patterns,
Mm. 12–16.

presented in sequential repetition. The third member is modified and
extended, and basically conforms to the rhythm of the theme. Each
melodic phrase member contains two descending thirds and consists of
a texture in thirds. In comparison to the melodic elaborations of the
preceding phrase, the musical impression of the melodic phrase
members in mm. 13–16 is one of *melodic compression*. A salient feature
of each melodic phrase member is the absence of appoggiaturas.

The theme occurs during the second antecedent phrase of Part I
(mm. 17–21). As shown in Example 7a, a linear pattern of descending
thirds (D^b–B^b–G^b) with intervening descending passing notes ($C^\natural$–A^b)

Example 7. Brahms. Opus 118, No. 6: Harmonic and Registral Similarities.

may be traced through the phrase and into the beginning of Phrase 1 of
the modified repetition of Part I. In contrast to the descending third
harmonic progressions of the preceding antecedent phrase, the second
antecedent phrase basically consists of an unfolding of b♭: i. An important feature of the phrase is the repetition of the note F which occurs in
the one-line, small, and great octaves on the first beats of mm. 17, 18,
and 19 and which is durationally extended throughout each measure.
The emphasis of F during the final phrase of Part I may be heard as
further intensifications of the pitch-class F. Furthermore, the
occurrences of F during the final phrase is a continuation of the melodic
extension (beginning in m. 16, second beat) of the third phrase member
of the preceding phrase. The connection between the first and second
antecedent phrase, which is shown in Example 7a, is achieved in
mm. 16–17 with the melodic succession of a major sixth (g♭–e♭¹) to an
octave (f, f¹).

While the final phrase of Part I begins with a *melodic* overlapping
from the preceding phrase, the final phrase of Part I concludes with a
harmonic overlapping into the first phrase of the modified repetition of
Part I. The harmonic progression in mm. 20–21 of b♭: i⁷–iv, shown in
Example 7a, brings about a subtle emphasis upon an E♭ minor triad
giving the impression of an apparent E♭ minor tonic. As shown in
Example 7b, the descending passing note A♭ in m. 40(second beat),
which moves to G♭ major harmony at the opening of Part II, appears
without B♭ harmonic support.[15] During Part II at the close of Phrase 3
(mm. 54–55), the modulation between the dominant and tonic key
areas, shown in Example 7c, is brought about with the harmonic
progression of a B♭ major-minor seventh chord to an E♭ minor triad, e♭:
V⁷–i. The progression of b♭: i⁷–iv in mm. 20–21 can be heard as a foreshadowing of the progression e♭: V⁷–i in mm. 54–55. These two

---

[15] The harmonically unsupported A♭ in m. 40 is one of the two modified
passages during the repetition of Part I (mm. 21–40). The other modification is
the figuration in the left-hand passage in mm. 23–24. Although the harmonic
setting for mm. 23–24 is b♭: vii°⁷, three G♭ triadic patterns may be traced
through the figuration as shown in the following example.

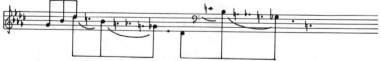

While the ascending G♭ triadic arpeggiation in m. 23(second beat) may be heard
as foreshadowing the arrival of G♭ major at the beginning of Part II (m. 41), the
descending semitones between B♭–G♭ in mm. 23–24 may be heard as foreshadowing the descent of A♭ in m. 49(second beat).

harmonic progressions not only exhibit similarities in their registral placement, but important formal and tonal features: b♭: i⁷–iv in mm. 20–21 occurs at the end of Part I and overlaps with the beginning of the modified repetition of Part I, the modulation involving e♭: V⁷–i in mm. 54–55 occurs between the penultimate phrase of Part II and its sequential repetition.

As illustrated in Example 7d, the final phrase of Part II concludes with a modified harmonic progression in fifths. The tonic-subdominant harmonic relationship employed at the close of Part I is retained. However, the tonic seventh in mm. 59–60 is a half-diminished seventh chord (e♭: i⁰⁷, the subdominant harmony in mm. 60–61 is an A♭ major-minor seventh chord (e♭: IV⁷). The IV⁷ is linearly related (A♭–A ♮ succession) to the A ♮ fully-diminished seventh chord which is reintroduced in m. 63 as e♭: vii°⁷/V and which establishes a sense of formal reprise. Nevertheless, the momentary harmonic impression of the modified tonic and subdominant seventh chords at the conclusion of Part II is that of an apparent progression of ii⁰⁷–V⁷ in D-flat major.

Throughout Part I and the modified repetition of Part I, it is possible to trace the *descending* third pattern of B♭–G♭–E♭–C ♮ with intervening descending passing notes. This recurring linear pattern with its various melodic and harmonic elaborations may be regarded as the unifying musical idea for Part I of the Intermezzo. During the B-flat minor key area of Part II, elaborations of an *ascending* third pattern of B♭–D♭–F–A ♮ may be observed. The final phrase of Part II, which is the first phrase of the E-flat minor key area, contains a transposition of the ascending third pattern, E♭–G♭–B♭–D ♮. An illustration of the melodic and harmonic outlines for each of the phrases of Part II is given in Example 8. Various third patterns are shown in all four phrases. The beginning of each phrase is indicated by the appropriate measure number; barlines are given in order to assist in comparing the analytical illustrations with the score.

The first and second phrases of Part II constitute a period with a half cadence in m. 44 and an elided perfect authentic cadence in mm. 48–49. A unifying harmonic feature of the last phrase of the modified repetition of Part I and the opening period of Part II is harmonic progressions in descending thirds (b♭: i–VI–iv–V/V). The extension and harmonic elaboration of the B♭–G♭–E♭–C ♮ third pattern of Part I into the opening phrases of Part II are combined with the initial melodic presentation of an *ascending* third pattern from B♭. In a broad sense, the basic harmonic progression during the antecedent phrase (mm. 41–44) is b♭: VI–V. A series of harmonic progressions in

Example 8. Brahms. Opus 118, No. 6: Melodic and Harmonic Outlines of Part II, Mm. 40–62.

ascending fifths (b♭: VI–III–VII) in conjunction with a melodic succession in ascending thirds (b♭¹–d♭²–f²) is introduced at the outset of the phrase.[16] These ascending fifth harmonic progressions foreshadow the harmonic progressions in *ascending thirds* introduced at the outset of the third and fourth phrases of Part II. An ascending passing note between b♭¹ and d♭² does not occur during the antecedent phrase; the phrase, however, concludes with a repetition of c ♮² with the harmonic support of b♭: V.

The consequent phrase in mm. 44–49 consists of a single ascending

---

[16] The occurrence of b♭: VII in m. 42(third beat) is the initial presentation of A♭ major in the Intermezzo. An A♭ major sonority (e♭: IV) is expanded during mm. 59–62 of the fourth phrase of Part II.

third span, b^{b1}–d^{b2}. While the antecedent phrase concluded with a repetition of c ♮², the consequent phrase commences with repetitions of b^{b1} supported by the descending third harmonic progression b^b: VI–iv. A conspicuous harmonic element of the consequent phrase is the occurrence of C major (b^b: V/V) in mm. 46–47. The introduction of the harmonic function b^b: V/V may be heard not only as an intensification of the cadence, but also as an intensification of the passing note c ♮² between b^{b1} and d^{b2}. Furthermore, the introduction of a C major triad instead of a C diminished triad may be heard as a signal for. the temporary cessation of descending third patterns from B^b.

Phrase 3 (mm. 49–55) of Part II is the only phrase within Parts I, II, and III that may be considered an independent phrase that is not organized within a period structure.[17] The phrase begins with b^b: i and concludes with a perfect authentic cadence in the tonic key of E-flat minor. The third phrase, however, is related through sequential repetition to the fourth (final) phrase of Part II. While the chromatic modulation in m. 54 may be considered one of the important harmonic features of the phrase, the incorporation of the theme of the Intermezzo during the final two measures is perhaps the most important melodic aspect of Phrase 3. The integration of the theme at this point in Part II may be regarded as a foreshadowing of reprise of the opening thematic and harmonic material of Part I. Phrase 3 may be analyzed as consisting of two subdivisions: the first subdivision (mm. 49–51) is comprised of a broad harmonic progression of b^b: i–V⁷, the second subdivision (mm. 51–55) contains a broad harmonic progression from b^b: V⁷ to e^b: i. The first subdivision is linked to the second subdivision through the expansion of b^b: V⁷ beginning in m. 51 (second beat) and the continuation of thirty-second note rhythmic subdivision.[18]

As illustrated in Example 8c, a harmonic progression in ascending thirds (b^b: i–III–V) occurs on the first beats of mm. 49–51. In addition, the triadic presentations of b^b: i ánd b^b: III are each followed with a descending third progression: b^b: i–VI, III–i. There are similarities between the opening measure (m. 41) of the first phrase of Part II and the opening measure (m. 49) of the third phrase which impart a sense of formal unity between the first and third phrases. While the rhythmic and registral features of m. 41 are retained in m. 49, the conspicuous

---

[17] The Coda (mm. 81–86) contains two independent phrases.
[18] The first and second subdivisions may be viewed as overlapping with b^b: V⁷, m. 51 (second beat), and the subsequent addition of a minor ninth, G^b, to the chord, m. 51 (third beat).

modifications in m. 49 include the contour inversion of the b♭: i arpeggiation in the left-hand figuration (first beat) and the durational compression of b♭: VI from three beats to two beats.[19] The first subdivision (mm. 49–51) of Phrase 3 may be viewed as consisting of three phrase members. The initial phrase member, which consists of the harmonic and melodic material in m. 49, is duplicated through modified sequential repetition in m. 50, and is finally duplicated through free sequential repetition in m. 51 with the preservation of rhythmic figuration during the first and second beats of m. 51. Whereas two ascending thirds (b♭1–d♭2) were melodically presented during the outset of the first phrase of Part II, the melodic content of the first subdivision (mm. 49–51) contains a succession of three ascending thirds, b♭1–d♭2–f2–a ♮2. As in Phrase 1 of Part II (Example 8a), Phrase 3 (Example 8c) does not contain a passing note c ♮2 between b♭1–d♭2.

The melodic emphasis during the second subdivision (mm. 51–55) is upon the descending third G♭–E♭, the interval pattern for the theme. The theme (commencing on g♭2) is introduced in mm. 53–54; however, at the point (eleventh note of the theme) where the descending passing note f2 would occur, e♭2 is sounded (m. 55, first beat) and is supported by e♭: i within the perfect authentic cadence. The registral preparation for the introduction of the theme in m. 53 is brought about through repeated emphasis of g♭2 in mm. 51–52 The arpeggiated recurrence in mm. 51–52 of an A ♮ fully-diminished seventh sonority, a sonority which was presented with the initial occurrence of the theme in Part I, is now heard as a harmonic component within b♭: V9 which occurs as a triadic simultaneity with the unfolding of the theme (m. 53, first beat). A striking feature of the harmonic support for theme is the appearance of an E♭ minor chord (b♭: iv) in m. 53(third beat). The appearance of this E♭ minor chord is emphasized through the linear succession of F–E♭ in the left-hand part on beats one and three of m. 53. The E♭ minor chord assists in the expansion of b♭: V9; however, an A ♮ fully-diminished seventh chord (b♭: vii°7) appears in place of b♭: V9 in m. 54. The metric placement and octave doubling of A ♮ in m. 54(first beat) clearly signals the melodic direction toward the B♭ major-minor seventh chord (e♭: V7) at the close of m. 54.[20]

---

[19] Beginning in m. 47(third beat), an octave doubling *above* the melody occurs.

[20] The tritone succession E♭–A ♮ in mm. 53–54 is presented in a doubling occurring in the great and contra octaves and can be considered a foreshadow-

The placement of a chromatic modulation at the cadence of Phrase 3 in conjunction with the sequential repetition of the phrase adroitly conceals the arrival of the tonic key area. Furthermore, the use of syncopation in m. 54 conceals the melodic descent of F to E♭ during the perfect authentic cadence. While the F of the theme in m. 54(third beat) appears as an ascending passing note between E♭–G♭, the syncopated occurrence of e♭: V⁷ with G♭ conceals the voice leading of F *down* to E♭. As shown in Example 8c, the thematic G♭ with e♭: V⁷ is a nonharmonic tone (escape tone) in relation to the preceding thematic F.

While the fourth (final) phrase (mm. 55–62) of Part II is basically a modified sequential repetition of Phrase 3, Phrase 4 is the first phrase in the tonic key area. As in Phrase 3, Phrase 4 contains two subdivisions: the first subdivision (mm. 55–57) consists of a broad harmonic progression of e♭: i–V⁷, the second subdivision (mm. 57–62) is comprised of a broad harmonic progression from e♭: V⁷ to e♭: IV⁷. As shown in Example 8c, a melodic succession of ascending thirds from E♭, E♭–G♭–B♭–D ♮, is presented during the first subdivision with harmonic progressions in ascending thirds (e♭: i–III–V). While the material in mm. 55–58 may be described simply as a sequential repetition a fifth lower of the material presented in mm. 49–52, it is significant that the tonic key area is confirmed with the material in mm. 55–58 being organized in ascending thirds from E♭.

As in Phrase 3 of Part II, the first and second subdivisions of Phrase 4 are linked by the harmonic expansion of a major-minor seventh chord. While the second subdivision of Phrase 4 does include the theme, the second subdivision from the second beat of m. 58 differs from the second subdivision of Phrase 3. By examining Example 8d, it can be seen that that the third note of the theme, g♭², is approached by a linear succession commencing on c♭² in m. 58(second beat).[21] In m. 59, the first note of the theme is modified (in comparison with the initial presentation of the theme in mm. 1–4) with regard to pitch (e♭² instead of g♭²), metric placement (syncopated occurrence on the second half of the first beat instead of on the first beat), and duration (eighth-note duration instead of a dotted eighth). However, in m. 59 the beaming in the right-hand part and the placement of the crescendo marking

---

ing of the succession of E♭–E♭ in mm. 60–61 which also occurs in a doubling appearing in the great and contra octaves.

[21] In mm. 7–9 of Part I (see Example 3) and mm. 27–29 of the modified repetition of Part I, a linear succession from G♭ *down* to C ♮ may be observed occurring on the beat in the left-hand figuration (great octave, G♭–F–E♭–D♭–C ♮).

clarifies the opening of the theme within the linear ascent to g^{b2}.

The harmonies presented during the linear ascent from c^{b2} to g^{b2} may be heard as elaborations of harmonic progressions occurring at similar formal locations. The harmony occurring with c ♮² (m. 58, third beat) is e^b: V^7/V and assists in the expansion of e^b: V. At the outset of m. 59, e^b: V is followed by the syncopated occurrence of A^b major (e^b: IV) with the modified first note of the theme, e^{b2}. The expansion of A^b major continues, with harmonic elaboration, until the conclusion of the theme in m. 62.[22] The expansion of A^b major during the final measures of Part II is accomplished by a harmonic progression in fifths, E^b half-diminished seventh chord to A^b major-minor seventh chord. During the expansion of A^b major in mm. 59–62, harmonic progressions may be analyzed within the temporary key area of D^b major: D^b: V_2^4–I_6–$ii^{ø7}$–V^7. While the progression of an E^b seventh chord to an A^b seventh chord (altered tonic to altered subdominant) at the close of Part II recalls the tonic to subdominant progression at the close of Part I, the *descending* fifth harmonic progressions (B^b major down to E^b seventh *down to A^b major*) at the close of Part II may be heard as a transformed recurrence of the *ascending* fifth progressions (G^b major up to D^b major *up to A^b major*) presented at the opening of Part II.

As shown in Example 1 (p. 217), all of Phrase 4 of Part II may be considered the first antecedent phrase of an enlarged period that concludes with a consequent phrase involving the expansion of e^b: i in mm. 77–81. The incorporation of the theme with the expansion of e^b: IV into the final phrase of Part II obscures an impression of reprise. Except for the modification of the theme in m. 59, the complete presentation of the theme in mm. 59–62 registrally corresponds to the two-line octave presentation of the theme stated during mm. 1–4. An interpretation can be made that the melodic content of Phrase 1 of Part III (which registrally corresponds to the melodic content of Phrase 1 of Part I) is integrated into the harmonic content (descending harmonic progression in fifths) of the second subdivision of the final phrase of Part II. Except for the modification of the left-hand figuration in mm. 63–64, a definite sense of reprise is established with Phrase 2 (mm. 63–67) of Part III which formally corresponds both melodically *and harmonically* to Phrase 2 (mm. 5–9) of Part I.

Phrase 3 (mm. 66–71) of Part III, like Phrase 3 of Part I, contains

---

[22] A similar harmonic situation of dominant harmony followed by subdominant harmony appears with the theme in the third phrase of Part II, m. 52 (b^b: V^9–iv).

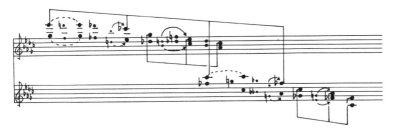

Example 9. Brahms. Opus 118, No. 6: Descending Thirds, Patterns, Mm. 66–70.

two phrase members: the first phrase member (mm. 67–68) contains a presentation of e^b: VI, the harmonic content of the second phrase member (mm. 69–70) is e^b: bII. As illustrated in Examples 4b and 4c (p. 220), Phrase 3 of each part contains a harmonic progression in descending fifths: C to F in Part I, C^b to F^b in Part III. The arrival of C^b major instead of a C ♮ diminished triad in m. 67 negates any impression of the dominant key area, while F^b major in m. 69 could be heard as a chromatic intensification of the pitch-class F.

The melodic material of Phrase 3 of Part III, as in Phrase 3 of Part I, consists of two phrase members that overlap. Each melodic phrase member employs the rhythm of the theme. In contrast to Phrase 3 of Part I, a texture in sixths is primarily used for the first six notes of each melodic phrase member. As illustrated in Example 9, on the basis of registral proximity a pattern of descending thirds down from E^b (e^{b2}–c^{b2}–a^{b1}–f^1) may be traced through the opening six notes of each melodic phrase member. Also in contrast to Phrase 3 of Part I, a pattern of consecutive descending thirds cannot be detected within each melodic phrase member. The opening six notes of each melodic phrase member may be analyzed as an elaborated arpeggiation from the *third* to the *root* of the harmony of each phrase member and as a foreshadowing of the harmonic support of G^b–E^b descending third within the final phrase of Part III and during Phrase 1 of the Coda.

While the unfolding of C^b major in mm. 67–68 contributes to the confirmation of an E-flat minor key area, the occurrence of the opening melodic note (e^{b3}) of Phrase 3 also confirms the establishment of the tonic key area. The e^{b3} in m. 66 can be perceived as the final note within a large-scale ascending line based upon ascending thirds that can be traced through Part II. Example 10 is an illustration of the ascending line which commences with b^{b1} in m. 41 with ascending thirds to a ♮^{2} (b^b: V, F MAJOR) in m. 51 which may be heard connecting with the octave doubling above b^{b1}, *b^{b2}* (e^b: III, G^b MAJOR) in m. 56. The

Example 10. Brahms. Opus 118, No. 6: Ascending Line, Mm. 41–66.

ascending line continues with an ascending third to d $\natural^3$ (e^b: V, B^b MAJOR) in m. 57 and finally to e^{b3} (e^b: VI, C^b MAJOR) in m. 66.

The most significant difference in the phrase relationships between Part III and Part I is that the enlarged period of Part III contains only a single consequent phrase (Phrase 5 of Part III, mm. 77–80), whereas Part I contains two consequent phrases. The change in phrase relationships between Parts I and III can be seen by comparing the fourth phrases of each part. Phrase 4 (mm. 13–16) of Part I commences with *B^b minor* harmony (b^b: i), in conjunction with the elided authentic cadence from the preceding phrase, and contains harmonic and melodic elaborations of the descending third pattern B^b–G^b–E^b–C $\natural$. The harmonic content of Phrase 4 (mm. 71–76) of Part III is basically the expansion of *B^b major* harmony (e^b: V) followed by A^b minor harmony (e^b: iv).

The general harmonic effect of Phrase 4 of Part III is an intensification of the dominant in preparation for the tonic expansion of the following consequent phrase. An illustration of third patterns contained in the melodic material of Phrase 4 is given in Example 11. An analysis of the third patterns within the melodic content of Phrase 4 corroborates the harmonic intensification. With the establishment of the tonic key area beginning in m. 55, harmonic and melodic elaborations of ascending and descending third patterns from E^b are employed. Example 11 reveals that third patterns commencing from E^b *and B^b* may

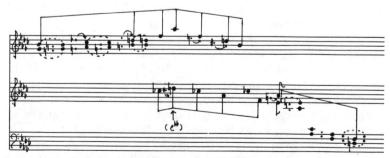

Example 11. Brahms. Opus 118, No. 6: Third Patterns, Mm. 71–76.

be traced through the melodic content of Phrase 4. In a cumulative sense, both formally and tonally, the melodic content of Phrase 4 may be heard as a combination of third patterns associated with the dominant key area (pattern initiated by B^b) and third patterns associated with the tonic key area (pattern from E^b). The outset of Phrase 4 recalls the linear melodic ascent from B^b to D^b heard during Phrase 2 of Part II (Example 8b, p. 226) while the ascending d ♮^{2}-f^2-a^{b2} arpeggiation recalls the linear melodic ascent (D^b-E^b-F, F-G ♮-A ♮) presented during Phrase 3 of Part II (Example 8c, p. 226).

A prominent melodic feature of Phrase 4 is the occurrence of tritones. Beginning in m. 73, the role of C^b within the expansion of e^b: V could be described as simply the addition of a dissonant ninth. The resultant diminished-seventh sonority (D ♮-F-A^b-C^b) and deceptive progression (e^b: iv$_6$) in m. 74(third beat) recall the opening harmonic progression of m. 7, b^b: vii^{o7}-iv. While a pattern of *ascending* thirds from B^b can be clearly detected, the pattern of *descending* thirds from E^b is more difficult to ascertain. As shown in Example 11, a series of descending thirds from e^{b1} can be traced from the occurrence of e^b: iv$_6$ (m. 74, third beat). In view of the descending thirds from e^{b3} during Phrase 3 and from e^{b1} during Phrase 4, an intervening succession of descending thirds could be conjectured by considering the d ♮^{2} in m. 73(second beat) as an enharmonic modification (d ♮^{2} = e^{bb2}) and a harmonic interlocking with e^b: V^7.

The occurrence of subdominant harmony has been observed as an important linking element between formal parts: b^b: i^7-iv in mm. 20-21, e^b: IV-IV^7 in mm. 59-62. The deceptive progression in m. 74 of Phrase 4 may be heard as not only a delayment in the presentation of e^b: i, but also as a linking harmony to the fifth (final) phrase of Part III. Example 12 is an illustration of the general melodic and harmonic content of Phrase 5 of Part III and Phrase 1 of the Coda. The theme (commencing on G^b) occurs complete in both phrases and is

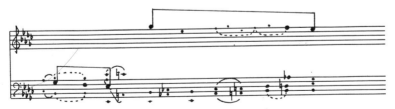

Example 12. Brahms. Opus 118, No. 6: General Melodic and Harmonic Content, Mm. 76-83.

represented in Example 12 by the descending third G^b–E^b with intervening passing note F. In m. 79 with the twelfth note of the theme, subdominant harmony occurs with a^b and c^{b1} and the subsequent chromatic linear successions great A $\natural$ and c $\natural^2$. The chromatic linear succession in mm. 79–80 recalls the linear succession (e^b: IV^7–$vii°^7/V$) between Phrases 1 and 2 of Part III. The first phrase of the Coda, as shown in Example 12, opens with the expansion of e^b: i with subdominant harmony and continues with the recurrence of the linear successions of A^b–A $\natural$ and C^b–C $\natural$ in conjunction with the harmonic progression e^b: $ii°_6$–V_6/V. In m. 83 the descending passing note of the theme is supported by e^b: V^7 and followed by e^b: i with great B^b as the lowest note which recalls the initial occurrence of an E^b minor triad, b^b: iv with great B^b, in m. 7(second beat). In a broad sense, Phrase 2 of the Coda with the simple arpeggiation of e^b: i may be heard as a modified rhythmic augmentation of the opening ascending figuration presented in m. 3.

In summarizing the tonal and formal features of Op. 118, No. 6, Karl Geiringer's word of "nebulous" seems an appropriate aesthetic description to bear in mind. The combination of the large-scale polarity of dominant and tonic key areas, which is accomplished primarily with the delayment in establishing the tonic key area, and the pervasive development of material through the elaboration of third patterns accounts for a work of subtle technical intricacy that manifests ostensibly indistinct harmonic relationships and fluctuant melodic configurations. While the ternary design of the Intermezzo conveys a large-scale impression of contrast and unity through the statement, digression, and restatement of material, the continuous elaboration of harmonic and melodic elements results in a piece that is formally dynamic. Perhaps it is the interaction of a progressive tonal structure (from dominant to tonic key area) with a variegated formal design (A B A') that accounts for a work whose technical features seem elusive and yet whose effectual qualities are ones of immediate dramatic intensity and profound pathos.

CHAPTER SIXTEEN

THE RELATIONSHIP OF ELECTRO-ACOUSTIC MUSIC TO PRE-1950S MUSIC AND IDEAS

Richard S. James

Bowling Green State University

> The fact is that every writer *creates* his own precursors. His work
> modifies our conception of the past as it will modify the future.[1]
> — Jorge Luis Borges

Electro-acoustic music[2] has been in existence now for nearly four
decades, and the initial impressions of an unprecedented, perhaps
threatening twist in the path of musical development have largely sub-
sided. Gradually it has been accepted into the mainstream of both
cultivated and vernacular musical styles. The reason is simple. Despite
superficial differences, this new medium is founded upon the same
acoustical, aesthetic and perceptual principles as all music, merely
augmenting them in some striking new ways. It is time, then, to move
beyond a chronicling of the events and techniques of electro-acoustic
music. It is time to establish its relationship to earlier music, to answer

---

[1] Jorge Luis Borges, "Kafka and His Precursors," trans. James E. Irby, in
Jorge Luis Borges, *Labyrinths: Selected Stories and Other Writings*, with a
Preface by André Mourois, ed. Donald A. Yates and James E. Irby (New York:
New Directions Publishing Co., 1962), p. 201.

[2] The term "electro-acoustic music" is now widely used, internationally, to
encompass the two initial schools of the field, *musique concrète* and
elektronische musik, along with such subsequent innovations as computer
music, cybersonic music, and live electronic music.

the question: Just how unprecedented is electro-acoustic music?

The following article is the result of attempts to address precisely this question. Unusual new ideas and experiments in early twentieth-century music were analyzed, pioneers were interviewed, and potential connections scrutinized. There emerged a diverse network of conjectures on and explorations into such areas as electric instruments, use of noise and percussion resources, sound recorded on photographic film, and phonograph record manipulation. Although no earlier instance of electro-acoustic music appeared and no essential first steps or foundational work were uncovered, there is ample evidence that electro-acoustic music was created by composers responding to musical interests, even imperatives that had already motivated significant though less extensive ventures.

In order to make a case for these relationships, it is necessary to begin by establishing, as a point of reference, just what has inspired nearly four decades of electro-acoustic music. What does it offer composers; what is its perceived potential? Answer to such questions fall into eight categories:

1. *New sounds*: Electronic equipment has expanded, to an extraordinary degree, the range of possibilities within all dimensions of sound: frequency, duration, amplitude, timbre, envelope, rhythmic relations, degree and rate of contrast, variety, complexity, and density.
2. *Greater control of sound*: It is also possible to exercise greater control over every dimension of the sound in electro-acoustic music. The composer can specify the most subtle distinctions and extreme contrasts, knowing that they will be faithfully reproduced.
3. *Sound manipulation*: One of the most distinctive capabilities of electro-acoustic music is sound manipulation, techniques wherein tape-recorded sounds or segments of music are cut, rearranged and spliced in any fashion. An important ramification here is the ability to control and experiment with the sound envelope itself.
4. *Sound location mobility*: By placing speakers about the concert hall, the composer of electro-acoustic music can cause sounds to originate from any or all directions and their point of origin to travel at any speed, in any fashion about the concert space, limited only by the architecture of the hall and the number of speakers.
5. *Complexity*: The ability to create and control an increasing quantity of sound events per unit time permits electro-acoustic music to convey a far greater density of information or meaning than more traditional music. This leads to the existence of considerably more

information in a piece than the listener can absorb in a single hearing and, thus, to the impression that the work changes markedly from one performance to another as the listener concentrates on different aspects of the work. To some degree this situation is the norm rather than the exception in music. The distinction here, as in the first category, is one of magnitude: the potential in electro-acoustic music for creating works of all but incomprehensible density is unprecedented.

6. *Reduced dependence on pitch considerations*: The composer of electro-acoustic music can more readily organize music in terms of timbre, texture or rhythm rather than pitch because the range and controllability of these traditionally secondary parameters is so expanded.

7. *Experimental approach to composition*: Conventional compositional techniques and training are largely inadequate preparation for the electro-acoustic music composer who is faced with countless available sounds, new techniques, and uncharted aesthetic territory. The ear becomes the composer's primary guide in an exploration of new resources and techniques that readily lends itself to comparison with the experimental method of modern science.

8. *Transcending performer and instrument*: In electro-acoustic music, composers can actually work with the sound itself rather than notation, put the sounds they select on tape and have this tape played for the audience, thus expressing themselves directly to the listener without fear of distortion. Equally significant is the fact that by allowing composers to bypass the performer, conventional musical instruments and notation, electro-acoustic music frees them from the physical and technical limitations of these intermediaries.

I — Sound Resource Expansion

The disparate prefigurements of electro-acoustic music discussed in this article transpired within the broader context of the composer's continuing search for increased subtlety and variety of musical expression, for new means of creating, manipulating and reproducing sound.[3] This

---

[3] While it would be imprudent to suggest that music history follows a course towards steadily increasing sophistication and range of expression, composers have regularly sought new possibilities as they leave others behind. The impression that resources are expanded is sometimes valid, as in twentieth-century music, but progress in expressive power is debatable.

quest, surely fundamental to Western musical creativity, is evident in the evolution of compositional styles and in the ever-changing demands placed upon performer and instrument. It is also well documented in prose. Writers from Francis Bacon and E.T.A. Hoffman, to Hector Berlioz, Ferruccio Busoni and Carlos Chavez have forecast, even demanded far-reaching new capabilities. Even so, composers have, during the past fifty years, exceeded most of these speculations. They have sought greater range and subtlety within every dimension of music and freedom from even the most basic limitations embodied in their sound sources, the performer's abilities and listener understanding.

When compared with the sound resource expansion in earlier periods, twentieth-century efforts take on a diversified, almost reckless character that cannot be dismissed as the mere distortion of chronological proximity. These qualities seem endemic to modern Western life. The tumult of an increasingly urban existence has been fed by a torrent of technological innovation that has fundamentally altered many aspects of the culture. Twentieth-century musical styles have exhibited similar chaotic change. The widely perceived paralysis of the harmonic language in the early decades spawned numerous new styles of unprecedented diversity. In the midst of all these initiatives, demand for new musical means and resources flourished.

An interest in expanding timbral resources has been especially prominent, just as timbre, itself, has been an increasingly important aspect of the music of this era. Schönberg's *Klangfarbenmelodie*, Bartók's "night music," and the colorful orchestrations of Ravel, Stravinsky and Scriabin come immediately to mind. Traditional instruments have come to be used in remarkable new ways, and considerable attention has been paid to a host of new instruments.

Musical change during the twentieth century has also been motivated, in part, by a desire to develop a music appropriate to or at least expressive of modern society. To many composers, such music demands new resources and even new approaches to composition. Claude Debussy, for instance, asked, "Is it not our duty to find a symphonic means of expressing our time, one that evokes the progress, the daring and victories of modern days? The century of the airplane deserves its music."[4] The modern technology to which Debussy refers has, of course, been critical to expanding musical resources. While its

---

[4] Quoted in Paul Griffiths, *A Concise History of Avant-garde Music from Debussy to Boulez* (New York and Toronto: Oxford University Press, 1978), p. 111.

incursion into music via the phonograph, radio, amplification and electrified instruments was greeted with a healthy wariness, its ultimate acceptance is seen in the success of electric instruments, works like Antheil's *Ballet mécanique* and Honegger's *Pacific 231*, and, eventually, electro-acoustic music itself. Some composers have found it a useful bridge between the unsettling experimentation of early twentieth-century music and new means of approaching and organizing sound, as well as a broader definition of music.[5] Perhaps most profound is the effect of the sound recording on music. It has brought the timbral diversity of the orchestra into every home,[6] and made possible the isolation of the individual sound, rendering it available for study, dissection, and manipulation.[7]

The remainder of this article is, then, a study of both the possible precedence for electro-acoustic music and the more far-reaching attempts to expand sound resources during the first half of the twentieth-century. Topics will include electric instruments, noise and percussion usage, manipulation of sound recorded on photographic film, and the creative uses of the phonograph and the player piano roll.

II — Electronic Instruments

In 1893, Ferruccio Busoni wrote an essay entitled "Insufficiency of the means for musical expression."[8] It is, in some ways, a classic statement; the progressives of any era rail against the limitations they have inherited. Busoni, however, proposed a provocative solution to this problem: a single instrument operated by a keyboard with a range of six octaves and the capability of "filling out all gaps in the sound and the technique of every individual instrument."[9] Busoni was not alone in such thinking. Figures as diverse as Arthur Honegger, Carlos Chavez, the Italian Futurists, Leopold Stokowski, Arnold Schönberg, John

---

[5] Interview with Otto Luening, composer, teacher, and writer, New York, 29 November 1978.

[6] Charles˙ Rosen, "Music and Technology" (Lecture presented at The University of Michigan, Ann Arbor, 19 October, 1978).

[7] Abraham Moles, "Machines à musique: l'apport de machines électronique et électro-acoustique a la nouvelle sensibilité musicale," *La Revue musicale* CCXXXVI (1957), 116–118.

[8] Ferruccio Busoni, "Insufficiency of the Means for Musical Expression" (1893), in Ferruccio Busoni, *The Essence of Music and Other Papers*, trans. Rosamond Ley (London: Rockliff Pub. Corp., 1957), pp. 38–39.

[9] Op. cit., p. 39.

Cage, Joseph Schillinger, and, of course, Edgard Varèse would dream of a "little black box" type of instrument which, filled with the marvels of science, would put literally unheard of resources at the composer's disposal. In 1939, Varèse presented a detailed explanation of what he expected from such an instrument, one that he felt would be based on electronic means of generating and manipulating sound:

> liberation from the arbitrary, paralyzing tempered system; the possibility of obtaining any number of cycles, or, if still desired, subdivisions of the octave, consequently the formation of any desired scale; unsuspected range in low and high registers, new harmonic splendours obtained from the use of sub-harmonic combinations now impossible, the possibility of obtaining any differentiation of timbre, of sound combination, new dynamics far beyond the present human-power orchestra, a sense of sound projection in space, by means of the emission of sound in any part or in many parts of the hall as may be required by the score, cross rhythms unrelated to each other, treated simultaneously . . . all these in a given unit of measure or time which is humanly impossible to obtain.[10]

Electricity did indeed become the primary means of realizing twentieth-century dreams of far-reaching new instrumental resources. During the 1910s, two critical breakthroughs in electronics made musical instruments based on electricity viable: the successful generation of acoustical oscillations (sound) using an electromagnetic oscillator, and an electronic means of amplifying sound. Although true electro-acoustic music, based upon the unique new possibilities which electronics brought to sound synthesis and control, was not realized until the late 1940s, the previous two decades saw many significant applications of electricity to musical instruments. Three representative examples will be discussed briefly: the Theremin, the Ondes Martenot, and the Electrophon/Sphaerophon.[11]

These and most other promising early electric instruments were based upon the heterodyne principle. Musicians know that two pitches which are very slightly out of tune from a consonant interval produce beats or pulses within the sound. The frequency of these beats depends on how out of tune the two pitches are. The same phenomenon results when two electrical currents of slightly different frequency are superimposed. The frequencies of the two currents so far exceed those audible to the

---

[10] Griffiths, *A Concise History*, p. 111.

[11] The best survey of these instruments for the non-engineer is Francis W. Galpin, "The Music of Electricity: A Sketch of its Origins and Development," *Proceedings of the Musical Association* LXIV (1937/38), 71–83.

human ear, however, that the resultant beats themselves may have an audible frequency.

Leon Theremin, a Russian acoustical engineer, was the first to construct a musical instrument based on the heterodyne principle. He unveiled his famous Aetherophone, also called the Thereminovox or simply Theremin, on 5 August 1920. Central to the Theremin is the fact that when an electrical current passes through a rod, it will generate a weak electromagnetic field around the rod. When the performer's hand moves within this field, the capacity of the field is changed because the hand acts as a conductor. If this rod is part of a heterodyne mechanism, the performer's hand functions as a variable condenser, thereby controlling the pitch being generated. The other hand is moved relative to a second rod where it effects another electromagnetic field and, in turn, the intensity of the current. In this way, the volume of the sound is altered. Completing the Theremin was a set of controls for regulating the intensity of the basic harmonics and, thus, the timbre of the sound.[12]

Despite the glowing accolades that greeted Theremin's demonstrations and the pioneer value of the instrument, the Theremin had severe limitations. Like most heterodyne instruments, it was strictly monophonic, and only later versions permitted the articulation of individual sounds as opposed to a continuous glissando. Precision, especially of intonation, was an ever-present problem, and its admittedly distinctive timbral range, contrary to some flowery descriptions, was confined to a rather hard, pure, dull quality.

By 1920, another electric instrument builder, Maurice Martenot, had begun to work toward an instrument, the Ondes Martenot, based on radio technology and the heterodyne principle. His primary goal was to significantly reduce the two major obstacles placed between the performer's expressive intent and the realization of that intent: the inherent limitations of the various musical instruments themselves and the technical difficulty involved in mastering them. He sought an instrument capable of great range and subtlety of expression, one that would, at the same time, place a minimum of technical demands on the performer. Martenot sought no radical departure from the prevailing aesthetic of music and musical instruments. He has, in fact, always

[12] The best readily available source for a technical description of this instrument is *The New Grove Dictionary of Music and Musicians*, s.v. "Theremin," by Richard Orton.

[13] From the program for a Theremin concert given by Vera Richardson, courtesy of Dr. Susan Cook Middlebury College.

Illustration 1. The Theremin[13]

disliked electro-acoustic music.[14] The inventor took pains, however, to describe and illustrate the new resources the instrument had to offer, rather than suggest that, like the electric organ, his instrument was a mere electrification of existing models.

Premiered on 21 April, 1928, the Ondes Martenot was a considerable improvement over the Theremin. Instead of waving both hands around in mid-air, the performer placed the right index finger through a ring

---

[14] Interview with Maurice Martenot, pedagogue, instrument designer, performer, and composer, Paris, 25 April 1979. For an excellent overview of Martenot's thoughts on and contribution to the field of electric instruments, see *Encyclopedie de la musique et dictionnaire du conservatoire*, s.v., "Electricité au service de la musique," by Maurice Martenot.

Illustration 2. The Ondes Martenot[15]

affixed to the end of a wire or metal ribbon. The wire served as the variable feature of the condenser, so that the length to which the performer extended it controlled the pitch of the sound. A false keyboard under the path of the wire facilitated pitch accuracy over the eight octave range. Other controls, operated by the left hand, were used to adjust volume, alter the harmonic makeup of the sound and thus its timbre, and also to turn the sound off and on (thus avoiding the continuous glissandi of the Theremin). In the past fifty years Martenot has made significant improvements to his original design. A functional keyboard, to be used independently or in conjunction with the wire, replaced the false keyboard by the early 1930s. The controls have been made increasingly simple yet more subtle and responsive, while the internal mechanism was eventually transistorized.[16]

---

[15] *Ibid*.

[16] For details on the Ondes Martenot and its construction see Galpin, ''The

The Ondes Martenot attracted a steadily growing number of composers in the 1930s and 1940s; its repertoire has continued to expand, even since the advent of electro-acoustic music. Dariuṣ Milhaud included the instrument in incidental music for two plays during the 1930s, while Arthur Honegger used it in two film scores and his oratorio *Jeanne d'Arc au bûcher* (1935). Not surprisingly, Edgard Varèse was also among the first attracted to the Ondes Martenot, though he used the instrument in only one work, *Ecuatorial* (1934).[17] Olivier Messiaen was so impressed by Martenot and his instrument that he wrote a piece for an ensemble of six Ondes Martenots. The resulting score, *Fêtes des belles eaux* (1937), is a thorough exploration of the range of timbres, articulations, and glissandi available on the Ondes Martenot. Messiaen has, of course, returned many times to the Ondes Martenot throughout his career.

Although one of the less well known figures in the field of early electric instruments, Jörg Mager may in some ways have been the most progressive. His training in electronics, instrument construction, and acoustics was more thorough than that of the previously mentioned inventors and he seems to have had a better grasp of the possibilities inherent in electric instruments. In the early 1920s Mager developed a heterodyne mechanism for sound generation that he called the Electrophon. By adding electronic filtering devices he could adjust the timbre of the sound, while a variable condenser with marked gradations was employed to prevent constant glissandi. Thus improved, the Electrophon, renamed the Sphaerophon, was demonstrated at Donauschingen in 1926 where it impressed, among others, Paul Hindemith. Mager then added a keyboard to the Sphaerophon and, in 1928, presented this Klaviatur-Sphaerophon at Darmstadt. With the help of government money, he established a laboratory near the latter town and, in 1929, founded an Electronic Music Society. Unlike Martenot, who was responding to existing, largely pedagogical needs, Mager pursued the ideal instrument, and his results, predictably less readily accepted, were clearly more far-reaching.[18]

Music of Electricity," p. 74, and *The New Grove Dictionary of Music and Musicians*, s.v. "Ondes Martenot," by Richard Orton.

[17] His original orchestration of *Ecuatorial* called for two Theremins but he soon replaced them with Ondes Martenot which he saw as a considerable improvement. Compared with the new musical instruments he foresaw, the Ondes Martenot and its contemporaries were too primitive to attract more than this one experiment on Varère's part.

[18] Abraham Moles, "Jörg Mager: un pionnier de la musique électronique," *Revue du son* (1955), p. vii.

In the final analysis, these and many other early electric instruments achieved at least modest success prior to 1940 yet failed to fulfill the dreams of progressives like Ferruccio Busoni and Edgard Varèse. The dramatic technological advances that followed World War II quickly rendered them obsolete and, in fact, painfully primitive. Those working in the field of electro-acoustic music have surpassed and largely disowned them. Only the Ondes Martenot has evaded relegation to the museum. Undeniably, a portion of this failure can be attributed to technological weaknesses. It was not until the second half of the twentieth century that electronic sound generation and amplification attained anything approaching perfection. A more serious difficulty stemmed from the severe and inherent limitations of electronic sound generation itself. Even the electro-acoustic music composers of the 1950s and 60s were forced to accept the fact that sound is a vastly more complex phenomenon than had previously been assumed. Experience has taught that the electronic generation of interesting sounds, such as a bowed note on the violin, is difficult and frequently beyond even our present technological means and understanding.

Electric instruments and electro-acoustic music are generally considered to be somehow closely related due, at least in part, to their common dependence upon electricity and the looseness with which the term electro-acoustic music is commonly used. So simplistic an association is easily drawn but of questionable accuracy. When compared with post-1950 electro-acoustic music, the use made of the early electric instruments is as elementary as the instruments themselves. Even the most innovative writing for Ondes Martenot is essentially conventional music that makes use of a few new possibilities offered by a new musical instrument. Electro-acoustic music was quite different from other music of the 1950s and can hardly be characterized as merely exploring a new instrument. It is the result of using electronic equipment to effect a comprehensive new approach to sound: to generating it, manipulating it, controlling it, presenting it, and even conceiving of it.

Electric instruments, then, can scarcely be seen as one of the essential steps in the evolution of electro-acoustic music, yet they do have several aesthetic motivations in common and offer composers some of the same benefits. A desire to create new timbres is one of the more obvious, as is the ability to place a high degree of control over a multitude of timbres in the hands of one person playing a single instrument. Electro-acoustic music and electric instruments attracted not only composers interested in exploring microtonal resources but others pursuing a higher degree of control over sound production in general, and a greater mobility of sound within the performance space. Both have served to make the realm of so-called non-musical sound much more accessible, too.

Finally, electric instruments are evidence of an increased intimacy between the arts and technology, an intimacy that would one day be essential to electro-acoustic music. In this increasingly technological climate with the unexpected new possibilities it brought to music, composers began to approach an experimental attitude towards composition, also integral to electro-acoustic music, about which so much would eventually be written.

III — Use of Percussion and Noise

The notion that noise[19] is appropriate to musical composition did not originate in the twentieth century. A variety of noise-making devices augments the percussion section in works of the standard repertoire, e.g., the "Anvil Chorus" from Verdi's *Il Trovatore* and the hammer blows and rattling of cowbells in Mahler's Sixth Symphony. In fact, increasing interest in such sounds contributed to the steady growth of both the size and variety of the orchestral percussion section during the nineteenth and twentieth centuries. Since 1900, the role of percussion and noise resources in music has expanded dramatically with composers writing music in which these resources are a major, even dominant force. In the more extreme cases, such works represent some of the most significant expansions of the sound resources available to Western composers and become distinct prefigurements of certain aspects of electro-acoustic music. The work of the Italian Futurists, Darius Milhaud's *Les Choéphores*, George Antheil's *Ballet mécanique*, and several pieces by Edgard Varèse have been selected to provide a broad cross-section of this tendency.

The artistically diverse and highly political Italian Futurist movement was founded by a poet and dominated by literary figures and artists. Only two men took part in creating a Futurist music: composer Balilla Pratella and painter/musician Luigi Russolo.[20] They wrote a number of manifestos and articles; presented concerts, invented a set of

---

[19] For the purposes of this article, noise may be defined as sounds traditionally considered to be outside of the scope of musical resources.

[20] For information on Futurist music see Michael Kirby, *Futurist performance* (New York: E.P. Dutton, 1971) and Rodney J. Payton, "The Music of Futurism: Concerts and Polemics," *Musical Quarterly* LXII (1976).

musical "noise" instruments, and wrote nationalistic, occasionally provocative music.

T,he most significant Futurist contributions to music are the radical notions for reforming music that are articulated in their manifestos and articles. Author of three Futurist manifestos, Pratella shared Marinetti's notion that art must express life itself, not decorate it.

> The annoyance attributed to a brusque passage, to a dissonance, to an excessive sonority, depends exclusively on the weakness of the nerves of the hearer habituated to bourgeois *grazioso*[21] music and instrumentation. Art, as revelation of life, can never be subordinated to limitations of this sort. It is absurd, therefore, to subtract from art any characteristic of life in preference to any other. If it is proper to life, it is proper to art: the strong and the weak, the good and the bad, the sweet and the violent.[22]

Luigi Russolo took this mandate as the point of departure for his famous treatise entitled *The Art of Noises*, published on 11 March 1913. In it he suggested that noise had become integral to the modern environment, while musical sounds seemed increasingly foreign and artificial. The latter had come to constitute, in his view, an exhausted resource whose limitations were stifling music; he found noise a more interesting and varied sound repertoire. At the same time, Russolo objected to using noise as a mere imitation of the real world and, thus, to noise compositions designed as collages of associated images. He felt that noise could and should be separated from its incidental, connotative associations so as to become abstract building blocks for musical works. Russolo's list of conclusions in this most central of Futurist music manisfestos includes the following:

1. The field of sound must be enlarged and enriched by the addition and substitution of noises.
2. Instruments must be developed which can reproduce a given noise at various pitches and intervals, including quarter tones.
3. These new instruments must allow for the manipulation of both tone and amplification as well as pitch and rhythm.[23]

---

[21] *Grazioso* was a popular Futurist term meaning insipid, shallow, and ingratiating.

[22] Rodney J. Payton, "The Futurist Musicians: Francesco Ballila Pratella and Luigi Russolo" (Ph.D. dissertation, University of Chicago, 1974), p. 44.

[23] Luigi Russolo, *The Art of Noises* (1913), in *Futurist Manifestos*, ed. and with an Introduction by Umbro Apollonio, trans. Robert Brain, R.W. Flint, J.C. Higgitt, Caroline Tisdall (New York: Viking Press, 1973), p. 87.

Illustration 3. The *intonarumori* ensemble[27]

Russolo's noise art was rapidly if only partially realized. With the help of fellow Futurist painter Ugo Piatti, he constructed his first *intonarumori* (noise generator) and presided over its public debute on 2 June 1913 in Modena. By the end of the summer he had completed a small *intonarumori* orchestra consisting of three buzzers, two bursters, one thunderer, three whistlers, two rustlers, two gurglers, one shatterer, one shriller, and one snorter (Illustration 3). Each had a range of ten notes to two octaves and an on-off switch. The first public concert by an *intonarumori* ensemble took place on 11 August 1913 in Milan's Red House. A number of similar concerts were presented throughout Europe, while the instruments figured in a few works by Pratella and augmented the background music for some Marinetti plays and Futurist skits. With a few riotous exceptions, they received tolerant and occasionally warm reception.

At least four compositions for *intonarumori* ensemble are known to have existed, written by Russolo's brother Antonio. Unfortunately, all that has survived of these works is one seven measure excerpt from "Awakening of a Capital," preserved in the pages of *Lacerba*, the

Futurists' official organic.[24] Both Varèse[25] and Maurice Ravel[26] expressed interest in using *intonarumori* in their music, but no works were forthcoming. More intriguing, though similarly without consequence, was a private demonstration of the instruments, some time in 1914 or 1915, that was witnessed by Sergei Diaghilev, Igor Stravinsky, and Sergei Prokofiev. Forty years later, Stravinsky recalled the event with some disinterest, claiming that he faked enthusiasm.[28] Furutist poet Francesco Cangiullo, also present that evening, gave a different account, reporting that Stravinsky expressed a desire to use some *intonarumori* in a ballet score while Diaghilev proposed bringing them all to Paris for a noise concert.[29] This pattern of passing interest is easily understood. Though wonderfully novel, the instruments suffered from insufficient volume — electronic amplification was still several years away. This, combined with their technical inflexibility, doomed them to limited success.

Darius Milhaud has provoked censure for his lack of self-criticism but never for his originality. In addition to the Ondes Martenot, he took a keen interest in expanded percussion and noise resources; wrote choruses in which the participants spoke, shouted, and groaned; and even manipulated sound directly by means of the phonograph. His experiments and his experimental attitude make him central to the present inquiry. The earliest and most significant of several works demonstrating his attraction to noise and percussion resources was *Les Choéphores* (1915), the centerpiece of his operatic trilogy, *L'Oresteia*. *Les Choéphores* deals with that portion of the Orestes story that begins with the lament over the death of Agamemnon and sets the stage for Orestes' revenge in the final opera. It culminates in a dramatic climax of great tension and horror. Milhaud described the expressive dilemma he confronted in setting this scene and the solution he came to in the following words:

> The savage, cannibalistic character presented us with one of the most complex problems to solve. The lyrical element was not musical. How to

[24] *Lacerba* 2 (1914), pp. 72–73.

[25] "La musique à travers le monde," *Le Joie musicale* II (1930), p. 32.

[26] "Echos — instruments nouveaux," *Musique et instruments* CXLIII (1921), 245.

[27] Michael Kirby, *Futurist Performance*, (New York: Dutton, 1971), p. 36.

[28] Igor Stravinsky and Robert Craft, *Conversations with Igor Stravinsky* (London: Faber and Faber, 1959), p. 93.

[29] Payton, "The Music of Futurism," p. 29.

convey, to focus this turmoil? It was then that I thought to have the text spoken in a measured fashion, punctuated and strung together as if it were sung; I wrote for speaking chorus supported by an orchestra composed entirely of percussion instruments.[30]

Milhaud directed the chorus to utter specific words and disjunct phrases, but notated only the rhythm. The percussion instruments he chose were also largely unpitched: drums, cymbals, whistles, whips, even a board and hammer. These vocal and instrumental effects are limited to two sections at the climax of the opera, 'Présage" and "Exhortations," with a brief recapitulation toward the close of the opera. Roland-Manuel, in a representative assessment, characterized the passages as "an infernal symphony which caused one's hair to stand on end and the effect of which was quite irresistible."[31]

Prior to a late 1920s retreat from the brink of modernism, George Antheil wrote a number of strikingly adventurous works. Most notable of these was his *Ballet mécanique* (1925), originally written to be recorded and synchronized with a Fernand Léger silent film of the same name. This synchronization was never achieved, but the music went on to enjoy independent and colorful success. It should be noted from the outset that Antheil had no intention of portraying machinery, but rather to reflect the "troubled and war-potentialed 1924 times . . . to warn the age in which [he] was living of the simultaneous beauty and danger of its own unconscious mechanistic philosophy, aesthetic."[32]

Antheil represented these images by means of jarring, percussive effects and an emphasis on rhythmic ideas and means of organization. Melodic concerns played a decidedly secondary role to rhythm and timbre. *Ballet mécanique* was scored for a percussion-dominated orchestra: eight player pianos, eight xylophones, four bass drums, two electric motors, one klaxon, one siren, two tin sheets, two steel sheets, and two octaves of electric bells. For the 1927 New York City premiere, an actual airplane propeller provided a visual supplement to the two motors; in a 1954 rescoring, Antheil replaced the motors with a recording of jet engines.

Surely the most serious pre-1950 innovator in the area of percussion resources and noise usage is French/American composer Edgard

---

[30] Paul Collaer, *Darius Milhaud* (Antwerpen: N.V. de Nederlandsche Boekhandel, 1947), p. 154.

[31] Roland-Manuel, "Les Choéphores," *Le Ménestrel* LXXXIX (1927), 122–123.

[32] George Antheil, *Bad Boy of Music* (Garden City, New York: Doubleday, Doran & Co., Inc., 1945), p. 140.

Varèse. While Milhaud used such resources to solve a particular dramatic need and Antheil's orchestration was somewhat programmatically motivated, Varèse made such sound a fundamental part of an abstract style. His departure from convention had roots in his childhood: he received a thorough education in the sciences and would always be inclined to think of music in scientific terms. By 1910, he already spoke of using noise in music, and was thinking in terms of organizing and manipulating rhythms, frequencies, and intervals. Not content with the melodic/harmonic orientation of Western music, Varèse formulated a remarkable new style in which rhythm, timbre and density played the central role. At the root of his rhythmic practice, as described by Elliott Carter,[33] was the rhythmic cell, a unit he developed and manipulated much as other composers work with melodic ideas. Varèse also spoke frequently of the spatial dimension in music, initially in reference to musical passages in which events or lines moved independently of one another, particularly at different rates of speed, thereby forming spatial relationships. By 1930 he was applying the term to music in which these independent musical events were physically separated by means of loudspeakers, and their point of origin made to move about from speaker to speaker.

Like the Futurists, Varèse felt that the aural richness of contemporary society necessitated radically new musical resources. He concluded that composers should turn to modern technology for the means to create instruments and music appropriate to the era. He even felt that the performer might advantageously be replaced by such machine instruments, but only in certain very modern music. In July of 1922 Varèse predicted that the composer and the electrician would have to work together on the instrument of the future, an instrument he hoped would be capable of producing a continuous sound at any frequency and with any timbral inflection. By 1930 he was proposing a musical laboratory where composers of advanced ability could, with the aid of technicians, study acoustics and the newest concepts, means, techniques and equipment of composition.

While waiting for technology to catch up with his idealism, Varèse contented himself with ensembles in which percussion instruments played an increasingly dominant role. Non-percussion instruments

---

[33] Elliott Carter, "On Edgard Varèse" in *The New Worlds of Edgard Varèse, a Symposium*, ed. Sherman van Solkema (New York: Institute for Studies in American Music, Brooklyn College of the City University of New York, 1979), p. 2.

included in these works were, in fact, frequently treated in a percussive manner as well. This "rhythmicized" orchestration[34] is evident even in his first major work, *Amériques* (1922). It is especially obvious in *Octandre* (1923), where a total lack of percussion (unique in his output) serves to highlight his percussive use of other instruments. The melodic capabilities of the eight instruments used in this work are largely ignored, while the piece is unified by repetitions of single pitches, intervals, or chords of varying densities. Although these motivic ideas were occasionally juxtaposed, his skill at separating them registrally, by means of stratified orchestration, makes them independently recognizable. His methods of manipulating blocks of sound are already evident in this work.

Perhaps most famous and significant of Varèse's output is *Ionisation*, a 1931 work scored entirely for percussion. Of the thirty-seven instruments he employs, only three — celeste, piano and chimes — are capable of multiple specified pitches. Rhythm, and, to a lesser extent, timbre, dynamics, and register, become the central musical factors of the piece. The demarcation of form, itself, is accomplished by means of timbre and register. In many ways, *Ionisation* is the culmination of Varèse's previous stylistic trends and the point of departure for his electro-acoustic works of the 1950s wherein timbral possibilities, rhythmic subtlety, manipulation of blocks of sound, and stratified orchestration would be exploited further.

The connection between electro-acoustic music and expanded use of noise and percussion resources seems obvious, though closer inspection reveals that the tie is unexpectedly subtle. The far-reaching implications of electro-acoustic music are only selectively and distantly suggested in the works just discussed. Many if not most other instances of increased percussion utilization have been motivated by an interest in mere sound effects, a desire to suggest jazz idioms, or a predictable and modest exploration on the frontier of traditional instrumental usage.

An association between electro-acoustic music and innovative percussion and noise scoring is harder to deny when confronted by Varèse who dealt with both. Varèse, himself, drew the parallel between his fascination with noise and his later work with electro-acoustic music, remarking that the former "led, in the later years of my life, to laboratory work in the discipline which they call, in France, *musique*

---

[34] *Ibid.*, p. 4.

concrète."[35] This association is equally strong in the case of the Futurists. Their theories and, especially, the *intonarumori* embody the most extreme expansion of timbral resources prior to the advent of electro-acoustic music, virtually the only one, aside from Varèse's music, of comparable magnitude.

While none of the pioneers discussed in this section, save perhaps Varèse, foresaw the broader revolution that electro-acoustic music would bring, their work reveals both techniques and ideas that composers and audiences would confront in electro-acoustic music. Most significant is the more dominant, even structural role given to non-pitched percussion sounds and noise. This, in turn, led composers to new means of musical organization not dependent upon pitch and harmonic factors, and, hence, a much greater awareness of the subtlety and power of rhythm. These innovators came to accept the use, in music, of sounds far outside the realm of traditional musical timbres, eventually finding that a broader definition of music was necessary. Thus, Varèse, Russolo, and the early electro-acoustic music composers shared some of the same problems of musical organization and coherence, as well as the redefining and the experimental attitude necessitated by such radical departure from accepted musical practice.

IV — Sound on Film Techniques

Since 1929, sound has been recordable on film as a series of black and white patterns. These patterns can take several forms, three of which are represented in Illustration 4. In the movie projector, the sound head contains a light source and a photoelectric cell. The latter device generates electricity when illuminated, while the amount of the resulting current varies with the intensity of the light. The sound track passes between the light source and cell so that the patterns on the sound track will cause changes in the amount of light reaching the cell and, consequently, the current the cell generates. Thus, the sounds recorded on film are converted to electrical impulses which can be made audible with an amplifier and loudspeaker.

Film music innovators soon discovered a number of intriguing secondary benefits to sound-on-film technology. For instance, it allowed one to freeze and visually preserve a sound for study. These

---

[35] Henri Barraud, *Pour comprendre les musiques d'aujourd'hui* (Paris: Editions du seuil, 1968), p. 155.

254   Richard S. James

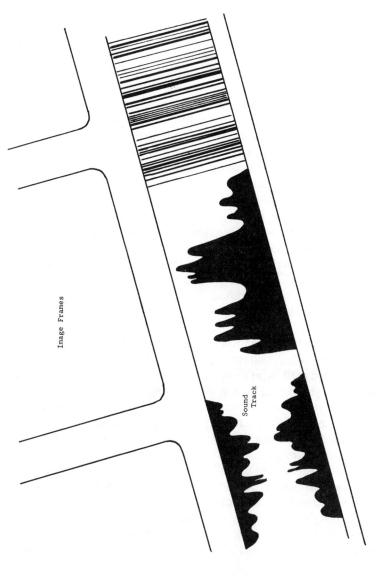

Image Frames

Sound
Track

Illustration 4. Sound Track Patterns

sound pictures could then be manipulated and altered, generating entirely new sounds and sound arrangements. Parts of a sound event might be excised while individual sounds and/or entire pieces of music could be reordered, reversed and superimposed by cutting, rearranging, and splicing the film. Sounds could also be altered by adding marks to the sound track by hand. Finally, the recording process itself could be circumvented completely, either by painting sounds onto the film or by taking pictures of various shapes and designs with an ordinary camera and then reducing and combining them like an animation sequence. Unusual as these notions must have seemed in the 1930s, all of them were tried by innovative film composers in Europe, Russia and North America.

One of the most gifted manipulators of filmed sound was French composer Arthur Hoérée. Hoérée's techniques are perhaps best illustrated in his accompaniment for the storm sequence in a 1934 film entitled *Rapt*.[36] This particular storm was both literal, a mountain thunderstorm, and figurative, a representation of the emotional and moral turmoil engulfing the movie's leading characters. Hoérée instructed the studio orchestra to improvise an imitation of the sounds of a physical storm: thunder, lightning, rain and wind. After recording their cacophony on about ten meters of film, Hoérée returned to his laboratory and there created a one hundred meter storm collage by means by duplicating, cutting, rearranging, reversing, and splicing the original material. The sound envelope, itself, was sometimes altered or reversed, the latter yielding a wonderful impression of distance. The result was far more subtle and expressive than real storm sounds. In Hoérée's words, "The total psychological content of the scene had been treated musically with fragments spliced together."[37]

Actual sound synthesis, as opposed to manipulation, was accomplished by applying the working methods of visual animation to the sound track. Most of the people involved with animated sound preferred to work with the aid of a camera, drawing what might be called pictures of sound, photographing them and then combining the photographs to produce a sound track. The earliest application of these ideas appeared around 1930 in Russia. There, music theorist and mathematician Arseni M. Avraamov experimented with sound tracks created by photographing drawings of repeated geometric shapes. N.V.

---

[36] Arthur Hoérée and Arthur Honegger, "Particularités sonores du film *Rapt*," *La Revue musicale* XV (1934), 90.

[37] Interview with Arthur Hoérée, composer, Paris, 25 April 1979. Similar sound collages are found in Vsevolod Pudovkin's 1933 film *Deserter*.

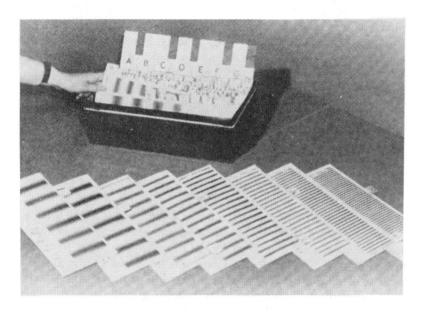

Illustration 5. Incrementally Varied Patterns[38]

Voinov, Avraamov's colleague and an animation specialist, took a given pattern and created a series of eighty-seven drawings in which the frequency of pattern repetition varied incrementally (Illustration 5). When combined in sequence, these drawings could be used to produce a chromatic scale of over seven octaves. Voinov then synthesized music by photographing arrangements of these drawings and actually did reproduce Rachmaninoff's C# minor Prelude and Schubert's *Moments Musicaux*.

In Germany, sound animators Oscar Fischinger, Laszlo Moholy-Nagy, and Rudolf Pfenninger paralleled these Russian initiatives, but it was Norman McLaren, the noted Canadian animator, who, in the late 1940s, expanded further on these techniques. Illustration 6 is a display of some of the repetition patterns he has employed, while in Illustration 7 the overlays that effect various sound envelopes are pictured, superimposed on splaying patterns used, with the envelope overlays, to create

---

[38] Roger Manvell and John Huntley, *The Technique of Film Music*, revised and enlarged Richard Arnell and Peter Day (London: Focal Press, 1975), p. 189.

[39] *Ibid.*, p. 188.

[40] *Ibid.*, p. 190.

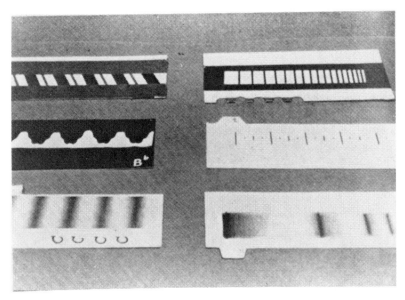

Illustration 6. Different Repetition Patterns[39]

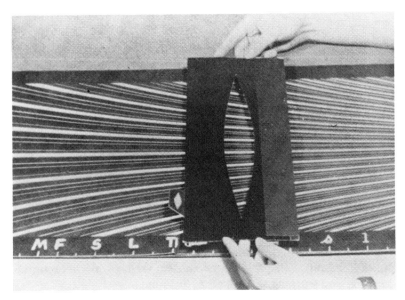

Illustration 7. Envelope Overlay and Glissaudo Pattern[40]

glissandi. By 1953, McLaren had refined his abilities to such a degree that he could specify tenths of a tone, about 100 dynamic shadings and durations of 1/50th of a second. He had six basic timbres and could mix these to create additional ones.[41]

Some of the parallels between these avant-garde sound-on-film techniques and electro-acoustic music are readily apparent. The above methods of splicing, rearranging, altering and reversing the direction of sounds recorded on photographic film have direct corollaries in electric-acoustic music in general and *musique concrète* in particular. The notion of sound collage was also inherent in much of the work at the early electro-acoustic music studios. On a more subtle level, sound-on-film techniques offered composers varying degrees of freedom from the limitations of the human performer, musical notation and conventional musical instruments, allowing direct interaction with sound. They also helped to broaden the range of sounds included in the category of musical resources and revealed fundamentally new ways of working with individual sounds. All of these possibilities would become important and attractive features of the electro-acoustic music field and most are nowhere more fully prefigured than in the avant-garde film scores of the 1930s. Finally, the range of radically new resources made available by sound-on-film techniques necessitated an experimental approach to composition similar to that seen in the early electro-acoustic music studios.

V — Miscellaneous

There remain a number of smaller topics in pre-1950 music — both techniques and ideas — that contribute to the precedent for electro-acoustic music. Experiments with the phonograph and the player piano, and various conjectures on transcending notation, performers and conventional musical instruments will be discussed briefly.

The phonography, along with radio, was the most visible incursion of electronic technology into the world of music during the early twentieth century. While the controversy over its long term impact on music and musicians raged, some writers began pointing to its potential as a creative tool. Abraham Moles observed that the recording process endowed sound with three new qualities: permanence, reproducibility, and indivisibility.[42] It provided composers with a way of capturing, studying, and working with all types of sounds.

---

[41] *Ibid.*, p. 193.
[42] Moles, ''Machines à musique,'' pp. 116–118.

In a 1930 article, French critic Raymond Lyon was more specific and, most importantly, insisted that the phonograph was clearly capable of more than the mere reproduction of sound: "One might conceive of the existence of an esthetic of the phonograph which permits the knowing instigation of deformation intended to produce certain effects."[43] He described several means of deforming phonographic reproduction: changing the speed at which the turntable rotates, reversing the direction of turntable rotation, and both juxtaposing and superimposing multiple recordings. He suggested further that these same manipulations could be applied during the recording process itself, and augmented by unusual adjustments to the microphone and microphone placement. Lyon concluded his list of creative uses of the phonograph with the question, "But suppose, for a moment, that a daring innovator recorded *other things* besides music and voice?",[44] suggesting that the phonograph would someday be, "the laboratory wherein researchers will utilize the characteristics of this instrument to create original ensembles and new sonorities."[45]

By the time of Lyon's article, however, techniques of manipulating sound recordings were no longer hypothetical. In 1922, Milhaud began five years of experimenting with the transformation of vocal sounds by means of phonograph speed changes.[46] Varèse, John Cage, and many others followed suit in the 1930s, at the same time that Hoérée, Jaubert and Honegger were incorporating work with reversible and variable speed turntables into their film scores. Similar notions were presented at Donauschingen in 1926. Two years later the Hochschule für Musik established a program for the exploration of creative uses of the phonograph and by 1930 Paul Hindemith and Ernst Toch were using techniques of manipulating phonograph recordings to create sound collages.[47]

The phonograph, then, provided these composers with the unprecedented ability to isolate sound and manipulate it directly. Until the late 1940s, when magnetic tape recording equipment became available,

---

[43] Raymond Lyon, quoted in "Le Phonograph d'avant-garde," *La Joie musicale* III (1930), 34.

[44] *Ibid.*

[45] André Coeuroy, "Le Phonographe, instrument de musique original," *L'Art vivant* III (1927), 53.

[46] Lowell Cross, "Electronic Music, 1948–1952," *Perspectives of New Music* VII (1968), 35.

[47] Otto Luening, "Origins," in *The Development and Practice of Electronic Music*, ed. Jon Appleton and Ronald Perera (Engle-wood Cliffs, NJ: Prentice-Hall, Inc., 1975), p. 10.

the phonograph was, in fact, the primary tool in Pierre Schaeffer's *musique concrète* work at the Studio d'Essais. The experiments of Milhaud, Cage, Hindemith and others establish a clear though rudimentary precedent for Schaeffer's breakthroughs, while Lyon's and Coeuroy's predictions reveal a remarkable premonition of what was to come.

Others were attracted to the creative possibilities of the player piano. One writer predicted the appearance, "sometime in the future, of new works written expressly for the automatic piano."[48] He seems not to have realized that such music already existed. One of the best examples, in fact, was Stravinsky's *Etude* for solo pianola (1917) which truly was not playable by any mortal pianist. Paul Hindemith, of course, worked with a tool for directly and manually cutting paper rolls for use in a mechanical organ. J.-A. André Sarnette described a similar tool, characterizing composition with such an implement as "juggling difficulties, I should say former difficulties. The rhythmic audacities are a game."[49]

From the perspective of the late twentieth century, it can be seen that all three of these men were quite open to capabilities that would eventually be among the most radical and highly touted of those offered by the electro-acoustic music medium: greater control over the sound material, the ability to exceed the limitations of the human performer, and the opportunity to present their ideas directly and precisely to the listener.

Placing an interpreter and a system of notation between the creator and his audience is fundamental to post-Medieval Western art music, and there are certain undeniable advantages to this dynamic. The performer's contribution is an unknown but often delightful, exciting, and even valuable variable in the musical equation. The line between enhancement and distortion is, however, a fine one. Even with the best, most well-meaning performer, there remains the less obvious yet potentially more impervious barrier of the finite agility, speed, and accuracy of the human anatomy. Most composers have, at least occasionally, entertained a desire to bypass the performer and musical notation entirely in order to express themselves directly and precisely to the audience.

---

[48] L.-E. Gratia, "Les Instruments de musique du XXe siécle," *Le Ménestrel* XC (1928), 478.

[49] J.-A. Sarnette, "Apercu sur la musique de l'avenir," *Le Ménestrel* XC (1928), 33. More recently of course, Mexican/American Composer Conlon Nancarrow has based his compositional techniques on manual cutting of player piano rolls.

Awareness of the possibility of bypassing human limitations via the perforated roll has already been noted. Related but far more fanciful, even prophetic thoughts on this subject are found in a 1928 issue of *Musique et instrument* wherein the author quoted, from *Allgemeine Musikzeitung*, the suggestion that the Berlin Opera orchestra be replaced by eighty-five Theremins. The French writer wondered if the innovators would be content to stop there and suggested that

> a central device, controlled by a conductor, will be activated, like the player piano, by a perforated music roll which will control the variable currents in diverse instruments. This "perfected" Theremin will therefore be entirely electro-mechanical. Designed in this way, it would allow us to [create] an "electro-mechanical" music based not on notes but on an uninterrupted assembly of sound currents.[50]

This begins to sound like Varèse's black box of scientific marvels, an instrument capable of placing vast sound resources under the control of one person whose use of them is limited only by his/her own imagination. The parallel to the synthesizers of today is crude but unmistakable.

Honegger, too, had strong, positive reactions to these possibilities. In a published debate over the broader topic of *musique mécanique*, he spoke of a similar mechanical orchestra, offering the following prediction:

> Composers, instead of writing their music according to the outdated and uselessly complicated system which constitutes modern notation, will write their work directly on perforated rolls . . . [and exceed] the limits forced upon instruments by human considerations."[51]

The perforated roll, the manipulation of various recording processes and, finally, the field of electro-acoustic music have provided progressively more successful options to human performers, conventional instruments and musical notation. Interestingly, live performers have suffered little from the availability of a means of circumventing them. Although many composers have been attracted to electro-acoustic music, few have wished to abandon the performer permanently. The

---

[50] "La Musique électro-mécanique," *Musique et instruments* CCXXVIII (1928), 991.
[51] Arthur Honegger, "La Musique Mécanique et l'artiste createur," *Figaro illlustré* IX (1932), 86.

262   Richard S. James

popularity, since around 1960, of live electro-acoustic music reveals how integral the performer remains to Western music.

VI — Conclusion

Electric instruments, noise and percussion resource usage, sound-on-film techniques, phonograph and perforated roll manipulation, and certain conjectures by early twentieth-century writers constitute a fascinating chapter in sound resource expansion, with provocative implications for our understanding of the origins of electro-acoustic music. Many of those involved in electro-acoustic music, especially its pioneers, are uncomfortable with the suggestion of any substantive precedence for their work. Two basic arguments emerge from their denials. First, they insist that electro-acoustic music is a completely new kind of music, based on wholly original techniques and concepts, not earlier work and ideas. Secondly, they feel that since they were not aware of any of these proposed precursors, their work could hardly have been derived from them.

It must be admitted that the techniques of electro-acoustic music composition involving the isolation, anatomical study, construction and manipulation of individual sounds are strikingly different from previous compositional methods, and virtually unforeseen, at least in their entirety, by even the most radical composers. The basic acoustical and psychological principles underlying electro-acoustic and non-electro-acoustic music remain, however, substantially the same. Form, time, contrast, length, meaning, the nature of human perception and the various acoustical properties of sound constitute considerable common ground. It is these concepts rather than transient matters of technique, style and the current aesthetic definitions of beauty, expression and musical sound that provide the foundation for all musics.

The suggestion that innovators must be aware of their precursors is, historically speaking, also untenable. This does not call into question the originality of the pioneers of electro-acoustic music, only the sensitivity of some of them to their historical position. The fact that they were unaware of prefigurements of their work merely clarifies the relationship. It emphasizes the necessity of avoiding implications of a direct, antecedent-consequent relationship between such prefigurements and electro-acoustic music. It remains possible and important, however, to assert that many of the ideas, techniques, and inherent possibilities of electro-acoustic music were, in varying and sometimes rudimentary fashion, a part of the musical milieu prior to 1940, that the pioneers of electro-acoustic music were responding to aesthetic motivations which had already inspired some of their predecessors to more modest yet significant work.

CHAPTER SEVENTEEN

OSCAR SONNECK'S LETTERS TO ALBERT STANLEY (1909–1911): THE COMPLETE TEXTS WITH INTRODUCTION AND COMMENTARY

Allen P. Britton

University of Michigan

In 1976, when Earl V. Moore, Dean Emeritus of the School of Music of The University of Michigan, first opened a box of newspaper clippings given him during the 1920's by his immediate predecessor at the University, Albert A. Stanley, he discovered a misplaced file folder containing thirty-five items pertaining generally to the earliest meetings and other activities of the North American Section of the International Musical Society, the progenitor of the American Musicological Society. During the summer of 1978, Moore turned the file over to me. It will be permanently located among the Stanley Papers in the Bentley Historical Library of The University of Michigan.[1]

In all, the file contains no less than sixteen hitherto unpublished

---

[1] A preliminary report on this material including excerpts from the letters was read on March 22, 1980 at the meeting of the Sonneck Society in Baltimore. An abstract entitled "Oscar Sonneck Writes to Albert Stanley, 1909–1911" appeared in the *Sonneck Society Newsletter*, VI (Summer 1980), 12–13. I am greatly indebted to Neal Hatch of the Manhattan School of Music for his secretarial assistance in the transcription of Sonneck's letters.

letters to Stanley, then president of the American Section, in the hand of Oscar G. Sonneck, then its secretary. These letters date from October 25, 1909, to March 7, 1911. Three additional items bear notations in Sonneck's hand: two copies of a four-page reprint from the *Proceedings of the Music Teachers National Association for 1907* headed, "Die Internationale Musikgesellschaft: First Meeting of the American Section" (Sent to Stanley with a long letter of August 10, 1910), and a printed communication addressed to "The President of the Landessektion," which had been sent to Sonneck "for information" and by Sonneck then sent on to Stanley with the notation, "My dear Professor: This obviously does not concern me but you the 'Vorsitzender.' Letter follows soon. O.G. Sonneck." Each subsequent letter begins with this salutation or "My dear Professor Stanley" and ends with this signature. The remaining sixteen items comprise letters to Stanley (mostly on IMS business) from Guido Adler (3), Oscar von Hase-treasurer IMS (6), Sir Alexander Mackenzie-president IMS (1), Charles Maclean-secretary IMS (4), and Professor Leo R. Lewis-vice-president MTNA (2), who was in charge of local arrangements for the Boston meeting of 1910.

It may be well at this point to provide a modicum of personal information concerning Sonneck and Stanley. Although a generation apart in age, they were alike in having been born in the United States and having pursued many years of advanced musical study in Germany. Each had subsequently returned to the United States to pursue distinguished scholarly careers in which, it should be pointed out, composition, administration, and performance nevertheless formed an important part. A native of Manville, Rhode Island, born in 1851, Stanley was a man in his late fifties during the period of the correspondence. He had occupied a position as professor of music and director of the School of Music at the University of Michigan since 1888. Sonneck was born in Jersey City in 1873. He had been serving as head of the music division of the Library of Congress since 1902. In his late thirties at the time, some twenty-two years Stanley's junior, he, like Stanley, enjoyed international distinction as a scholar.

Turning to a description and characterization of the documents themselves, we shall begin with the two copies of the reprint from the MTNA Proceedings for 1907, containing an account of the first meeting of the American Section. No papers were read at this essentially social gathering, which took place in New York, at the "happy suggestion" of Dr. Frank Damrosch who was vice-president of the section, and who succeeded in assembling six other members for an informal luncheon held at the Hofbräuhaus on December 27, 1907. The account gives the names of those in attendance as well as nine absentees. The latter included both Sonneck and Stanley. Each of the reprints contains proposed revisions of the section constitution in Sonneck's hand, one version providing only for "active" members, another allowing for an additional category of "associate" members. Page four of the document contains the text of a circular "sent out by the courtesy of the Music Teachers National Association in the hope of learning the names and addresses of those who may be interested in the work of the International Society". In addition to those already mentioned, the officers of the American Section included a treasurer, Waldo S. Pratt of the Hartford Theological Seminary.

Since this paper has taken Sonneck as its principal focus, the sixteen non-Sonneck items must be dealt with much more briefly than is warranted by their intrinsic interest. They concern three different topics: the formation of IMS *Ortsgruppen* (local chapters), the Vienna IMS Congress of 1909, the MTNA meeting in Boston of 1910, and the London IMS Congress of 1911.

The formation of local chapters was naturally of special interest to Stanley, but Sonneck was interested also, as we shall see. The earliest and the latest items of the non-Sonneck group concern this subject. A handwritten letter of October 22, 1908, sets forth Charles Maclean's problems as head of the Section of Great Britain and Ireland with his three *Ortsgruppen*. One problem stemmed from lack of special dues at the local level. the last item in this group, dated at Leipzig, January 5, 1911, is handwritten, and expresses Oscar von Hase's thanks to Stanley for the latter's success "über die Bildung der Ortsgruppe Ann Arbor-Detroit," expressing also the hope that New York and other places would soon form similar groups.

Both Sonneck and Stanley had attended the Vienna Congress of the IMS in 1909. Adler's letter of June 26, 1909, discusses a report prepared by Stanley and includes a very personal expression of regret that he had not succeeded in having Stanley elected vice-president of IMS.

The two letters from Professors Leo R. Lewis of Tufts College deal with local arrangements for the American Section meeting during the MTNA meeting in Boston in December of 1910.

Several communications from London giving information concerning the London IMS Congress of 1911 possess incidental interest, since both Sonneck and Stanley planned to attend.

Let us turn now to consideration of the sixteen letters in Sonneck's clear hand. As a whole, they provide us an intimate glimpse of

Sonneck's participation in the beginnings of musico-logical organization in the United States, and more particularly, of the wit, the mildly sardonic humor, and the minute attention to detail that characterized his approach to everything he undertook. That he and Stanley worked together on the friendliest and frankest of terms is evident throughout.

The first letter, dated Washington, October 25, 1909, deals hardly at all with IMS business, but it best reveals the close relationship that Sonneck and Stanley had developed.

Washington D.C. Oct. 25. 09

My dear Prof. Stanley:

With the help of Prof. Pratt I have deciphered your "neumes" and assure you that your handwriting beats mine, indeed, that of the late Mr. L. van Beethoven.

Mir geht's ganz gut, nur habe ich soviel zu thun, dass mir der Kopf wackelt.

That I shall be able to join you all at Evanston is very doubtful. I don't have the funds. Consequently I think that it will be much better if *you* relate our Viennese experiences. All the more so, because the editor of the New Music Review got me to write an article on the subject for that magazine (See November number).

In the meantime Cole has been after me for a paper. In meiner Gutmütigkeit I suggested one on: 'Favourite Songs. A curious chapter in the history of Pasticcio opera' providing that he has nothing against such a paper. I hope that he will advance weighty reasons why such a "Vortrag" would be out of place because it struck me afterwards that I was getting myself into trouble. The thing is not so easy as it first seemed to me and I feel very much like retreating. Really, you ought to give the other fellows a chance. Instead of making us old members work, why not commit the new members like McWhood etc. to a more matrimonial interest in our I.M.S. affairs, by giving them the floor. They would appreciate it and it might help us to understand better just where the natural channels of development are in this country.

My mother was not very well this summer but seems to be pulling herself together lately. She insisted that you are much more charming and nicer than I am. Well, de gustibus non est disputandum. Perhaps she is right. All the more ground for jealousy. After all, I am not responsible for myself. My own generation is a failure anyhow in many respects, so that I take my mother's comparative criticism of you and me very calmly. Another jolly week in your company might improve me wonderfully, but, as I said above, mancano i denari.

Nevertheless a rivederci some day in the near future

Yours very sincerely
O. G. Sonneck

The next two letters are quite short, but they introduce us to a Sonneck who was quite capable of poking fun at Germans, at least in personal correspondence with a friend who, like him, had spent many years of study in Germany. He is happy that a "balance of power" will be maintained against the Germans in the IMS, and he finds "life too short" to explain to them the differences, (geographical, climatic, esthetic, etc) between a country like ours and "Tschermanie." Nothing he says here or later can be taken as representing a serious chauvinism, and yet a certain pique is evident. All of this is particularly ironic in view of accusations of "pro-Germanism" later made against Sonneck during the War. Although born in the United States, his upbringing in Germany made him suspect in the context of war-time fear and suspicion.

LIBRARY OF CONGRESS
MUSIC DIVISION

ALL CORRESPONDENCE SHOULD BE ADDRESSED
"THE LIBRARIAN OF CONGRESS
WASHINGTON, D. C."

WASHINGTON, D. C. Jan. 29. 10.

In reply quote file No. MU

My dear Prof. Stanley:
    Just keep "Nuova vita" for another week or more.
    As I am responsible for the invitation to the Germania Club dinner on Feb. 3, I accept your regrets with regrets and shall notify the Secretary. (I happen to be second vice-president of the Club, what we call in our club jargon "Zweites Unter-Laster". The President is

nicknamed "Herr Oberlaster".) So I know all about it and am glad that I can save you the trouble of writing a letter.

Hurrah for Kroeger. We'll get third place yet in the I.M.S. and together with the English and French will be able to hold the balance of power.

Yours in haste but "con amore"
O. G. Sonneck

On April 17, 1910, Sonneck first mentions the matter of forming *Ortsgruppen* (local chapters), revealing at the same time his opinion that Germans had difficulty in understanding Americans.

Washington, D. C. April 17. 10

My dear Prof. Stanley:

Dr. Maclean sent me a postal card informing me that he had written you about something that would interest me. What is it?

Br[eitkopf] & H[ärtel] (or as v. Bulow called them Schwalasch u. Weichel) sent me a letter in German-English (Leipzig Brand) and circulars about Ortsgruppen to be founded in U. S. A. Well, they will have a hard time to accomplish much in that direction. Seven members, I believe, is the minimum and New York City and Ann Arbor are about the only places where the thing could be done. Why not try it in Ann Arbor?

I have not answered their letter because life is too short to explain to them the differences, (geographical,˙ climatic, esthetic, etc) between a country like ours and Tshermanie.

I hope that you are O. K. bodily and mentally and that your new house is a bing-bang success. When does that London meeting take place?

With I. M. Gruss

Yours gloomily
O. G. Sonneck

He returns to these matters again and again in a subsequent series of eight letters, all quite long, all dealing primarily with planning a

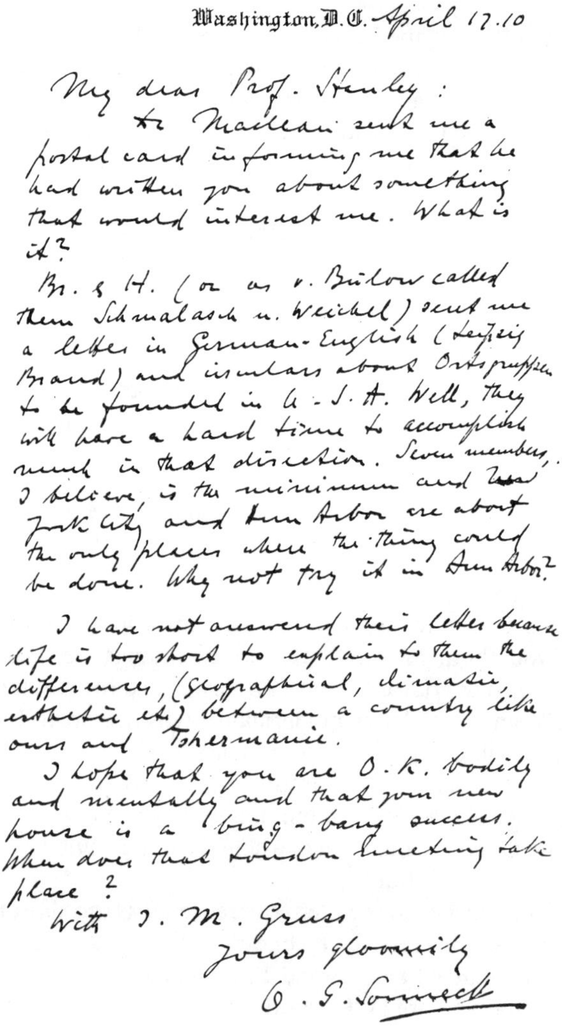

Washington, D.C. April 17.10

My dear Prof. Stanley :

Dr. Maclean sent me a postal card informing me that he had written you about something that would interest me. What is it?

Br. & H. (or as v. Bülow called them Schmalosch u. Weichel) sent me a letter in German-English (Leipzig Brand) and circulars about Ortsgruppen to be founded in U. S. A. Well, they will have a hard time to accomplish much in that direction. Seven members, I believe, is the minimum and New York City, and Ann Arbor are about the only places where the thing could be done. Why not try it in Ann Arbor?

I have not answered their letter because life is too short to explain to them the differences, (geographical, climatic, æsthetic etc) between a country like ours and Tshermanie.

I hope that you are O. K. bodily and mentally and that your new house is a 'bing-bang' success. When does that London meeting take place?

With I. M. Gruss
yours gloomily
O. G. Sonneck

Illustration 1. Sonneck's letter of April 17, 1910, on "German-English (Leipzig Brand)" and related matters.

program for the coming meeting of the American Section of IMS at Boston in December, 1919, a meeting to be held during the regular convention of the MTNA. The relationship then between the larger and the smaller group is entirely parallel with that of the American Musicological Society and the Sonneck Society today. In fact, many problems to which Sonneck refers are quite similar in general nature to some which have arisen within more recent memory.[2]

The letter of August 10, 1910, was enclosed with two copies of the MTNA reprint described above and which contained Sonneck's penned-in suggestions for revising the constitution. [The following was crowded in above, around, and below the date line:]

Hotels: The Raleigh is not quite so expensive as the New Willard, but not cheap. The St. James is well spoken of. It is cheaper than the two others but not so defaut, though still above the average. These three on Pa. Ave. The Riggs (opposite the Treasury) is about like the St. James. *I do not recommend orthodox dry rot. [emphasis original]*

Washington, D. C. Aug. 10. 10.

My dear Professor:

In as much as Br. & H. have inundated you with circulars etc, it might be just as well to use them. Speaking for myself, I doubt the efficacy of circulars boosting the I. M. S. in America and in particular of a circular as sent you by Br. & H. Britannia rules the waves, but Germania certainly rules the world. At least she thinks she does and even an international firm like Br. & H. will not see nor understand that the German way of doing things might be neither customary nor effective in other countries. If Br. & H. were so anxious to spread the gospel of the I. M. S. in America, they should have asked either you or me, just what kind of a circular might possibly do the work. The one in question is a cross between England and Germany and will not appeal to American investors of $5. On the contrary, the long distance titles of the German professor on the third and fourth page will inevitably arouse an American's sense of humor. (Their craze for titles has even led them to prefix a *Dr.* to my name and it helps me not to protest and assure them that I am not a *Dr.*) However, perhaps this title business could not be avoided when

---

[2] For more on this, see Nicholas Tawa's editorial, "The Limits of Tolerance," *Sonneck Society Newsletter*, V (Summer 1979), 7.

giving a list of the Sections, but that "Ortsgruppen" list is totally out of place in America. Instead, one of the four pages should give a survey of subjects and articles actually contained in the publications, so that the "serious"-minded American musician may see for himself that he is not being handed a gold brick, framed up by a bunch of learned professors for whom there may be something in this deal. Furthermore, a circular intended for America, should contain a paragraph or two which will appeal more strongly to the sense of pride in their serious mind of those American musicians, who have gotten beyond the vicious self-advertising habit of the musical profession in America. Etc. Etc. In short, Br. & H. should, as business men, have had sense enough to ask us to formulate a circular at their expense for American consumption, instead of, as I suspect, taking their cue from hustling but thoroughly British Dr. Maclean, who is the crown jewel in the affairs of the I. M. S. but who surely cannot understand our conditions here. In fact, I shall propose this to Mr. von Hase, if you concur in my views. Probably, it is too late to do anything this fall and therefore the present circular will have to do, though I doubt its efficacy, unless accompanied by an extra circular as outlined by you and which I return without amendments. By all means, include a franked postal card, but let it be addressed to Pratt. We should keep our administration as simple as possible and the modus vivendi should be that all checks be made out to Pratt, who then sends me a list of the new members and the money for Br. & H. in New York. Even that temporary method is too complicated and at Boston we should hit upon some scheme eliminating all unnecessary (for us unnecessary) expenses. Pratt should be molested with money matters only that refer to the cash $1 of the American Section and which $1 does not concern Br. & H. at all. The $5 really do not concern us and we should not be bothered with it. My suggestion would be to call Pratt Financial Secretary and Br. & H. in New York Treasurers. The only difficulty about it is this that those who deal directly with Br. & H. might not consider themselves bound by our own American constitution and might refuse to pay the $1 if conditions compel Pratt to call for it. On the other hand, nobody can properly, not even Br. & H., be called a regular member of the American Section, though he might have sent his $5 to Br. & H. in New York, who has not accepted the conditions framed by the American Section! So there we are!

I think that the whole matter can be regulated easily enough, if Br. & H. in New York are made Treasurers and if an ironclad working agreement (if necessary *via* headquarters of the firm in Leipzig) is reached between them and us, that will absolutely recognize us as the "powers that be" in America.

Doch, halt bei geschlossener Barriere! I have just read our own constitution, and now see more clearly where the difficulty lies. According to this circular which I enclose, Pratt is practically treasurer only for the $1 and Br. & H. for the $5. It is not made clear that the one dollar, *if* called in, is to be paid to Pratt. The thing reads as if actually every year one dollar has to be paid, which is, as we know, not the case. Of course, associate members *have* to pay $1, (because they surely cannot become associate members for nothing) whereas active members need only pay if requested. There's the trouble. So far the idea of associate members has been a failure and I do not believe that it can be made a success in building up the I. M. S. as such. Why not simply drop the associate membership idea! At any rate it is a point, which, I believe, should be taken up at Boston and be settled once for ever.

If we recognize straight regular members of the I. M. S. only, then all applications for membership should be made to, at any rate referred to (even by Br. & H.) the Secretary of the American Branch. He should then send whatever circular or printing matter (containing our constitution) has been decided upon to the applicant who will then, if he so cares, register as member by way of a postal card, officialy provided by the Secretary and addressed to Br. & H. in New York City. They will receive the monies and they should be obliged, as *treasurers of the American Section*, to make a financial report for the annual meeting (and they should in each case report to the Secretary any new members). As Br. & H. cannot be expected to be present at each annual meeting, they should forward their report in due time to the Financial Secretary who will read it at the annual meeting. The Financial Secretary shall further report on the $1 which might have been necessary to collect in order to defray special expenses of the American section. These $1 do not concern Br. & H. at all, nor, indeed, any monies that are "extras". In other words, even as Treasurers they have to do only with "publication" monies not with "administrative" monies.

If, however, the proposition to drop associate members, is voted down, well, then we shall have to chew our stew. Perhaps as follows:

1. All applications for active or associate membership are to be made (and to be referred to) the Secretary.

2. Active membership applications are to be dealt with as above.

3. Associate membership is secured by payment to the Financial Secretary, without Br. & H. in it at all.

4. Br. & H. report a) to the Secretary every new active member b) to the Financial Secretary on the finances of active membership timely enough for him to read this report at the annual meeting.

5. The financial Secretary reports in addition on the associate membership and all $1 collected also from active members.

How do these propositions strike you? I have amended two copies of our constitution (one for active and associate membership, the other for active only) as I think it should be done.

The constitution should appear on the circular which we may reasonably expect Br. & H. will print for American distribution. I even believe that it is their interest to mail such a circular broadcast at their own expense. At the same time, I think it about time to protest at headquarters in Leipzig any printed matter which is to draw members and which has not previously been approved by us as likely to help the I. M. S. in America. I shall to [sic] that to-morrow and at the same time ask, if they are willing to print (and mail) a circular such as we shall decide upon at Boston.

Now, please let me know your opinion about all this. I, too, believe that you should stir up Lewis to make Boston a success and to "collect" a goodly number of new members. Tell me your ideas about a program for Boston and I shall tell you mine. A list of Washington musicians would be useless. There are hardly any here of I. M. S. caliber and inclinations.

Sincerely yours with "Auf Wiedersehen" here

O. G. Sonneck

He wrote again on October 4, and now began to make specific suggestions concerning the Boston program.

Washington, D. C. Oct. 4. 10

My dear Professor Stanley:

Home again, I suppose, and not too much in work for giving the annual meeting of the I. M. G. some thoughts.

My intention is to send postals to each member with query whether he will be in Boston or not and whether he has an address up his sleeves or not. What do you think of asking Dolmetsch to give us some old lute music? Indeed, what program suggestions do you have for the I. M. G. meeting quite apart from the M. T. N. A. meeting? Don't you think that we should be able to have an afternoon with annual dinner devoted to our own affairs. Of course, if we can get a few interesting papers together and induce Dolmetsch as member of the I. M. G. to do his share, we should keep open house and let all who care to attend our meeting, attend. If we offer something worth while and attractive, that will help to rope in a few more members. I have about decided to go to Boston and shall, if necessary, contribute a paper to kill time.

Our business meeting will last a little longer this year on account of the constitutional questions etc Just a few days ago I had a letter from Mr. v. Hase, in which he agreed to print for us next year an Americanized circular. He further agreed that the New York branch of his firm would accept any reasonable offer of a more businesslike cooperation. Then there are some points about the Zeitschrift and the Sammelbände which should be voted on in view of the London Congress. I do not think, therefore, that our business meeting will last less than an hour or an hour and a half. Add an hour and a half for papers and Dolmetsch, if we can get him, half an hour for intermissions and a margin — Schon haber wir 3½ Stunden.

Supposing we start at 2½ — we don't get through before six. We simply need one whole afternoon for our own affairs and I suggest that you get busy and make arrangements accordingly with the Program Committee of the M. T. N. A.

At any rate, please let me hear from you as soon as possible and give me "instructions." I do not even know the exact date of the M. T. N. A. meeting and with whom to get in touch, if the necessity arises. After hearing from you I want to request suggestions from the other members of the Executive Committee of the I. M. G. How about Lewis? Would he not be a good man to put in charge of the more local affairs?

Perhaps I am a little "previous" but I like to have things in some shape ahead of time. It's a vice, I know, but I cannot help it.

Beste Grüsse

Yours sincerely
O. G. Sonneck

His next letter of November 2 again mentions Lewis, but this time with some disgruntlement.

If Sonneck was willing with some reluctance to relinquish responsibility for the local arrangements, he certainly did continue to supply Stanley with detailed suggestions regarding every other feature of the program. So far as I can determine, Stanley must have followed Sonneck's suggestions. There is no evidence of disagreement. Specifically, Sonneck suggests the names of speakers, agenda topics for the business meeting, the precise allottment of time to be given each activity, including the budget to follow, and he goes to the extent of suggestings several alternate arrangements, depending upon who could and who could not be persuaded or dissuaded from speaking.

The letters of November 3, 7, 10, and 20 speak for themselves.

Washington, D. C. Nov. 2. 10

My dear Prof:

I did write you a letter but it contained a few good-naturedly sarcastic remarks about the summersault Lewis made over my head and I tore it up. Of course, it is best that the whole business be centralized and I quite agreed with you that Lewis should be given a free hand, but he might have had the tact to write me a few lines and tell me what he proposed to do. I received sundry communications after he had done things which ordinarily a secretary does and had I received his letters one day later our members would have heard from me to a similar effect with the result that they would have thought the I. M. S. had *two* American Secretaries. Lewis was so kind as to leave me the job of sending out programs to applicants for such. I could not quite see why I should act as a kind of post-office if the real work is to be done by the Local Committee and I told him that he can lick stamps just as well as I. In other words I urged him not to invite confusion by letting even the routine business out of the hands of the local committee. They should do either everything or nothing and since, for good reasons, they have commenced to do everything, they should continue to do so. We better leave the whole business in Lewis' hands, except to certain suggestions affecting the I. M. S. *in toto*.

I noticed that Dr. Friedlaender is down with a paper for the M. T. N. A. It was my idea to have him, one of the most prominent members of the I. M. G., read a suitable paper to us. Imagine my disappointment when I saw him down for the M. T. N. A. Nevertheless

I wished Lewis to switch his paper over to us, on the grounds that the I. M. S. has more "rights" on Friedlaender than the M. T. N. A. You see, my paper is not exactly of the attractive kind and its scientific but depressing effect should be offset by something more interesting, especially if that part of our meeting is to be open to non-members. If we do not get Friedlaender, the danger will be that only yours truly will read a paper and that would be a rather poor showing for a Section that now counts over fifty members. I fear, that if you do not stir up Lewis, vice-president of the M. T. N. A., on this point, that our I. M. G. meeting will practically sink to the level of a mere business meeting, because my paper will not take up more than half an hour. We need absolutely *two* papers at least.

Our business meeting should surely be a closed meeting but unless the members attend very punctually at 2 o'clock, we shall not be able to "open the doors" at 3. Why not start with the papers at 2 and close the doors at 3 or a little after for a business meeting which then can last as long as necessary. The three matters to be brought up and to be discussed are: 1. Canvassing Committee. 2. Changes in the Constitution, amounting principally to the abolition of associate members, to the change of our now Treasurer to a Financial Secretary and the election of Br. & H. in New York as Treasurers with a number of details of administration connected with this change. 3. The matter of suitable circulars.

To settle all this, one hour will not be sufficient and the things are very important. 4. Local Boston Group.

As to the circulars, Dr. v. Hase is inclined to be very liberal, but my advice is to drop the matter until our meeting because I have written him to that effect and he might otherwise become quite confused. It follows that this piece of advice extends as far as suggesting that you should not waste further energy before the meeting on an increase of our membership. In order to expedite matters at the meeting, I shall have my matter in such shape that a waste of time will not be my fault. According to our constitution proposed amendments must first be submitted to the Executive Committee for approval. Therefore I shall address the proposed amendment with arguments to you with the request that you forward it with your vote to Damrosch, he to Pratt and Pratt to Gow, and Gow back to me. If the Executive Committee disapproves, well, — they will have committed a blunder.

I can't make out your P.S. about Prof. "Dam" *[probably Hollis Donn]* of Cornell. Please try again.

Certainly, pry v. Hase open as to the nigger in the woodpile, and do it so that you can report results at Boston, possibly in an official announcement to the M. T. N. A. but only after we have roped in a few more *regular* members. See the point? Yours sincerely O. G. Sonneck.

Washington, D. C. Nov. 3. 1910

My dear Professor:

Last evening I wrote you a letter and this morning I received this letter from Mr. Lewis which I beg to return to me in your next letter to me.

Lewis' letter is a clear cut document, but I ask you to compare it with his pink copies of circular letter, dated October 25th and especially with the one sent to Br. & H. I must be utterly stupid, but it seems to me that in the Br. & H. letter he decidedly goes beyond what he proposes to do in his letter to me of Nov. 1. If I am to send out programs etc, why does he want the list of members from Br. & H. for purposes of publicity? However, now he says that the invitation for lunch, program-outline, answers to inquiries etc are to issue from me. Very well, but sofar I know very much less about what is going to happen than he does. On the basis of Lewis' letter of Nov. 1, I shall attend to the outlined routine business, once I know what to do.

Br. & H. should not be mixed up in this affair because they have nothing to do sofar with the official business of the American Section.

As matters stand now, the I. M. S. has its meeting on Dec. 28th, at the Harvard Musical Association.

Program

a) 2–3 Papers. (one by Sonneck, theme: "Caractacus" not Arne's "Caractacus.")
b) 3–4 Business meeting
        (or vice versa)
c) 4– Formation of Local Group
        B. and c. require no further comment whereas a. calls for further work.

Most of our prominent members read papers before the M. T. N. A. Consequently they are not to be counted on. And again I come around to Friedlaender and urge you to influence the Program Committee in accordance with my suggestion of yesterday. If you consider that suggestion hopeless or inadvisable, for pity's sake, drum up somebody who will read an attractive and worthwhile paper of the I. M. S. kind. If everything else fails, I shall, with your consent, urge my assistant here Dr. Bruno Hirzel, one of the star-pupils of Sandberger and of course a member of the I. M. S., to hold something in reserve which I can read for him, if his means do not permit his trip to Boston. For instance, we bought for the Library of Congress the only known, or rather one of the two existing, mss. librettos of Wagner's "Liebesverbot." Hirzel is concocting an article on this for "Die Musik". Possibly it might interest our members to hear it read (in translation) before they read it, if they read it, in "Die Musik". Perhaps he has something else up his sleeve. I can ask him in due time, after you see no other way to fill the hour.

As regards the publication of I. M. S. papers, I think that we should see to it that publication in the M. T. N. A. Proceedings (which I personally do not favor, I mean *our* own stuff) does not militate against publication in the organ of the I. M. S. As for my own paper, I shall send it, in fact, next week to Leipzig for the Sammelbände, though not knowing whether they will print it or not. The point I make is this: It is about time that more worth-while American stuff appears in the Zeitschrift and in the Sammelbände. Of course, "wo nichts ist, da hat der Kaiser sein Recht verloren." So far, I am, I believe, the only American member who has had his messages printed in Leipzig.

Do not make a mistake about it, my dear Prof., the I. M. S. meeting, so far as its literary side is concerned, will be a dead failure in contrast with the apparently fine program of the M. T. N. A., if you do not exercise pressure on somebody to read something really fine. Do not give much publicity to our meeting, unless we can make an excellent showing. Otherwise keep it *entre nous* as much as possible.

Yours sincerely
O. G. Sonneck

Washington, D. C. Nov. 7. 10.

My dear Prof.
I have nothing to add to my previous letters except concrete suggestions.

1. Libraries are counted as members and therefore they can send anybody they please to represent them.

2. The Luncheon. Is it to be before our meeting or after or when? If on the 28th before 2 o'clock it will surely knock a hole into our meeting calculations. You better find out about that. Also you better ask if Friedlaender gets an invitation. Of course he should, but somebody might forget the fact that he is an I. M. S. man.

3. Simply decide on your own authority whether business meeting or paper function at 2 o'clock to 3.

4. Papers. I advise to find out if the M. T. N. A. will transfer Friedlaender to us. Of course, then our paper functions should be open to all members of the M. T. N. A. and such persons who by payment of M. T. N. A. affair obolus have the right to attend this meeting. Our meeting (I mean the literary part) should be open only to such persons and ourselves. Our business meeting should not be open to anybody except members of the I. M. G. Please decide definitely that point. If the M. T. N. A. does not transfer Friedlaender, I am strongly in favor of making our meeting as much as possible an I. M. S. affair but I would extend the invitation or at least let it be known that members of the M. T. N. A. are welcome to our literary function.

Afterthought! Perhaps you better drop the transfer idea of Friedlaender but ask him personally as American president if he will not honor us with an address. My plan would then be this

1) 2–3 Business meeting, (to be transacted expeditiously)

2) 3–4 or a little later Papers.

a. Introductory remarks by you of a *general* character (about 5 minutes)

b. A paper by somebody (perhaps Canon Douglass if you can get him). 15 minutes.

c. Sonneck's paper. (25 minutes)

d. Friedlaender on the aims of the I. M. G., its accomplishments abroad etc and emphasis on importance of local groups.

3) 4– Formation of Boston group.

Do you see the point? Friedlaender could easily make such a propaganda speech in fifteen minutes. It need not even be a set speech but we could have a stenographer who would take it down for revision by him for the Proceedings of the M. T. N. A.!

If you cannot get Friedlaender to do this nor to read any paper, then you would simply elaborate on your own introductory remarks. These should then be followed by my paper and this in turn by a paper which will be more interesting.

Or again, if Friedlaender prefers to read a paper on some special topic, then you would start in with about 10 minutes on the I. M. G. I would follow you and the climax would come with Friedlaender. In other words, if he does not make a speech on the I. M. G. but delivers a paper on some special topic then the program would not require an additional paper at all, nor would time permit it.

These are the possibilities, as I see them. It therefore seems to me that your first and immediate step should be to get in touch with Friedlaender. Further arrangements will depend on his answer. If you get him down for either a speech on the I. M. G. or for what might be better still a corking good and interesting address, then the situation is saved and you really would not need a further paper beyond his, mine and your introductory speech. If he refuses, then go immediately for somebody else, whether the theme be Indian Music or the proper instrumentation of an Egyptian oyster cock-tail.

If I can send word to *our* members between Dec. 1st. and 5th, that will be time enough. Please send me the completed program in type-written form. I shall then have it printed more or less elegantly under the heading I. M. S. on swell cards and send it out. It should of course contain (for our members only) date and place of the Luncheon, which, I hope, will not be on prohibition lines.

Yours sincerely
O. G. Sonneck

Nov. 10. 10
Library of Congress

My dear Prof.

Just received your letter of Nov. 8. I believe *my* last letter which you must have received in the mean time covers the points mentioned in your last few communications. "Liebesverbot" not possible, because Hirzel cannot finish it. However, he is willing to have read by me a 10 minute affair from a large work which he is compiling. This excerpt (with introduction) deals with the musical impressions of an English lady on the Continent and, from what he tells me, will be an attractive Scherzetto in our Suite. Definite title yet to be settled. *I have accepted his offer*, because it is just what we need to fill in. Now please address a few appropriate lines to Dr. Bruno Hirzel, Library of Congress, thanking him and hoping that he will be able to personally read the paper. (The trip to Boston is, I fear, too expensive for him and so, I shall, *trotz* your hope, probably have to read the paper for him.

Aldrich out of the question because he stutters terribly, the poor fellow. Otherwise excellent. Still, though you would have to run the risk that he would attend personally and try to read his paper, I suggest that you ask him point-blank if he would not contribute something 10–15 minutes. He must know his unfortunate defect and I am sure that he would rather have the thing read (by staying in N. Y.) than read it himself. By getting Aldrich's active interest, it might help to draw the other critics of standing to our ranks! At any rate try!! and try immediately.

If Aldrich says no, then tackle either Dickinson or Andrews for something (10–15 minutes on a fitting subject close to their hearts). You see, we cannot keep the interest alive amongst our more recent members when [i.e. unless] they are made to feel that they are welcome and important members of the organization!! I feel sure that one of the three gentlemen mentioned will say yes. Accordingly the program should then be as follows:

1. 2–3 Business meeting. (If necessary the job to be finished by the Executive Committee on proper motion)

2. 3–4 ½ Papers.

with dis-
cussion
not more
than
1 ½ hours

a. Stanley: Introductory Remarks (5 minutes)
b. Aldrich or D. or A. (10–15 minutes)
c. Sonneck (25–30 minutes)
d. Hirzel (10 minutes)
e. Friedlaender on the I. M. G. 10 min.

4 ½ Formation of Local Boston group.

That would be a corking good program. Try to settle it in that form.

Yours sincerely
O. G. Sonneck

Washington, D. C. Nov. 20. 10.

My dear Prof.

By all means "Growth of musical form in Plain Song", if he can settle that in 15–20 minutes. Otherwise "Methods of research in the Solesmes Laboratory". Sofar then the program reads:

Stanley, Hirzel, Douglass, Sonneck or whatever order you prefer.

Now, if Friedlaender refuses, the question will be, do we have enough?

In reading my stuff as already sent to Leipzig, it took 45 minutes. Well, I got busy and just slashed it to pieces, at the same time improving the paper as a "Vortrag." I have now got it down safely to 30 minutes, but even with further amputations I can't get it below 25 minutes. Let us say then, 30 minutes, Hirzel 10 minutes, Douglass 15 minutes, your introductory remarks 5–10 minutes. Let us say 65 minutes without Friedlaender and for intermission and discussion 15 minutes = 80. If Friedlaender accepts for a talk not to exceed 10–15, then you would limit yourself, as planned, to five minutes. *Ergo*: 5 + 10 + 30 + 15 + 15 + 15 = One hour and a half. So that we are saved, no matter whether Friedlaender, of course asked to be present, accepts to read paper or not. Therefore I move Schluss der Debatte. As soon as you hear from Friedlaender and Canon Douglass, please send me typewritten titles of your introduction and their addresses. I shall then immediately get the program printed and send it out. Of course, I also need definite information about date and place and host of luncheon.

As to the business meeting, the Secretary will have practically nothing to report. My report will not take more than five minutes, Treasurer's report and your opening remarks will not take more than five minutes. This leaves 50 minutes. If the Executive Committee has approved my proposed amendments and unless some crank begins to introduce tape-wormy discussions of the subject, the acceptance etc of the proposed amendments should not consume more than 15 minutes. This leaves 35 minutes. Election of officers, not more than five minutes. We still have 30 minutes. Appointment of Propaganda Committee not more than five minutes. This should, in order to expedite matters, be put in charge of (wording and publishing at Br. & H.'s expense) a proper circular. What I have to produce in form of suggestions from Br. & H. will not take more than five minutes. Now, I think that the matter of propaganda and circular should be put, upon timely motion, entirely into the hands of either the new Executive Committee or of a propaganda committee. Personally, I prefer the former, as I do not believe in breaking up things into too many committees. The committee decided upon can then easily find about an hour before we all return home, to settle the matter right then and there at Boston.

In brief, we should be able to close the business meeting before 3 o'clock, or at any rate, we should be able to start the papers punctually at three. I have an idea, that if we announce papers for 2.45, it might help to cut down useless discussions at the business meeting. If we start the business meeting at 2 or not later than 2.5–2.10, we should still be able to begin papers before three. The point is to not protract the luncheon. We should be punctually ready at 2 o'clock to go ahead. It might also be well, to say 4.15 Formation of local Boston group, instead of 4 or 4.30.

Now please, after hearing from Friedlaender and Canon Douglass, just send me a typewritten program with dates, time etc as you consider it advisable. I am sure, that it will not require further discussion.

Very sincerely yours
O. G. Sonneck

On December 18 a week and a half before the meeting, Sonneck wrote Stanley at some length. This was the last letter written prior to the meeting. It mentions some of the recurrent concerns and can serve as a summary of them.

Washington, D. C. Dec. 18. 10.

My dear Prof:

Your letter received with the news of local group.-the first in the United States. The East has been beaten out of it after all. I suppose the gentlemen at Boston will feel sore but that is their private business. As the rules call for at least seven members for the formation of a local group and as so far there are only about two in Boston, they must have done some hustling, if they are about to form a local group there. However, we shall see.

Not counting a New York gentleman who wants to become a member in time for Boston, I find that we have, institutions included, sixty-four members of the I. M. G. in our country. That is a pretty good showing everything considered. It would not surprise me if, after the Boston meeting, we shall have run the total up to about eighty. At that rate we shall soon be in fourth position, with only Germany, France and England ahead of us, because Austria–Hungary cannot properly be called Germany. In other words, our voice should have weight in the council of nations and at London we should stand on our rights and not allow ourselves to be considered back-numbers any longer. Just for the fun of it, I "soeben" counted up Austria-Hungary as in the list of August 1909. They then had seventy members. With just a little energy we should be able to run ahead of them even though they, too, have gained in numbers since August 1909.

Now to Boston. I have received sofar fifteen affirmative answers. They do not include Lewis, Cole and Gòw. I figure that we shall have about twenty of our members present if not more. Sofar only three have answered in the affirmative who were not members on July 1. I sincerely hope that our Harvard Friends will not adhere to their very embarrassing time limit. That restriction of theirs was about the most tactless thing that ever came out of the East. At any rate, such a restriction should not apply to members who come from afar! Either one is a member of the I. M. S. or one is not and *all* members should be welcome at such a luncheon. A few dollars more or less should not be a consideration, if they wish to honor us and at any rate they should not give us a luncheon with such a string to it which would cause bad blood among those whom they wish to honor! As you will have noticed, I, as Secretary, did not feel justified in insulting some of our members by quoting the Harvard luncheon conditions. Instead, I wanted to see just how many of the "undesirables" would attend, trusting that afterwards Lewis would arrange matters satisfactorily. I shall send him the complete list on Dec. 21 with the urgent request that the three "undesirables" not be barred. Who knows but such "undesirables" may turn out later to be our best members. How very unwise and inconsiderate to make such a restriction! Indeed, of the three, for all I know, two may have applied for membership before July 1. Furthermore, supposing that Parker, Chadwick, Converse, Dickinson etc. had become members in October, would the Harvard people want them barred, too? Pshaw!!

I am to attend personally *and* as *official* representative of the L. of C., as a member and Hirzel, too, will come in person. (Accordingly Harvard ought to give me two meal tickets instead of one!) I expect to be at the Copley Square Hotel on Dec. 27th in the morning.

As to the program, Friedlaender's informal address is *not* new. He printed an essay on this topic a year ago in the Peters Jahrbuch, I can't see for the life of me, how he can get through with his address in fifteen minutes. Mine will take at least twenty minutes, but, in case Friedlaender works overtime, I shall not read my stuff, but merely give the arguments and results of my thesis. That should not take more than ten minutes. Of course, if Canon Douglass disappoints us, then I shall read my paper as cut down mercilessly from the original which, I hope, will be printed in the Sammelbände.

Also "Auf baldiges Wiedersehen"

Mit herzlichen grüssen
O. G. Sonneck

Stanley's file contains five letters written subsequent to the Boston meeting. On January 1, 1911, Sonneck wrote, "We had a corking good time, didn't we?". He then mentions what turned out to be a problem in getting George Chadwick to join. The matter is mentioned again in subsequent letters. The full story is best told in Sonneck's own words.

January 1, 1911: "I shall go after Chadwick and feel certain that he will join, even if only to enrich the New England Conservatory Library."

January 12, 1911: "Please write Chadwick asking him if you understood correctly that he wishes to join the *International Musical Society*. He did not say anything of the kind, but that is the way to get him. Request him to drop *me* a line to that effect."

January 26, 1911: "At least we now have a swell letterhead and swell envelopes even if our friend Chadwick gave us the cold shoulder . . . . . Chadwick will get the circular and he will see that we are alive."

We learn also from these letters that the Section had increased in size to eighty-eight members. Stanley and Sonneck by this time were planning to leave for London for the International Congress. The full text follows.

Washington, D. C. Jan. 1. 1911

My dear Prof.

Here is the list of names of new Ann Arbor and Detroit members. Please correct it, add to it, give me the exact addresses and return it at your earliest convenience. I shall then tell the gentlemen, how to deal with Br. & H. After Lewis returns the Boston list, I shall send to Br. & H. a complete list of new members.

Milliken, H. A.
Howland, William
Hughes, Edwin, Detroit, Mich.
Lockwood, Albert

Biggs   Detroit, Mich.
Peace, Marshall
Any others?
We had a corking good time, didn't we? I shall go after Chadwick
and feel certain that he will join, even if only to enrich the New
England Conservatory Library.

In haste

Yours sincerely
O. G. Sonneck

P.S. Do you think that a special executive vote is necessary to accept
invitation to meet at Ann Arbor? Or, in as much as you, Pratt and I
were at Boston, would not our "yea" be sufficient? PP. SS. What is
Bowman's address? Whom else did you rope in besides Faelten and
Foote?

83 members sofar!!

Washington, D. C. Jan. 12. 11.

Dear Prof.:

1) All checks for regular membership to Breitkopf & Härtel, New
   York City. Pratt gets only $1 if he calls for it.
2) Have insisted that Pratt have regular North American Section writing paper printed. It's the only dignified way for doing things now
3) Please send *me* London Congress circulars for distribution if
   necessary *but not* the old English circulars
4) Tell your friend Maclean in London please to forward the bulk of
   such stuff always to me, the Secretary.
5) Send Ann Arbor-Detroit names to Br. & H., N.Y.C.
6) Am waiting for the rest of 'em.
7) Our Constitution will be printed in our own circular which will go
   to all of our members besides, as Br. & H. have already promised,
   to M. T. N. A. members, to the persons on their business mailing
   list and to a large number of libraries. We shall then feel the results
   or "nit."
8) Kicked about delay in our getting the Zeitschrift etc. Br. & H. have
   instructed Br. & H. in Leipzig to send to all members direct instead
   of via New York.
9) Shall send complete list as soon as all names are in.
10) Please write Chadwick asking him if you understood correctly that
    he wishes to join the *International Musical Society*. He did not say

anything of the kind, but that is the way to get him. Request him to drop *me* a line to that effect.

11) Insisted that Br. & H. send to all new members the back numbers of the year as they are entitled to them for their $5.

12) Enclose Local Constitution for forwarding to the rest of the Executive Committee.

Sincerely yours
O. G. Sonneck

After E.-C. has approved Local Branch draw off names of officers for me so I can send them on to Leipzig.

International Musical Society
NORTH AMERICAN SECTION

PRESIDENT, ALBERT A.
  STANLEY, UNIVERSITY OF
MICHIGAN, ANN ARBOR, MICH.
SECRETARY, OSCAR G.
  SONNECK, LIBRARY OF
CONGRESS, WASHINGTON,
D. C.

VICE-PRESIDENT, FRANK
  DAMROSCH
  120 CLAREMONT AVE.,
  NEW YORK CITY
FINANCIAL SECRETARY,
  WALDO S. PRATT,
  86 GILLET ST.,
  HARTFORD, CONN.

TREASURERS
BREITKOPF & HAERTEL,
24 WEST 20TH ST., NEW YORK CITY

Washington, D. C. Jan. 26, 1911

My dear Professor:

    At least we now have a swell letterhead and swell envelopes even if our friend Chadwick gave us the cold shoulder.

    How about Gautvoort. Please tackle him as I am not sure that he saw our immediate usefulness.

Chadwick will get the circular and he will see that we are alive.

Have just written President Hutchins accepting officially the invitation.

April 4–11 I am due at Rome, carrying the official U. S. brand to the Congress Internazionale Musicale.

A shame if we cannot muster half a dozen strong ones for London.

Sincerely yours,
O. G. Sonneck

Lento lamentoso   Allegro spiritoso

Chicago and Evanston members
Cole, Prof. Rossetter G. 1363 [i.e. Hyde] Park Boulevard Hackett, Karleton. Kimball Hall
Hattstardt, John J. American Conservatory of Music. Kimball Hall
Middelschulte, Wilhelm 3232 South Park Ave.
Weidig, Adolf 243 Wabash Ave.
Evanston
Lutkin, Prof. Peter C. Northwestern University
White, Prof. Wm. A.   ,,   ,,

Lutkin should be able to get half a dozen more without difficulty.

Pratt sent me name of Prof. Carl Paige Wood, Denison University, Granville, O. as new member whom please add to the list which I requested Br. & H. to send to you.

We have *eighty-eight* now!

International Musical Society
NORTH AMERICAN SECTION

PRESIDENT, ALBERT A. STANLEY, UNIVERSITY OF MICHIGAN, ANN ARBOR, MICH.
SECRETARY, OSCAR G. SONNECK, LIBRARY OF CONGRESS, WASHINGTON, D. C.

VICE-PRESIDENT, FRANK DAMROSCH
120 CLAREMONT AVE., NEW YORK CITY
FINANCIAL SECRETARY, WALDO S. PRATT,
86 GILLET ST., HARTFORD, CONN.

International Musical Society

NORTH AMERICAN SECTION

PRESIDENT, ALBERT A. STANLEY,
UNIVERSITY OF MICHIGAN, ANN ARBOR, MICH.

SECRETARY, OSCAR G. SONNECK,
LIBRARY OF CONGRESS, WASHINGTON, D. C.

TREASURERS
BREITKOPF & HAERTEL,
24 WEST 20TH ST., NEW YORK CITY

VICE-PRESIDENT, FRANK DAMROSCH,
120 CLAREMONT AVE., NEW YORK CITY

FINANCIAL SECRETARY, WALDO S. PRATT,
86 GILLETT ST., HARTFORD, CONN.

Washington D. C. Jan. 26, 1911

My dear Professor:

At least we now have a swell letterhead and swell envelopes even if our friend Chadwick gave us the cold shoulder.

How about Gantvoort. Please tackle him as I am not sure that he saw our immediate usefulness.

Chadwick will get the circular and he will see that we are alive.

Have just written President Hutchins accepting officially the invitation.

April 4 – 11 I am due at Rome, carrying the official U. S. brand to the Congresso Internazionale Musicale.

A shame if we cannot muster half a dozen strong ones for London.

Sincerely yours

O. G. Sonneck

Chicago and Evanston members
Cole, Prof. Rossetter G. 1363 High Park Boulevard
Hackett, Karleton. Kimball Hall
Hattstaedt, John J. American Conservatory of Music. Kimball Hall
Middelschulte, Wilhelm 3232 South Park Ave.
Wendig, Adolf. 243 Wabash Ave.
Evanston
Lutkin, Prof. Peter C. Northwestern University
White, Prof. Wm. A.

Lutkin should be able to get half a dozen more without difficulty.

Pratt sent me name of Prof. Carl Paige Wood, Denison University, Granville, O. as new member whom please add to the list which I requested Br. & H. to send everyone.

We are eighty-eight now!

Illustration 2. Sonneck's letter of January 26, 1911, written on the new "swell letterhead" and mentioning that "Chadwick gave us the cold shoulder."

Washington, D. C. Feb. 10, 11

My dear Professor:

1. Boston Section — Punk, unless they get together. One of the gentlemen on Prof. Lewis' list (and I believe he was at present at our meeting) refused to honor Br. & H.'s bill because he neither is nor wants to be a member.

2. Envelopes. Pratt thinks we should have envelopes printed locally. You for your purposes, I for mine etc.

3. Representative at Rome of the I. M. S. Very well, on condition that I do not make use of it, unless other Sections have done the same and delegated somebody.

4. We two certainly are aristocrats. I go abroad with the "Kaiserin Auguste Victoria," you with the "Empress of Britain." I expect to arrive at London May 24th or 25th, but I do not know yet where I shall take "Kost und Logis." All preliminaries will therefore have to be settled by correspondence. As you arrive before May 29th we can easily settle upon a place of meeting together with the other American gents.

5. Circular. Br. & H. are awaiting the pleasure of young Dr. von Hase, now in America. He is to decide about it. I fail to see what he has to say about it, if his father has sanctioned the thing, but what can I do. At this rate, the circular will not be out before I quit America for Europa. Probably I shall have to request Dr. Hirzel to act as Secretary pro tem.

This is about all for to-day.

Yours very sincerely
O. G. Sonneck

International Musical Society
NORTH AMERICAN SECTION

PRESIDENT, ALBERT A.
  STANLEY, UNIVERSITY OF
MICHIGAN, ANN ARBOR, MICH.
SECRETARY, OSCAR G.
  SONNECK, LIBRARY OF
CONGRESS, WASHINGTON,
D. C.

VICE-PRESIDENT, FRANK
  DAMROSCH
120 CLAREMONT AVE.,
NEW YORK CITY
FINANCIAL SECRETARY,
WALDO S. PRATT,
86 GILLET ST.,
HARTFORD, CONN.

TREASURERS
BREITKOPF & HAERTEL,
24 WEST 20TH ST., NEW YORK CITY

March 7. 11.

My dear Prof. Stanley
  Why bother about reprints of the Proceedings. However, if you and Pratt are of a different opinion, just go ahead. But please leave me out of it just now. I am getting ready for my song "Ich hab mich ubergeben mit Herz und mit Hand" and really could not attend to the business, if I wanted to: I leave here next Wednesday.
  The circulars have been sent to Leipzig! I am to read proof there. Br. & H. wanted to save some few dollars. That is also the reason why they ship the magazines from Leipzig to America by freight together with other stuff, and not by mail. I have not gotten the February number yet. Young Dr. v. Hase, who was here, a few days ago could see nothing objectionable or annoying in this. The truth is, he does not care a d—— for the I. M. S. and does not like the fact, that the firm has lost over 36000 Mk sofar on the proposition.
  Neither Farwell nor Clippingen have written to me but Zielinski,

who does not appear in the membership list, did. We dropped him because he did not send his dues to New York though repeatedly asked to do so. He informs me that he is in the habit of making payment to Leipzig. I told the Br. & H. in New York to get into touch with the Leipzig crowd or rather their headquarters. If I am correctly informed and I have no reason to doubt Pratt's word, they can't get any money out of Zielinski for the M. T. N. A. either. Does he send his fees for the M. T. N. A. to St. Petersburg?

What a crazy notion to pay by way of Europe and get the whole thing mixed up.

Enough for to-day. Auf Wiedersehen.

Yours sincerely
O. G. Sonneck

World War I soon put an end to international musicology. The Americans did not get themselves organized again until the 1930's, when still another German-educated American, Otto Kinkeldey, the third generation as it were, succeeded in founding the American Musicological Society.

ICONOGRAPHIC AND ARTISITIC TRADITIONS

CHAPTER EIGHTEEN

THE TWENTY-FOUR ELDERS IN THE SOUTH OF SPAIN

Thomas F. Taylor

University of Michigan

> There was a rainbow encircling the throne, and this looked like an emerald. Around the throne in a circle were twenty-four thrones, and on them I saw twenty-four elders sitting, dressed in white robes with golden crowns on their heads. Rev.4:3–4
>
> The Lamb came forward to take the scroll from the right hand of the One sitting on the throne, and when he took it, the four animals prostrated themselves before him and with them the twenty-four elders; each one of them was holding a harp and had a golden bowl full of incense made of the prayers of the saints. They sang a new hymn. Rev.5:7–9

Thus John describes the twenty-four elders in his vision of the Apocalypse. It is a vision which was used by Medieval church authorities to remind their flock of the elevated position held by Christ in the universe. He was the King of Kings and Lord of Lords. To have a full twenty-four elders wearing crowns serving as vassals made the figure of Christ seem greater even still. And the elders all played harps, bringing to mind the Old Testament figure of King David, the harpist and singer of psalms.

Throughout the Middle Ages, there was a great fascination with the elders of John's apocalyptic vision, particularly in the Iberian peninsula. ''The Apocalypse itself had a peculiarly cherished place in Spanish religious life. This fact was officially stated as early as the fourth Council of Trent. 'The Apocalypse is a canonical book and should be read in the church from Easter to Pentecost'."[1]

The apocalyptic vision was widely discussed in Medieval literature, and illustrated in manuscript illuminations and sculpture. For instance, the *Commentaries* of Beatus of Liebana devote some of their most sumptuous illuminations to that vision. Beatus(d.c.798), a monk of northern Spain, was teacher and advisor to Queen Adosinda, wife of King Silo of Leon, 774–783. The *Commentary on the Apocalypse* is an affirmation of hope, an invitation to put faith in Christ, who speaks and acts as Victor.

By the time the Beatus *Commentaries* were copied in subsequent centuries, the harps had been changed to guitars in the illuminations of several of the twenty-four manuscripts which are known to be extant. Madrid, Bibl. Nac. Olim, B. 31 (fol.6), dated 1047, for instance, has six elders playing guitars to the lamb at the foot of a large cross. Fourteen

Illustration 1. Beatus of Liebana, *Sancti Beati a Liebana in apocalypsin codex Gerundensis* (facsim. Urs Graf, Olten and Lausanne, 1962), ff. 189v.–190.

---

[1] John Williams, "The Beatus Commentaries and Spanish Bible Illustration," in *Actas del simposio para el estudio de los codices del "Comentario al Apocalipsis" de Beatus de Liebana* (Madrid, 1980), 218.

elders are seen on folio 122v of Madrid Archivo Historico, S4V6, dated 968–970. Seven of them are playing guitars, and the others seem to be playing tambourines.

Curiously, the number of elders in the illumination does not seem to be significant to author or artist. Elders increase in number in the magnificent scene pictured on ff. 189v–190 of the Codex Gerundensis of about 975 in Gerona cathedral in northeastern Spain (*Illus.* 1), where twenty-nine elders are seen holding eighteen guitars (perhaps fiddles, although no bows are visible).

As gothic cathedrals were conceived and construction commenced in the eleventh and twelfth centuries, the tradition of the twenty-four elders was transferred from parchment to stone with the French cathedral builders at Moissac, and particularly beautiful Chartres, adorning the stone archivolts around the royal portal with carvings of elders and angels. The curved form of the doorway lent itself well to John's image of the rainbow. As with Beatus, "harps" were broadly interpreted to include a variety of stringed instruments.

A study of the royal portal at Chartres cathedral makes clear the connection with Beatus. "The second coming of Christ combines tympanum, lintel, and archivolts in one grandiose scene. His return in glory is witnessed by the angels and twenty-four elders, as it had been represented before in illuminated manuscripts of the Beatus Apocalypse and in the tympanum of St. Pierre in Moissac."[2]

> It was perhaps because of its harmonic, chordal capacity, as well as for its use in sacred music and in instruction in the cloisters, that the hurdy-gurdy was frequently given the place of honor in the assemblage of the twenty-four elders in so many French and Spanish tympanums of the 11th and 12th centuries. . . . The elders, it seems, preferred the apparently nobler instruments, the stringed ones, perhaps because of the string instruments mentioned in Revelation 14:2–3; as far as the writer can see, they did not touch a bagpipe.[3]

Thus, Emanuel Winternitz describes the choice of instruments used by the elders. The example he uses is the *Portico de la Gloria* at the 12th-century cathedral of Santiago de Compostela. That portico contains only string instruments. Indeed, most of the Spanish doorways which depict the elders have them playing stringed instruments; however, in

---

[2] Adolf Katzenellenbogen, *The Sculptural Programs of Chartres Cathedral* (Baltimore, 1959), 25.

[3] Emanuel Winternitz, *Musical Instruments and their Symbolism in Western Art: studies in musical iconography* (New Haven, 1979), 71.

Illustration 2. Burgos cathedral, South portal detail. See note 5.

some cases, winds and a few percussion instruments may also be found.

The elders around the south door of the cathedral at Burgos are in very much the same orientation and organization as those in Chartres, however the instruments are of a greater variety than those in the French cathedral. Some of the instruments are broken, but one can clearly make out the signs of wind players with their cheeks puffed out to blow. Two of the instruments are quite possibly bagpipes. This conjecture is supported in the case of the instrument on the lower left of the outer archivolt by its being paired with a hurdy-gurdy next to it in the inner arc (*Illus.* 2). Winternitz discusses the similar iconography of these instruments, both of which are drone instruments.[4] The instrument two elders above the hurdy-gurdy on the left-hand inner arc at Burgos is a wind also — possibly a recorder or shawm, judging from the position of the musician's arms, which are partially broken, as is the lower portion of the instrument. Above that, an elder plays a traverse flute, and a positive organ is also included in the scene, situated high above the flute player in the outer arc (*Illus.* 3).[5]

    [4] *Ibid.*, 71–85.

    [5] Hannschubert Mahn, *Kathedralplastik in Spanien: Die Monumentale Figuralskuptur in <Alt = >Kastilien, Leon und Navarra zwischen 1230 und 1380* (Reutlingen, 1931). Abb. 13.

Illustration 3. Burgos Cathedral, South portal detail. from Mahn, plate 16.

Even more wind instruments are to be found around the door at Sasamon Cathedral, which is also in northern Spain, thirty kilometers west of Burgos. In organization and style, that door is very similar to the one in the larger city, and is probably derived from it. Here, at least nine of the elders may be seen playing trumpets, shawms, bagpipes, and a transverse flute. As at Burgos, one elder plays a positive organ, assisted by a youth to pump the bellows.[6]

A map in Hannschubert Mahn's *Kathedralplastik in Spanien* shows that the tradition of sculptured portals depicting the Apocalypse was concentrated in the north-western part of the country.[7] This is under-

---

[6] *Ibid.*, Abb. 93–4.
[7] *Ibid.*, 80.

Illustration 4. General picture of Orihuela, *Porta de Loreto*.

standable, since it is to that part of the country, along the pilgrim route to Santiago, that the French influence is most pronounced in cathedral design in cities such as Leon and Burgos.[8]

Thus, it is of some interest that a set of musicians encircle the south door (*Porta de Loreto*) of Orihuela Cathedral, in Alicante province in the south-eastern corner of the country (*Illus.* 4). Whereas the Burgos, Santiago de Compostela and Sasamon apocalyptic doors occupy prominent positions in the cathedral plan, opening on to relatively large squares, the south door at Orihuela cathedral faces a narrow street so that one is likely to miss the significance of the sculpture to be viewed there.

Several questions come to mind as one views these sculptures around the door in Orihuela:

1. What are they doing here in the south?
2. Who brought the idea down from France or northern Spain?
3. Were the artists who sculpted them French or Spanish?
4. Do the figures represent the elders of the apocalypse?
5. Can the instruments portrayed tell us anything about types of instruments used locally, or about the manner in which they were played?

---

[8] O.N.V. Glendinning, "The visual arts in Spain," in *Spain, a companion to Spanish Studies*, edited by P.E. Russell (London, 1973), 479.

A few historical details about Orihuela can perhaps help to answer some of these questions. During Roman times, it was probably the site of the important city of Orcelis, being in an easily defended position between the Segura river and à steep mountain, looking over a fertile *huerta*, or plain, which contains the largest palm grove in Spain. Under the Visigoths, the city was apparently renamed Aurariola, and in 579, became the capital of one of the eight provinces into which Leovigild divided the peninsula. During the Moorish period, which began in the eighth century, duke Teodormiro obtained a special privilege to maintain an independent Christian territory, which lasted for nearly a century. The Christians retook the city in 1262, and by the first years of the fourteenth century, a large collegiate church was under construction. It was that building which became the cathedral when a bishopric was established in Orihuela in 1437.[9]

Influence from the north was made more likely when Orihuela was reattached to the realm of Valencia by the treaty of Torrijos. That was in 1304, just the year before construction was begun on the collegiate church, thus opening the way for artisans from farther north to be imported for work on the project. The identity of those artisans has yet to be determined. They could have been either French or Spanish, as were the men who built the cathedrals in the north. Even if they were known by Spanish names, they might not have been Spanish, as was most likely the case with Maestro Esteban and Maestro Mateo, who did the statues and bas-reliefs at Santiago de Compostela. To complicate the issue, Spaniards were sometimes trained under French master stoneworkers.[10] Perhaps the most likely possibility for the Orihuela door is that local sculptors were used. Judging from the primitive simplicity of the carving, it would seem that the artists had not learned their trade from the same source as those who worked at Burgos, Santiago or Sasamon. In the Orihuela work, hands and heads are often too large for the bodies — details are far less adventurously and realistically handled — the bodily positions are more wooden and less varied.

Whereas the programs of the doors at Burgos and Santiago de Compostela are easy to determine and are clearly laid out, there seems

---

[9] "Orihuela" in *Enciclopedia Universal Ilustrada Europeo Americana*, (Madrid, 1920).

[10] Glendinning, p. 476. For further discussion of the masons who worked on Spanish cathedrals, see George Edmund Street, *Some Account of Gothic Architecture in Spain*, new edition by G.G. King, (London, 1914).

to be a mixture of elements in the plan of the *Porta de Loreto* at Orihuela. Around the more well-known doors in the north, angels and elders are clearly distinguished from each other. At Burgos, the angels occupy an inner ring, and the elders encircle them in two outer rings. In the plan at Santiago, angels stand on either side of the composition, and the elders are in one large arch with their heads radiating out from the central scene. The orientation at Orihuela has elders and angels mixed in two concentric arches with their bodies moving around the tympanum as at Burgos and Sasamon. Perhaps the sculptor knew the north door of Valencia cathedral which was being worked on at about the same time (first half of the fourteenth century), and pictures angels around the figure of the Blessed Virgin.[11]

Illustration 5. Left side of Orihuela portal.

---

[11] Mahn, 58.

Illustration 6. View of top, Orihuela portal.

The principal obstruction to determining the full plan at Orihuela however, is that the entire composition is no longer in place. Elders and angels make music around the doorway, but there is no scene for them to glorify in the center. At the other cathedrals where this scene is displayed, Christ is in the center in his glory as a judge or king, and around him are various arrangements of the four beasts, the four evangelists at their desks and sometimes some angels. (See the two beasts and one evangelist in *Illus.* 2.) At Orihuela, the center contains no sculpture — just a timpanum in a patterned decoration with a lintel to support it. These two elements seem more recent than the archivolts, both in condition of the stone and in style. Thus, it is principally through obvious connections with the tradition established by Beatus, and continued in stone at Moissac, Chartres and the northern Spanish cathedrals that one can deduce that it is the vision of John that is being depicted here.

It is possible that the artist at Orihuela chose to include the evangelists among the elders, as three of the figures are holding what appear to be large quill pens (*Illus.* 5–6). Their places in the portal are Numbers 26, 30 and 42 in *Figure 1*, a diagram which identifies the sculptures, and places them in the overall design. Number 26 is the fourth figure up on the right side of *Illus.* 5. Number 30, third from the top of the inner left-hand arch in *Illus.* 6 is possibly wearing a bishop's miter, in which case he would be Mark, who by tradition was the first bishop

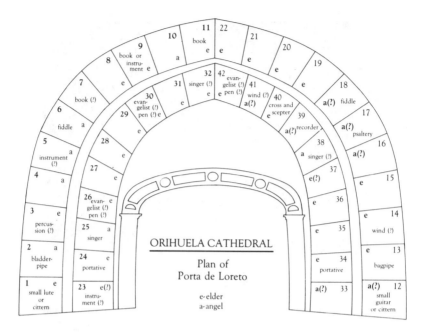

The plan labels (reading the arch from outer to inner rings):

Outer ring: 11 book e · 22 e · 21 e · 10 a · 20 · 9 book or instrument e · 8 e · 19 e · 7 e · 18 · 6 book (?) a · 17 · fiddle · 5 instrument (?) a · 28 · 16 · psaltery a(?) · 4 a · 27 · 15 e · 3 percussion (?) e · 26 evangelist (?) pen (?) e · 14 · wind (?) e · 2 bladder-pipe a · 25 singer a · 13 bagpipe e · 1 small lute or cittern e · 24 portative e · 12 small guitar or cittern a(?) · 23 instrument (?) e(?)

Inner ring: 32 singer (?) e · 42 evangelist (?) pen (?) e · 41 wind (?) a(?) · 31 e · 30 evangelist (?) pen (?) e · 40 cross and scepter e · 39 recorder a(?) · 29 e · 38 a singer (?) · 37 e(?) · 36 e · 35 e · 34 portative e · 33 a(?)

ORIHUELA CATHEDRAL

Plan of
Porta de Loreto

e- elder
a- angel

Figure 1.

Illustration 7. No. 1, small lute or cittern.

Illustration 8. No. 12, cittern or small guitar.

of Alexandria. If the three figures are indeed holding pens rather than vials of incense "made of prayers of the saints" (Rev.5:7-9), then the fourth evangelist would be one of the other figures who could easily have lost his quill to the ravages of time.

The sculptor's placement of instruments around the doorway at Orihuela exhibits an element of symmetry. The small lute or cittern on the lower left (No. 1, *Illus.* 7) is balanced by a plucked string of similar size, but slightly different shape on the lower right (No. 12, *Illus.* 8) The playing positions used for these instruments is slightly different as well. Above those, are a bladder pipe (No. 2, *Illus.* 9), and a bagpipe, the bag broken off, but the player's hands clearly in place on the chanter (No. 13, *Illus.* 10). In the inner arch next to the bagpipes are portative organs of different sizes (No. 24, *Illus.* 11; No. 34, *Illus.* 12). Two fiddles are also placed in nearly symmetrical positions in the outer arches (Nos. 6 + 18, *Illus.* 5 + 6). Such a concern for symmetry of musical instruments does not appear to be operative in the northern Spanish depictions of this scene.

The intermingling of angels and elders, also unusual in apocalyptic portals, is also evident from *Figure 1*. Those considered to be elders are wearing crowns in accordance with John's description and the elders in northern Spanish depictions of the scene. The angels, of course, have wings. However, in some cases the stone work behind a figure makes it difficult to determine whether the sculptor intended to depict wings or a

Illustration 9. No. 2, bladderpipe.

Illustration 10. No. 13, bagpipe (broken).

Illustration 11. No. 24, portative organ.

Illustration 12. No. 34, smaller portative organ (or hurdy-gurdy?)

curved backdrop. In some, a feathery texture gives the indication of wings. However, there seems to be no clear distinction between elder and angel in many cases, in either placement or function. In contrast to the door at Burgos, some angels here make music, while some elders don't. Various figures seem to have both crowns and wings while others have neither. Thus, several of the indications in *Figure 1* are quite subjective.

While most of the instruments depicted in the northern Spanish porticos are strings, fewer than half the elders around the *Porta de Loreto* play instruments in that category. As can be seen in *Figure 1*, there are only five stringed instruments which can be identified: two plucked strings (Nos. 1 and 12), two fiddles (Nos. 6 and 18), and a psaltery (No. 17). Due to the deteriorated condition of some of the statues, and considerable evidence of repair, it is possible that one or another of the instruments are misidentified. No. 34, for instance, could possibly be a hurdy-gurdy. Other symmetrical or programmatic elements may have been intended, but several of the elders who originally held instruments may have lost them over time — by accident or intent.

Harps and full-sized guitars, which are customarily featured in the apocalyptic doorways of northern cathedrals, are missing in Orihuela. (See the Burgos harpist in *Illus.* 2.) This is of particular interest in the evolution of the scene, as those are the string instruments which are the most common in the earliest representations of john's vision. It is likely that such a change in choice of instruments is a result of contemporary instrumental practice. The locale of influence is difficult to ascertain, since it is possible that the sculptors were brought in to plan and execute the work. The place of their origin and training would be very difficult to determine.

The wind instruments played by the elders around the *Porta de Loreto* are not substantially different in type from those at the cathedrals at Burgos, or Sasamon. They are the bagpipe and bladder-pipe (Nos. 13 + 2), the two portatives (Nos. 24 + 34), and a recorder (No. 39, *Illus.* 6 — fourth from the top in the inner right-hand arch). As is the case with apocalyptic portals elsewhere, some of the figures in the inner arch seem to be singing (Nos. 25, *Illus.* 13; 32 and 38), and at least one is probably playing a percussion instrument (No. 3, *Illus.* 5). Thus, just as elders and angels are intermingled, so are instruments traditionally considered to have secular or sacred connotations.

A comparison of the Orihuela organs with those in the doors at Burgos and Sasamon reveals that far less elaborate instruments are

Illustration 13. No. 25, singer.

depicted at the cathedral in the south-east: a portative, which the player holds in his lap, pumping the bellows with one hand. The music played on the keyboard with the other hand is assumed to be primarily mono-phonic. (Is the player on the left side of the doorway (*Illus.* 11) really playing with the left hand while pumping with the right — and if so, did the sculptor depict a real musician in the act of playing?) The bellows on the instrument on the right side of the door (*Illus.* 12) seems to be a round concertina-like device. These instruments contrast markedly with the larger positive instruments depicted at the northern cathedrals, which sit on a table, and are pumped by assistants, freeing the player to use both hands on the keyboard. One would like to be able to draw some conclusions regarding period or provenance from the differences between the organs as just described, however both sizes of organ existed during the thirteenth through early sixteenth centuries in Italy, Spain and France as well as in other countries, and so we must be content to note the differences. Suffice it to say that the smaller type of instrument might be more readily encountered in a city on the edge of Christendom than would a more cumbersome one.

The question remains — does the *Porta de Loreto* illustrate instru-ments played by local musicians, and thus give us precise information about the kinds of instruments used in southern Spain in the early four-teenth century? A critical reading of the Spanish poets of the late Middle Ages can serve to bring us a word of caution regarding specific information we may attempt to glean from opulent displays of instruments in paintings or sculpture of the period.

It seems that as poets such as Juan Ruiz described fiestas and the musical instruments used in them, they would wax eloquent, adding instruments to enhance the general effect. In his *Libro de Buen Amor*, Ruiz lists no fewer than thirty instruments, including a grand conglomeration of western and arabic instruments.[12] The event described was clearly one of great rejoicing, and

> the literature naturally seized on that detail. The court poets and romancers did not neglect to give us the complete list of instruments which would enhance the festival they described; it was for them an occasion to detail their memories. [However they were] less than lexicographers in musical matters, and so soon, it appears that they extablished a sort of rivalry between themselves, and with time, their enumerations stretched so as to lose touch with reality and verisimilitude (32 categories of instruments, for instance, in the famous list of Machaut).[13]

Surely the vision of the Apocalypse represents the greatest fiesta of them all: the ultimate scene of rejoicing for those who sing the new song. And so, one must assume that such poetic license would be taken by sculptors of the period — the instruments represented in such a scene would mostly likely not represent local musical practice, but a grand collection of instruments such as that described by Juan Ruiz, or pictured in.the *Cantigas de Santa Maria* from the thirteenth-century court of Alfonso el Sabio.

A grand collection is not the case with the *Porta de Loreto*. The

---

[12] Juan Ruiz, *Libro de Buen Amor.*, ed. Jean Ducamin (Toulouse, 1901), 220–222.

[13] Felix Lecoy, *Recherches sur le Libro de Buen Amor*, (Paris, 1938), 258. Quoted in Daniel Devoto, "Le enumeracion de instrumentos musicales en la poesia medieval castellana" in *Miscelanea en Homenaje a Monsenor Higinio Angles* I (Barcelona, 1958), 215. (Translation by author)

> la litterature s'empara tout naturellement de ce detail. Les poetes courtois et les romanciers ne manquent pas de nous donner la liste complete des instruments qui rehaussent de leur eclat les fetes qu'ils decrivent; c'etait au reste pour eux l'occasion d'etaler leurs connaissances, au moins lexicologiques, en matiere musicale; bientot meme il semble qu'il s'establit entre eux une sorte de rivalite, et l'on voit, avec le temps, leurs enumerations s'allonger, au point de perdre certainement tout contact avec le realite et la vraisemblance (trente-deux categories d'instruments, par exemple, dans la fameuse liste de Guillaume de Machaut).

instruments are of a number and type which might have enlivened any fiesta or church feast in a city the size and importance of Orihuela. However, "poetic" license is indeed probable, and so romantic notions of local musicians posing for portraits in stone should probably be cast aside. The door thus represents something of an enigma for us. In its state of incomplete preservation, it does not give the full program intended by the artists who conceived and brought it into being. It presents us with more questions than answers, and yet it documents the spread of Christian doctrine to an area which had been retaken from the Moors only a short time before. The portal also represents the continuing use into the fourteenth century of the vision of John as a focus for Christian teaching: a reminder of the heavenly glory to which the artistic accomplishments of humans can only point.

CHAPTER NINETEEN

A BOOK OF HOURS FOR POPE LEO X

John Constant

University of Michigan, Dearborn

Among the collection of books and manuscripts of the Toledo Museum of Art, Toledo, Ohio, is a brilliantly illuminated Book of Hours made for Pope Leo X.[1] Upon examining this manuscript one of the texts immediately recognized is a hymn attributed to St. Bonaventura, *Christum ducem qui per crucem.* This text was chosen by Josquin des Pres as the final *pars* of the six-*pars* motet, *Qui velatus facie fuisti.* Even though there has been considerable attention given to this hymn text and to Josquin's setting of this Passion text, the fact that there appears to be so little information about the Office of the Passion and/or Office of the Holy Cross is puzzling.[2] So many of the motet texts chosen by Renaissance musicians are accessible for examination within their place in the liturgy as a part of the whole unit. Neither of these Offices is a part of the modern liturgy and neither is available in editions of

---

[1] The manuscript is identified as *Officium Beatae Mariae Virginis*, Acc. No. 57.23.

[2] See David M. Gehrenbeck, "Motetti de la Corona: A Study of Ottaviano Petrucci's Four Last-Known Motet Prints (Fossombrone, 1514, 1519), with 44 Transcriptions" (unpublished S.M.D. dissertation, Union Theological Seminary, 1971), pp. 575–592; Jacquelyn A. Mattfeld, "Some Relationships between Texts and Cantus Firmi in the Liturgical Motets of Josquin des Pres," *Journal of the Americal Musicological Society* XIV (1961), 159–183; and, Helmuth Osthoff, *Josquin des Pres*, 2 vols. (Tutzing, 1962), 1:124–128; 2:30–31, 80–84.

liturgical books prior to the reforms of Pope Pius V in 1570.[3] I will describe this devotional book, identify the miniaturist, describe the Offices, and show the variants between the hymn from this Italian source and the text chosen by Josquin des Pres.

The Book of Hours is made of fine vellum measuring 5 7/16 inches by 3¾ inches; the leaves are edged with gold. It is bound in green velvet and can be fastened closed with a brass clasp. There are 246 folios with the original guard of heavy parchment at the beginning and a modern guard at the end. Folios 96v–100r, 156v–157r, 184v–188r, 202v–203r, 237r–240r, 244v–246v are blank but are lined for the placement of text. Pencil foliation can be found in the lower right hand corner of each page. The prevailing pattern of organization is by quinternion: folios 14 to 93 — eight quinternions; folios 111 to 150 — five quinternions; folios 158 to 187 — three quinternions; folios 189 to 198 — a single quinternion; and folios 204 to 233 — three quinternions. The practice of collating music manuscripts in this manner is peculiar to Florence.[4] The above physical evidence may suggest Florentine provenance for this book, even though it is not a music manuscript. The remaining gatherings of this manuscript are single, double, or triple bifolios. Single sheets of heavier parchment are tipped-in to accommodate the full-page illuminations.

The lettering of the text is Gothic. It is, however, unlike the Gothic lettering found in manuscripts north of the Alps because it is angular, almost round. Therefore the scribe was probably an Italian.[5] There are thirteen lines of text on each page. The lettering is black, blue, and red. A gold initial is reserved for the beginning of the different hours in the Office of the Blessed Virgin and Sext of the Office of the Holy Cross.

A Book of Hours is a devotional book intended for private contemplation and prayer, rather than liturgical use, and may include

---

[3] Three of the manuscripts cited by Mattfeld where the Office and/or hymn text can be found are: *Centum meditationes passionis domini nostri ihu xpristi.* Netherlands, ca. 1440, (Boston Public Library, MS 1587); *Officium passionis.* Written in Marches, Italy, ca. 1330, (Boston Public Library, MS 1554); and, *Hymni et collectae, item evangelia, epistolae, introitus, gradualia, et sequentiae. . . .* Cologne: Quentel and Calenius, 1566. (Harvard University, Widener Library.) See Mattfeld, *op. cit.,* pp. 175–176.

[4] H. Colin Slim, *A Gift of Madrigals and Motets,* 2 vols., (Chicago, 1972), 1:17–20. Professor Slim cites the Florentine non-music manuscript, the *Pandects of Justinian* (Biblioteca Nazionale Centrale, MSS. Magl. XXIX, no. 16, Banco rari 24–26) as having a gathering structure of quinterns.

[5] James Hayes, *The Roman Letter,* (Chicago, 1951), p. 33.

texts of special significance to the individual for whom it was intended.[6] Since it was common to recite votive offices to the Virgin, the Litany of Saints, and Office of the Dead, in addition to the regular services of the liturgical year, the inclusion of these texts in a Book of Hours was rather pragmatic. In certain instances the commemorative office of the Holy Cross and that of the Blessed Virgin had additional significance; the Office of the Holy Cross was assigned to Friday and that of the Virgin to Saturday.[7] The inclusion of the above offices and texts in a Book of Hours might stem from the recitation of the Gradual Psalms, Penitential Psalms, and the Litany of Saints as a private devotion outside of the choir in monastic practice.[8]

The Book of Hours of Leo X begins with the Calendar, folios 1r–12v. The offices and other texts found in the manuscript are:

Office of the Blessed Virgin, folios 14r–96r
Office of the Dead, folios 101r–156r
The Seven Penitential Psalms, folios 158r–184r
The Gradual Psalms, folios 189r–202r
The Office of the Holy Cross, folios 204r–236r
The Little Office of the Cross, folios 241r–244r

With the exception of the Office of the Holy Cross and the Little Office of the Cross, all of the other texts are usually expected to be included in a Book of Hours.

At the beginning of each of the Offices or the special psalms there are elaborate illuminations. The scene depicted for the opening of the Office of the Blessed Virgin is the *Adoration of the Shepherds* (Plate 1a). The Virgin, dressed in blue with golden halo, and two of the three shepherds are kneeling in adoration of the Child. Golden rays project into the scene from the blue sky above. The stable and distant hills are seen in the background. The scene is framed within a green border with gold trim. At the bottom of the folio is the Medici coat of arms, a gold shield with five red balls and one blue ball on a red background. The balls and shield are enclosed in a green laural wreath with a gold trim

---

[6] David M. Robb, *The Art of the Illuminated Manuscript*, (New York, 1973), pp. 331–332.

[7] Andrew Hughes, *Medieval Manuscripts for Mass and Office: A guide to their organization and terminology*, (Toronto, 1982), p. 13; and J.B.L. Tolhurst, *The Monastic Breviary of Hyde Abbey*, 6 vols., A publication of the Henry Bradshaw Society, vols. 69, 70, 76, 77, 78, 80 (London, 1942), 6:101–107.

[8] Tolhurst, *The Monastic Breviary of Hyde Abbey*, 6:57–72.

Plate 1a.   folio 13v   Adoration of the Shepherds
Plate 1b.   folio 14r   Initial D (Virgin)

guarded by two angels on a green and blue background. On the top border of blue is a gold medallion with the three red balls and one blue ball. White pearls are attached to two smaller golden medallions and a larger medallion in the center. The decorations of the right and left border appear to be blue, white, and gold lanterns or vases on a red background.

On the facing folio, folio 14r, is the opening text of the Office of the Blessed Virgin, "Incipit officium beatae Mariae virginis. Ad matutinum. *Versus.* Domine labia mea aperies" (Plate 1b). Enclosed in the large initial "D" are figures of the Madonna and Child. The initial is of blue and red acanthus leaves framed in gold. On the bottom is a blue shield on red background within a green laural wreath trimmed in gold. The inscription on the shield is "Leo X, PO. M." Two *putti* guard the shield. The right hand border is decorated with blue and gold lanterns or vases with two *putti* on a dark red background. At the top and bottom of this margin are portraits of two unidentified women, hands folded in prayer. They are probably saints since each has a golden halo. The left border is decorated in a similar manner without the portraits. On the dark blue background of the top border is a central golden jeweled medallion with light red and blue pearls attached to either side.

The next section of the book is the Office of the Dead. The full folio

Plate 2a.   folio 100v   Raising of Lazarus
Plate 2b.   folio 101r   Initial D (Death)

illumination opening this office is the scene of the *Raising of Lazarus* (Plate 2a). The Christ, dressed in blue and red, faces Lazarus who is standing in a marble sarcophagous. Martha who is kneeling is turned away from Lazarus. She is dressed in orange robes. Beneath the scene is a dark blue shield encircled by a wreath. The gold inscription reads: "Leo X, PO. M." On either side of the wreath are blue cornucopia trimmed in gold. The narrow ends of the horns of plenty extend into the lower margin of the book. The background is dark red. The three remaining borders are decorated with blue and pink flowers and gold seeds. The flowers are probably strawberry, violets, and stylized lilies and *fleur-de-lis*. On the top border is a blue circle with the gold monogram "YHS," (IHS) the abbreviation of the name Jesus in Greek. On the top of the right and left border are portraits of two unidentified men.

On the facing folio, 101r, is the ornamented initial "D" with the opening of Psalm 114, *Dilexit quoniam exaudiet Dominus.* (Plate 2b). The initial is made with pink, blue, and green acanthus leaves within a gold frame. Inside the initial is Death holding a scythe. The borders are decorated with blue and pink flowers, and gold seeds as in (Plate 2a). In the center of the top border is a death mask. A portrait of a monk dressed in a cowl is found in the bottom center of the folio. He is

Plate 3a.   folio 157v   David in Prayer
Plate 3b.   folio 158r   Initial D (David)

holding a banner with the word *memento* of *memento more*. This miniature is framed in gold by a square superimposed on a diamond. The lower end of the diamond extends from the picture frame into the margin of the book.

The opening of the Penitential Psalms is illustrated with King David in prayer (Plate 3a). On the ground lay a psaltery. In the foreground is a hill which gives the illusion of a Roman arch. Blue sky, green hills, and blue mountains appear in the background. On the lower border is a gold shield of the Medici with the five red balls and one blue ball with three gold *giglie*. On top of the shield is the Papal tiara. The shield and the tiara are encircled by a green laural wreath decorated with gold. This symbol of Pope Leo X is guarded by two *putti* with red wings. It is also decorated with gold. On the top border is a blue medallion with the gold monogram, "YHS". The remaining borders are decorated in blue and pink flowers with yellow centers as well as with three dimensional blue and pink stylized acanthus leaves. At the bottom of the left border is a bird, perhaps a pelican.[9]

---

[9] The pelican symbolizes Christ's sacrifice on the cross symbolizing the

The beginning of the text of the Penitential Psalms, folio 158r, is decorated with an illuminated initial "D," for Psalm 6, *Domine, ne in furore* (Plate 3b). The initial is formed by pink, green, and blue acanthus leaves within a gold frame. In the opening of the initial is King David holding a psaltery. In the center of the top margin is a gold psaltery; in the center of the bottom margin is a violet-blue monogram with the gold letters, "Leo X PO. M." The borders are decorated with light and dark blue flowers with yellow centers and dark pink flowers. Gold seeds are interspersed throughout.

The section of the Book of Hours containing the Gradual Psalms opens with the Presentation of Mary on the Steps of the Temple (Plate 4a).

> And there was about the Temple, after the fifteen psalms of degrees, fifteen steps or degrees to ascend up to the Temple, because the Temple was high set . . . And then Our Lady was set on the lowest step, and mounted up without any help . . . they left their daughter in the Temple with the other virgins . . . And the Virgin Mary profited every day in all holiness, and was visited daily of angels . . .[10]

The young Virgin dressed in orange garments ascends the steps toward the high priest Zacharias. Joachim and Anna observe from below. A group of onlookers observe the scene from the left. The borders are decorated with pink and blue flowers and acanthus leaves with gold seeds throughout. There are two portraits of young women one each in the right and left borders. On the bottom border is a portrait of the prophet Isaiah within a gold and blue circle. On the banderole carried by the prophet are the letters "ISAIE PR."

The facing folio, 189r, is the first of the Gradual Psalms (Plate 4b). There is an illuminated initial "D" similar to the initials on folios 14r, 101r, 158r. In the interior portion of the letter is a portrait of the Virgin holding a book. Pink and blue flowers with yellow centers surrounded by gold seeds decorate the borders. On the bottom border is an unknown prophet holding a banderole. The portrait is framed in a gold square on a diamond. The lower part of the diamond intrudes into the white border of the folio.

Eucharist. This interpretation is supported by Psalm 102: 6, "I am like a pelican of the wilderness," an accepted allusion to Christ. According to the Book of Matthew, David is a direct ancestor to Christ. See George Ferguson, *Signs and Symbols in Christian Art*, (New York, 1954), p. 23; and, James Hall, *Dictionary of Subjects and Symbols in Art*, (New York, 1977), p. 92.

[10] Hall, *Dictionary of Subjects and Symbols in Art*, p. 252.

Plate 4a.   folio 188v   Presentation of Mary
Plate 4b.   folio 189r   Initial D (Virgin)

The next full page of artwork is found on folio 203v — *Christ Carrying the Cross* (Plate 5a). Christ is dressed in red garments highlighted with gold. The Virgin, in blue, stands to the left. A man in a short dress stands on the right with his back to the spectator holding the bottom of the cross. He is probably Simon the Cyrenian. Distant hills and trees and blue sky are seen in the background. On the bottom border is a gold Greek cross on a dark blue background within a green laurel wreath encircled with gold. On either side stand two birds, probably pelicans since the pelican became the symbol of the sacrifice of Christ on the cross.[11] This would be an appropriate place for such a symbol since the Office of the Holy Cross begins on the facing folio. On the top border is a smaller Greek cross on a dark blue background encircled with gold. On either side is a violet cornucopia decorated with gold and filled with flowers. It was customary to kiss the crosses before beginning the private devotion that followed. It may be for this reason that the blue background of the Greek crosses show a very slight discoloration or staining. Blue and dark pink flowers with yellow

---

[11] Hall, *Dictionary of Subjects and Symbols in Art*, p. 238. (f.note 9 above).

Plate 5a.   folio 203v   Christ Carrying the Cross
Plate 5b.   folio 204r   Initial P (Adoration of the Cross)

centers decorate the borders. Again gold seeds are part of the decoration.

A large illuminated letter "P" is found on the facing folio, 204v, *Per signum crucis* (Plate 5b). Blue, green, and pink acanthus leaves form the letter on a gold frame. The scene inside the initial is an empty cross with nails and a crown of thorns. Mary Magdalene is kissing the cross. On the bottom border is another empty cross on a light blue background with nails on the terminals and foot of the cross; at the top of the cross there is a crown of thorns. This scene is framed by a gold square superimposed on a diamond. Again the bottom part of the diamond enters the margin of the book out of the frame of the illuminated page. Pink and blue flowers with yellow centers decorate the borders. There are also green leaves and gold seeds.

The final illuminations are found on folios 240v–241r (Plates 6a–b). The full folio scene, 240v, is Christ on the Cross (Plate 6a). Mary, dressed in blue with a halo, is to the left of the cross. Her face is turned from the cross. John is standing at the right. A landscape of hills and blue sky form the background. Christ hangs on the cross, blood dripping from his wounds. In the center of the lower border within a gold circle is an empty cross; on the right is a spear and on the left, a sponge. A small gold cross is found in the center of the top border. Two

Plate 6a.   folio 240v   Christ on the Cross
Plate 6b.   folio 241r   Initial P (Dead Christ)

portraits are found in the right and left border. On the right is a young
man; the banderole identifies the man as "ISAIE." The portrait on the
left is that of an old man; perhaps also Isaiah. Blue and pink flowers
decorate the borders. On the facing folio, 241r, is an illuminated initial,
"P" (Plate 6b). The half-naked figure of the dead Christ is depicted
within the initial. Blue, green, and red acanthus leaves form the letter.
In the center of the lower border is an empty cross with nails and a
crown of thorns; all are within a gold circle. The background of both
scenes is a light blue. Again the border decorations are blue and dark
pink flowers and gold seeds.

*   *   *

Visual evidence indicates that the illuminations were those of
Giovanni Boccardi il Vecchio (b. Florence, 1460–d. March 1, 1529).[12]
He was a Florentine and favorite miniaturist of Pope Leo X. It is known
that he worked in Florence, Perugia, and Montecassino. Manuscripts

---

[12] See Mirella Levi D'Ancona, *Miniatura e miniatori a Firenze dal XIV al
XVI secolo*, (Florence, 1962), pp. 149–154. Giovanni Boccardi was the miniaturist who illuminated the Newberry partbooks, see Slim, *A Gift of Madrigals
and Motets*, 1:31–40.

illuminated by Boccardi include several Books of Hours, breviaries, and antiphonaries. The *Breviarium romanum* (Florence, Biblioteca Mediceo-Laurenziana, MS. Pluteus XVII.1), known to be by Boccardi, was specifically written for Pope Leo X. Another manuscript illuminated by him, *Hippocratis De morbis vulgaribus* (Florence, Biblioteca Mediceo-Laurenziana, MS. Pluteus LXXXIII.12) is dedicated to Leo X.[13] Stylistic traits of Boccardi found in the illuminations of the Book of Hours in the Toledo Institute of Art include: some disproportion among the figures, the use of gold in the drapery, the pale color of the faces, and the repetition of scenes.[14] A comparison of illuminations known to be Giovanni Boccardi's with those in this manuscript helped identify him as the miniaturist.

Disproportion among the figures is found in the *Adoration of the Shepherds* (Plate 1a). The other figures are small when compared with the Virgin. In the scene, *Christ Carrying the Cross* (Plate 5a), one would think that Simon were a young boy because of his small size in comparison to the size of either Christ or the Virgin. Another example of disproportion is found in the scene *The Raising of Lazarus* (Plate 2a). Lazarus appears to be the size of a child when compared with others in the scene. Christ dwarfs Martha in the same scene. In each of the illuminations found in this manuscript this stylistic trait of Boccardi can be found.

The most remarkable use of gold to highlight drapery is found on the garment worn by Christ (Plate 5a). The lines are so fine that they appear as gold thread on the dark red robe of Christ. Similar use of gold can be found on the garments of the Virgin (Plates 1a, 4b, and 6a) and King David (Plates 3a–b).

When one opens the manuscript to the illuminated folios the wide range of color used by the miniaturist is striking. However, upon closer examination it is noted that by contrast some of the faces are without detail of color. On folio 13v, the Virgin's face appears pale against her gold halo and textured blue mantle (Plate 1a). A notable characteristic of the two unidentified women saints, folio 14r, is the paleness of their faces (Plate 1b). The same lack of color can be found in most of the illuminations particularly so with the portraits of the two unidentified men (Plate 2a). The lack of contrast in facial detail is also a trait of Boccardi.

---

[13] For a list of manuscripts illuminated by Giovanni Boccardi see, Slim, *op. cit.*, 1:37–40.

[14] Levi D'Ancona, *Miniatura e miniatori*, p. 152.

Professor Levi D'Ancona suggests one way to determine Boccardi's work from that of another famous Florentine miniaturist, Attavante degli Attavanti, is that "he (Boccardi) repeats himself, having poor imagination for his scenes."[15] Whether or not he had a "poor imagination" is rather difficult to measure; however, there is repetition of subject in this manuscript. The empty cross is found four different times, folios 204r (twice), 240v, 241r (Plates 5b, 6a–b). Nails and a crown of thorns are found in two of the four scenes.

Repetition of another kind helps to further corroborate that this is Boccardi's work. In four manuscripts known to be by this Florentine miniaturist there are scenes of King David in prayer.[16] In all of the scenes David is facing the same direction; on the left in the immediate background is a mountain with the distant landscape on the right. In three of the scenes the mountain on the left has an opening similar to a Roman arch. All of these characteristics are similar to the scene of David in the Toledo manuscript. The closest resemblance to the scene of David in this Book of Hours is found in the Yates Thompson MS. 30, folio 66v, British Museum. In both of these illuminations the instrument on the ground in front of David is the psaltery. (In the other scenes of King David either a harp or lute is pictured.) There is an airy, open uncluttered landscape, and the stature and pose of the central figure is the same. On the top border of another illumination in *Officium Beatae Marie Virginis*, folio 117r, there is a psaltery identical to the ones in the Toledo Book of Hours and the Yates Thompson MS. 30. Also on the same folio of the Yates Thompson manuscript, David is holding a psaltery.

The styles of the border decorations, the portraits, and placement and highlighting of symbols in manuscripts known to be decorated by Boccardi are similar to those found in this manuscript. The visual similarities of the strawberry flowers and violets with yellow centers, the use of gold seeds to fill in the spaces, the bold strokes of the acanthus leaves in initials and borders, and identical stylized lilie and *fleur-de-lis* are found. The portrait of Isaiah in this manuscript (Plates 2b, 4a, and 6a) and those portraits of older men found on Plates 17, 20,

---

15 Livi D'Ancona, *Miniatura e miniatori*, p. 152.

16 Salterio dei Sancti, Inv. 544, folio 1v, Museo di San Marco, Florence (Plate 15, Slim, *A Gift* vol. 1.); Salterio T, folio 5, Basilica di San Pietro, Perugia (Plate 16, Slim, *op. cit.*); Officium Beatae Mariae Virginis, folios 116v–117r, formerly in the Sidney Cockerell collection (Plate 17, Slim, *op. cit.*); and Breviary, MS. Lat. 8879, folio 10v, Bibliotheque Nationale, Paris (Plate 20, Slim, *op. cit.*)

and 21 of Professor Slim's study are similar in style. A comparison of
the placement and treatment of symbols in the known Boccardi manuscripts and this Book of Hours of Leo X shows them to be the same.
One of the frames found to hold portraits in the Toledo manuscript is
the square superimposed on a diamond found on folios 101r, 189r, 204r
(Plates 2b, 4b, and 5b). A similar frame is found on the lower border of
the Pandects, MSS. Magliabecchi XXIX, no. 16, B.R. 24, Biblioteca
Nazionale Centrale, Florence. Several other manuscripts in Boccardi's
hand were also consulted to examine his stylistic characteristics.[17] These
observations through comparison indicate Boccardi was the miniaturist
of this Book of Hours.

In the manuscripts opening calendar, folios 1r–2v, the capital letters
"KL" (Kalendar) are written in blue ink. Red ink is used to indicate
principal feasts, and black ink for the others. Red and blue line decorations are found on the left margin of the folio of each new month.
Calendars of liturgical books not only indicate feasts of the universal
Roman Church, but also feasts celebrated by the different orders,
diocese, or individuals for whom the book is intended. Several of the
feast days indicated in the calendar suggest an Italian provenance for
the manuscript.[18] These feast days may have been of special importance
to Pope Leo X: the feasts of Antony of Padua (June 13), Clare (August
12), Ludovici, and Francis (October 4). Also, these saints are associated
with the Franciscan Order. Two other feasts listed in the calendar that
may also have some special significance are Pudentiana (May 19) and
Elizabeth of Hungary (November 19).

Immediately following the calendar is the Office of the Blessed
Virgin, folios 14r–96r. All of the texts in this portion can be found in
modern liturgical books. The texts of these hours are taken from the
Common of Feasts of the Blessed Virgin, the Office of the Blessed
Virgin on Saturdays, and the Little Office of the Virgin.[19] Most of the

---

[17] Most useful was Slim, *Op. Cit.*, Plates 15, 17–8, 20–2, and 24; also, see
David Diringer, *The Illuminated Book*, (London, 1967), Plate VI–34b; Livi
D'Ancona, *Miniatura e miniatori*, Plates 18, 19, and 20; and, Mario Salmi, *La
miniatura Italiana*, (Milan, 1956), Plate XLV b.

[18] In attempting to isolate feasts of special significance in this devotional
book, I compared its calendar with the calendars of two early English
breviaries — the monastic breviary of Hyde Abbey and the Hereford Breviary.
See Tolhurst, *The Monastic Breviary of Hyde Abbey*, 5:G4r–G9v; and Walter
Howard Frere, *The Hereford Breviary*, 3 vols., (London, 1904), 1:xi–xxiv.

[19] *Breviarium Monasticum Pauli V jussu editum Urbani VIII . . . Regula S.
Patris Benedicti Militantibus*, 4 vols., (Belgium, 1953), pp. (278–326). This
citation will be abbreviated "BM" in the text.

texts are those of the Little Office of the Virgin. There are only a few excursions from the Little Office as is currently found in the *Breviarium Monasticum*, (pp. 315–326). This portion of the manuscript appears to be subdivided in the following manner: a complete monastic office (folios 14r–76r); Matins, feria ii and iii with three psalms and antiphons (folios 76v–81v); Matins, feria iv and Sabbato with three psalms and antiphons (folios 81v–87r); and the Office of the Blessed Virgin to be said during Advent, all hours, (folios 87r–96r).

Following the Office of the Virgin is the Office of the Dead (folios 101r–156r), the Penitential Psalms with Litany, (folios 158r–184r), and the Gradual Psalms (189r–202r). The same liturgical texts and sequence of psalms is found in the corresponding sections of *Breviarium Monasticum*.[20] The few differences found in the Toledo manuscript from the modern edition were reversals of words, spelling variances, and shortened rubrics.

The next section in Pope Leo X's Book of Hours is the Office of the Holy Cross, folios 204r–236v. There is a liturgy for all of the hours. Matins, folios 204r–214r, begins with Psalm 94. Following this opening psalm is the hymn, three additional psalms with antiphons, three lessons with responsories and the *Te Deum*. The other hours have only one psalm and antiphon, a hymn, a reading, and a prayer in addition to appropriate responsaries. The *Benedictus Dominus, Magnificat*, and *Nuns dimittis* are found in their respective offices.

There was an attempt made to identify the texts of the Office of the Holy Cross as a unit within the modern liturgy. Since there are only two feasts of the Cross in modern liturgical books, the Finding of the Holy Cross (May 3) and the Exaltation of the Holy Cross (September 14), and since both of these feasts have been celebrated in the liturgy since the thirteenth century, one would expect that there would be common texts. None of the hymns, specific order of psalms for the office, lessons, proper responsories, or antiphons from the Finding or Exaltation of the Cross are found in the Toledo manuscript. In fact, even the *Te Deum* of Matins is an unfamiliar text in this Book of Hours. The only text in common is the Communion of the Mass for the Finding of the Holy Cross: *Per signum Crucis de inimicis nostris libera nos Deus noster*.[21] This is the opening sentence of all the hours of the Cross except

---

20 *Breviary Monasticum*: Office of the Dead, pp. (326–354); the Gradual Psalms, pp. (355–356); and the Penitential Psalms with Litany, pp. (356–367).

21 *The Liber Usualis*, (Tournai, 1950), p. 1457. Whenever this citation is given in the text it will be abbreviated "*LU*."

for Lauds. (Perhaps the scribe inadvertently left it out.) It is immediately followed by *Deus in adjutorium* or, for Matins, *Domine labia mea aperies.*

Some additional texts of the Office of the Holy Cross can be identified in the modern liturgy. Again, they are not from any one celebration of mass or office. The common sentiment is that of the Passion of Christ. Searching through the modern liturgies of Lent, Passion Sunday, or Holy Week proved fruitless in finding a liturgy or part of a liturgy that would correspond to the Office of the Holy Cross. Antiphon and responsory texts from this Office found in the modern liturgy follow:

Matins (folio 208r) antiphon, 2, Psalm 2 *Quare fremuerunt Gentes* Astiterunt reges terrae, et principes convenerunt in unum adversus Christum ejus.

[Matins, Good Friday, antiphon 1, *LU*, p. 665; Matins, Holy Saturday, responsory 7, *BM* (Verna), p. 465. (The versical that follows is *Quare fremuerunt Gentes*.)]

Matins (folio 210v) responsory and versicle 1 *Seniores populi* consilium fecerunt, ut Jesum dolo tenerent, et occiderent et exierunt tamquam ad latronem. Collegerunt pontifices et pharisaei consilium ut Jesum occiderent. Et exierunt cum gladiis et fustibus tamquam ad latronem.

[Matins, Maundy Thursday, responsory 9, *LU*. p. 645–646.]

Matins (folio 211v) responsory 2 Tristis est anima mea usque ad mortem sustinete hic, et vigilate mecum nunc* autem turba multa vallabit me. Neque fugam capietis et ego vadam immolari pro vobis.

[Matins, Maundy Thursday, responsory 2, *LU*, p. 630 (same to *).]

Matins (folio 212v) responsory 3 Tu autem Domine, miserere mei.

[Matins, Holy Saturday, versicle, *LU*, p. 726.]

Matins (folio 213r) Tenebre facte sunt dum crucifixissent Jesum Judei et circa horam nonam exclamavit voce magna dicens: Deus meus ut quid dereliquisti me. Et inclinato capite emissit spiritum.* Tunc unus ex militibus lancea latus eius aperuit, et continuo exivit sanguis et aqua. *Versicle.* Cum ergo accepisset acetum dixit consumatum est et inclinato capite emisit spiritum. Tunc.

[Matins, Holy Thursday, responsory, *BM*, p. 444, (Verna) same to * except "Jesus voce magna".

Lauds (folio 214r) antiphon 1
Attendite universi populi et videte* Jesum vulneratum ligatum laudantes eum in excelsis.

[Matins, Holy Saturday, antiphon 3, *LU*, p. 736 (same to *).]

Lauds (folio 217r) responsory
Tradetur enim gentibus ad illudendum et flagellandum et crucifendum.

[Vespers, Commemorations of the Sunday or of the Feria, antiphon 1, *LU*, p. 1087.]

The lessons at Matins are taken from the Passion of the four Gospels with most of them from the book of Matthew. There are many additions to the Vulgate texts and some of the lessons are a paraphrase of a selection of many texts. For example Lesson iii of Matins (folios 212r–212v) is assembled from selections of Matthew 27: 1–50. The readings of the other Offices refer to the Passion of Christ: Prime, (folio 219v) from Peter 2:21, *Christus passus est pro nobis, vobis relinquens exemplum, ut sequamini vestigia ejus,* or Terce, (folio 222r) from Philippians 2:8, *Christus factus est pro nobis obediens usque ad mortem, mortem autem crucis.*

None of the prayers of the offices in the Toledo Book of Hours can be found in the modern liturgy. However, two prayers found in a Book of Hours (Salisbury) for Office of the Passion of Christ have almost identical wording to those for None and Vespers of the Office of Holy Cross.[22]

The text of the *Te Deum* of Matins (folio 213v–214r) is similar to the standard hymn, however it still remains unidentified:

Te Christum laudamus. Te Jesum benedicimus. Te regem regum et dominum confitemur. Te crucixum colimus gloriosum ducem et amabilem redemptorem. Qui nos aspersionem tui sanguinis redimisti.

---

[22] [Book of Hours (Salisbury)]: *Enchiridion preclare ecclesie Sarum: de votissimis precationibus ac venustissimis imaginibus,* (Paris, 1530), folios 115v and 116v.

Dignus est domine jesu christe accipere laudem et benedictionem et gloriam et honorem. Exultet in te omnis caro. Omnis vivens glorificet nomen tuum. Humilietur omnis facies sub pedibus tuis. Omnis creatura iubilet tibi. Serviat et laudet et extollat in eternum.

This *Te Deum* is also found in the Salisbury Book of Hours for the Matins Office of the Passion of Christ, folio 116v, however it begins *Te Deum laudamus* instead of *Te Christum laudamus*.

The hymn for the Office of the Holy Cross in Pope Leo X's Book of Hours is Bonaventura's single hymn-sequence *In passione Domini*. It is divided into eight sections and each section is assigned to a specific liturgical hour of the Office: Matins, *In passione Domine*, (folio 206r); Lauds, *Christum ducem*, (folio 215r); Prime, *Tu qui velatus*, (folio 218r); Terce, *Hora qui ductus tertia*, (folio 220v); Sext, *Crucem pro nobis*, (folio 223v); None, *Beata Christi passio*, (folio 226v); Vespers, *Qui pressura mortis dura*, (folio 229v); and Compline, *Qui iacuisti mortuus*, (folio 234v).[23] This hymn-sequence is found in the Salisbury Book of Hours for the Office of the Passion of Christ and is divided in the same manner as the Toledo manuscript.[24]

Josquin des Pres used exerpts of Bonaventure's hymn-sequence for his six-part motet *Qui velatus*.[25] The texts for all of the hours are not used in the motet. The hymn text and hours are: i, Prime, *Qui velatus*; ii, Terce, *Hora qui ductus tertia*; iii, Sext and Vespers, *In flagellis*; iv, Vespers, *In amara crucis ara*; v, Compline, *Qui jacuisti mortuus*; and, vi, Lauds, *Christum ducem*. It has been suggested that Josquin's motet was probably used during the Office of the Passion.[26] This statement should be amended to include the Office of the Holy Cross since there are many similarities between the two.[27] It appears that northern liturgical sources associated the Bonaventura hymn with the Office of the Passion; Italian sources assigned it to the Office of the Holy Cross.

There is no way of determining exactly what textual sources Josquin consulted for his motet. The Toledo Book of Hours dates from 1513-1521 and was a contemporary source. The following shows the

[23] Guido Maria Dreves, ed., *Analecta Hymnica Medii Aevi*, (Leipzig: 1886-1922), L, 568-570.

[24] See [Book of Hours (Salisbury)]: *Enchiridion*, folios 111r-122r.

[25] Albert Smijers, ed., *Josquin Motetten*, (Amsterdam, 1925), 1:41-47 (for parts 1-5); and 1:21-23 for part 6.

[26] Mattfeld, "Some Relationships between Texts and Cantus Firmi in the Liturgical Motets of Josquin des Pres," *JAMS* XIV (1961), 175-176.

[27] See Gehrenbeck, *Motetti de la Corona*, pp. 580-587.

differences between Bonaventura's hymn and the text found in Josquin's motet. The text used by Josquin shows marked differences:

Pope Leo X's Book of Hours	Josquin
i, Prime	
Tu qui velatus facie	Qui velatus facie fuisti
fuisti sol iustitie	Et penurias sustinuisti,
felxis illusus genibus	Sol justitiae, flexis
	illusus genibus,
ut sis nobis propitius	Esto nobis propitius
ii, Terce	
gravem ferendo humeris	Christe ferendo humeris
Fac nos sic te diligere	Fac sit nos diligere,
carnem mumdumque vicere	Sanctamque vitam ducere,
ut mereamur requie	Ut valeamus requie
frui celestis glorie.	Frui coelestis patriae.
iii, Sext-Vespers	
Qui suo nos supplicio	Qui suo supplicio
redemit ab egyptio.	Nos redemit ab inferno.
bibisti amarissime	Bibisti amarissium
Nostre genti	Omni genti
iv, Vespers	
deus homo quem	Jesu Christe,
adoro	rex benigne,
nos conducas	Fac nos ire
et inducas	et venire,
v, Compline	
et te redemptor querere.	Semperque laudes reddere.
redemptis tuo sanguine	Quos redemisti sanquine,
educ nos de miseria	Et duc nos ad coelestia,
et dona pacis gaudia	Aeternae pacis gaudia.
vi, Lauds	
gaudet cetus	Laudet coetus
nos damnatos	corda terrant

reddat gratos	ut te quaerant:
sunt collata	sint collata
sumus loti	sumus laeti
qui fidelis	ac etiam

Several of the variations in the text are particular to the Toledo source and different from the hymn text printed in Dreves, *Analecta Hymnica Medii Aevii*. Those variances as cited in Dreves are from an Italian manuscript from the fifteenth century.[28] One of the variants unique to this Book of Hours is the portion of the Vespers text *deus homo quem adoro*. The variations in the hymn text in the Toledo manuscript are significantly different from the portions of text set by Josquin. It can be assumed that the Book of Hours of Leo X was probably not the source consulted by Josquin.

The last Office in the Book of Hours of Leo X is also one of the Holy Cross (folios 241r–244r). It begins *Incipit officium primum (parvum?) sancte crucis*. The entire text is in manuscripts of English provenance as a devotion for the Memorial of the Passion.[29] The origin of this devotion was probably from lay sources, however one manuscript has the following notice: *Commemorationes dominice passionis facte a papa iohanne uicessimo secundo dicende post horas canonicas.*[30] If the attribution is correct, the devotion was written between 1316 and 1334. It eventually became a part of hours as the "last amplification of the monastic office as said in monasteries of the English Congregation before the suppression in 1539."[31] The text that follows is from the Book of Hours of Leo X:

Hymnus.	Patris sapientia veritas divina deus homo captus est hora matutina. A votis discipulis cito derelictus a iudeis traditus venditus afflictus.
Antiphon.	Adoramus te christe et benedicimus tibi.
Response.	Quia per sanctam crucem tuam redemisti mundum.
Oratio.	Domine iesu christe fili dei uiui pone passionem crucem et mortem tuam inter iudicium tuum et

---

[28] See Dreves, *Analecta Hymnica*, L. 568–570.
[29] Tolhurst, *The Monastic Breviary of Hyde Abbey*, 6:134–137.
[30] *Ibid.*, p. 135.
[31] *Ibid.*, p. 134.

animas nostras nunc et in hore mortis nostre largiri
digneris . . . .

(Rubric.)   Antiphonia et oratio ut supra (?) ad omnis horas.

Ad primam hymnus.

Hora prima ductus est iesus ad pilatum.
falsis testimoniis multum accusatum.
in collo percuciunt manibus ligatum.
uultum dei conspuunt lumen celi gratum.

Ad tertiam hymnus.

Crucifige clamitat hora terciarum.
illusus induitur veste purpuratum.
caput eius pungitur corona spinarum.
crucem portat humeris ad locum penarum.

Ad vi hymnus.

Hora sexta dominum iesus est cruci conclauatus
et est cum latronibus pendens deputatus.
pre tormentis sitiens felle saturatus.
agnus crimen diluit sic ludificatus.

Ad nonam hymnus.

Hora nona dominus iesus expiravit.
hely clamas spiritum patri commendauit.
latus eius lancea miles perforauit.
terra tunc contremuit et sol obscurauit.

Ad vesperas hymnus.

De cruce deponitur hora vespertina.
fortitudo latuit in mente divina.
talem mortem subiit uite medicina.
heu corona glorie iacuit supina.

Ad completorium hyumnus.

Hora completorii datur sepulture.
corpus christi nobile spes uite future.
conditur aromate complentur scripture.
iugis sit memoria mors est michi cure.

(Rubric.)   In finem omnium horarum. Oremus.

Oratio.   Has horas canonicas cum devocione
tibi christe recolo pia ratione.
ut qui pia ratione pro me passus es
amoris adore sis michi solacium in
mortis agone.

The study of such a magnificent Renaissance manuscript reveals the nature of the private devotion through a book of remarkable beauty and high artistic value. The brilliant illuminations augment the emotional and contemplative texts. The fact that this Book of Hours was prepared for a leading religious figure, Pope Leo X, makes the manuscript even more exceptional.

CHAPTER TWENTY

DAMNED MUSIC: THE SYMBOLISM OF THE BAGPIPES IN THE ART OF HIERONYMUS BOSCH AND HIS FOLLOWERS

John H. Planer

Manchester College

Symbolism in the art of Hieronymus Bosch has been the subject of widely-differing interpretations. Some scholars assert that Bosch, who died in 1516, was a devout and orthodox believer whose art depicted the sins of the flesh and their inevitable consequences — eternal punishment in the flames and ice of hell.[1] Others, following the lead of Wilhelm Fränger, argue that Bosch was a heretic — that he hid his Adamite heresy and membership in the Brotherhood of the Free Spirit behind a cover of orthodoxy and membership in the confraternity Illustre Lieve Vrouwe Broederschap at the Sint Jans Kirk at s'Hertogenbosch.[2] Fränger based his interpretations upon only a few references, and his thesis relies heavily upon the record of a trial held in Cambrai in 1411, at least two generations before Bosch was born.[3]

---

[1] Max J. Friedländer, *Early Netherlandish Painting*, vol. V, *Geertgen tot Sint Jans and Jerome Bosch*, trans. by Heinz Norden (New York: Frederick A. Praeger, 1969), pp. 59–65.

[2] Wilhelm Fränger, *The Millenium of Hieronymus Bosch*, trans. by Eithne Wilkins and Ernst Kaiser (New York: Hacker Art Books, 1976). Sandra Orienti and René de Solier, *Hieronymus Bosch* (New York: Crescent Books, 1979).

[3] Fränger, *Millenium*, pp. 16–31.

Hans Lenneberg refuted Fränger's interpretations of Bosch's musical symbolism by citing numerous misunderstandings and inaccuracies.[4] Recently some art historians have approached Bosch's art through the study of alchemy and astrology.[5] They have assembled significant evidence but have not yet discovered any document linking Bosch directly with alchemy or astrology. And although we know relatively little about Bosch's life, what we *do* know does not support an alchemical or astrological interpretation.[6] Other studies of Flemish proverbs have helped in interpreting Bosch's ambiguous symbolism in some works.[7] Yet other scholars have concluded that if Bosch were not directly involved in practicing witchcraft himself, at least he knew much about it.[8] To understand Bosch's imagery, they have studied treatises of those who practiced witchcraft as well as those who prosecuted it. Finally, others have suggested that Bosch's imagery resulted from the use of drugs.[9] Studies of sixteenth-century recipes of witches reveal that their salves and elixers included strong hallucinogens.[10] Thus

---

[4] Hans H. Lenneberg, "Bosch's Garden of Earthly Delights: Some Musicological Considerations and Criticisms," *Gazette des Beaux-Arts*, ser. VI, vol. LVIII (September, 1961), 135–44.

[5] A. Boczkowska, "The Lunar Symbolism of the Ship of Fools by Heironymus Bosch," *Oud-Holland*, vol. 86 (1971), pp. 47–69. A. Spychalska-Boczkowska, "Materials for the Iconography of Hieronymus Bosch's Triptych the Garden of Delights," *Studia Muzealne* V (1966), 49–95. Jacques Combe, *Jheronimus Bosch*, trans. by Ethel Duncan (London: B.T. Batsford, n.d.), pp. 27–38. Andrew Pigler, "Astrology and Jerome Bosch, *The Burlington Magazine* XCII (1950), 132–36, reprinted in *Bosch in Perspective*, ed. by James Snyder (Engelwood Cliffs: Prentice-Hall, 1973), pp. 108–17. See also Orienti and Solier, *Hieronymus Bosch*.

[6] Biographical data are summarized in Mia Cinotti, *The Complete Paintings of Bosch*, in the series *Classici dell'arte* (New York: Harry N. Abrams, n.d.), pp. 83–85 and are printed in Charles de Tolnay, *Hieronymus Bosch* (New York: Reynal and Company, 1966), pp. 407–8.

[7] For example, the central panel of the *Tripych of the Hay Wain* has been interpreted by means of proverbs. See Tolnay, *Hieronymus Bosch*, p. 355. In addition see the bibliography in Robert L. Delevoy, *Bosch*, trans. by Stuart Gilbert (Geneva: Skira, 1960), pp. 131–32 and the references in Friedländer, *Netherlandish Painting* V, 105, notes 170–72.

[8] Charles D. Cuttler, "Witchcraft in a Work by Bosch," *Art Quarterly* XX (1957), 128–40.

[9] Delevoy, *Bosch*, p. 76.

[10] H.J. Norman, "Witch Ointments" in Montague Summers, *The Werewolf* (New York: Bell Publishing Company, 1966 — a reprint), pp. 291–92. See also Robert Fletcher, "The Witches' Pharmacopoeia," *Bulletin of the Johns*

Hieronymus Bosch and his art are the subjects of a lively scholarly debate. I propose to study the symbolism of musical instruments in the art of Bosch and his followers in order to ascertain which of these interpretations the musical symbolism supports.

In the art of Hieronymus Bosch and his followers, musical instruments appear frequently and prominently. Because Bosch's instruments are often fantastic and are often played in bizarre manners, his art reveals less about the construction of instruments and performance practices than it does about instrumental symbolism. Instruments often appear singly; only two instruments infrequently appear in the same panel. Table One lists single and paired instruments. Table Two lists works in which three or more instruments are gathered into ensembles or are scattered throughout. In some paintings cited in these tables the attributions to Bosch rest secure; nevertheless art historians disagree whether most of the other works are originals, copies, workshop productions, or imitations by followers.

Table Three lists the instruments found in works by Bosch and his followers, but excludes paintings by Pieter Huys, Jan Mandyn, and Pieter Bruegel the Elder. From this information we may draw the following conclusions. First, few instruments appear only in heaven or are associated only with saints. One example, however, is the psaltery which appears only once in Bosch's works (Cinotti catalogue 2), played by an angel seated outside the heavenly gates. Second, some instruments appear in both good and evil settings. For example, while one angel plays the harp outside the heavenly gates (Cinotti 2), another harp appears elsewhere in the same work under the vice of lust and the instrument occurs in numerous scenes of hell; in earthly settings Bosch's harpists are obviously evil, degenerate, or foolish (Cinotti 16). Third, Bosch usually reserves busînes for angels (Cinotti 50D), although occasionally a demon plays a busîne in paintings whose attributions to Bosch are doubtful. Fourth, Bosch reserves for demons the curved trumpets, often with fire emerging from the bell. (Cinotti 30D) Perhaps the source for Bosch's distinction between straight and curved trumpets is Isaiah 40:4, where the voice crying in the wilderness proclaims "Prepare ye the way of the Lord" — indeed an appropriate text for the Last Judgement — and asserts that "the crooked shall be made

---

Hopkins Hospital VII, no. 65 (August, 1896), 147–56 and Michael Harner, "The Role of Hallucinogenic Plants in European Witchcraft" in Michael Horner, ed. *Hallucinogens and Shamanism* (New York: Oxford University Press, 1972), pp. 127–50.

TABLE I. Single and paired instruments found in the art of Hieronymus Bosch and his followers

Title (Cinotti catalogue)	Location	Instruments	Attribution	Dates
Marriage at Cana (3)	Rotterdam: Boymans-van Beuningen Museum	bagpipes (drawing includes a bladder)	Bosch	1475–80
Death of the Reprobate (13B)	New York: Private Coll.	curved trumpet	Bosch?	?
Ship of Fools (16)	Paris: Louvre	lute	Bosch	1490–1500
Allegory of Pleasure (17)	New Haven: Yale Art Gallery	curved trumpet	Bosch	1490–1500
Ascent of Calvary (20)	olim London: Arnot Gallery	curved trumpet	Follower of Bosch	c. 1500
Path of Life (21A)— Hay Wain Triptych	Madrid: Prado Variant: Escorial	bagpipes	Bosch	1500–02
Hell (21D)— Hay Wain Triptych	Madrid: Prado Variant: Escorial	curved trumpet	Bosch	1500–02
Battle Between Carnival and Lent (23)	The Hague: Cramer Gall.	bagpipes	Copy of a lost work?	?
Evil World (25A)— Flood Triptych	Rotterdam: Boymans-van Beuningen Museum	lute	Bosch	1500–04
Temptation of Saint Anthony (29B)	Valenciennes: Musée des Beaux-Arts	lute	Bosch or a Follower	?
Passion (33B)	Berlin-Dahlem: Staatliche Museen	curved trumpet	Bosch	1504–05
Small St. Christopher	Madrid: Private Coll.	busîne (played by a demon)	Bosch?	?
St. Anthony (40A)— Hermits Altarpiece	Venice: Palazzo Ducale	curved trumpet	Bosch	c. 1505
Seizing of Jesus (43A) Anthony Triptych	Lisbon: Museu Nacional de Arte Antigua	curved trumpet	Bosch	1505–06
St. Anthony (43C) Anthony Triptych	Lisbon: Museu Nacional de Arte Antigua	bagpipes	Bosch	1505–06
St. Anthony (43E) Anthony Triptych	Lisbon: Museu Nacional de Arte Antigua	curved trumpet	Bosch	1505–06
Ascent of Calvary (44)	Madrid: Royal Palace	curved trumpet	Bosch	1505–07

TABLE I. *Continued*

Heaven (51C)—Last Judgment Triptych	Bruges: Musée Groeninge	harp, busîne	Workshop of Bosch	?
Last Judgment (52)	Baytown, USA: Princess Kadjar Collection	busînes (angels); curved trumpets (demons)	Copy or imitation	?
Crowning with Thorns (58)	Escorial: Monastery of San Lorenzo	bagpipes	Bosch	c. 1510
Temptation of St. Anthony (60)	Berlin-Dahlem: Staatliche Museen	curved anus-pipe (demon)	Follower of Bosch	·?
Donor and St. Peter (62B)—Epiphany Triptych	Madrid: Prado	bagpipes	Bosch	c. 1510
Adoration of the Magi (62C)—Epiphany Triptych	Madrid: Prado	bagpipes, busîne	Bosch	c. 1510
Adoration of the Magi (63C)—Epiphany Triptych	Anderlecht: Church of SS Peter and Guyon	bagpipes	Follower of Bosch	?
Adoration of the Shepherds (65A)	Philadelphia Museum of Art	recorder	Workshop of Bosch	?
Adoration of the Magi (66)	New York: Metropolitan Museum of Art	bagpipes?	Workshop of Bosch	?

TABLE II. Multiple instruments found in the art of Hieronymus Bosch and his followers

Title (Cinotti catalogue)	Location	Instruments	Attribution	Dates
Seven Deadly Sins (2)	Madrid: Prado	Last Judgment: busînes Luxuria: harp, pipe and tabor Heaven: harp, psaltery, recorder (busîne?), busîne	Bosch	1475–80
Concert in the Egg (7)	Lille: Musée Wicar	lute, harp, singers, brass or reed instrument, music book, cornetto?	Copy after Bosch	1475–80

TABLE II. *Continued*

Valve Boat (after 16)	—	bagpipes, grill-harp, lute singers, music book	After Bosch	1562
Hay Wain (21C)— Hay Wain Triptych	Madrid: Prado Variant: Escorial	bagpipes, lute, nose-pipe, singers, music book	Bosch	1500–02
Hell (30D)— Garden of Earthly Delights Triptych	Madrid: Prado	drum, lute, harp, pommer, singers, organistrum, recorder, music book, 3 curved trumpets, 2 bagpipes, 2 bells, sackbut	Bosch	1503–04
Job (42B)—Job Triptych	Bruges: Musée Groeninge	bowed skull, bladder-pipe, reed pipe with pirouette, busînes—one with curved extension	Follower of Bosch	?
St. Anthony (43D) Anthony Triptych	Lisbon: Museu Nacional de Arte Antigua	harp, lute, organistrum, pommer (nose-pipe), singers, music book	Bosch	1505–06
Last Judgment (50D)—Last Judgment Triptych	Vienna: Akademie der bildenden Künste	angels: busînes demon: busîne bagpipe, 2 lutes	Workshop of Bosch	?
Hell (50D)—Last	Vienna: Akademie der bildenden Künste	lute, harp, pommer or bagpipe, anus-pipe, curved trumpets, pipe and tabor, singers, music book	Workshop of Bosch	?
Last Judgment (51D)—Last Judgment Triptych	Bruges: Musée Groeninge	lute, harp, bagpipes, bell, busînes (angels), curved trumpet	Workshop of Bosch	?
St. Martin (129) print after a lost grisaille	—	4 lutes, bagpipes, 2 harps, drums, 1 busîne, 2 curved trumpets	Print after Bosch	?
Burlesque Concert (drawing)	Paris: Louvre	lute, bagpipes	Follower of Bosch	?
Temptation of St. Anthony	Antwerp: Mayer van den Bergh Museum	harp, lute, curved trumpet	Pieter Huys?	1577

TABLE II. *Continued*

Temptation of St. Anthony	New York: Metropolitan Museum of Art	bagpipes, nose-pipe, 2 lutes, drums, busine	Pieter Huys?	?
Trials of Job	Douai: Musée des Beaux-Arts	bagpipes, kettle drums, bell, lute, pipe and tabor, busîne	Pieter Huys or Jan Mandyn	?
Fall of the Rebel Angels	Brussels: Musées Royaux des Beaux-Arts	pommer, busine, organistrum, curved trumpets	Pieter Bruegel the Elder	1562

TABLE III. Musical instruments in art by Bosch and his followers[1]

Instrument	Heaven	Earth[2]	Hell
Lute	—	7, 16, 21C, 25A	29B, 30D, 43D, 50D, 50E, 129
Harp	2, 51C	2, 7, 16	30D, 43D, 50E, 51D, 129
Psaltery	2	—	—
Organistrum	—	—	30D, 43D
Bagpipes	—	3, 16, 21A, 21C, 23 58, 62B, 62C, 63D, 66?	30D, 43C, 50D, 51D, 129
Recorder	2[3]	42B?, 65A	30D
Pipe and Tabor	—	2	50E
Bladder Pipe	—	3 (drawing), 42B	—
Sackbut	—	—	30D
Pommer	—	—	30D, 43D, 50E?
Busîne	2, 50D, 51C, 51D, 52	42B?, 62C, 66	37, 129
Curved trumpet	—	17, 20, 33B, 43A, 44	13B, 21D, 30D, 40A, 51D, 52, 60, 129
Bells[4]	—	—	30D, 51D
Drums	—	—	30D, 129
Singers	2?	7, 16, 21C	30D, 43C, 50E
Nose pipe	—	—	21C, 43D, 50D, 53
Anus pipe	—	—	50E
Bowed Skull	—	42B	—

[1] Numbers refer to Bosch's works as cited in the Cinotti catalogue. These numbers are also identified in the preceding tables.
[2] Earthly subjects often depict evil, lust, greed, or folly.
[3] Kathi Meyer-Baer (*Music of the Spheres and the Dance of Death*, p. 161) identifies this instrument as a busîne, but the embouchure suggests that a reed pipe or recorder might be more likely.
[4] The attribute of St. Anthony was the bell, in addition to the Tau cross, pig, rosary, and habit. In this list the bell is not cited as a musical instrument when it appears as an attribute of St. Anthony.

straight" (*et erunt prava in directa*). Artists other than Bosch, however, often did not observe this distinction. For example, in Pieter Bruegel's *The Fall of the Rebel Angels*, all the angels blow curved trumpets, while a demon blows a straight one. Fifth, most of Bosch's instruments appear in settings of human folly or evil, such as enthusiastic soldiers or citizens (Cinotti 44) participating in the Crucifixion of Jesus; Job's tormentors (Cinotti 42B); the seven deadly sins (Cinotti 17); the lovers atop Bosch's Hay Wain (Cinotti 21) accompanied by a demonic obligato nose-pipe; or in scenes of hell and demonic torment, as in the Musical Hell (Cinotti 30) from the *Garden of Earthly Delights*, the hell from the Last Judgment Triptych in Vienna (Cinotti 50); and the hell from the Last Judgment Triptych in Bruges (Cinotti 51D).[11] In general, Bosch associated the lute with sensuality and passionate love.[12] Thus in Bosch's art angels do not play lutes, although other artists did indeed depict angelic lutenists.[13] Bosch's iconography and symbolism thus appear extremely conservative. Sixth, Bosch depicted many ensembles composed of sinners, as in the print of the *Valve Boat* after a lost work of Bosch (Cinotti 16); the *Concert in the Egg* (Cinotti 7); Job's comfortors (Cinotti 42B); the print of Saint Martin (Cinotti 129); and the various musical hells. Ensembles appear in four works depicting earthly dissolution and in five works depicting hell or assaults by

---

[11] See Reinhold Hammerstein's excellent study *Die Musik der Engel* (Bern: Francke Verlag), pp. 100–15 for sources describing the music of hell, which provided the literary tradition for Bosch's depiction of demonic and damned concerts.

[12] The etymology of "lewd" is uncertain. The *Oxford English Dictionary* suggests a possible derivation from *laigo* — ecclesiastical Latin — and hence from *laicus*, laity. Perhaps a derivation from "lute" might be possible. Certainly the lute is a favorite instrument of lovers. For examples see the prints "The Large Garden of Love," "A Pair of Lovers and a Fool at a Fountain," and "A Pair of Lovers at a Fountain," engravings 102, 493, and 534 respectively, in the collection *Late Gothic Engravings of Germany and the Netherlands*, comp. by Max Lehrs (New York: Dover Publications, 1969).

[13] Angels playing lutes appear frequently in the works of Hans Memling. For examples see paintings 1C, 15o, 29A, 35A, and 81 in the catalogue raisonné by Maria Corti, *L'opera completa di Memling*, vol. 27 in the series *Classici dell'arte* (Milano: Rizzoli Editore, 1969); see also A.P. de Mirimonde, "Les Anges musiciens chez Memlinc," *Jaarboeck van het Koninklijk Museum voor Schone Kunsten* (Antwerp: Musée Royal des Beaux-Arts, Annuaire), 1962–63, pp. 5–55. Angels playing lutes appear frequently in the art of Gossart and others. There are numerous illustrations of angelic lutenists in Kathi Meyer-Baer, *Music of the Spheres and the Dance of Death: Studies in Musical Iconology* (Princeton University Press, 1970), figs. 55, 63, 65, 67, 69, etc.

demons. In earthly settings, the sinful play upon traditional instruments or parodies of them, such as the grill-harp (Cinotti 16) or the spider-web harp (Cinotti 16). In hell either demons play upon instruments to torment the damned or else the instruments torment the damned directly by imprisoning them (Cinotti 30); penetrating their orifices; or ensnaring them (Cinotti 51D). When damned souls rather than demons sing or play instruments, they do so unwillingly.

The second most popular instruments, after curved and straight trumpets, are the bagpipes; they appear in fourteen works. Art historians have found sexual symbolism in Bosch's bagpipes. Cinotti calls them "obscene";[14] Bax referred to them as male and female emblems;[15] Orienti and Solier call them an "impious instrument with sexual connotations" and refer to the "sexual symbol of the red bagpipes";[16] to Tolnay they were the "emblem of the male sex";[17] to Combe they were an "instrument which Bosch often uses as a symbol of carnal lust";[18] Gibson called them "an emblem of the male organ of generation."[19] Fräenger went further: ". . . these bagpipes are idle nothingness, blowing and squeaking only as long as living breath inflates the bag, and wretchedly collapsing as soon as the breath fails. . . . the bagpipe represents the essence of human foolishness."[20] Since Bosch depicts this instrument frequently and since its very scale suggests major importance, we shall explore its symbolism in detail. We shall survey the mythic origin of the instrument; its sexual associations; the functions at which pipers played; their social status; and literary and artistic traditions.

According to a legend recounted in Ovid's *Metamorphoses* and elsewhere, Athena invented the bagpipes, but when she discovered that playing them distorted her features and thereby amused the other gods, the embarrassed Athena cast them away. Marsyas, a satyr, discovered them. He learned to play them well and boasted that his skill exceeded that of Apollo. Apollo accepted the challenge. Marsyas nearly won, but Apollo resorted to trickery, and Marsyas lost. The victorious Apollo

[14] Cinotti, *Bosch*, p. 101, no. 30D.
[15] Cited in Cinotti, *Bosch*, p. 101, no. 30D.
[16] Orienti and Solier, *Bosch*, pp. 54, 95.
[17] Tolnay, *Bosch*, p. 32.
[18] Combe, *Bosch*, pp. 12, 19, 38, 91.
[19] Walter S. Gibson, *Hieronymus Bosch* (New York: Praeger Publishers, 1973), p. 98.
[20] Fränger, *Millenium*, p. 69.

flayed Marsyas alive for his *hubris*.[21] A woodcut of 1501 from the *Ovidio metamorphoses volgare* depicts the entire legend.[22]

The shape of the bagpipes does indeed suggest male genitalia, and Bosch often stresses their sexual resemblance by painting them pink or red (Cinotti 3, 30D). In addition, as Curt Sachs noted, "Most of the instruments reserved for men have a harsh, aggresive, indeed ugly tone; most of the instruments preferred by women have a muffled timbre."[23] Thus the shrill, piercing tones of the bagpipe suggest the male sex. And indeed, aside from rare representations of angels, goddesses, or allegorical figures, the bagpipes were virtually the exclusive domain of male pipers in the fourteenth, fifteenth, and sixteenth centuries. This statement, however, contradicts a passing observation made by Professor Edith Borroff in her paper "Women and Secular Music in Gothic Europe," read before the Midwest Chapter of the American Musicological Society in the fall of 1978.[24]

Aside from angels, who rarely play bagpipes and who are generally depicted as male,[25] the only woman bagpiper I have found prior to the seventeenth century is the goddess Athena, shown in the Apollo–Marsyas contest.[26] An illumination from the *Roman de la Rose* from a manuscript in the Bodleian Library illustrates a variant passage

---

[21] The story is recounted in Book VI of Ovid's *Metamorphoses*, lines 385–400, and elsewhere. See Emanuel Winternitz's article "The Curse of Pallas Athena," reprinted in Winternitz's *Musical Instruments and Their Symbolism in Western Art* (New Haven: Yale University Press, 1967), pp. 150–65.

[22] Winternitz's *Musical Instruments*, p. 158; plate 70A is an anonymous, sixteenth century, Italian painting of the Marsyas-Apollo contest preserved in the National Gallery in Washington. See also Athena playing the bagpipes in plate 71A. The periodical published by graduate students in art history is entitled *Marsyas*. Whether the title refers to Marsyas's skill, Apollo's trickery, or being flayed alive, I do not know.

[23] Curt Sachs, *The History of Musical Instruments* (New York: Norton & Company, 1940), p. 52.

[24] Bismarck Hotel: Chicago, Illinois: November 18–19, 1978.

[25] Gustave Davidson, *A Dictionary of Angels Including the Fallen Angels* (New York: Free Press, 1967), pp. 112–13. Davidson notes the existence of female angels in the Jewish tradition. Shigebumi Tsuji, "Angels: 4. Iconography," *New Catholic Encyclopedia*, vol. 1 (1967), pp. 515–16 notes that in the scriptures angels are male and that female angels are a development of renaissance art. Indeed the names Raphael, Michael, and Gabriel are male.

[26] Winternitz, *Musical Instruments*, p. 158, plate 70A, plate 71A, and the detail in plate 69C.

preserved in a small group of manuscripts.[27] The passage, however, recounts the story of Marsyas, and the woman thus is the goddess Minerva, playing her bagpipes before the gods.

Evidence for female pipers comes either from medieval glossaries or else from the seventeenth and eighteenth centuries, when dressing as shepherds and shepherdesses was considered *chic*.[28] The Latin terms for bagpipes were *tibia utricularis, pandora, chorus*, and *musa*.[29] The term *fistillator* referred to a player of pipes, though not necessarily bagpipes;[30] the term *fistillatrix*, a female piper, does occur — once — in a fifteenth-century *nominale*.[31] R.E. Latham, in his *Revised Medieval Word List*, noted that he had found no reference to the term

---

[27] Oxford: Bodleian Library, MS Douce 195, f. 77r, available on color microfilm 211G, frame 9, from the Bodleian Library. The insertion occurs after line 10,830 in the composite, critical edition by Ernest Langlois, *Le Roman de la Rose* (Paris: Honoré Champion, 1921), III, p. 176, pp. 305–7.

[28] Edith Borroff, *Music in Europe and the United States: A History* (Englewood Cliffs: Prentice-Hall, Inc., 1971), p. 443. I am grateful to Professor Borroff for calling this engraving to my attention.

[29] For a reference to the *pandora* see the treatise of Joannis Aegidius *Ars musica*, printed in Martin Gerbert's *Scriptores ecclesiastici de musica sacra potissimum* (reprint: Hildesheim: Georg Olms, 1963), vol. 2, p. 390: "Et ideo instrumentum fistularum ab eo inventum Pandorium est vocatum, ut dicit Isidorus. Est etiam Pandorium instrumentum rotundum, cum pergameno extento super lignum, quod manibus tangatur. Ad hoc fistulis se excitant vigiles, et earum melodiae suavitate ad dormiendum ocyus et suavius provocantur in lectulis quiescentes." The *chorus* may well refer to a bladderpipe, rather than bagpipes. Sibyl Marcuse (*A Survey of Musical Instruments* (New York: Harper & Row, 1975), pp. 666–67) cites Martin Gerbert (*De Cantu et musica sacra* (reprint: Graz: Akademisch Druck- und Verlagsanstalt, 1968), vol. 2, pp. 150–51 and plates 22 and 24), who examines the letter of Pseudo-Jerome to Dardanus (J.-P. Migne, ed., *Patrologia Latina*, vol. 30, cols. 219–22). Helmut Giesel (*Studien zur Symbolik der Musikinstrumente im Schrifttum der alten und mittelalterlichen Kirche* (Regensburg: Guatav Bosse Verlag, 1978), pp. 186–87) concludes that the instrument resembled the bagpipes. The letter to Dardanus links the *chorus* with the Jewish people and their narrow understanding of scriptures. Thus there is a precedent for associating Jewish musicians with the bagpipes well before the time of Bosch.

[30] Henry Holland Carter, *A Dictionary of Middle English Musical Terms*, ed. by George B. Gerhard (Bloomington: Indiana University Press, 1961), p. 358.

[31] *Anglo Saxon and Old-English Vocabularies*, ed. by Thomas Wright, "A Nominale (Of the Fifteenth Century)" (London: Trübner & Co., 1883), col. 693. Francis Collinson (*The Bagpipe: The History of a Musical Instrument* (London: Routledge & Kegan Paul, 1975), pp. 18, 30, 36, 41) cites female pipers of antiquity, yet in these instances Collinson refers to single or double reed pipes — not bagpipes.

in literature.[32] Likewise the French term *cornemuseresse* refers to a female bagpiper, but according to Godefroy's *Dictionnaire de l'ancienne langue française*, the term appears only in a Latin–French glossary.[33] To date I have found no art in the middle ages or renaissance depicting mortal woman playing the bagpipes; and the two terms for female pipers appear only in glossaries rather than literature. Clearly in Bosch's time the bagpipes were considered male instruments.[34]

The function of a musical instrument partly determines its symbolism. In the twelfth, thirteenth, and even fourteenth centuries, evidence exists that the nobility used bagpipes in their entertainments, as in the Heidelberger manuscript; the instruments appear in several miniatures in the *Cantigas* of Rey Alfonso el Sabio;[35] French authors cite the instruments of their courtly poetry;[36] Machaut mentioned that organs, bagpipes, and other instruments might be used in his polyphonic music,[37] and indeed a bagpipe appears in a miniature in Machaut's *Remède de Fortune*;[38] miniatures of courtly gatherings and

---

[32] R.E. Latham, *Revised Medieval Latin Word List from British and Irish Sources* (London: Oxford University Press, 1965), pp. xx and 193.

[33] Frédéric Godefroy, *Dictionnaire de l'ancienne langue française*, vol. 2, p. 305, "Cornemuseresse"; see also *Tobler-Lommatzsch altfranzösisches Wörterbuch*, vol. 2 (Berlin: Weidmannsche Buchhandling, 1936), col. 875, where Godefroy is cited. Neither Godefroy nor Tobler cite a feminine form for players of the *estive, muse, veze, musette*, or *chevrete*. Godefroy does list a masculine form for a *chevrete* performer, however: *chevreteor*.

[34] In Edmund A. Bowles's *Musikleben im 15. Jahrhundert*, in the series *Musikgeschichte in Bildern* (Leipzig: VEB Deutscher Verlag für Musik, 1977), bagpipes appear in at least twelve plates. In nine of those examples the bagpipers are male; in three instances I cannot identify the sex of the players. In Walter Salmen's *Musikleben im 16. Jahrhundert* in the same series (Leipzig: VEB Deutscher Verlag für Musik, 1976) bagpipes appear in at least twenty plates. In each instance the bagpiper is male. Additional illustrations appear in Collinson, *The Bagpipe*, pp. 65–97 and plates 10–19; when the sex of the piper can be determined (excluding angels), it is male. For female pipers in Scotland in the eighteenth century see Collinson, pp. 193–94.

[35] *Cantigas de Santa Maria*. The miniatures containing bagpipes are gathered and printed in plate 22 of Winternitz's *Musical Instruments*.

[36] Godefroy and Tobler cite numerous examples; see the entries and variants for *chevrete, cornemuser, muse*, and *veze*. The *estive* probably referred to a hornpipe, as Marcuse (*Survey*, p. 665) suggests.

[37] Machaut's letter to Péronne d'Armentières (Letter X, c. 1361) is cited in Armand Machabey, *Guillaume de Machault 130?-1377; La Vie et l'oeuvre musical* (Paris: Richard Masse Editeur, 1955), vol. 1, p. 171.

[38] Karl Michael Komma, *Musikgeschichte in Bildern* (Stuttgart: Alfred Kröner Verlag, 1961), p. 58.

musical allegories depict an occasional piper;[39] and John of Afflighem reports that the bagpipes are the most excellent (*superexcellens*) of all musical instruments because they are inflated by human breath, as in the *tibia*; operated by hand, as in the fiedel; and actuated by a bag or bellows (*folle excitatur*), as in an organ.[40]

Yet by the fifteenth century bagpipes had lost many of their aristocratic associations and were rapidly becoming the instrument of rustics. In the fifteenth and sixteenth centuries peasants used the instrument to accompany processions, fairs, and weddings.[41] Such rural dances were often erotic — hardly chaste. For example, in Bruegel's *Wedding Dance* in Detroit, the piper and the two men dancing in the foreground have obvious erections. Bagpipes frequently appear in scenes of degeneracy, as in Bruegel's print *Lust* (Luxuria) and in his drawing of *Gluttony* (Gula), both in the series *The Seven Deadly Sins*. And in a German woodcut 1535, a devil blows into a bagpipe whose sack clearly resembles the head of Martin Luther; the blowpipe attached to the ear symbolizes heresy.[42] In Bosch's *Battle Between*

---

[39] As in the miniature for Boethius's *De Musica*, preserved in the Biblioteca Nazionale in Naples. The miniature is reproduced in color on the record jacket of "Secular Music circa 1300" in the series *Das alte Werk* (Telelfunken SAWT 9504). The red hose and relatively short gown of the piper suggest that he is male.

[40] *Johannis Affligemensis: De Musica cum Tonario*, ed. by Jos. Smits van Waesberghe, in the series *Corpus Scriptorum de Musica*, vol. 1 (Rome: American Institute of Musicology, 1950), p. 54: Musa, ut diximus instrumentum quoddam est omnia musicae superexcellens instrumenta, quippe quae omnium vim atque modum in se continet: humano siquidem inflatur spiritu ut tibia, manu temperatur ut phiala, folle excitatur ut organa.

[41] The *Abbildungsverzeichnis* in Bowles's study (*Musikleben im 15. Jahrhundert*, pp. 175–84) reveals the functions of bagpipes in the fifteenth century. Bagpipes are rare in coronations, military activities, and church music. They appear seldom at banquets (3 out of 75 examples), tournaments (4 out of 50), receptions and festive processions (5 out of 148), weddings (3 out of 31, but see p. 30), gatherings of friends (4 out of 91), court dances (6 out of 62), and town bands (5 out of 48 — but they were common at executions). Bagpipes most often appear in the theater (3 out of 11), dances of burghers (3 out of 14), and peasant dances (10 out of 15). Since instruments are not cited for some works, these figures are approximations.

[42] Winternitz, *Musical Instruments*, p. 78, fig. 10. For additional examples see Ernst and Johanna Lehner, *Devils, Demons, Death and Damnation* (New York: Dover Publications, 1971), p. 160, where a print from the anti-Lutheran pamphlet *Catalogus haereticorum omnium pene* (Cologne, 1526) is reproduced. Lucas Cranach the Elder used the same symbol for the Roman Catholic Church in his colored woodcut *Der Unterschied zwischen dem*

Carnival and Lent (Cinotti 23), known only through a grissaille copy, the gaity and eroticism of Carnival contrasts with the austerity of Lent; in Bosch's painting a bagpiper accompanies the dances of Carnival.

Literary evidence reinforces the strong non-religious and erotic associations of bagpipes. For example, the Bible does not mention bagpipes, save for the book of Daniel, where the *sumponyah* is cited three times (3:5, 10, 15). King Nebuchadnezzar ordered that all officials assemble and bow before his golden image when various instruments, including the *sumponyah*, sounded. Scholars disagree whether or not the *sumponyah* was a bagpipe. Alfred Sendrey carefully weighs the evidence; his conclusion that the *sumponyah* was definitely not a bagpipe, however, is stated far more definitely than that evidence warrants.[43] The Vulgate translates *sumponyah* as *symphonia*, which in the middle ages usually referred to the organistrum, but in some instances it referred to bagpipes.[44] In any event, the association of the *sumponyah* with Nebuchadnezzar's egotism and idolatry was hardly a positive recommendation for the instrument.

Classical and patristic sources also mention the bagpipes in secular, erotic contexts.[45] In Aristophanes's *Lysistrata*, a piper accompanies the final dance (line 1242); the women return to their husbands and lovers; their union is joyous, for the women have ended the long war between Athens and Sparta by withholding sexual relations.[46] In Aristophanes's *The Acharnians* (line 862), a bumpkin from Boeotia enters with pipers. Translators differ whether the lines read, "You pipers who are here from Thebes, with bone pipes blow the posterior of a dog"[47] or whether the name of the pipers tune was "The Dog's Arse."[48] Neither translation is flattery. Athenaeus, reporting the licentious revelries of

---

Evangelischen und Katholischen Gottesdienst c. 1545; it is reproduced in *The Age of the Renaissance*, ed. by Denys Hay (New York: McGraw-Hill Book Company, 1968), p. 203.

[43] Alfred Sendrey, *Music in Ancient Israel* (New York: Philosophical Library, 1969), pp. 325-32.

[44] Marcuse, *Survey*, p. 676; Gerbert, *Scriptores*, I, pp. 22-23. Sendrey, *Music*, p. 296, notes that Isidore defines *sambuca* as a bagpipe, but his translation of *sambuca in musicis species est symphoniarum* is not literal. The term *zampugna* (*zampogna*) is a type of bagpipe, as Sendrey notes on p. 325.

[45] See the numerous references in Sendrey, *Music*, pp. 325-32 and in Anthony Baines, *Bagpipes* (Oxford University Press, 1960), pp. 63-68.

[46] Baines, *Bagpipes*, p. 63.

[47] Baines, p. 63.

[48] *The Complete Greek Drama*, ed. by Whitney J. Oates and Eugene O'Neill (New York: Random House, 1938), vol. 2, p. 458.

Antiochus Epiphanes, mentions instruments which may have been bagpipes.[49]

Educated Romans held bagpipes in low esteem.[50] Suetonius and Dio Chrysostomos both note that the dissolute and infamous emperor Nero played the bagpipes (*utricularium*).[51] Anthony Baines concludes, ". . . the early bagpipe, with the possible exception of a brief spell of novelty in Rome, was the equipment of a beggar, perhaps not frequently seen and its music certainly rated of no kind of interest whatsoever."[52]

Literary references to the bagpipes are frequent in the thirteenth, fourteenth, and fifteenth centuries.[53] At best the context is rustic or chivalric love; often the context is sin and debauchery. Eustache Deschamps referred to bagpipes as *cet instrument des hommes bestiaulx*.[54] In lines 545-66 of the Prologue to the *Canterbury Tales*, Chaucer describes a brawny miller who played the bagpipes:

> He was a janglere, and a goliardy
> And that was the moost of synne and harlotries.

In two of the three Macro Plays bagpipers appear. In "The Castle of Perseverance," *circa* 1425, clarions and bagpipes sound as Belial summons his troops — Pride, Envy, Wrath, Flesh, Gluttony, Sloth, Lechery, and Lust — to attack the castle, symbolizing faith and virtue (line 2199).[55] In "Wisdom," *circa* 1460, a bagpiper accompanies the entry of six perjurors: Wrong, Sleight, Doubleness, Falsehood, Ravine, and Deceit (lines 728-31).[56]

Sebastian Brant often mentions bagpipes in his *Ship of Fools*, published in 1494 in Basel.[57] Bosch's painting *The Ship of Fools*

---

[49] Sendrey, *Music*, p. 326.

[50] Sendrey, *Music*, pp. 326-27.

[51] Sendrey, *Music*, p. 328.

[52] Baines, *Bagpipes*, p. 67.

[53] See note 36.

[54] Marcuse, *Survey*, p. 677.

[55] *The Macro Plays*, ed. by F.J. Furnivall and Alfred W. Pollard in the series Early English Text Society, vol. 91 (London: Kegan Paul, Trench, Trübner & Co., 1904), p. 143, line 2199. For the association of bagpipes as the devil's instrument in folklore see Oskar Dähnhardt, *Natursagen*, Band 1 (Leipzig: B.G. Teubner, 1907), p. 189.

[56] *The Macro Plays*, p. 59, lines 727-30, including the stage direction.

[57] Facsimile edition by Franz Schultz in the series *Jahresgaben der Gesellschaft für Elsässische Literatur*, vol. 1, *Sebastian Brant: Das Narrenschiff* (Strassburg: Karl J. Trübner, 1913).

(Cinotti 16) was probably derived from Brant's work. To Brant the bagpipes symbolized folly. For example, the tercet preceding chapter fifty-four, entitled "Of Impatience of Punishment" reads:

> If bagpipes you enjoy and prize
> And harps and lutes you would despise
> You ride a fool's sled, are unwise.[58]

Brant recalls the folly of Marsyas in the tercet preceding chapter sixty-seven, entitled "Not Wishing To Be A Fool":

> How did the silly Marsyas fare
> He lost his hide and lost his hair
> And yet his bagpipe was still there.[59]

The tercet preceding chapter eighty-nine, "Of Foolish Trading" (Brant 89), reads:

> Whoe'ver for bagpipes trades his mule,
> Will not enjoy his trade, the fool,
> He'll walk when riding's been his rule.[60]

In chapter sixty-one Brant notes the folly of dancing. By the fourteenth and fifteenth centuries bagpipes carried strong pejorative connotations. The lower classes played them in rural settings to accompany dances, and from such dances probably arises the erotic symbolism of the bagpipes.

Additional iconographic evidence supports these interpretations. Artists rarely depicted angels playing bagpipes, but frequently angels do play harps, lutes, trumpets, psalteries, organs, and fiedels. The few examples of angelic pipers are either from the twelfth of thirteenth centuries[61] or else generally appear in large groups of angels playing

---

[58] Wem sackpfiffen freüd kurzwil gytt
Und acht der harpff und luten nytt
Der ghört wol uff den narren schlytt.
The excellent rhyming translation is by Edwin H. Zeydel, *The Ship of Fools by Sebastian Brant* (New York: Dover Publications, 1962), p. 186.
[59] Der narr Marsyas der verlor
Das man im abzoch hut und hor
Heilt doch die sackpfiff noch als vor.
[60] Wer syn mul umb eyn sackpfiff gytt
Der selb syns tusehens gnüsset nytt
Und muss offt gan so er gern rytt.
[61] Baines, *Bagpipes*, p. 60, figs. 32 and 33; Komma, *Musikgeschichte*, p. 55,

many different instruments, as in Exeter Cathedral[62] and in Geertgen tot Sint Jans' painting *The Virgin and the Child*.[63] I have never seen any of the twenty-four elders of the Apocalypse playing bagpipes, though they do play lutes, harps, psalteries, organs, bells, and even reed pipes.[64] On the other hand, shepherds, particularly in representations of the Annunciation to the Shepherds and the Adoration of the Magi (Cinotti 62C), usually carry bagpipes.

Finally neither art historians nor musical iconographers have noted the Jewish musicians or *klezmorim* in Bosch's works. *Klezmorim* were itinerant Jewish musicians, both men and women, who often played at Jewish and Christian festivities.[65] We can generally identify Jews by the pointed *Judenhut* or by the badge, often a yellow circle, which the Fourth Latern Council in 1215 forced them to wear.[66] In addition, the scorpion often symbolized the Jewish people,[67] just as the crescent (Cinotti 57) symbolized the heresy of Judaism, Islam, or both.[68]

---

fig. 131; Winternitz, *Musical Instruments*, plates 21C, 23, 65, 68. For statues of Giovanni Balduccio da Pisa from the early fourteenth century see Donald J. Grout, *A History of Western Music*, rev. ed. (New York: Norton and Co., 1973), p. 73. See also *Studia instrumentorum musicae popularis*, ed. by Erich Stockmann, vol. IV, Bericht über die 4. Internationale Arbeitsagung der Study Group on Folk Musical Instruments des International Folk Music Council in Balatonalmádi, 1973, pp. 72, 77.

[62] Komma, *Musikgeschichte*, p. 55.

[63] Reproduced in Winternitz, *Musical Instruments*, plate 65 and Friedländer, *Early Netherlandish Painting*, vol. 5, plate 120, and Meyer-Baer, *Music of the Spheres*, p. 168.

[64] Hammerstein, *Musik der Engel*, pp. 196–98. Other paintings showing the twenty-four elders playing musical instruments are the Master of the St. John Vision, *Vision of St. John the Evangelist* (Cologne: Wallraf-Richartz Museum), 1450–1500 and the Master of the Enthroned Mary, *Coronation of the Virgin* (Cologne: Wallraf-Richartz Museum), *circa* 1450; both works show the elders playing fidels and harps only. For examples of the elders sculpted in the archivolts of church portals see Meyer-Baer, *Music of the Spheres*, pp. 87–119; none of her plates show elders playing bagpipes.

[65] Abraham Zevi Idelsohn, *Jewish Music and Its Historical Development* (New York: Schocken Books, 1967), p. 456.

[66] Bernhard Blumekranz, "Badge, Jewish," *Encyclopedia Judaica*, vol. 4, cols, 62–71. See also "Head Coverings" in the *Jewish Encyclopedia*, vol. 6 (1904).

[67] Marcel Bulard, *Le Scorpion: Symbol du peuple juif dans l'art religieux des XIVe, XVe, XVIe siècles* (Paris: E. de Boccard, 1935).

[68] Frequently a crescent appears above the Temple in Jerusalem, as in a work by a follower of Bosch, number 73 in the Cinotti catalogue. In another work, an

Many references to Jews appear in Bosch's art, and nearly all are uncomplimentary. In his *Ship of Fools* (Cinotti 16), the fool wears a yellow badge. The pointed *Judenhut* appears frequently in scenes of the passion of Jesus (Cinotti 27), and perhaps Bosch's symbol of folly, the inverted funnel worn as a hat (Cinotti 1), directly parodies the *Judenhut*.[69] In the infernal concerts of Bosch and his followers, demons often sport Jewish attributes. In some works, such as those by Pieter Huys and Jan Mandyn, followers of Bosch, the High Priest appears; he may be identified by the bells and pomegranates alternating on the hem of his garment (Exodus 28:34); he blows a curved trumpet, a parody of the shofar.[70]

Bosch also refers directly to Jewish bagpipers. For example, in *The Marriage at Cana* (Cinotti 3), the bagpiper wears a circular, yellow badge containing a crescent, while he leers at the marriage party and Jesus. In *The Hay Wain* (Cinotti 21C), a nun with wimple and rosary chases a Jewish piper wearing a yellow badge, an obvious reference to lust and perhaps apostasy.

Iconographic evidence from various sources links Jewish *klezmorim* with bagpipes. On a woodcut from *Die Juden Erbarkeit* of 1571, three Jewish devils appear to be wearing the badge.[71] The third plays the bagpipes and straddles the *Judensau*, a scatological and anti-semitic symbol common in the thirteenth through eighteenth centuries.[72]

Jewish manuscripts also depict bagpipers. For example, in the

---

anonymous painting of the Crucifixion attributed to the Master of St. Veronica (Chicago: Art Institute), the high priest holds a broken staff with a crescent at the top; the priest is blindfolded and a devil whispers in his ear. Perhaps the crescent became associated with Judaism through the mitre of the high priest, which artists of the fifteenth century frequently depicted as having a crescent affixed to the front.

[69] Carl Linfert (*Bosch* (New York: Harry N. Abrama, n.d.), p. 46) interprets the funnel as a symbol of folly. Delevoy, *Bosch*, p. 27, considers it a symbol of deception. Tolnay, *Bosch*, p. 54 calls it "the funnel of wisdom." Anthony Bosman (*Bosch* (New York: Barnes & Noble, 1962), p. 18) calls it a symbol of the charlatan. If the scorpion appears on the man's yellow brooch, this interpretation is greatly strengthened (Tolnay, *Bosch*, p. 56.)

[70] Lotte Brand Philip identifies the central figure in Bosch's *Triptych of the Epiphany* (Madrid: Prado) as the Jewish Messiah in her study "The Prado Epiphany by Jerome Bosch," reprinted in *Bosch in Perspective*, pp. 88–107.

[71] For the links which some Christians made between Jews and devils see Joshua Trachtenberg's excellent study *The Devil and the Jews* (New York: Harper & Row, 1966 reprint of the 1943 edition).

[72] Isaiah Shachar, *The Judensau: A Medieval Anti-Jewish Motif and Its History* (London: Warburg Institute, 1974).

Barcelona Haggadah from the fourteenth century, a bagpiper stands among other musicians.[73] The Book of Job in the Rothschild Miscellany, from Northern Italy, *circa* 1470, depicts Job's wealth; a piper sits in the lower left corner.[74] Thus the identification of Jewish bagpipers in the art of Bosch and his followers is supported first, by the appearance of Jewish pipers in Christian art; second, by the appearance of bagpipes in Jewish manuscripts from the fourteenth and fifteenth centuries; third, by the frequent appearance of Jews in non-musical settings in works by Bosch; and fourth, by evidence documenting that *klezmorim* often played at Christian festivities.

Our survey of Bosch's musical symbolism, therefore, suggests that Bosch was not an Adamite heretic or an alchemist: he was a devout, orthodox believer. His membership in the Lieve Vrouwe Broederschap at s'Hertogenbosch was not a cover for witchcraft or astrology. The records of the confraternity, published by Dr. Smijers, indicate that the brotherhood commissioned and performed only choral and organ music.[75] Bosch thus associated most instruments with secular functions. Although Bosch might depict angels playing straight trumpets at the Last Judgment or, in a *Jugendwerk*, even show them playing an occasional harp or psaltery, as sanctioned by biblical texts, nevertheless Bosch associated most instruments with damnation, often through the deadly sin of lust. As for bagpipes, their literary tradition, sexual shape, harsh sounds, function accompanying erotic dancing, and occasional associations with Jewish *klezmorim* indicated clearly to Bosch that bagpipes seduced the foolish and led directly to the concerts of hell.

---

[73] Bezalel Narkiss, *Hebrew Illuminated Manuscripts*, p. 65, plate 12.

[74] Narkiss, p. 153, plate 56.

[75] A. Smijers, *De Illustre Lieve Vrouwer Broederschap te s'Hertogenbosch* (Amsterdam: G. Alsbach & Co., 1932). See also A. Smijers "Meerstemmige muziek van de Illustre Lieve Vrouwe Broederschap te s'Hertogenbosch," *Tijdschrift der Vereeniging voor Nederlandsche Muziekgeschiedenis* XVI (1941), 1–30.

PROVINCIAL PERSPECTIVES

CHAPTER TWENTY-ONE

JOHN WYETH AND THE DEVELOPMENT OF SOUTHERN FOLK HYMNODY

David Warren Steel

University of Mississippi

The tunebooks of John Wyeth stand at an important threshold in American psalmody. They mark the end of the age of New England composer-compilers (1770–1810) and the beginning of the age of southern collector-compilers (1816–1860). Their contents, like their dates and place of publication, illustrate the transition, and the essential continuity, between these two schools of psalmody. *Wyeth's Repository of Sacred Music, Part Second* (1813) has been shown to be an important source for an influential body of folk hymns appearing in later collections.[1] Wyeth's original *Repository* (1810) has been cited chiefly for its derivative character.[2] The present paper deals with the

---

[1] Irving Lowens, "John Wyeth's *Repository of Sacred Music, Part Second*: A Northern Precursor of Southern Folk Hymnody," *Journal of the American Musicological Society* V (Summer 1952): 114–131; reprinted in Irving Lowens, *Music and Musicians in Early America* (New York: W.W. Norton, 1964), pp. 138–155. See also Lowens's introduction to the facs. reprint of the 2nd ed. of *Wyeth's Repository of Sacred Music, Part Second* (New York: Da Capo, 1964). Lowens here defines the folk hymn as "basically a secular folk-tune which happens to be sung to a religious text (p. v)."

[2] Irving Lowens and Allen P. Britton, "*The Easy Instructor* (1798–1831): A History and Bibliography of the First Shape Note Tune Book," *Journal of Research in Music Education* I (Spring 1953): 30–55; reprinted in Lowens,

358   David Warren Steel

first edition of the *Repository*, the sources of its music, and its influence on later tunebooks. The significance of the *Repository* will be considered in the light of the varying musical and religious preferences of Wyeth's day.

There is little in the biography of John Wyeth (1770–1858)[3] to suggest that his interest in psalmody was any more than that of an amateur. As a boy in Cambridge, Massachusetts, he may have attended a singing-school during the 1780s, an important decade in the growth of native psalmody. As a printer's apprentice he may have been aware of current developments in music printing, including the introduction of movable type for musical notation, an innovation from which he would later profit considerably.[4] Wyeth's printing career led him to the West Indies, then briefly to Philadelphia, and ultimately to Harrisburg, Pennsylvania, where in 1792 he took over the publication of a newspaper which he renamed *The Oracle of Dauphin*. No indication of musical activity can be found until 22 September 1810, when Wyeth advertised in *The Oracle of Dauphin* that he would shortly issue "a new work entitled 'the Harrisburgh Repository of SACRED MUSIC,' which will contain (besides all the tunes of merit in Smith and Little's collection) many additional tunes, selected from the most eminent and celebrated authors. . . ." By time the copyright was registered on 10 October and the work was "just published, and for sale" on 24 November, the collection had been retitled *Wyeth's Repository of Sacred Music*.

In the preface to this work, Wyeth claims three qualifications as a compiler of sacred music: (1) "many years attention to the charms of church music," (2) "an extensive acquaintance with the taste of teachers of the first eminence in the United States," and (3) "the

---

Music and Musicians, pp. 115–137, see p. 134. See also Lowens's introduction to the facs. reprint of the 5th ed. of *Wyeth's Repository of Sacred Music* (New York: Da Capo, 1974).

[3] *Dictionary of American Biography* (New York: Scribner's, 1936), s.v. "Wyeth, John", pp. 575–576.

[4] American printers had printed music from movable type as early as 1750. However, the method was not firmly established until Isaiah Thomas brought out *The Worcester Collection* (Worcester, 1786). By the years 1800–1810, 72 percent of all sacred tunebooks issued in the United States were printed typographically, including *Wyeth's Repository*. See Richard Crawford and D.W. Krummel, "Early American Music Printing and Publishing," in William L. Joyce *et al.*, (eds.), *Printing and Society in Early America* (Worcester: American Antiquarian Society, 1983), pp. 195–196.

[5] John Wyeth, *Wyeth's Repository of Sacred Music* (Harrisburg, Pa.: J. Wyeth, 1810), p. [2].

possession of some thousand pages of selected music to cull from." To these credentials, Irving Lowens adds a fourth, an "adventurous opportunism" which recognized the financial rewards to be gained from the publication of a popular tunebook.[6] The first two suggest some early musical training in the Boston area, where Wyeth indeed may have known "teachers of the first eminence" or studied their taste indirectly through books such as *The Worcester Collection* (1786). Wyeth's "thousand pages of selected music" represent a choral library that may be defined with some precision on the basis of the music contained in the *Repository*. The significance of Wyeth's "adventurous opportunism" is that, not being a musician himself, he chose the contents of his book chiefly for non-musical considerations, including the popularity of a tune in earlier collections and the suitability of a text or poetic meter to established traditions of denominational psalmody and hymnody.[7] An analysis of the format and contents of *Wyeth's Repository* may demonstrate how well Wyeth catered to the taste of his public.

The appearance and format of *Wyeth's Repository* were shared by numerous earlier collections of sacred music. The oblong shape, the open score with the melody in the tenor, and the pedagogical introduction were all solidly within the tradition to which Wyeth was contributing. In only one aspect of Wyeth's presentation was there any element of novelty or risk: the employment of a system of four character notes, or shape notes. This system, introduced in William Little and William Smith's *Easy Instructor* (Philadelphia, 1801), used four differently-shaped note heads to indicate the four singing syllables (*fa, sol, la* and *mi*).[8] This system was but one of several notational experiments that appeared in America during the first decade of the Nineteenth Century.[9] That it prevailed in the South and West during the following decades was at least partly due to Wyeth's efforts.

---

6 Lowens, *Music and Musicians*, p. 134.

7 The tune DAUPHIN may have been chosen for its title, which it shared with Wyeth's newspaper and the county in which Harrisburg is located.

8 This notation was invented by Philadelphia merchant John Connelly, who on 10 March 1798 signed over his rights to the system to Little and Smith. See William Smith, *The Easy Instructor, Part II* (Hopewell, N.J., 1803), p. [2], also Richard Crawford, *Andrew Law, American Psalmodist* (Evanston, Ill.: Northwestern University Press, 1968), p. 175.

9 As early as 1785, Benjamin Dearborn had published a musical notation requiring only letterpress characters to indicate pitch and duration, in *A Scheme for Reducing the Science of Music to a More Simple State*

Before John Wyeth began printing music in 1810, only two tunebooks had appeared in the Little and Smith notation: *The Easy
Instructor* itself, printed in several editions from 1805 to 1809 by an
Albany, New York firm, and William Smith's *Easy Instructor, Part II*,
issued in 1803 and 1806. Although Little and Smith claimed exclusive
rights to their shape-note system,[10] this claim was challenged by
Andrew Law, who had printed tunebooks in a similar notation.[11] Other
compilers of shape-note tunebooks chose variant shapes, either to
avoid infringe on another's claims,[12] or perhaps to enable themselves to
claim proprietary right to their own system if it proved popular. By
1810, however, Wyeth, evidently sensing that such claims would not
prove legally binding, acquired a font of music type in Little and
Smith's notation. Wyeth's choice of notational system was probably
based on the established popularity of *The Easy Instructor* among the
audience for which he wished to compete.[13]

The music in *Wyeth's Repository* consists of New England composi-

---

(Portsmouth, N.H.). Other systems introduced during the period 1800–1810
resembled that of Little and Smith in providing distinct symbols to indicate the
four singing syllables currently in use in America. Andrew Law, *Musical
Primer* (Cambridge, Mass., 1803) was the first of Law's collections to use a
staffless notation with heighted note-heads similar to those in *The Easy
Instructor*. Charles Woodward and John Aitken, *Ecclesiæ Harmonia*
(Philadelphia, [1806]) is printed in four new shapes. Copies of Andrew Adgate,
Philadelphia Harmony, (9th ed., Philadelphia, 1807 and later) contain handwritten or printed strokes whose angles denote the singing syllables. Nathan
Chapin and Joseph L. Dickerson, *The Musical Instructor* (Philadelphia, 1808;
2nd ed., 1810) combines the Little and Smith shapes with strokes distinguishing
the two *fa*'s, etc., in each octave. Timothy Olmsted found it necessary to justify
his use of conventional notation in his *Musical Olio* (Northampton, Mass.,
1805), p. [3]: "These characters are not only our old acquaintance, but that of
the whole musical world, in which all nations can read and probably never will
discard."

[10] Smith, *Easy Instructor, Part II*, p. [2].

[11] Crawford, *Andrew Law*, pp. 170–176.

[12] Andrew Law, a litigious defender of his own claims to notational reform,
considered even Woodward and Aitken's *Ecclesiæ Harmonia* to be an infringe-
ment on his own patent, and contemplated legal action against its publishers.
See Crawford, *Andrew Law*, p. 174.

[13] *Vokal Musik* (advertised for sale on 27 October 1810), aimed at
Pennsylvania's German-speaking population. Through this and three later
tunebooks, Wyeth established a preference for shape notes among
Pennsylvania Germans. German and bilingual tunebooks in four shape notes
appeared in Pennsylvania as late as 1883.

tions, together with a variety of pieces of foreign origin: in short, a distillation of the New England taste in sacred music during the years 1770–1810. New England singing-masters and tunebook compilers had found Pennsylvania a fertile field for their activities since the 1780s. As early as 1783, Andrew Law of Connecticut had taught singing-schools and sold tunebooks in Philadelphia.[14] Compositions by William Billings of Boston had been performed in concert and favorably reviewed in the Philadelphia press during the years 1786–1788.[15]. New Englanders had published popular tunebooks in Philadelphia: Andrew Adgate's *Philadelphia Harmony* (1789) went through some nine editions, the last as late as 1808, while Nehemiah Shumway's *American Harmony* (1793) introduced several new tunes by New England composers. Interest in New England psalmody was not confined to Philadelphia: a manuscript copy-book in the Bucks County Historical Society shows that a sizable number of New England tunes were copied and sung in rural Pennsylvania within a few years of their first publication.[16]

The sources for the music in *Wyeth's Repository* were eclectic collections which included both American and British tunes.[17] Foremost among these was *The Easy Instructor*, which was also the source of Wyeth's notation. Wyeth evidently preferred to copy tunes out of *The Easy Instructor* where possible: the *Repository* reproduces several errors and misattributions otherwise found only in *The Easy Instructor*.[18] Another shape-note source used by Wyeth was William Smith's *Easy Instructor, Part II*, from which Wyeth took at least one tune, MONTVILLE, not found in any other printed source before 1810. Of 129 compositions in the 1810 *Repository*, no fewer than sixty-four had previously appeared in *The Easy Instructor*. Five more had appeared in *Part II*. Thus, sixty-nine tunes in Wyeth's collection had been published in shape notes before 1810.

---

[14] Crawford, *Andrew Law*, pp. 36–37.

[15] David P. McKay and Richard Crawford, *William Billings of Boston: Eighteenth-Century Composer* (Princeton: Princeton University Press, 1975), pp. 152–154.

[16] The manuscript, signed John Mathias, 1789, is described in Richard Rosewell, "Singing Schools of Pennsylvania, 1800–1900" (Ph.D. diss., University of Minnesota, 1969).

[17] A few continental tunes like OLD HUNDRED were printed in popular American collections, but these had long been associated with English psalmody.

[18] For example, Sansum, for Tans'ur, as the composer of ST. MARTINS, and an attribution of REPENTANCE to Peck (elsewhere Rollo).

Of the pieces in *Wyeth's Repository* not previously published in shape notes, most can be found in various editions of two popular New England anthologies. *The Worcester Collection* (eight editions, 1786-1803) and *The Village Harmony* (ten editions, 1795–1810, with further editions to 1821) were among the most successful tunebooks of their time.[19] *The Worcester Collection* is the likely source of the eight tunes attributed to Oliver Holden, *The Village Harmony* for several tunes by rural composers from northern New England. Both were printed from movable type in relatively large editions, whose frequent revisions were sensitive to changes in taste.[20] A rough measure of this sensitivity is the Core Repertory, comprising the 101 sacred compositions most frequently printed in America to 1810, as defined by Richard Crawford. Of the 129 compositions in *Wyeth's Repository*, sixty-two come from the Core Repertory, among the highest totals of any tunebook of the period.[21]

The printer-compilers of the popular eclectic tunebooks like *The Worcester Collection* and *The Village Harmony* drew most heavily on tunes of established popularity: they typically included few, if any, previously unpublished tunes. Only six pieces saw print for the first time in the pages of *Wyeth's Repository*.[22] Three of these, NEW JUBILEE, PASTORAL ELEGY and PENITENCE, are attributed to composers who are otherwise unknown. The three unattributed tunes,

---

[19] See Karl Kroeger, "The Worcester Collection of Sacred Harmony and Sacred Music in America, 1786–1810" (Ph.D. diss., Brown University, 1976).

[20] Other sources for individual tunes in *Wyeth's Repository* include Supply Belcher, *The Harmony of Maine* (Boston, 1794) for CONVERSION, David Merrill, *The Psalmodist's Best Companion* (Exeter, N.H., 1799) for CLAREMONT, Bartholomew Brown, *Columbian and European Harmony* (Boston, 1802) for SARDIS, and John Cole, *The Beauties of Psalmody*, 2nd ed. (Baltimore, 1805) for BALTIMORE. This information is derived from Richard Crawford's card-file index of compositions printed in American sacred tunebooks to 1810.

[21] Richard Crawford, *The Core Repertory of Early American Psalmody* (*Recent Researches in American Music*, vols. XI–XII) (Madison, Wis.: A-R Editions, 1984) p. lxxviii.

[22] Information of first printings is from Allen P. Britton, Irving Lowens and Richard Crawford, *Bibliography of Sacred Music Published in America through 1810* (Worcester: American Antiquarian Society, in press), consulted in manuscript through the kindness of Richard Crawford.

SUPPLICATION, COMMUNION and WESLEY, will be discussed later.

The choice of hymn texts for *Wyeth's Repository*, and for other eclectic tunebooks, may be more significant than previously thought. James C. Downey has distinguished three doctrinal streams within American Protestantism in the late eighteenth century and suggested distinctive types of religious poetry favored by each.[23] (1) The "Old Side" Calvinists, who had opposed the evangelical movements of the 1740s, had by 1800 become either Unitarians or Anglicans. They were largely confined to the urban upper classes, their clergy were educated at Harvard, and they tended to use Brady and Tate's *New Version* of the Psalms.[24] (2) The "New Side" or moderate evangelicals had largely inherited the Congregational and Presbyterian structures of New England and the Middle States following the "Great Awakening" of the 1740s. Their clergy were trained at Yale, Nassau Hall (Princeton) and Rhode Island College (Brown), as well as in less formal "log academies." They overwhelmingly favored the Psalms and Hymns of Isaac Watts, supplemented by the hymns of other English evangelical poets.[25] Most of the New England composers of the period 1770–1810 were at least nominally associated with this party. (3) Radical evangelicals, often called Separatists, frequently joined Baptist and Methodist groups, especially on the frontier, where a continuing revival movement developed. Their preachers were mostly uneducated, but by 1800 they had produced a distinctive body of devotional poetry in a popular style.[26] According to Downey, "early folk song, inspired by revivalistic religion, was at its greatest vigor in the period 1780 to 1830 among the Baptists."

In preparing a tunebook "for the use of Christian churches of every denomination," a compiler had first to provide at least one tune for

---

[23] James Downey, "The Music of American Revivalism" (Ph.D. diss., Tulane University, 1968), pp. 43–45.

[24] Nicholas Brady and Nahum Tate, *A New Version of the Psalms of David* (Worcester: I. Thomas, 1788).

[25] Isaac Watts, *The Psalms of David, Imitated in the Language of the New Testament* and *Hymns* and *Spiritual Songs, In Three Books* (Exeter, N.H.: J. Lamson, 1794). American editions of Watts usually contained an appendix of "Select Hymns" by other British authors.

[26] A representative early collection containing Separatist poetry is Joshua Smith and Samuel Sleeper, *Divine Hymns, or Spiritual Songs* (Portland, T. Clark, 1803). A tunebook designed for Separatists is Jeremiah Ingalls, *The Christian Harmony; or, Songster's Companion* (Exeter, N.H.: H. Ranlet, 1805).

each of the meters used in church psalmody and hymnody. In English-speaking churches, the meters most frequently used were the iambic 8686, 8888 and 6686, known as Common Meter, Long Meter and Short Meter respectively.[27] Together, these meters account for 99 of the 122 texts in *Wyeth's Repository*. The remaining texts provide a scattering of other psalm and hymn meters such as 6666.4444, 668.668, six 10s, four 10s, 7777, 8787, and amphibrachic 8s (v – v), all known collectively as Particular Meter; also two set pieces of fluctuating meter, and five prose anthems.

John Wyeth, though himself a Unitarian, clearly prepared his *Repository* with the needs of moderate evangelicals in mind. At least 79 of the 122 texts can be traced to Isaac Watts; 53 of these are psalm paraphrases. Only ten texts come from Brady and Tate's *New Version*, sanctioned by the Protestant Episcopal Church. Of the remainder of the metrical texts that have been identified, most come from British poets such as Charles Wesley, Thomas Flatman, Anne Steele and Joseph Addison, all represented in John Rippon's *Selection of Hymns*, a well-known supplement to Watts.[28] The subjects of the hymns are drawn from a wide range of evangelical themes; however, Wyeth, like other tunebook compilers, avoided texts that treated controversial or sectarian doctrines, such as strict predestination, total sanctification, or specific modes of baptism.

In addition to providing tunes for Protestant worship, *Wyeth's Repository* was intended to meet the needs of "singing schools and private societies." As Richard Crawford has pointed out, the existence of groups of musically literate singers in America created a demand for more varied and complex forms of music, a demand which would strain the bounds of traditional congregational psalmody.[29] The fuging-tune, with its strong rhythmic momentum and overlapping vocal entries, appealed to many in singing-schools and churches alike, but came under increasing attack by educated clerics and musicians after 1790.[30]

---

[27] The figures represent the number of syllables in each line of a stanza.

[28] An American reprint is John Rippon, *A Selection of Hymns from the Best Authors, Intended to Be an Appendix to Dr. Watt's Psalms and Hymns* (New York: W. Durrell, 1792).

[29] McKay and Crawford, *William Billings*, pp. 23–24.

[30] The fuging-tunes of 18th-century England and America generally consist of a homophonic opening section, followed by imitative entries in each voice-part, working up to a homophonic close. The spellings "fuge" and "fuging-tune" distinguish this form from the classical fugue. See Lowens, *Music and Musicians*, p. 237n. For condemnation of fuging-tunes, see Allen P. Britton,

That *Wyeth's Repository* contains no fewer than forty fuging-tunes suggests an effort to maintain the interest of singing-school pupils, and perhaps implies that condemnation of this form had not yet reached Wyeth's rural audience.

Another way in which Wyeth catered to needs not strictly liturgical was his inclusion of many compositions whose texts, though taken from Watts's Psalms, represented stanzas other than the first of a given psalm or section, and had evidently been chosen for their vivid imagery or their suitability to the American scene. Among these are VIRGINIA, OCEAN and POOL, all taken from the "nautical" section of Psalm 107, with appropriate musical illustration:

> At thy command the winds arise,
> And swell the towering waves.
> The men astonish'd mount the skies,
> And sink in gaping graves.   (OCEAN, p. 30)

The evocative text of WINTER comes from Psalm 147:

> His hoary frost, his fleecy snow
> Descend and clothe the ground;
> The liquid streams forbear to flow,
> In icy fetters bound.   (P. 28)

The verses of WHITESTOWN, from Psalm 107, must have reminded Americans of their own history as well as that of the ancient Hebrews:

> Where nothing dwelt but beasts of prey,
> Or men as fierce and wild as they,
> He bids th'opprest and poor repair,
> And build them towns and cities there.   (P. 39)

The factional struggles of the young republic found themselves mirrored in RUSSIA, with its text from Psalm 62:

> False are the men of high degree,
> The baser sort are vanity;
> Laid in the balance both appear
> Light as a puff of empty air.   (P. 34)

"Theoretical Introductions in American Tune-Books to 1800" (Ph.D. diss., University of Michigan, 1949), pp. 357–362; also Richard Crawford, *American Studies and American Musicology: A Point of View and a Case in Point*, ("I.S.A.M. Monographs," no. 4 [Brooklyn: Institute for Studies in American Music, 1975]), pp. 23–24.

The success of *Wyeth's Repository* may be judged by its public reception, and by its influence on later collections. Reissued four times in its
first decade, the *Repository* was available as late as 1834 in a stereo-
typed edition. The total circulation is reported to have reached
120,000.[31] In 1813, Wyeth, noting the "very flattering manner" with
which his *Repository* had been greeted by the public, brought out a new
tunebook entitled *Wyeth's Repository of Sacred Music, Part Second*.

From its contents, *Part Second* appears to have been designed, as
Irving Lowens put it, "to supply the musical needs of the vast market
created by the revivals and camp-meetings prevalent in Pennsylvania at
the time."[32] Compared to the *Repository*, it contains far fewer texts by
Isaac Watts, and a greater number of revivalistic texts. It contains
examples of two styles of composition known to have been favored by
Methodists and Baptists: florid hymns and set pieces derived from the
British theatrical tradition, and folk hymns, that is, melodies drawn
from or resembling secular ballads or dance tunes, harmonized in a
native idiom giving equal weight to all parts. For twenty-five hymns
(largely those not found in Watts and other moderate evangelical
hymnbooks) additional stanzas are supplied, making the book equally
suitable for singing-school, church service and revival meeting.[33] Both
the original *Repository* and *Part Second* contain instructional
rudiments; the repertories in the two books do not overlap. Hence, the
books are mutually complementary: the *Repository* for the evangelical
mainstream, and *Part Second* for Separatists and radical evangelicals
who expressed their piety in fervent and frequent revivals.

---

[31] *Dictionary of American Biography*, XX, p. 575. *Wyeth's Repository*
underwent relatively few thorough revisions. Editions numbered 2 to 5
appeared with various imprint dates from 1811 to 1823; 12 pages were added to
the original 120-page volume in 1812, and 12 more pages in the stereotype
editions of 1826–1834. See Richard J. Stanislaw, *A Checklist of Four-Shape
Shape-Note Tunebooks*, ("I.S.A.M. Monographs," no. 10 [Brooklyn:
Institute for Studies in American Music, 1978]), pp. 42–43; also Irving Lowen's
introduction to the facs. reprint of the 5th ed. of *Wyeth's Repository*, p. x.

[32] Lowens, *Music and Musicians*, p. 143. Lowens suggests E. K. Dare of
Wilmington, Delaware, a Methodist minister, as the musical editor of *Part
Second*.

[33] Tunebooks normally underlaid a single stanza of text to each composition.
While this was adequate for singing-schools, public worship required additional stanzas for each psalm or hymn, a requirement that was met by pocket
editions of Watts or "Select Hymns." Since these editions generally lacked the
new revivalistic poetry, *Wyeth's Repository, Part Second* attempted to include
the necessary texts, as had the Baptist-oriented *Christian Harmony* of Jeremiah
Ingalls.

From his base in Harrisburg, Pennsylvania, John Wyeth was well situated to take advantages of new developments in psalmody on the American frontier. The dissemination of New England music westward and southward took place along two major routes of settlement. The first proceeded east of the Alleghenies, from Harrisburg into the Valley of Virginia. The second, west of the Alleghenies, went from Pittsburgh down the Ohio Valley and into Kentucky and Tennessee. During the period 1810–1825 a sizable number of sacred tunebooks, all in shape notes, was compiled and published along these routes, as shown in Figure 1. A list of these collections is given in Table 1.[34] Of the seven Harrisburg imprints, all but the last were products of Wyeth's press; many others show the influence of his two collections.

The publications of Ananias Davisson (1780–1857) have long been recognized for their role in transmitting the New England repertory, as well as folk hymns, to points further south.[35] Like Wyeth, Davisson printed two major collections with similar titles. *Kentucky Harmony* (1816), like *Wyeth's Repository*, contains mostly New England tunes, also a selection of folk hymns, many claimed by Davisson himself. Of the 137 texts in the first edition, fully 124 have been traced to Isaac Watts or to Rippon's *Selection*,[36] showing that Davisson, a Presbyterian, intended his collection for moderate evangelicals. Of the tunes printed in the various editions of *Kentucky Harmony*, 73 had appeared in *Wyeth's Repository*. In his preface, Davisson acknowledged the work of past compilers, including Little, Smith, Wyeth, Billings, Holyoke, Adgate, Atwell and Peck.[37]

The *Supplement to the Kentucky Harmony* (1820) is an entirely distinct tunebook, compiled so "that his Methodist friends may be furnished with a suitable and proper arrangement of such pieces as may seem best to animate the zealous Christian in his acts of devotion."[38]

---

[34] Based on George Pullen Jackson, *White Spirituals in the Southern Uplands* (Chapel Hill: University of North Carolina Press, 1933; reprint ed., New York: Dover, 1965), p. 25; Charles Hamm, "Patent Notes in Cincinnati," *Bulletin of the Historical and Philosophical Society of Ohio* XVI (October 1958): 293–310; Stanislaw, *Checklist*.

[35] Jackson, *White Spirituals*, pp. 29–30; Lowens, *Music and Musicians*, pp. 139–141.

[36] Harry Lee Eskew, "Shape-Note Hymnody in the Shenandoah Valley, 1816–1860" (Ph.D. diss., Tulane University, 1966), p. 30.

[37] Ananias Davisson, *Kentucky Harmony*, (4th ed.; Harrisonburg, Va.: A. Davisson, 1821), p. 4.

[38] Ananias Davisson, *Supplement to the Kentucky Harmony* (Harrisonburg,

368   David Warren Steel

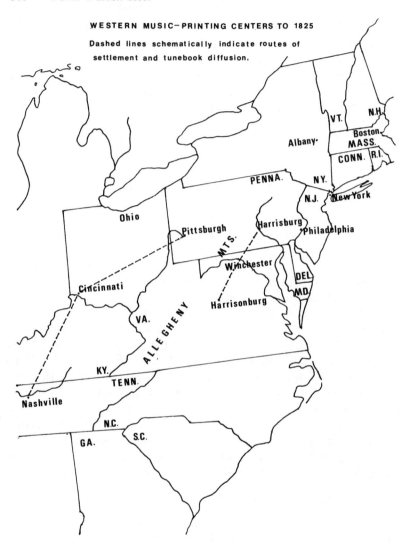

Figure 1. Western Music Printing Centers, 1810–1825. Dashed lines
schematically indicate routes of settlement and tunebook diffusion.

TABLE 1. Western shape-note tunebooks, 1810–1825

A. East of Alleghenies.

Date	Compiler	Short Title	Place
1810	J. Doll	Leichter Unterricht	Harrisburg, Pa.
1810	J. Wyeth	Wyeth's Repository	Harrisburg
1813	J. Wyeth	Wyeth's Repository, Pt. 2nd	Harrisburg
1815	J. Doll	Leichter Unterricht, Bd. 2	Harrisburg
1816	J. Funk	Choral-Music	Harrisonburg, Va.
1816	A. Davisson	Kentucky Harmony	Harrisonburg
1817	W. Gillet	Virginia Sacred Minstrel	Winchester, Va.
1818	J.M. Boyd	Virginia Sacred Musical Repository	Winchester
1818	Gerhart & Eyer	Choral-Harmonie	Harrisburg
1820	A. Davisson	Supp. to Kentucky Harmony	Harrisonburg
1821	J.P. Carrell	Songs of Zion	Harrisonburg
1821	J. Rothbaust	Franklin Harmonie	Harrisburg
1821	A. Davisson	Introduction to Sacred Music	Harrisonburg
1821	S. St. John	American Harmonist	Harrisburg
1825	A. Davisson	Small Collection	Mt. Vernon, Va.

B. West of Alleghenies

Date	Compiler	Short Title	Place
1813	R. Patterson	Patterson's Church Music	Cincinnati
1814	F. Lewis	Beauties of Harmony	Cincinnati
1815	J. McCormick	Western Harmonist	Cincinnati
1816	T. Flint	Columbian Harmonist	Cincinnati
1816	J. Armstrong	Pittsburgh Selection	Pittsburgh
1818	S. Metcalfe	Kentucky Harmonist	Cincinnati
1818	A. Johnson	Tennessee Harmony	Cincinnati
1819	Little & Smith	Easy Instructor	Cincinnati
1820	A.D. Carden	Missouri Harmony	Cincinnati
1822	S. Ely	Sacred Music	Cincinnati
1824	F. Lewis	Songs of Zion	Pittsburgh
1824	Carden & al.	Western Harmony	Nashville
1825	W.C. Knight	Juvenile Harmony	Cincinnati
1825	W. Moore	Columbian Harmony	Cincinnati

Only a small proportion of the 144 texts are the work of Isaac Watts; nearly half of the texts are unidentified.[39] Not only, then, was Davisson familiar with Wyeth's tunebooks, not only did he borrow extensively

Va.: A. Davisson, 1820), preface, quoted in Eskew, "Shape-Note Hymnody," p. 45.

[39] Eskew, "Shape-Note Hymnody," p. 46.

from their repertory, but his very plan of providing two independent though mutually complementary tunebooks for different sectarian groups was essentially the same as Wyeth's plan, and may have been inspired by it.

The influence of Wyeth's tunebooks was not confined to compilers east of the mountains. Within a few years of Wyeth's publication, western compilers were making use of their music and their pedagogical introductions. Alexander Johnson in *Tennessee Harmony* (1818) and Allen D. Carden in *The Missouri Harmony* (1820) both acknowledge a debt to "Mr. 'Wyeth's Repository — part second' for many of the rules and remarks contained in his introduction."[40] The contents of both collections show their compilers to be familiar with both of Wyeth's tunebooks. Johnson's book, with 100 tunes, contains 39 tunes from *Wyeth's Repository* and 28 from *Part Second*. Carden's larger collection of 185 pieces had 61 from the *Repository* and 38 from *Part Second*. The influence of Davisson's work upon Carden has been cited,[41] but is not sufficient to account for many of the correspondences between *The Missouri Harmony* and Wyeth's tunebooks.

Of the six tunes which made their first appearance in *Wyeth's Repository*, five were reprinted in later collections. PENITENCE by T. Smith was printed in Robert Patterson's *Church Music* (Cincinnati, 1813) and in Freeman Lewis's *Beauties of Harmony* (Cincinnati, 1814). PASTORAL ELEGY by Knapp appears in Davisson's *Supplement to the Kentucky Harmony* and in Carden's *Missouri Harmony* (both 1820). SUPPLICATION, COMMUNION and WESLEY are unattributed in *Wyeth's Repository*. Their reprintings show anomalies whose investigation may help demonstrate the relationship of southern compilers to their sources.

The melodies of SUPPLICATION and COMMUNION share traits consistently linked to folk hymns.[42] Both exhibit gapped modal scales: the sixth degree of the natural minor mode occurs not at all (COMMUNION) or only in unaccented position (SUPPLICATION). In later printings the tunes appear in varying melodic and harmonic versions; their titles and texts likewise vary. Unlike northern psalm-tunes, which were reprinted as complete polyphonic compositions,

---

[40] Alexander Johnson, *Johnson's Tennessee Harmony* (Cincinnati: Morgan, Lodge & Co., 1818), p. xiii; Allen D. Carden, *The Missouri Harmony*, (Stereotype ed.; Cincinnati: E. Morgan & Co., 1839), p. 12.

[41] Jackson, *White Spirituals*, pp. 40–41.

[42] Jackson, *White Spirituals*, pp. 161–163; Dorothy D. Horn, *Sing to Me of Heaven* (Gainesville: University of Florida Press, 1970), p. 19.

Example 1. Supplication, from *Wyeth's Repository of Sacred Music* (1820 ed.)

Example 2. Supplication, from A.D. Carden, *The Missouri Harmony* (1839 ed.)

these tunes must have circulated in oral tradition or in manuscript as bare melodies, perhaps with an underlying bass part or a persistent title. Each arranger or compiler felt free to notate the tunes as he remembered them, and to add his own harmonies and preferred text.

SUPPLICATION first appeared in *Wyeth's Repository* in a setting for three voices, shown in Example 1. In 1813, Robert Patterson printed a four-voice setting of the same melody as THE SEASONS. Ananias Davisson brought out a new four-voiced setting in 1816, with an attribution to "Chapin." This version, reprinted by Carden in 1820, is shown in Example 2. Alexander Johnson (1818) of Tennessee and William Walker (1835) of South Carolina printed yet other settings of the tune.

COMMUNION, like SUPPLICATION, first appeared in *Wyeth's Repository* in a setting for three voices (Example 3). Under the title LIBERTY-HALL, the tune was included in a small untitled pamphlet printed in 1812 by Andrew Law for John Logan, a Virginia singing-master, in Law's staffless shape notation.[43] The new setting, in four

---

[43] Two copies of this untitled sheet, containing sixteen tunes (eight attributed to Lucius and Amzi Chapin) were bound in a copy of Law's *Harmonic Companion*, 2nd ed., now in the William L. Clements Library, University of Michigan. They represent the first known attributions to the Chapin brothers, and the first publication of folk-hymns instigated by a Southerner. For correspondence about this publication, see Crawford, *Andrew Law*, pp. 215,

372   David Warren Steel

Example 3. Communion, from *Wyeth's Repository of Sacred Music* (1820 ed.)

Example 4. Liberty Hall, from A. Davidson, *Kentucky Harmony* (1816 ed.)

Example 5. Wesley, from *Wyeth's Repository of Sacred Music* (1820 ed.)

voices, was attributed to L[ucius] Chapin. Further printings by
Patterson (1813), Lewis (1814) and Davisson (1816, Example 4)
continue the new designation. The four-voiced versions in Logan,
Patterson and Davisson vary from each other in harmonic details, most
frequently in the upper two voices. Wyeth's setting was not forgotten,
however: Johnson (1818) printed the tune as COMMUNION in the
original three-voiced setting.

If later printings of SUPPLICATION and COMMUNION exhibit variations that suggest oral transmission, the treatment of WESLEY

219–220. For more on the Chapins' pioneering rôle as singing-masters in the
South, see James W. Scholten, "The Chapins: A Study of Men and Sacred
Music West of the Alleghenies, 1795–1842" (Ed.D. diss., University of
Michigan, 1972).

Example 6. Jerusalem, from W. Walker, *The Southern Harmony* (1854 ed.)

shows conscious remodeling of an entire composition. As printed in
Wyeth's Repository, WESLEY is a fuging-tune in Common Meter,
shown in Example 5. Its four voice-parts are the work of a composer
unknown to Wyeth.[44] In 1835 William Walker, in *The Southern
Harmony*, reprinted the tune without change. Yet, in the same collection, Walker published an original adaptation of WESLEY under the title
JERUSALEM.[45] JERUSALEM, shown in Example 6, is a "revival spiritual
song" with a fuging refrain, for three voices. The homophonic opening
section is sung twice, to accommodate a full quatrain of John Cennick's
Long Meter text, requiring the omission of the slur in the third measure.
The fuging section follows, also with a busier text and slurs omitted.
The new text is not drawn from Cennick's poem, but is a rollicking
revival chorus repeated after each stanza. The part-writing of

---

[44] Ananias Davisson reprinted the tune in his *Kentucky Harmony* (1816),
attributing it to "Moore," perhaps Josiah Moore, who contributed a set piece
entitled *PRODIGAL SON* to the same collection.

[45] A manuscript tunebook compiled by William Walker for Elizabeth
Adams, now at Furman University, includes *JERUSALEM* in a section of tunes
dated 29 June 1833. See Milburn Price, "Miss Elizabeth Adams' Music Book:
A Manuscript Predecessor of William Walker's *Southern Harmony*," *The
Hymn* XXIX (April 1978): 70–75. In his *Christian Harmony* (Philadelphia:
Miller, 1867), p. 217, Walker claims to have "arranged" the tune in 1832.

WESLEY is retained with little change other than a reduction in texture in the third measure of the fuge.

Though not a musician, John Wyeth played a major role in the musical development of the American frontier. Following the example of New England printer-compilers like Isaiah Thomas, Wyeth established a flourishing musical press at a strategic location on an important migration route to the south and west. Sensitive to variations in musical and religious tastes, he defined distinct markets for tunebooks, and sought to provide tailor-made products for each. While his *Repository* summed up the New England tradition of psalmody, his publication of folk hymns in both major collections suggests an enterprising and original effort to keep abreast of changes in religious practice and musical taste. The continued reprinting of pieces from Wyeth's tunebooks demonstrates his influence on later compilers on both sides of the mountains. At the same time, the variations in tunes like SUPPLICATION, COMMUNION and WESLEY suggest new rôles for Wyeth's successors: not merely as anthologizers, nor yet as original composers, but as collectors, adapters and reworkers of material from diverse oral and written sources. It was in this area that Ananias Davisson and William Walker excelled during the years 1816–1860, and here also that they differed from their New England predecessors.

On 29 June 1815 Conrad Speece of Staunton, Virginia, writing in *The Republican Farmer*, complained of the music being taught in singing-schools in the Valley region. He singled out two styles of music for condemnation: fuging-tunes like OCEAN, MONTGOMERY and SHERBURNE, and "ballad tunes, vamped up with accompanying parts, and applied as the vehicles of religious sentiment." He acknowledged, however, that "angular notes" were effective agents of musical learning, despite their uncouth appearance.[46] The juxtaposition of New England favorites and folk hymns, printed in shape notes, was precisely the synthesis that Wyeth pioneered in his two *Repositories*. It would become the norm in more than thirty tunebooks compiled by Southerners in the decades up to the Civil War.

---

[46] Conrad Speece, *The Mountaineer*, (New ed.; Staunton, Va.: I. Collett, 1823), pp. 123–127. The three fuging-tunes mentioned by Speece are all in *Wyeth's Repository*.

CHAPTER TWENTY-TWO

SEKI AKIKO: THE RED PRIMADONNA OF JAPAN

William P. Malm

University of Michigan

Choosing a Japanese subject for an article in honor of Gwyn McPeek is difficult because: 1) there is so much yet to be said about Japan for western readers and 2) McPeek is a scholar of exceptionally broad interests. A review of his vitae will show that the topic could be on musical instruments, notation, iconography, transcription, or a host of other things. Any one of those subjects is open to research in Japan. However, since musicology is becoming increasingly ethnomusicological in its concern for music in its socio/political context, I have chosen a topic that I think Professor McPeek will appreciate and I hope will accept in his honor.

Let us begin this gift with a picture of another music teacher receiving a gift (Plate I).[1] A Western observer would not be surprised to learn that the kimono clad, middle aged lady with glasses and short hair is a music teacher and that the flowers are from her students. They were given to her at a banquet in her honor on December 22, 1955. She is the choral conductor, Seki Akiko but the banquet is not in honor of her retirement, rather it is in celebration of her receiving the Stalin Peace Prize of 1955 for her work with people's music and choruses. We obviously are

---

[1] The author is grateful to the 1984 staff of the Ongaku Center 2–16 Okikubo, Shinjuku-ku Tokyo for their help in locating this picture as well as generous cooperation throughout the completion of this study.

Plate 1.

not observing the typical Japanese music teacher. Instead we have
found an excellent example of how music careers can be used to reflect
the socio/political spirits of a period and hopefully we have also found
an appropriate gift for Gywn McPeek.

Seki Akiko (also Kanko or Kaneko) was born in 1898, the oldest of
seven children of a former chief retainer of the Koriyama fief.[2] During
the Meiji restoration period (1868–1910) he became a teacher of English
at what was to become Tokyo University. He also became a newspaper
journalist on art under the *nom de plume* of Nyorai Sanjin. A true man
of the Meiji era, he knew Chinese classics as well as masses of English
and European literature. He was said to have made a good living but
money was not plentiful despite the frugal efforts of her "very
progressive" mother. It was mother who determined that Akiko should
have a profession of her own so that she would not have to depend on a
man all her life. In this spirit Akiko was given a music tutor

---

[2] The biographical information that follows is derived from articles in a
special issue of the magazine *Chisei* (April, 1956) responding to the Stalin Prize.
See also chapters one and two plus the time chart in Inoue Yoritoyo's *Oki na
kobara* (Tokyo: Ongaku Center, 1981).

before she went to elementary school. Throughout her elementary and high school period her keen interest in singing was matched by intensive reading in the Western classics from Turgenev and Heine to Gide and Sinclair. In keeping with the Tolstoyan humanitarian spirit of the period among many Japanese intellectuals, Akiko fell in love at the age of 12 with Simonson, the husband of Katchusha in the Tolstoy novel *Resurrection*. Her dream from that point on had two goals: 1) to be a great opera singer and 2) to marry a Japanese revolutionary.

It is said that Akiko did poorly on her entrance examination into the Tokyo School of Music, but the quality of her voice allowed her to matriculate and become a favored student of a German voice teacher, Mrs. Hanka Petzwald.[3] The diligence of her practice is noted in the fact that many college students boarded in the neighborhood of her family home and the landlords complained to the school and to the police that her piano and voice practice was driving the students away. The police informed her that she could only practice until midnight and at anytime in the morning. With this order in mind she rose at 4 a.m. and sang every day.

Seki Akiko's recital at the school was successful and by graduation in 1921 she was set for a concert career. During this period of her life her only "radical" activity, outside her practice hours, was to teach music at a nursery of a settlement house founded by Tokyo University teachers. Apparently it was through such work that she met Ono Miyakichi, the son of a Mitsui bank director and then a Tolstoyan working in drama at the Tsukiji Little Theater.[4] After a five year engagement they were married in 1926. Ono had broken from the Tsukiji theater under Osanai Kaoru and, with Senda Koreya, founded the Zengo theater. His continued association with socialist drama seemingly fulfilled Akiko's childhood desire to marry a revolutionary. However, in the context of government reactions to such movements during the 1930's, it should be noted that their ten years of marriage

[3] Hanka Petzoldt (ne Christensen) was a Norwegian soprano who came to Japan in 1909 as the wife of a German journalist, Bruno Petzoldt. She taught voice and piano at the Tokyo Music Academy until 1924 and died in Tokyo August 18, 1937. See "Petzoldt," *Encyclopedia Musica* (Tokyo: Heibonsha, 1983), V, p. 2234. Also Tatsuhide Akiyama, (ed.), *Nihon no yogaku hyakunen-shi* [One hundred years of the Western music in Japan], (Tokyo: Daiichi Hoki shuppansha, 1952), p. 238.

[4] The Tsukiji Theater played an important role in the development of new theater in Japan throughout this era. See "Tsukiji," *Encyclopedia Japonica*, (Tokyo: Kabushiki kasha, 1970) vol. 12, p. 406. Also Mizushina Haruki, *Tsukiji shogekijo* (Tokyo: Nichinichi shobo, 1931).

included two and one half in which Ono was in prison and two in which he was in the hospital before his death in 1937, apparently from tuberculosis. Akiko herself had suffered from an unsuccessful throat operation so her own career as a singer was ended. Thus in 1937 Akiko was left with a daughter, Teruko (born 1927), a thorough training in an aspect of Western music she could no longer pursue directly, and with direct experience in the politically oriented musical activities of the period.

The first unified organization of literary, theatrical, and musical proletarian movement in Japan is said to be the Japanese Proletarian Liberal Arts League (*Nihon proletaria bungei renmei*, nicknamed the Pro-ren), founded on December 6, 1925.[5] It merged with the Marxian Arts Study Group (nicknamed Maru-gei) to form in 1926 Pro-gei, the Japan Proletarian Arts League (*Nihon proletaria geijitsu renmei*). Music was part of the first league but Pro-gei is generally given credit as having the first organized music division. It specialized in strike songs. In Japan, the musical problems of this effort were different from those of similar workers' movements going on at the same time in the West. Euro/American workers groups could base their music on European styles and claim to be using music of the people. In Japan, Western public school and military music had been part of the people's experience for barely fifty years. At the same time, traditional Japanese music did not fit into the so-called international (but musically Western) revolutionary mode. This should be kept in mind as we study the growth of proletarian music in Japan in relation to the career of our remarkable women.

The first major musical/political event in Seki Akiko's career occurred in October of 1926. An "Evening for Proletarians" (*Musansha no yube*) was held by Pro-gei in honor of the first anniversary of the founding of a newspaper, the *Musansha shimbun*.[6] During that evening the song "Our Endless Rut" (*Kurumeku wadachi*) was performed by Seki Akiko. As seen in Example 1,[7] it was a German-style folk song from the IWW little red songbook; a source that McPeek may have seen at the time.

Seki Akiko had already appeared in newspaper reviews where she

---

[5] The following historical materials are primarily derived from the article "Nihon minshu ongaku-shi" in *Chisei* (April, 1956), 38–40.

[6] Inoue, *op. cit.*, 356.

[7] The source of notated examples is the book accompanying the record set *Kaiho no utagoe* MLS 2003–2004 (Tokyo: Ongaku Center, 1972) in which each piece can be heard.

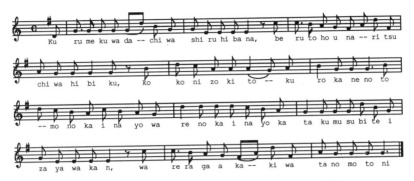

I.   The endless rut, the running spark,
        The factory belt roars, the hammer resounds.
        Here let us make a prayer of iron!
chorus: My comrade's arm in mine,
        Firmly linked, let us advance,
        Beneath our red flag!

II.   Although the whip of exploitation is mighty,
        Although the storm of tyranny is mighty,
        We fervently pray:
        chorus

III.   Now, in the thick of battle,
        Although the comrade at my side is fallen,
        I cross his corpse and carry the flag onward!
        chorus

IV.   The path we follow is not easy,
        The bettter day for which we strive is not close.
        Still, boldy let us advance with heroic shouts:
        chorus

Example 1: Our Endless Rut (Kurumeku wadachı)

was noted for her renditions of Schubert and opera arias. However, her fame really may be said to have begun when, in response to calls for an encore at the Waseda Music Festival of 1926, she sang again "Our Endless Rut." Thereafter writers called her the Red Primadonna. By that time, she, along with her husband Ono Miyakichi and with Kaji Wataru, had formed the music division of Pro-gei. Since Pro-gei's ideological base was Marxist and Akiko's training was in Western music, it is not surprising that the group used no Japanese music but rather concentrated on providing Japanese texts for foreign revolutionary songs like "Comrades Have Fallen," "I am a Blacksmith," "Hymn to the Freedom of Russia," and "The Melting Pot of Hate." Example 2[7] is the latter, the most long-lived of such pieces in Japan except perhaps "The International" and "The Red Flag".

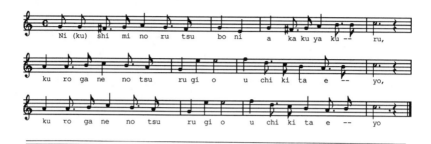

I.   In the melting pot of hate, burning red,
      Temper our iron swords
      Temper our iron swords.

II.   Although strong the fortress of opprssion,
      Although fierce the storm of tyranny,
      (repeat second line)

III. Comrades, firmly let us link our arms,
      Comrades, loudly let us make our pledge.
      (repeat second line)
IV.   Bring an end to the history of our humiliation.
      Let is fight the final battle.
      (repeat second line)

V.   See the flag of crimson,
      See it over the fortress made of corpses.
      (repeat second line)

Example 2: The Melting Pot of Hate (Nikushimi no rutsubo)

Proletarian movements continued to merge for solidarity against increasing government suppression. The March, 1928 creation of the All Japan Proletarian Arts League (Ren-mei) included a musicians' league that used the acronym PM (Proletarian Music). Seki Akiko was a founding member of this tiny group. The first public performance of the "PM chorus" was, in fact, a quartet with Akiko the alto. Their debut was at a public lecture on April 30, 1930 in the Ueno Autonomy Hall where they sang "The Melting Pot of Hate".[8] The use of singing groups at other events increased and in June the PM chorus was able to hold its own Proletarian Vocal Concert at the Tsukiji Little Theater. Of the ten songs on the proposed program seven were foreign revolutionary songs previously used by Pro-gei, one was a more recent soviet import "Let Us Hoist Up the Red Flag", and two were Japanese

---

[8] Inoue, *op. cit.*, 357.

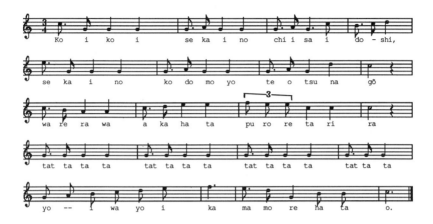

Come!Come! Little comrades of the world,
Children of the world, let us join hands.
We are the red flag proletariat.
Tattatata tattatata
Everybody ready? Let us guard the flag.

Example 3: The Little Comrades (Chiisai doshi)

composed pieces; "The Power of Unions" by Ishii Goro and "The Little Comrades" by Morita Masayoshi. The latter is shown in Example 3.[7]

Given Seki's thorough Western training it is pleasant to note that, at one Pro-gei central committee meeting she suggested that the group sponsor a search for Japanese folk songs as a better medium for use in factory singing circles. The idea was rejected by the internationally-oriented committee. However, they did produce three records[9] of "traditional" revolutionary songs. In 1932 a soviet children's operetta, "Construction" was staged; translated by Ono and accompanied by Akiko at the piano. A May Day operetta, "Red May" was created by a joint action with the Pro-gei literary division and childrens' songs were produced for use in workers' circles.

In addition to concerts, PM was able to mimeograph the PM News.[10] Seki and Ono were appointed as the first chairman and secretary

---

[9] These have been partly re-recorded in the record listed in footnote 7.
[10] The author was able to secure copies of the originals in 1968.

general of the PM central committee. An Itinerant Music Troupe (*Ido ongakutai*) was formed in the style of a former mobile theater in order that P.M. could perform with labor and student groups and, hopefully, with less police censorship. From such small organizations there was progress in the teaching of workers to sing songs themselves and to form singing "circles" at their place of employment.

PM held bi-annual concerts in March and December of 1931 and 1932 but the police harassment became more intense and PM was dissolved in 1934.[11] During World War II the surviving musicians (including Seki Akiko) became involved in national patriotic efforts through the placing of choruses and bands in factories.[12]

The cease fire was issued on August 16, 1945, and in September the Japanese Music Culture Association was formed.[13] On October 10th the old IWW song, "The Red Flag" was heard in Hibiya Hall as part of the anniversary of the Bolshevik revolution. In 1946, under the democratic surveillance of Allied censors, the Japanese National Broadcasting Corporation (NHK) produced an April program of music for May Day. The conductor was Seki Akiko. In March, 1947 a Democratic Chorus and a World Labor Delegates Welcoming Music Group appeared. By March of 1948 a Central Chorus under the guidance of Seki Akiko had split from the Democratic Youth Movement and, following pre-war PM methods, organized workers' and student choruses. While two/thirds of the music used was still foreign there was less emphasis on the old revolutionary songs. The most romantic addition was the Soviet popular song "Katchusha," the name of the girl so important in Akiko's impressions at the age of twelve. By 1949 the Central Chorus claimed to have some five hundred circles established throughout Japan and May Day records were on the market. In June of that year the Central Chorus published its official organ, *Utagoe*, The Singing Voice. A year later they built The Music Center in Tokyo with offices, rehearsal rooms, and a studio for Seki Akiko.

---

[11] Details of this action are found in the author's article, "A Century of Proletarian Music in Japan," in *The Transactions of the Asiatic Society of Japan*, 3rd Series, Vol. 19 (June, 1984), 175–196.

[12] An interesting article on the function of traditional musicians during the war is found in *Kikan hogaku* XXXV (June, 1983), 67–80.

[13] The following post-war information was first derived from the quarterly journal *Nihon no utagoe*, no. 3 (Sept., 1971) and Fujimoto Yo, *Uta hatatakai to tomo ni*, (Tokyo: Ongaku Center, 1971). It now is available in Inoue Yoritoyo's *Utagoe yo yoku hirogete* (Tokyo: Shin nihon shuppansha, 1978).

The Central Chorus was now firmly established and by 1951 it was quite active in the World Youth for Peace movement. In 1952 the chorus' slogan became "Utagoe wa, heiwa no chikara" (The singing voice, the power of peace). From this came the new name for the entire movement, the Japanese Singing Voice (*Nihon no utagoe*) or later just the Singing Voice. As its director, Seki Akiko seems to have put her basic energies towards music. However, in the *Chisei* magazine honoring her award of the Stalin Peace Prize she did publish one article, "The Theory of the Utagoe Movement"[14] This article opens with a standard phrase, "Music was created out of the daily life of the masses." Recalling the pre-war rebuf she received concerning Japanese music, the statements that follow are more interesting:

> The old folk songs left in various parts of Japan sing of man's noble talents. Music changes over in time due to religion, social class, etc., but the people always have music of some sort. After Meiji there arose the erroneous legend that the Japanese couldn't sing. This developed when they put [Western] music into the school curriculum. When grammar school choruses were started, the traditional Japanese scales were ignored and European scales were introduced. Thus Western music spread quickly but it bore no relation to the music people heard at their mother's knee. An additional problem was that people were taught to sing Western music but not how to listen (understand) or how to create it. Since people forgot what they learned in school they turned to vulgar and popular music but the masses had not really lost their music during this period.

This surprising thrust towards traditional music is soon contradicted as she refers to the post-war activities saying that, "the music taught was the same as that used by workers of progressive countries." Thus we see in Seki Akiko the continuing cross that school-trained Japanese musicians have had to bear since the Meiji Era; a powerful drive to absorb Western culture nailed to the crossbeam of a desire for national culture.

Akiko goes on to say that she did not really want to participate in the first post-war May Day activities because labor, government, newspapers, and broadcast companies were all involved, giving her a feeling that the whole affair might look like the work of intellectuals and specialists rather than a "sincere" gesture of the workers. Her interest in the people's music is further evident in the section that follows:

---

[14] Seki Akiko, "Utagoe undo no riron," *Chisei* (April, 1956), 65–67.

> It is impossible to lecture the masses on how to sing properly. In choral singing, one teaches by letting the workers lock their arms and sing happily together. Occasionally one can suggest to them how it might be done better. Such a system works well with the masses but the intelligensia can't understand it. The role of the specialist is to step in when the people can't fully express themselves. Japanese professional composers are eighty years behind the times . . . the workers needed songs to express their emotions when striking and so they began to write their own . . . The activists should consider themselves [musical] specialists.

Akiko's view of her own program is that, "Since Utagoe is not political it cannot be called Red." It is involved in, "the notion of peace expanded until it included patriotism, love of nature, home, family, and friends, etc." In her view of the future she predicts that Utagoe, "will open schools for the study of folk music and instruments from early childhood. The movement and the songs it sings must be popularized throughout the world."

The compelling question that McPeek would certainly ask is, "What actually happened?" We have already mentioned the building of a Music Center in Tokyo. From the Center cheap song books and plastic records were produced and shipped to the many circles set in schools and factories throughout Japan. In 1966 the central office claimed a membership near ten million and large national choral meetings were held frequently.

A more intimate application of the tradition could be seen in special coffee houses such as one in the Shinjuku ward of Tokyo named Katchusha after the heroine of Akiko's favorite Tolstoy novel. Within the Russian decor there is a place for an accordionist to stand and lead group singing. In addition to coffee, tea or beer one can buy a small booklet that contains texts of favorite Utagoe pieces.

Perhaps the most powerful example of Utagoe applied to action is a scene in June of 1960 when U.S. Ambassador Douglas MacArthur, Jr. and presidential envoy James Haggerty were seated in a car between Haneda Airport and the U.S. embassy. It could not move because of the mass of people who had locked arms and were singing the peace loving songs they knew so well like "American Go Home" and "Ban the Bomb." This event helped cancel President Eisenhower's visit to Japan and topple the Kishi government. Personal observations of the 1968 May Day parade in Tokyo revealed the continued use of singing though the old revolutionary songs were gone except for "The Red Flag" which, being set to the tune of "O Tannenbaum", seems to play an ambiguous role in any meeting.

Our final example may represent the highest point to which the movement developed; the creation of a communally composed message opera. Former opera singer Seki Akiko had spoken of traditional music in her 1956 statement. In 1966 the Utagoe central committee, of which Akiko was director, searched for the proper role of opera in the proletarian music movement. During this same period there was considerable pressure from both the left and right wing of Japanese politics to re-occupy Okinawa. Thus an opera story was chosen concerning a 1955 event in which U.S. military forces evacuated villagers from a section of Iejima island in order to use their farm lands for a bombing range.[15] The August, 1966, statement by the opera committee[16] said first that the Japanese proletariat must work to support the struggle for the return of Okinawa. It next set three goals for its own work: 1) learn from the past music tradition and the many musical accomplishments of Utagoe, 2) seize hold of Okinawa's musical assets, and 3) let collaborative specialists cooperate. Okinawa was visited and by November of 1967 it was possible to perform an "Okinawa" opera prologue at the annual Utagoe festival. The libretto was complete by 1968 through the labors of a commune of eight Utagoe personnel plus a collaborator from the Okinawa Liberation Movement. The music committee consisted of thirteen persons of whom one was from the Okinawan Youth Chorus. A professional European-trained conductor, Yamada Kazuo, joined the music committee. At the head of this complicated and ambitious operation one finds the name of Seki Akiko.

It took some three years of composition and group criticism for the teams of create one full-length opera. The result, "Okinawa," was premiered in Tokyo on December 10, 1969. The program gives credits to no individual composer, librettist, or singing star. The concept of such communal cooperative action and its results are mind boggling to artists of the Western "genius"-oriented society, though they might seem quite natural in modern China. Nevertheless, McPeek might ask, "Was it a good opera?"

Before answering that question let us look at the background of some of the members of the composition committee.[17] Kinoshita Sonki is

---

[15] Details of the actual event can be read in Gibe Keishun, *Sengo Okinawa no rekishi* (Tokyo: Nihon seinen shuppansha, 1971) and in *Okinawa nenkan* (Naha: Okinawa Times honsha, 1970), 357–358.

[16] Inoue Yoritoyo, "Kagekki Okinawa to nihon no utagoe undo," *Okinawa* [souvenir program of the opera] (Tokyo: Seisakujoenchuo jiko-iinkai, 1972), 17.

[17] *Okinawa* (souvenir program cf. fn. 16), 25.

identified in the opera program as a transfer from a Nara Utagoe circle to a position as the leader of a Shinjuku chorus and the writer of choral pieces such as "In Flowers, the Sun, in Children, Peace." It was his piece "Return Okinawa" that won him a prize in 1965 and perhaps placed him on the committee. Matsunaga Yuji came from the Shizuoka prefecture to the Central Chorus and studied vocal music and conducting through the Center as well as played the piano and accordion for them. Mori Manbu moved from singing in the Nagoya Youth Chorus to being an Utagoe conductor and prize-winning composer in Utagoe contests. All three members show obvious commitments to music that are based more on belief than on formal training. One might shudder at the thought of hearing an opera composed by such sincere young devotees to peoples' songs and choruses. These were my thoughts when I attended a June, 1972 performance, staged in celebration of the "liberation" of Okinawa from U.S. to Japanese occupation.

My first impressions were rather bourgeoisie as I entered the new auditorium in the Shibuya ward and bought the large souvenir program and a LP album of the complete opera.[18] The funding of such an expensive enterprise as an opera is implied by the eleven organizations besides Utagoe that are members of the organization committee as well as the fifty-eight people and nineteen unions that are listed as sponsors. After the credits one finds a smiling picture of Seki Akiko as well as congratulatory notes from the governor of Tokyo and urban governor of Kyoto. In addition to performers names and a resume of the plot there also is a historical essay on the actual Iejima affair and on the manner in which the opera was communially composed (cf. fn 15-17).

The music of the first act is basically that of a European romantic opera with a brief reference to Okinawan folk rhythms in the opening chorus that speaks of the hardship of living under a military occupation. The pathos of relocation camp living and lost identity provide excellent vehicles for the kinds of pathetic or vengeful arias and duets that are essential to this European idiom. The first scene of Act II is ethnomusicologically more interesting. It is set in the capitol of Okinawa, Naha, in which the farmers from Iejima have come to ask for help. Peasants, urbanites, local gangsters, and vendors with their street calls are mixed with American soldiers with their cokes and Okinawan girl friends. Perhaps to literally add color or an additional message, the soldiers in this scene have black faces and are non-aggressive towards

---

[18] The album was an Ongaku Center release MLS 2001-2 and was soon out of print. A copy is available at the University of Michigan.

the oppressed nationals (the soldiers during the forced evacuation and in confrontation scenes are white). In the midst of the market scene one hears an actual Okinawan instrument, the *jamisen*, used to accompany a section in the *kuzuchi* form of folk music from which the drama is sometimes said to have been inspired. Its text is given in Okinawan dialect with a Japanese translation. For this Western viewer it was as effective as the Catsfish Row scenes in Gershwin's "Porgy and Bess."

Other scenes have their better arias or duets though the stilted romantic opera form makes dramatic tension difficult. It should be noted, however, that the drama is not unduly anti-American, the villains in Verdi's opera usually faring much worse. Rather, the major stage confrontation in "Okinawa" is between two leaders of the protest movement, one being aggressive and the other more hesitant. It is the latter who is killed when the farmers attempt to reoccupy their village and there is a fire. The lament of the villagers, led by a wise old man, is matched by a dedication to continue the struggle by the other leader (remember that the opera was written before Japan reoccupied Okinawa). In such big scenes throughout the opera there always is a large chorus, often placed behind a scrim to become visible when necessary and reinforce the message of the moment. The use of large choruses is a convention of Western operas and oratorios but its use and placement here is more similar to modern Chinese operas during the Cultural Revolution period.

Another important function of the chorus was to involve members of Utagoe in the production. Interviews with other members of the audience revealed that many came because a friend was in the chorus or because they were members of an Utagoe circle that had members on stage. Many of the basic songs of the opera had been distributed earlier to the Utagoe circles so one could observe many moving lips in the audience as the same pieces appeared in the production.

When the curtain rose in response to the final applause, Seki Akiko appeared on stage and led the chorus and the audience in the piece "Return Okinawa." The fact that Okinawa was already returned took nothing out of the power and pleasure of this event. Compare it with other situations in which memories of a struggle can be musically encased and used anew with equal or greater power as, for example, in the uses of the "Star Spangled Banner." Think also of the value of being able to involve generally passive listeners into musical action. McPeek would suggest the use of chorales in Bach's Passion settings and his cantatas. In the opera "Okinawa" these factors can be put together with all the previous musical and sociological goals discussed earlier and then we can return to the question, "Is it a good opera?" From a purely musical standpoint it is an impressive joint effort in an idiom that is not encumbered by the illusion of originality. It was designed to communicate with the musically conservative audience for which it was built and it did so. Sociologically we must reply to the question first by adding a question, "Good for what?" As "art" music the opera is no "masterpiece" but neither of these terms seems germane to the function of such music in society. The same could be said of most Western operas that now fill the needs of many musicological theses. In both cases a message was sent in a medium that was built on the tastes and background of the targets. In that sense both forms of opera were "good." In the case of "Okinawa," many of the theories and aspirations of Seki Akiko seem to have come to fruition.

Seki Akiko was true to her beliefs to the very end. After conducting Utagoe selections at an open air May Day concert in 1973, she suffered a stroke while leaving the stage and died the next day. A special concert was held in her honor on May 23rd and the Utagoe movement carried on as best it could without her. A visit to their Music Center in February of 1984 found a rebuilt building with a commercial recording studio upstairs and new sets of song books and records. The Utagoe song book contained handwritten new choral pieces and arrangements. A second set of song books made no reference to the movement but included such titles as "The Peace March" and "Never Again the A Bomb" plus "We shall Overcome" and "It's a Small World". The texts and chords for old socialist songs are found in the back along with instructions for group dance movements while the cover is a capitalistic pop art picture of a car, bank, liquor store and a quarter pounder hamburger.

Further interviewing produced news of no major events except a May Day festival at an amusement park in Tokyo and an annual national choral meeting in Osaka in November. A copy of the Utagoe weekly newsletter showed a picture from last years meeting. It did not seem to be a huge assemble of the size seen in the Utagoe movement during the Seki period. Nevertheless, young people were there and they were singing as was the Central Chorus whose records were still available. The only new books for sale were two sets of comments and memories; one on the history of the Utagoe movement from 1948 to 1978[19] and the other in memory of Seki Akiko.[20] The latter is entitled *The Big Red Rose*.

[19] Inoue, *Utagoe yo yoku hirogete* (see fn. 13), 208–210.
[20] Inoue, *Oki na kobara* (see fn. 2).

The Utagoe movement itself may have lost some of its mass appeal and drive as Japanese affluence has softened the need for it and more radical proletarian groups have formed separate music programs. The legacy of the Seki tradition in Utagoe includes Akiko's younger brother, Seki Tadaakira (b. 1915), who became the vice president of the Music Center and her daughter, Teruko, who relates to the movement, not as a conductor but as a singer of Soviet songs in Russian. However, it is the life and work of Seki Akiko herself that best represents the movement. They also provide us with excellent, consistent materials for the study and appreciation of some fifty years of proletarian music in Japan.

INDEX